THE CINEMA OF SARA GÓMEZ

Sara Gómez, circa 1964. © ICAIC

NEW DIRECTIONS IN NATIONAL CINEMAS

Robert Rushing, editor

THE CINEMA OF SARA GÓMEZ

REFRAMING REVOLUTION

Edited by
Susan Lord and María Caridad Cumaná with
Víctor Fowler Calzada

INDIANA UNIVERSITY PRESS

This book is a publication of

Indiana University Press
Office of Scholarly Publishing
Herman B Wells Library 350
1320 East 10th Street
Bloomington, Indiana 47405 USA

iupress.org

© 2021 by Indiana University Press

All rights reserved
No part of this book may be reproduced or utilized in any form or by any means, electronic or mechanical, including photocopying and recording, or by any information storage and retrieval system, without permission in writing from the publisher. The paper used in this publication meets the minimum requirements of the American National Standard for Information Sciences—Permanence of Paper for Printed Library Materials, ANSI Z39.48-1992.

Manufactured in the United States of America

First printing 2021

Library of Congress Cataloging-in-Publication Data

Names: Lord, Susan, 1959- editor. | Cumaná, María Caridad, 1964- editor. | Fowler Calzada, Víctor, 1960- other.
Title: The cinema of Sara Gómez : reframing revolution / edited by Susan Lord and María Caridad Cumaná with Víctor Fowler Calzada.
Description: Bloomington, Indiana : Indiana University Press, [2021] | Series: New directions in national cinemas | Includes bibliographical references, filmography, and index.
Identifiers: LCCN 2020047890 (print) | LCCN 2020047891 (ebook) | ISBN 9780253057044 (hardback) | ISBN 9780253057051 (paperback) | ISBN 9780253057068 (ebook)
Subjects: LCSH: Gómez Yera, Sara—Criticism and interpretation. | Motion pictures—Cuba—History—20th century. | Documentary films—Cuba—History and criticism. | Women motion picture producers and directors—Cuba—Biography. | Women, Black—Cuba—Biography.
Classification: LCC PN1998.3.G37343 C56 2021 (print) | LCC PN1998.3.G37343 (ebook) | DDC 791.4302/33092—dc23
LC record available at https://lccn.loc.gov/2020047890
LC ebook record available at https://lccn.loc.gov/2020047891

CONTENTS

Acknowledgments vii

Introduction: New Women, Old Worlds / Susan Lord 1

1. **"We Have a Vast Public"** / Interview for *Pensamiento Crítico* by Sara Gómez Yera 32

2. **"Sara Is So Very Sara!"** / Inés María Martiatu Terry Interviewed by Lourdes Martínez-Echazábal 35

3. **Inquisitive Gazes:** Sara Gómez's Perspectives on Social Marginality from and within the Cuban Revolution / Odette Casamayor-Cisneros 58

4. **Sergio Giral Interviewed by María Caridad Cumaná** 80

5. **Neither Farms nor Coffee Plantations:** Urban Spaces and Cultural Contours in the Script and on the Screen / Víctor Fowler Calzada 87

6. *Residential Miraflores* (Script for *De cierta manera* / **One way or another**) / Sara Gómez Yera and Tomás González 123

7. **Luis García Mesa Interviewed by Lourdes Martínez-Echazábal and María Caridad Cumaná** 181

8. **Sara Gómez:** *AfroCubana* (Afro-Cuban Women's) Activism after 1961 / Devyn Spence Benson 223

9. **Racial Identity and Collisions:** Gómez and Guillén Landrián / María Caridad Cumaná 251

10. **Rigoberto López Interviewed by Víctor Fowler Calzada** 260

11. **Information and Education:** Sara Gómez and Nonfiction Film Culture of the 1960s / Joshua Malitsky 270

12. **Virtual Heroes in the Midst of Shortage:** Sara Gómez Confronts the New Man / Ana Serra   287

13. **Iván Arocha Montes de Oca Interviewed by Ricardo Acosta**   306

    Illustrated Essay: Rumba by Sara Gomez   317

14. *Sabor* and *Punctum*: Music in Sara Gómez's Films / Alan West-Durán   328

15. **The Santiago of Two Pilgrims:** F. G. Lorca and Sara Gómez in Search of Eastern Cuba / Lourdes Martínez-Echazábal   341

16. **Her Contribution** / Sandra Abd'Allah-Alvarez Ramírez   362

17. **Conclusion:** Transculturation, Gender, and Documentary / Susan Lord   372

    Epilogue: "As Time Goes By, We Are Less of a Polite, Aesthetic, Static, Sexual, and Passive Object" / Sara Gómez Yera Interviewed by Marguerite Duras   395

    Filmography   403

    Index   417

Acknowledgments

The story of this collection of texts about Sara Gómez could be compared to the long return of Ulysses to his birth home in Ithaca. More than ten years have passed since the project began, and some of those who contributed are, alas, no longer with us: Inés María Martiatu Terry ("Lalita," 1942–2013) and Rigoberto López (1947–2019). We still feel the loss of Julio García Espinosa (1926–2016), who was an early supporter of this project and of Sara. Still, I believe it was worth waiting for this concert of dissimilar voices to usher in the light, reeling from documentary and fictional work that, at the time it was filmed, envisioned the future and continues to provide inspiration for tomorrow.

The singularity of Sara's films is uncovered in the research of each of the authors as they examine and interpret the themes exposed in her films. Sara's legacy should establish a starting point for a larger study of the contributions of women filmmakers within the context of Cuban audiovisual productions after 1959.

I want to thank my mother, María Antonia González, who continues to gift my life with a shining light, a light that emanates from women like her, who inspired and created a singular space on the big screen, through the work of Sara Gómez.

—*María Caridad Cumaná*

In 1992 at the Euclid in Toronto, Ontario, Sara Gómez's documentaries saw the light of a projector—some for the very first time, all on videotape with wonky subtitles. This project was inspired by that event, programmed by Ricardo Acosta and David MacIntosh. It changed my life in ways I could not have imagined at the time. I anticipated that researchers with more preparation than I had in matters of Cuban and Latin American cinema would take on this project. Several years later, in Havana, Gloria Rolando took my hand, became my friend, and gave me encouragement, advice, and introductions. A project that started, naively, as a single-author monograph became a rich and complex montage of voices, perspectives, arguments, memories, and hope thanks to my coeditor María Caridad. It became clear that Sara's legacy deserved much more that I could honor alone. We called Caridad *la llave*, the key, because she held the confidence of so many in the ICIAC and the world of Cuban cinema. And thanks to her, the project was launched in the form it has taken. Víctor Fowler found the script of *De cierta manera* entitled *Residential Miraflores* and supported the project in many ways. And the women of the colloquium "Sara Gómez, imagen múltiple: El audiovisual cubano desde una persectiva de género" in Havana in 2006 have kept working on Sara, encouraging and pushing for this project to see the page: they are Sandra del Valle, Sandra Abd'Allah-Alvarez Ramírez, Karen Rodríguez López-Nussa, Norma Guillard, and Danae C. Diéguez. At the ICAIC, Luciano Castillo, Lola Calviño, Katy Casanova, and the late Pablo Pacheco offered advice, archives, and permissions with enthusiasm and kindness.

Sara's children, Iddia Veitía Gómez and Ibis Hernández Gómez, gave us encouragement and permission. This book is dedicated to their brother, Sara's and Germinal Hernández's son, the musician Alfredo Hernández Gómez, who passed away in 2013.

The numerous and seemingly endless stops and starts on this journey are due, in part, to the ever unfolding possibilities of contributors, documents, images, interviews, translations, and commentaries. The contributors to this book deserve all our gratitude for their wisdom, patience, and support. Nearly every article, interview, and document required translation. Helen Dixon, Joan Donaghey, Paul Kelley, Miguel Ángel Pérez, and Zaira Zarza did tremendous work translating and advising as I worked through the texts with the authors, copy editors, transcribers, and proofreaders. Tim Pearson is an extraordinary editor—he helped get through the first five hundred pages with a sharp eye and good humor. Freddy Monasterio Barso, Shawn Newman, May Chew, Jessica Jacobson-Konefall, Ozlem Atar, and Xenia Reloba de la Cruz all pushed this along with intelligence and hard work. A special thanks to Xenia for the professional, painstaking work with the index. The next generation of care for the work of Sara Gómez is happening as this book goes to press, with the digitization and subtitling of Sara's documentaries in our Vulnerable Media Lab, thanks to Dairon Luis Morejón Pérez, Melissa Noventa, and Michelle O'Halloran.

Thank you to the seemingly infinite patience from the people at Indiana University Press, including Allison Chaplin, Robert Rushing, Janice Frisch, Carol McGillivray, and Lesley Bolton. And special thanks to the two reviewers who helped put new wind under our sails with suggestions and positive remarks.

ACKNOWLEDGMENTS

The research for this book was undertaken with the financial support of the Social Science and Humanities Research Council of Canada.

Over the years, friends in Havana have offered loving support and laughter—and flan. Those individuals include Mirta Carreras Díaz, Emilia Fernández, Inés and Olguita Rodríguez, Dannys Montes de Oca Moreda, Laura Cisneros, Manuel Piña, Lourdes Pérez Montalvo y la familia de calle 17, Omar Morejón Guerra, Jorge León Sanz, Vanessa Chicolo, Aldo Peña, Joel del Río, and Marta Díaz. During many evenings over many years, Karen Dubinsky, Susan Belyea, Jordi Belyea Dubinsky, Scott Rutherford, Sayyida Jaffer, Mary Caesar, and Dorit Naaman have listened to my hopes and fears for this project here in Kingston and on the balconies of Havana. And thank you to Paul Kelley and Kurt Kelley-Lord for keeping me fed and loved all the way.

—*Susan Lord*

THE CINEMA OF SARA GÓMEZ

Introduction

New Women, Old Worlds

Susan Lord

ONE SCENE FROM SARA GÓMEZ'S 1968 documentary *En la otra isla* (On the other island) provides a touchstone for many of the contributions to this book and offers a guide for viewing much of her film legacy.[1] In the scene, Gómez interviews a young black man, Rafael, about his desire to be an opera singer. She listens and waits, gently prompting him to speak. A beautiful two-shot with Rafael's body turned to the camera, his head turned to Gómez, and Gómez's back to the camera with her head turned to Rafael is perhaps one of the most nuanced and complex moments in documentary cinema. It performs an equalization but not a sameness of relations between filmmaker and subject where they complete each other. It embodies the image of utopia, it documents a new way of belonging, and it offers a horizon of that which is not yet here.

New forms of belonging and engagement available to women and people of color in the 1960s in many parts of the world were quickly threatened by national, patriarchal, and racist traditions that formed both their context and their subjective terrain. The symbolic burden Cuba bore for most of the freedom-seeking world at this time was amplified within the spheres of race and gender, making certain images both vibrate with hope and collapse from symbolic saturation. Sara Gómez came to represent this combination of forces. She was a young, free, black, beautiful, talented, revolutionary in a miniskirt, with an afro, holding a camera. *The Cinema of Sara Gómez: Reframing Revolution* attempts to understand this image of Gómez and the films she made. What difference did they make in the 1960s and 1970s? And what do they offer us today? Each contributor to this volume gives weight and complexity to the life and cinema of Sara Gómez. Together, these multiple views assemble a history, criticism, biography, methodology, and theory of Gómez's work in scholarly writing, interviews, images, a film script, and a detailed and complete filmography. The anthology reorients how we tell Cuban cinema history and how we think about the intersections of race, gender, and revolution.

The contributions pivot on two fulcrums: Gómez's 1972 reflexive documentary, *Mi aporte* (My contribution), and the telling and retelling of her life as filmmaker, daughter, mother, lover, and friend. The reasons are simple. *Mi aporte* demonstrates that Gómez's contribution to cinema and to the Cuban Revolution are tethered and, in her own words, "determined by awareness [*toma de conciencia*]; it will be the result of a determined attitude when we confront our problems, when we confront the necessity of decolonizing ourselves politically and ideologically, and of freeing ourselves of traditional values whether economic, ethical, or aesthetic" (chap. 1). Her life is told and retold by the contributors as part of their own stories and positions as scholars, friends, filmmakers, and coworkers. Never described in quite the same way, Gómez's biography and work are shown to be part of a living archive that continues to move us. The translations of interviews with Gómez herself that open and close the book provide readers with a sense of the robustness of her analysis, the fearlessness of her speech, and the determination of her commitment.

Sara Gómez Yera was born in 1943 to Juana Yera and Carlos Gómez, members of an extended middle-class black family of artisans and musicians from Central Havana and Guanabacoa.

> She grew up in the home of her paternal family in Cerrada del Paseo between Zanja and Salud, Centro Habana, La Habana. She was cared for by her aunts, Aleida, Lupe, Delia, and Cuca, who educated her in the style of the time. Innumerable photos of her childhood reveal the growing Sara Gómez: black girl, small nose, bright eyes, and sculpted mouth. She stuttered and she was asthmatic. Sara took music classes for seven years at the municipal Conservatory and spent many hours of the day studying the piano at home. The revolutionary emerged when she was in her third year of high school—she left school to participate directly in the new social process. (Abd'Allah-Alvarez Ramírez 2008, n.p.)

Gómez participated in the formation of a new society initially through work as a journalist with the newspapers *Hoy Domingo* and *Revista Mella*. In 1961, she began working at the Instituto Cubano del Arte e Industria Cinematográficos (ICAIC, or Cuban Film Institute) when both the institute and Gómez herself were very young. She also was part of an ethnology study group associated with the National Theatre. During her years at the ICAIC, she directed twenty films and she had three children: Iddia Veitía Gómez with her first husband,

Figure I.1 Sara Gómez filming *De cierta manera*, circa 1973. © ICAIC

Héctor Veitía, a prolific documentary filmmaker; and Ibis Hernández Gómez and the late Alfredo Hernández Gómez (1971–2012) with her second husband, Germinal Hernández (1944–2007), a brilliant sound technician.[2]

We learn via the interviews that are interspersed throughout this anthology a great deal about Gómez's intensity of commitment and her high spirit. Here, in the words of her eldest daughter, Iddia, we learn something about the primacy of love:

> For Sara, life hurt her more than it did Don Quixote. However, perhaps she felt the most important things that happened to her were the clearest evidence she had of her existence. That incredible pain, which only she could revert back to love, placed her right there, in the understanding that the only thing that really matters in a person is their humanity. And that was her work: an irrepressible concern with the fate of all people, together with the need to proclaim that the "others" are not outside of "us," that we all are folded in a "we." And that was her life: that eagerness to find a rational explanation at the very edges of our experience.
>
> Only in this prismatic worldview can her memory and the significance of her work remain alive. She believed herself to be constantly evolving in

a world of possibility, which led her to throw herself out there incessantly, and this was the only thing that enabled her to transcend. But we still haven't reached that level of transcendence; it is so risky, so committed. This is why I think—personally—that when we evoke Sara, whether just from nostalgia, through memory or censorship, she will continue to be constrained within each of us, we will never really know how to understand her. We owe this unbelievably cheerful girl—which is just how I remember her—that evocation of herself in, and from, a spirit of hope. She remains with us in the love whose only desire is to risk losing ourselves in the other. (I. Gómez 1989, 36)

Iddia's reflection on her mother provides us with threads that weave a tension between Gómez's commitment to the particularity of a person and their belonging to a project larger than any one individual. The stories of her way of working, her relationships, and the challenges she faced as well as those she dealt out are told throughout this book in multiple dimensions and with profound feeling by the contributors. Acosta and McIntosh (1992, n.p.) write: "Sara once admitted to a friend: 'The blues and agrarian reform keep me working in this country. That's my philosophy now, with apologies and acknowledgements to Kant and Hegel.'"

Gómez's death from asthma at the young age of thirty-one on June 2, 1974, was a painful and traumatic loss for her family, friends, and colleagues. And like Gómez herself, her passing has become legendary. It is recounted in interviews published here with her friends "Lalita" Inés María Martiatu Terry (chap. 2) and with Iván Arocha (chap. 13). Arocha, who was also Gómez's editor, describes Gómez's funeral in very spiritual terms: "There's something lovely that happened at Sara's funeral. Sara was the daughter of Yemayá, and the day of the funeral was beautiful, sunny. All her friends and colleagues, all of us, were there. When they lowered her coffin so it could be buried, the sky suddenly darkened, a tremendous thunderclap sounded and it broke open the sky and an impressively heavy rain fell. When the rainstorm was over and we left the cemetery, the sun was shining just as it had been when we had entered."

It is indeed worth underscoring the impact of her short life, not just on those who knew her but also on the formation of the ICAIC; on ethnographic and autoethnographic filmmaking practice; on political discourses of race, gender, and revolution; and on the limits of that which could be represented. The ICAIC was created in March 1959 as one of the first acts of the new revolutionary government of Cuba after the overthrow of the Batista regime on

January 1, 1959. By August 1961, Gómez had left her job at *Revista Mella* to make her contribution through cinema. The first paragraph of Act 169, published on March 24, 1959, in the *Gaceta Oficial de la República* paper, reads, "Cinema is an art." These words were meaningful to Gómez, and she took up the challenge to build a new society through cultural forms. The document contained the essence of the new industry, and it was approved by the government as a matter of principle. Many experienced the ICAIC, overseen by Alfredo Guevara and Julio García Espinosa, as an "island on the Island" because of Guevara's ability to maintain *relative* freedom for artists working at the institute.

The ICAIC established two entrance routes for emerging filmmakers to learn their craft: *Noticiero ICAIC Latinoamericano* (Latin American news of the ICAIC, or ICAIC newsreels) with Santiago Álvarez as the founder and director; and *Enciclopedia popular* (Popular encyclopedia), where Gómez, Nicolás Guillén Landrián, and numerous others trained.[3] Working with the filmmakers inside the ICAIC was an impressive group of musicians, known as the Grupo de Experimentación Sonora del ICAIC, who created the soundtracks and performed the music for much of Gómez's work as well as for that of Guillén Landrián, who was noted for his experimental, ethnographic style in image and sound.

The ICAIC realized its mandate to build a nation through images by experimenting with new modes of documentary; historical dramas that were meant to rebuild history (new citizens, new stories, new forms); transformations in contexts of production, reception, and distribution; and the production of discourse in the form of manifestos ("The Viewers' Dialectic" by Tomás Gutiérrez Alea and "For an Imperfect Cinema" by Julio García Espinosa) and *cine-debates* (forums for discussion of the films).

As well, Alfredo Guevara wanted to "make a huge cine-club out of the island" (Guevara cited in Piñera and Cumaná 1999, 58), thus bringing films by Ingmar Bergman, Orson Welles, Luis Buñuel, Sergei Mihailovich Eisenstein, Akira Kurosawa, Charlie Chaplin, and others to screen in Cuban cinemas and on the backs of trucks throughout the island. The ICAIC also invited international filmmakers to present their work, make new films, and present workshops and classes for the emerging cohort of Cuban filmmakers. It was in this context that Gómez became assistant director to the French filmmaker Agnès Varda in 1962, whose film *Salut les Cubains* includes footage of a young Gómez doing the cha-cha with editor Nelson Rodríguez (see the interview with Rigoberto López in this anthology for more on the relationship between Varda and Gómez).

Sara Gómez is recognized by scholars, filmmakers, and cinephiles as having made profound and lasting contributions to Cuban cinema, women's and

Afro-descendent cinema, postcolonial cinema, and world cinema. However, her legacy ebbs and flows like the tide: on and off the island, inside and outside cinema. For example, interest in her work surged in 2018, when the extraordinary Grammy-nominated musician/*rappera* Telmary Díaz worked with young filmmakers in Cuba to create a dynamic music video that remediates images of Gómez and her films. "Fuerza Arará" refers to the "force" of the Arará—a population located primarily in the provinces of La Habana and Matanzas and descended from Fon, Ewe, Popo, Mahi, and other ethnic groups in Dahomey. The music video uses fragments from Varda's film, including the segments of Gómez dancing the cha-cha, as well as fragments from Gómez's own oeuvre. The layered colors and textures, almost like a hand-processed film, are synchronized to a soundtrack that revives the archive of Afro-descendant music and cultural forms, bringing Gómez's legacy to life in a surprising, joyous, and insistent present tense.

However, alongside this flow, I present an example of the ebbing of Gómez's legacy. In November 2017, I was invited to give a talk at an event focusing on the work of young diasporic Cuban filmmakers working off the island. The event was in chilly Edmonton, Canada, and the filmmakers arrived with ski jackets from Germany, Spain, Switzerland, Mexico, and Canada. Organized by Zaira Zarza, it was a transformative event for all of us. Cuban film scholar Ruth Goldberg gave a paper about the link between the current generation and Nicolás Guillén Landrián. The reason they could be in such a conversation is because Guillén Landrián's work had been digitized and shared in the early 2000s by artist Juan Carlos Alom, in whose work a conversation with Guillén Landrián clearly exists.

I remember when artists and filmmakers, including Alom, started to see the Guillén Landrián films the early 2000s. They were amazed and inspired; and deeply saddened that Nicolasito's work had been in a vault, neither shown in Cuba publicly nor distributed, because he was a "complicated" figure, both politically and psychologically. He had an inventive and unique cinema style that bridged experimental cinema and documentary by assembling material from the ICAIC cutting room floor—the stuff nobody wanted or wanted to be seen. This style was combined with his unflinching gaze at everyday life, at complex social relations, and at black experiences, which in the 1960s and early 1970s was a problem for state socialist modernity. As discussed by Caridad Cumaná in this volume, Guillén Landrián was one of three black filmmakers working in the ICAIC at the time—Gómez and Sergio Giral were the other two. But, as was the case for the women filmmakers, no black filmmakers except Gómez and Giral were given the opportunity to make feature films. At the Edmonton event, I spoke about Gómez and showed images from her work. It is striking that although her feature film was well known and a source of inspiration, not one of the young filmmakers had seen any of Gómez's documentaries. They, too, were deeply saddened by what they and their generation had missed.

Until the 2008 release of Rebeca Chávez's film *Ciudad en rojo* (City in red), Gómez was the only woman to have made a feature film in Cuba. She remains one of only a few Afro-descendant Cubans to have made films at the ICAIC about contemporary issues facing Afro-descendent Cubans in general, and women in particular. Yet her work has inspired many Cuban filmmakers (as I discuss in more detail in this book's conclusion), and her 1974 feature film *De cierta manera* (One way or another) presented North American and British feminist film critics and theorists with one of the first "non-Western" films by a woman, thus marking a shift from North American and European authorship in the then relatively small canon of women's films. When Gómez died in 1974, she was in postproduction for *De cierta manera*, the only feature-length film she made after ten prolific years as a director of documentaries (the filmography at the end of this volume provides detailed information on Gómez's work). The feature was completed by Gómez's colleagues at the ICAIC in 1977, went on to receive tremendous critical and scholarly attention, and continues to focus attention on, and debate about, Cuban culture and society.[4]

All this well-deserved attention, however, has strangely done little to encourage distribution or analysis of Gómez's earlier documentary work either inside or outside Cuba,[5] such that Iván Arocha in his interview with Ricardo Acosta talks about her films as "ghosts." Nineteen documentaries of between eight and forty minutes in length, including the five she made for the *Enciclopedia popular* addressing a range of themes from Afro-Cuban musical traditions to family ethnography, critically engage with explicitly political matters, such as volunteer labor, *poder popular* (literally "popular power," a system of local government), social housing, racism, machismo both in the workplace and at home, youth marginalization, childcare, and prenatal care.[6] As a result of recent and renewed interested on and off the island in her work and in the intersectional themes of race and gender she addresses, several initiatives are underway to digitize her work. At Queen's University (Kingston, Canada) in my Vulnerable Media Lab (vulnerablemedialab.ca) we are working with the ICAIC to digitize and subtitle all of her documentaries for a 2021 release; Arsenal—for Film and Video Art (Berlin) is restoring a version of *De cierta manera*; and Eirene Houston of the Havana Glasgow Film Festival digitized and subtitled *En la otra isla* in 2020.

There are a few exceptions to this historical dearth of public viewing of her documentaries.[7] The first was a festival curated by Canadian David McIntosh and Cuban Ricardo Acosta for the Euclid Theatre in Toronto in 1992. I was fortunate to be involved in the Euclid at this time, so I worked with the programmers and saw Gómez's documentaries for the first time. An ambitious and groundbreaking project, *"Crónicas de mi familia*: New Cuban Film and Video" presented Gómez as the foundational figure for an emerging generation of filmmakers, including Jorge Luis Sánchez, Magda González Grau, and Enrique "Kiki" Álvarez. The program was coproduced with the support of organizations such as the Asociación Hermanos Saíz, a cultural organization established in 1986 to support young artists and musicians. It was "created by young artists to guarantee them a cultural infrastructure as well as a broadening arena for discussing ideas and aesthetic issues. This is an organization which is rooted in self-representation and which provides a mechanism for dialogue with other cultural institutions and artists from previous generations" (Acosta and McIntosh 1992, 10). The film program at the Euclid was a predigital labor of love with everything copied onto video and subtitled into English in Havana. The program also included a film homage to Gómez by Acosta, who was an emerging film editor and is now an award-winning editor and producer. As they wrote in their program notes, Acosta and McIntosh understood Gómez's legacy in terms that echo Iddia Veitía's words:

> This feverishly sensitive and unquestionably committed woman has left a legacy of complete honesty, which offers us a starting point and example for considering how we can proceed to produce art which combines innovative professionalism with truly popular concerns, making no concessions, seeking no facile solutions.... Over all, this series has been constructed to offer insights and respond to questions which we all share as artists despite the particular nature of our practice. All of the work you will see represents the firmly held position of an individual director, but also an honest approach to understanding common realities. As we grow we learn that the "other" is not outside of "us," we are all "us." (Acosta and McIntosh 1992, n.p.)

In Cuba, attention to Gómez beyond her feature film is sparse. In 1989, a significant portion of the journal *Cine Cubano* was dedicated to Gómez; yet ten years later in a special issue celebrating the fortieth anniversary of the ICAIC, neither Gómez's name nor her image nor stills from her films were given a place in those pages. However, Jorge Luis Sánchez González's 2010 book *Romper la tensión del arco* offers sensitive readings of some of the documentaries, and at

Figure I.2 Program cover for program *Crónicas de mi familia/Chronicles of my family: New Cuban Film and Video*, 1992. © Susan Lord

about the same time as the "rediscovery" of Nicolás Guillén Landrián (whose work is discussed by Cumaná in chap. 9) in the early 2000s, Gómez's work was also revived on the island with the release of a DVD of *De cierta manera* and *Iré a Santiago*. But the most significant event for Gómez's public memory is the one that brought the full range of Gómez's work and legacy into view in Havana for the first time. In November 2007, *Coloquio Sara Gómez: Imagen múltiple; El audiovisual cubano desde una perspectiva de género* (Sara Gómez colloquium: Multiple images of Cuban audiovisual culture from a gendered perspective) was organized by Sandra Abd'Allah-Alvarez Ramírez, Sandra del Valle Casals, and Norma Rita Guillard Limonta. The event was a first for its screening series, with presentations of analyses of Gómez's legacy and a broader inquiry into issues of gender in Cuban media.[8] In 2017, Ediciones ICAIC published *Sara Gómez: Un cine diferente* by Cuban researcher Olga García Yero, offering the first comprehensive overview of Gómez's work and context. The current volume, *The Cinema of Sara Gómez: Reframing Revolution*, is the first scholarly resource on Gómez's work, providing a biographical palimpsest of Gómez herself and multiple perspectives on her work and her legacy from Cuban and international researchers and colleagues.

From her biography through to the structures of her documentary films, we find in Gómez a filmmaker who continuously reevaluated the promises of modernity and of the Cuban Revolution, and the values inherited through popular memories of families, streets, and altars. She did not settle on a positive, unequivocally affirmative image. And the contributions to this anthology reflect this unsettled character, offering diverse and even conflicting evaluations of the films. Gómez insisted on, and persisted in, process, embodying the *cine imperfecto* (imperfect cinema) theorized by Julio García Espinosa in 1969 in the sense of an open system, a continuous and reflexive critique—what Gómez herself referred to as "decolonizing" (see chap. 1).[9] This work of decolonization was always grounded in political, personal, and historical realities as well as in memory and in acts of appearance or making visible under- and unrepresented figures, stories, and discourses. The essays and interviews in this book therefore comprise a conversation between these realities, offering new information and insights about Gómez's biography and her family, about how she worked as a filmmaker, and about the sociopolitical histories she represents and interrogates.

A central element of Gómez's social and political context that she speaks to throughout her films is the Revolution's ostensible commitment to the advancement of women's rights, which is taken up by several of the writers in this anthology. And the discourse about women's rights was constrained and complicated by the discourse of the "New Man." As Ana Serra writes in chapter 12: "'Socialism and Man in Cuba,' [Che] Guevara's foundational document on the Cuban Revolution, stressed the idea of a 'new man,' 'a new society,' and a 'new consciousness' with 'new values.'" Later in the chapter, she writes, "Revolutionary activity allowed men, according to Guevara, to become 'the highest rank in the human species' and to 'graduate as men' (quoted in Guillermoprieto 2001, 85). The ultimate expression of masculinity was thus achieved in combat. In the framework of the traditional bourgeois ideal of a heterosexual family, Guevara calls for total dedication to revolutionary duties, which, among other things, results in women having to shoulder all the responsibilities of home and children." The main institutional mechanism charged with overseeing, implementing, and advancing women's rights was the Federación de Mujeres Cubanas (FMC, or Federation of Cuban Women), established in 1960 by Fidel Castro and Vilma Espín. The FMC's crucial work for the rights of women, both inside and outside the home, was not unequivocally embraced by the women themselves; nor is the federation's history without contradiction.

As new research is demonstrating, the top-down accounts of women's gains in the Revolution overlook the activism of women after the 1959 victory, particularly in the urban centers. As Michelle Chase (2015, 7) notes: "Activist women of different political stripes pushed the leadership to address problems within the private sphere, such as food provisioning, domestic labor, and child rearing. In doing so, they raised more transformative notions of women's liberation and gender reform. Thus, in many important ways, women led rather than followed." Thanks to the FMC (which, as Chase reminds us, was a federation of a diverse range of women's groups that eventually were subsumed by the FMC's unifying agenda), women could divorce more easily, put their children in childcare centers so they could work, and be recognized in law and policy as equal to men in terms of wages, access to education, and more.[10] The FMC also encouraged marriage (but not housewifery), traditional forms of feminine behavior, heteronormativity, and sexual austerity.

This profile of the New Man's new woman was something Gómez refused to accommodate. Lillian Guerra (2012, 244) cites Gómez as saying, "Women did not elect to practice sexual austerity any more than they elected to work three jobs—in the home, 'on the street,' and in the political tasks set by the state. Women's denial of their own 'erotic universe' was, she said, 'a collective disease of which we are not even conscious.'" As described in the interviews with Inés María Martiatu Terry (chap. 2), Luis García Mesa (chap. 7), and Iván Arocha (chap. 13), and in Benson's contribution (chap. 8), Gómez had a complicated relationship to the FMC. Perhaps the most fractious moment was when the FMC commissioned the film *Mi aporte* and then censored it upon its completion. Gómez's unbending determination to decolonize gender and race, to particularize personhood, and to remediate popular memory brought her into conflict with vice ministers, ICAIC directors, and the FMC leadership.

The contributions to this anthology also discuss Gómez's aesthetic practice. The degree of self-reflexivity in her films is consistent with a radical, autoethnographic, feminist, and experimental cinema (see Lord and Martínez-Echazábal). Her use of music is a counterpoint, a guide, and/or alternative social history (West-Durán, chap. 14). The moments of interactive/reflexive subjectivity—such as the young boy mugging at the camera in the beginning of *Una isla para Miguel*, or the playful exposure of the camera in *Iré a Santiago*—extend to more developed forms, such as when the filmmaker enters the frame as a participant-observer in *Mi aporte*. Or, as Víctor Fowler Calzada (chap. 5) discovered through his analysis of the script for *De cierta manera*, Gómez's intention was to take down the fourth wall and display the apparatus of filmmaking. This impulse of radical filmmakers around the world at the time was particularly significant for Gómez and the context of the Cuban Revolution's claims for full participation, because it challenges the prevailing operating system of censorship and containment in the 1970s. And so it is no surprise that this scene in the script (reproduced in chap. 6) did not make the cut in the film:

> The camera pans and we discover the environment of the filmmaking. Lights, cameras, makeup artists, etc. Mario in the center of this environment speaks to the audience:
> Balmaseda as actor: This could be an ending for the film.

Gómez developed a very particular form of authorship, one connected to feminist and "third cinema." She put herself in the frame in acts of relinquishing directorial power to a collective imaginary but never abdicating responsibility for voice, frame, montage, and subject matter. As I discuss in the concluding chapter, the role of consciousness-raising films was central for feminist and antiracist movements of the time, for they offered an affective vocabulary and an image of collective overcoming. Gómez was the first to develop an aesthetic that brought this consciousness-raising practice together with the decolonizing language of third cinema. She refused to use the camera as a weapon, as in the "cinema as gun" trope of the period; rather, for her the camera was a mirror of affection. In this, Gómez refused what Lillian Guerra (2012) hypothesizes as a binary of authenticity and hyperreality. Instead, leading us through and back into complexities is something Odette Casamayor-Cisneros (chap. 3) perceives as Gómez's attachment to revolution in the Arendtian sense of an "irresistible movement" of people, with their "individual particularities sustained as men and women." During a 1998 lecture delivered at an international symposium on "Popular Memory and Changes," Gómez's friend and colleague Gerardo Fulleda León argued, "She does not try to teach us. . . . She grasps, listens, shows. . . . There are no slogans or ideological sermons, so fashionable at the time." *Crónicas de mi familia*, he suggested, "is a cinematographic poem that takes [the woman's] authenticity out of the trunk, where all black families have wanted to hide all our false aspirations, our mediocre existence and our little human miseries as miserable evils that we cannot show. Sober and bitter way of building our dignity, of being what we are" (Fulleda León 1998, n.p.).

Víctor Fowler Calzada's essay (chap. 5) on *De cierta manera* offers a provocative renewal of the film by connecting it directly to the tensions and expectations about urban poverty and planning in the early 1970s, a decade after the first brigades set out to build the Miraflores housing project, and within the context of the "Laws against Idleness" of 1971. This urban landscape—its spaces of unequal development and its places of belonging—was always at the forefront of Gómez's interests. For example, *Iré a Santiago* is not about going to Santiago; it is about the city itself, its streets, and cinema's recording of and reflection on public life and cultural memory. *Crónicas de mi familia* is not just about Gómez's family; it is about locatedness and the urban genealogy and cultural history of an Afro-descendant family. *Y... tenemos sabor* is at once an Ortizian ethnography of *son* and an urban soundscape. In *En la otra isla*, the urban ethnographer goes to the Isle of Pines (soon to be renamed the Isle of Youth) to which urban youth have been moved so they can be cared for—or rehabilitated, depending on the viewpoint. She does not interview campesinos or *pineros* (inhabitants of the Island of Pines) in this film (although she does in *Una isla para Miguel*); she interviews youth who have become homeless or stateless (in a variety of ways) in Havana. The final argument in the street between Yolanda and Mario in *De cierta manera* meets the demolition at the beginning—the city as a space of contestation, love, and citizenship. The liminal spaces between home and street in *Mi aporte*, between work and street, the spaces of argument—a public space in process—are key to Gómez's articulation of a *cine imperfecto* aesthetic. The framing in *Mi aporte* of the black, urban woman on the threshold between tradition and modernity, where both spaces differently offer possibility and constraint, is seen across Gómez's work.

In her 1962 contribution to *Enciclopedia popular*, right away we see the cinematic imagination at work, producing layers of discourse between images and the voice-over. At times, we can perceive a contrary position; at others, a nuancing. In *Historia de la piratería* (1963), for example, the voice-over talking about the new achievements of the Revolution accompanies an image track that adds depth to the forward-moving sense of time and progress in the discourse. The image shown in figure I.3 of a woman at the threshold between private and public, framed by the film, the doorway, and a tableau of didactic posters, is followed by an image of a woman crossing the street (fig. I.4) with an energetic gait and a broad smile. These types of montage are common in Gómez's work and tell us something important about her reflections on the relationship between art and politics. The unequal, uneven, and nonidentical processes of agency and social change require a cinematic imaginary capable of communicating across cultural difference and social distance.

As mentioned earlier in this introduction, Gómez and the ICAIC were both young when she joined the organization in 1961; so, too, was the Cuban Revolution. And, of course, globally, youth were rebelling against wars, white supremacy, coloniality, patriarchy, authority, and economic disparity. In Cuba, Julio García Espinosa made a film titled *The Young Rebel* about the training of a young man to become a "New Man"—a disciplined revolutionary as postulated by Che Guevara to think with his head and not his sex. Much could be said about this film for the way it genders and whitens revolutionaries and represents the condensation of discipline in the body.

However, here I want to set the film beside three other sets of "youthful" images that contextualize Gómez's time: a literacy campaign, the Zafra de los Diez Millones (ten-million-ton harvest; a government program to improve Cuba's economy by producing a record amount of sugarcane), and the Isla de Pinos project. Images of the literacy campaign, especially Manuel Octavio Gómez's film *Historia de una batalla* (1962), give citizenship to youth—particularly young black girls and women.[11] And few images from the early 1960s are more exhilaratingly hopeful than that of a black teenage girl wearing a military uniform armed with a pencil.

Toward the end of the decade, on the cusp the *quinquenio gris* (five gray years, 1971–76), Gómez turned her camera on the Isle of Pines, where marginalized groups (young, female, black, poor) were not only to work for but also benefit from and, indeed, *make* the Revolution. In turn, these "pioneers of the future" would become the ageless face of the Revolution. Gómez made three documentaries there: *En la otra isla*, *Una isla para Miguel*, and *Isla del tesoro*. This site, a mid-1960s experiment in currency-free, communist living, was a world ruled by young people where women were central organizers, and it embodied many of the dreams and failures of the larger island's experiments that came in the post-1968 gray years.[12] The first two films are ethnographic

Figure I.3 *Historia de la piratería*, 1963. © ICAIC

Figure I.4 *Historia de la piratería*, 1963. © ICAIC

documentaries (excellent examples of direct cinema) about the island's new inhabitants: thousands of people under age thirty-five who arrived in waves over the first seven years of the Cuban Revolution to populate an island that had been abandoned by earlier governments. Some of these young people were sent to study or arrived as *brigadistas* to help after Hurricane Alma destroyed great portions of a fertile and productive agricultural area cultivated by previous waves of immigrants on farms or for American orchard owners. Others, the subjects of Gómez's documentaries, were sent there because they were perceived to be in need of reform because their values (sexuality, religion, long hair, and marginalization due to racism or abandonment) stood in contradiction to the values of the Cuban Revolution.

Let us return to the scene from *En la otra isla* with which I opened this introduction. The two-shot in cinema is a conversation shot in which the gaze is not the property of either of the filmed subjects. In mainstream fiction, the two-shot surveils, providing an image of intimacy or privacy as a moment in a cessation of power dynamics usually preceding the classic shot reverse shot that tells the viewer about social and semiotic control. In documentary, the two-shot is used as a sign of interactive or reflective practice on the part of the filmmaker, as an equalization of the planes of power between the social subjects of the documentary or between the documentarist and her subject. The two-shot democratizes the screen; perspective is forgone in favor of horizontality. Viewers are offered a privileged point of view and gain a sense of listening in, of knowledge for which they are responsible as intimate witnesses. Viewers see a vulnerability to which they are invited to attend to, and possibly to protect or take care of.

A qualitatively different type of two-shot was used in documentaries around the same time by voyeuristic directors such as Fredrick Wiseman, where the intimacy is really a privacy. Participating instead in the verité networks that moved from the streets of Montreal, Paris, and Algiers to Havana, Gómez is in the picture, on an equal plane not just aesthetically but also ethically. This two-shot presents a moment of autoethnography—a young black man and a young black woman, an opera singer and a filmmaker—brought to this moment of vulnerability with each other through the near unspeakability of race. In the dialogue, Gómez waits for Rafael even as he wants her to speak for him. She is his mirror and interlocutor to whom he can speak the pain of racism and bring it out into the public world—a world not owned by any, a world shared by all. As Casamayor-Cisneros writes in her essay (chap. 3), "By spurring on young Rafael against his inertia and the kind of resentful shame he demonstrates, the filmmaker seems to ask him to shake off his fear of exposure. She wants

Figure I.5 Sara Gómez and the opera singer Rafael discussing racism *En la otra isla*, 1968. © ICAIC

him to talk fearlessly about the suffering he experiences as a subject of racial discrimination—to speak out rather than struggle against his own voice. In other words, Gómez places herself in opposition to the silence that envelops the issue of racism in postrevolutionary Cuba."

These documentaries share with *De cierta manera* the open ending, the unresolved argument about the coming community. In all of Gómez's films, windows, thresholds, and doorways speak volumes. They are spaces of emergence; they are interior frames that function to mediate or create a density of mediation through which we literally see the emergence of a new subjectivity. In *Mi aporte*, women are often at thresholds; in *Crónicas de mi familia*, the door and window frames allow the material measure of difference versus the universal discourse of equality; in *De cierta manera*, the privacies of race and gender enter the classless streets. These cinematic acts of emergence take place during the *quinquenio gris*. Coined by Ambrosio Fornet, this period saw the first widespread restrictions on intellectuals and artists. It officially began in 1971, but many argue that it came on the heels of the Havana Cultural Congress in 1968. This era represented a significant change from the relative freedom of the 1960s in the atmosphere and working process for artists, and it meant for Gómez in particular a multifaceted set of struggles over her critical engagement with issues of marginalization of specific social groups (see Fornet 2007 for a reflection on this period).

In the 1960s, Havana became a project for the international Left and the decolonizing populations. It was a home for those with nowhere to belong, a screen on which to project utopian imaginaries, an experimental city, a stage for the apex of Cold War drama, and an expanded media space in which new images and sounds of burgeoning nations were invented. Havana saw an intensification of culture's role in the making of citizens and connecting them to, and shaping their contributions toward, the global imaginary. This activity produced a new form of cosmopolitanism—a decolonized cosmopolitanism, theorized elsewhere (Lord, Montes de Oca, and Zarza 2015), through networks built across previously unbridgeable cultural, social, and national borders. Political theorists, activists, journalists, philosophers, poets, painters, filmmakers, and students came to Havana from Paris, Montreal, Santiago, Harlem, Rome, Istanbul, Berlin (East and West), Moscow, Buenos Aires, and Kingston (Jamaica). Among those who came were C. L. R. James, Andrew Salkey, Aimé Cesaire, Simone de Beauvior, Jean-Paul Sartre, Amiri Baraka, Margaret Randall, Pablo Neruda, Charles Wright Mills, Octavio Paz, Hans Magnus Enzensberger, Mario Vargas Llosa, Allen Ginsberg, Max Aub, Julio Cortázar, Jorge Semprún, Oscar Lewis, Gabriel García Márquez, Michel Leiris, Graham Greene, Carlos Fuentes, Marguerite Duras, Miguel Ángel Asturias, Rosa Prado, and Italo Calvino.

Until the Soviet army quashed the Prague Spring (which Castro did not denounce), Havana was perhaps the most dynamic city in the world, attracting thousands of campesinos, political tourists, solidarity brigades, Black Panthers, and new Soviet residents—as well as counterrevolutionary attacks. Indeed, two hundred thousand elite Cubans left the island nation, abandoning their property, which was then redistributed to campesinos and students. Monuments to imperialism were destroyed. Banks were turned into hospitals, hotels into headquarters of the newly formed government. New graffiti of literacy campaigns and rebel youth replaced advertising meant to attract the moneyed class and tourist gazes. Military Units to Aid Production—forced labor camps—were operated by the state from 1965 to 1968, and to them were sent people who did not seem to belong to the portrait of the New Man—primarily gay men and those perceived to be counterrevolutionary. Publications such as *Lunes de Revolución* (1959–61) were closed down and folded into state-run publications. Afro-Cuban societies were closed and nationalized as folklore centers opened in their place. Operación Pedro Pan (Operation Peter Pan) saw fourteen thousand children airlifted from Cuba to the United States by the Catholic Church and the US Central Intelligence Agency between 1960 and 1962. And, of course, a full embargo against Cuba by the United States arrived in 1962. These events set the stage for a complex, contradictory internal condition of crisis, fear, solidarity, trauma, hope, dependence, autonomy, suspicion, and hospitality.

Gómez worked with Agnès Varda when Varda came to Cuba in 1962, and Marguerite Duras interviewed her when Duras came as part of the delegation to the Salon de Mayo in 1967.[13] Gómez worked at the ICAIC during a period of its most intense cosmopolitanism. She was a member of a group that studied ethnography and black history (Seminario de Etnología y Folclore del Teatro Nacional de Cuba). She read Frantz Fanon (a quotation from *The Wretched of the Earth* forms the epigraph of *Una isla para Miguel*),[14] Malcolm X, and Aimé Césaire. She was connected to the Black Power movement and received a telegram from Stokely Carmichael congratulating her as the "first free head" in Cuba. And she walked Havana with Jamaican novelist Andrew Salkey and Trinidadian poet John La Rose when they attended the Havana Cultural Congress of 1968. Referring to Gómez as "Sarita," Salkey writes in his fascinating *Havana Journal*: "Sarita, in her very early twenties, has eight important documentaries to her and ICAIC's credit.... She gave the impression of going dynamically ahead of her field, and yet both John [La Rose] and I wondered if she wasn't just a little too imaginatively vital and aspiring for the confines of the cultural blockade and its aftermath in Havana which I had, so far, very narrowly peeked at since my arrival. In her conversation we both spotted a mind about to 'crash,' if their wider concerns weren't allowed maximum room for exploration, comparative criticism and development" (1971, 27–28). Six years after this encounter, at the age of thirty-one, Gómez died, leaving behind her three children, two husbands, loving friends and comrades, nineteen documentaries, a feature film, and an image of utopia.

In a book project of this scope—with conversations, histories, and analyses—repetition is complicated to manage. Yet we believe some repetition is both useful and inevitable in a comprehensive collection, with various documents and voices from academia, filmmaking, and journalism. The overlaps are not typically pure repetition but rather are associated with memories or points of emphasis. This overlapping, combined with some cross-referencing, gives this volume a sense of a community conversation. Similar information is provided by various authors in various ways and for different purposes. Removing the overlaps, in some cases, could result in a change of meanings or make arguments difficult to follow, especially if (as often happens) selected essays might be used for teaching purposes. With an overall focus on Gómez's documentaries, the authors here each address a set of films, providing differences in interpretation, methodology, biography, and historical context. These analytical essays are interspersed with interviews in which the biographical detail provided by Gómez's coworkers and friends is rich and even sometimes startling. Most of these interviews provide a history of the ICAIC and the Cuban cultural scenes from a perspective we do not often hear from—that of the film crew. The invaluable, granular narratives help us understand the working method, the theory of cinema, the complexities of work at the intersection of revolution and art, and the profound meaning and value of friendship.

The scholarly essays in this collection attempt to match Gómez's deeply intersected work, with contributors investigating the following topics: the provocations of racial consciousness and feminist aesthetics; critiques of machismo, masculinity, and the New Man; deep listening and the role of music in Gómez's documentaries; the place of her documentaries in the context of the ICAIC's documentary production and next to her colleagues; and her specific formulations of ethnography and autoethnography.[15] Gómez's documentaries are analyzed in these pages by various authors, and often by more than one contributor. For example, *En la otra isla* and *Una isla para Miguel*, films from the Isla de Pinos/Isla de Juventud trilogy, appear in chapters by Odette Casamayor-Cisneros, María Caridad Cumaná, and Devyn Spence Benson. For our part, this shared archive indicates the central role these films play in understanding the era and Gómez's life and work.

Casamayor-Cisneros, a specialist in Afro-descendent studies and Cuban cultural production, gives us "Inquisitive Gazes: Sara Gómez's Perspectives on Social Marginality from and within the Cuban Revolution." We place it first among the analytical essays because it offers a survey of Gómez's work, pivoting on the autoethnographic portrayal of family as a lens through which to view the complexity of Cuban society that makes up *Guanabacoa: Crónicas de mi familia*. Casamayor-Cisneros's attention to marginality in the films is presented by reading a number of Gómez's documentaries in terms of both contemporary and historical discourses of race and gender. Working with and against the morality of the New Man, Casamayor-Cisneros brings new understandings of the documentary project in the production and representation of a tension between cultural citizenship and personhood.

In "Racial Identity and Collisions: Gómez and Guillén Landrián," Cuban film scholar María Caridad Cumaná shifts to a comparative, auteurist study of the documentary productions of these two filmmakers whose practices represent the radical experiments of the time. Cumaná attends to issues of race and cultural difference through a cinema studies lens that records the ways in which filmmakers engage with modes of institutional practices. Social and cultural historian Devyn Spence Benson's intersectional analysis of race and marginalization is organized around the theme of Afro-Cuban women's activism after 1961. Benson's chapter, "Sara Gómez: *AfroCubana* (Afro-Cuban Women's) Activism after 1961," is an extension of her groundbreaking book *Antiracism in Cuba: The Unfinished Revolution* (Benson 2016). Offering here a history of Afro-descendency and race politics in the post-1959 context, Benson deepens our understanding of both the films' representational strategies and their context of production and reception.

Another group of contributors who share engagements with the film *Mi aporte*, a documentary that directly chronicles issues facing women at the time of the sugar harvest, are Sandra Abd'Allah-Alvarez Ramírez, Ana Serra, and me. Abd'Allah-Alvarez Ramírez's "Her Contribution" and my concluding essay, "Transculturation, Gender, and Documentary," accompany each other to complete the analyses of Gómez's contribution to gender, culture, and ethnographic practices as visible through *Mi aporte*. Abd'Allah-Alvarez Ramírez's chapter interweaves biography, autoethnography, and self-inscription practices. Abd'Allah-Alvarez Ramírez, one of Cuba's most renowned journalists and bloggers, runs the blog *Negra cubana tenía que ser* and participates in the archive *Afrocubanas*. She provides valuable primary materials from interviews she conducted and archives she accessed that are not covered in the other essays. Building on the previous chapters, my concluding essay raises some theoretical and methodological problems concerning the cross-cultural encounter particular to an analysis of Gómez's documentaries. I consider the documentary studies paradigms from several contexts (feminist, first world, "third cinema," Latin American, and Cuban) to reveal strategies for translating and recognizing the profound transcultural proposals at the heart of Gómez's project.

Serra addresses Gómez's films about the voluntary labor program (*Sobre horas extras y trabajo voluntario*, Extra hours and voluntary work; 1973) and local people's government (*Poder local, poder popular*; 1970), in the context of gender and the New Man. Serra, author of the book *The "New Man" in Cuba: Culture and Identity in the Revolution* (2007), completes and extends the discussion initiated by Casamayor-Cisneros on the New Man in her chapter titled "Virtual Heroes in the Midst of Shortage: Sara Gómez Confronts the New Man." Serra takes the reader through key historical moments (the ten-million-ton harvest and the volunteer labor movement) and their social and economic contexts as Gómez engaged with them in order to theorize a gendered critique and reevaluation of the New Man and cultural citizenship. Focusing on documentaries such as *Mi aporte*, *Sobre horas extras y trabajo voluntario*, and one about the first daycare centers in Cuba, Serra produces a new paradigm for understanding revolution and gender in the Cuban context.

Other documentaries receive singular but nonetheless rich and important analyses by other contributors. Joshua Malitsky frames Gómez's *Enciclopedia popular* films in terms of the role of documentary and educational films in postrevolutionary society. Malitsky, a documentary film theorist and historian, analyzes Gómez's encyclopedia films and documentaries in terms of the educational project of Cuba in the early 1960s in "Information and Education: Sara Gómez and Nonfiction Film Culture of the 1960s." He traces how teaching, instructing, informing, and persuading became not only goals but objects of thought. He focuses on Gómez's narrational choices—selecting, organizing, and rendering nonfiction film material to produce a certain effect on the viewer. It is at the level of narration that we can see her resonances with contemporary education policy, some of her most urgent political concerns, and where she at times subtly but also more overtly marks her films in relation to both Western and dominant Cuban models.

The place of music in Gómez's films, but especially in the 1967 film *Y... tenemos sabor*, is Alan West-Durán's focus. West-Durán is a Cuban cultural and music studies specialist who brings together a panoramic musicology of both the representation of music and the use of music as cinematic structure, West-Durán provides a new and surprisingly—because of its integrity of music and image—underrepresented perspective on Cuban cinema. His chapter, "*Sabor* and *Punctum*: Music in Sara Gómez's Films," analyzes five films through their soundtracks, considering her use of music in different contexts and how it intersects with her view of a revolutionary cinema. West-Durán's contribution follows what is perhaps one of the most striking contributions to this collection: a reproduction of an extended illustration by Gómez on rumba originally published in *Cuba* (similar to *Life* magazine) in 1964, which clearly shows the depth of her research for *Y... tenemos sabor*.

These themes of performance studies, music, carnival, and Afro-Cuban culture in *Iré a Santiago*, Gómez's first film for the ICAIC documentary division, are extended in the chapter by Latin American and Cuban studies scholar Lourdes Martínez-Echazábal. Her essay combines the history and geography of Cuba by focusing on the city of Santiago de Cuba. *Iré a Santiago* is Gómez's homage to the city, its people, and the Spanish poet Federico García Lorca, whose sound poem *Iré a Santiago* Gómez both directly referenced and counterpointed in the film. Martínez-Echazábal's historical geography and postcolonial perspective offers a comparative and transnational methodology.

At the heart of this anthology is the screenplay for *De cierta manera*, Gómez's only feature film, written by Gómez and Tomás González. Discovered in the ICAIC archives by Víctor Fowler Calzada, the script is published here for the first time. It provides enormous insight into the project of the film and the aesthetic strategies of the filmmaker. As Fowler Calzada describes at the beginning of chapter 5: "In the Documentation Center of the Instituto Cubano del Arte e Industria Cinematográficos (ICAIC, or Cuban Film Institute) is a mimeographed copy of a film script called *Residencial Miraflores* with argument and dialogue by Sara Gómez and Tomás González Pérez. Alberto Pedro Díaz and Tomás Gutiérrez Alea also appear as advisers. Inexplicably ignored for four decades, the script is 110 pages long, and although it lacks a date, a reference on the reverse of the authors' details page says it was donated to the ICAIC Documentation Center in 2006." *De cierta manera* is a remarkable film for its portrayal of complex social, racial, and gender relations and for its inventive strategies of giving such relations a mode of representation adequate to their complexities. The film is renewed with each passing decade by new questions (or old questions but new tools for asking them) about the structures, histories, spaces, everyday practices, and experiences of racialization, gender inequity and violence, machismo and masculinity, marginality, and poverty; and about resistance, decolonization, and anti-imperialism, collective work and dreaming, and the limits and possibilities of the Revolution as a project of modernity and national identity. Fowler Calzada also notes: "The enormous ambition of this project—which proposes a fusion of documentary and fiction, questions and revises the cinematographic apparatus itself, and employs such extensive textual references that feed into and interact with the project to create its own story—as well as the wealth of positions embodied by the diverse characters creates one of the most dense, lively, and disquieting works of national filmmaking and, in general, of all the culture produced during the time of the Cuban Revolution."

While most of the chapters provide some references to, or analysis of, *De cierta manera*, Fowler Calzada's chapter offers the first analysis of the transition from script to screen. His essay also provides a rich historical context of the film's focus on urban development in Havana. In "'Neither Farms nor Coffee Plantations': Urban Spaces and Cultural Contours in the Script and on the Screen," Fowler Calzada, one of Cuba's most respected and renowned intellectuals, provides a profound analysis of the film. Focusing on the question of citizenship and marginality in Cuba in the pre- and postrevolutionary periods, Fowler Calzada reads the original screenplay against the finished film and excavates some of the most difficult questions Gómez faced in her work of entering the marginal, black neighborhoods of Havana. Bridging urban studies and cinema studies, this essay is a major contribution to how we understand both the filmmaker and her time.

In addition to these incisive texts, we are fortunate to have an oral history of Gómez's life and work provided through intimate and deeply touching interviews with some of her friends and colleagues. Inés María Martiatu Terry, known as "Lalita," was interviewed by Lourdes Martínez-Echazábal just before Lalita passed away. Structured more like a conversation between two colleagues, "Sara Is So Very Sara!" functions both as a critical biography of Gómez and as an account of Cuban politics of cultural production in the decades of the 1950s, 1960s, and 1970s. A key member of the reformation of cultural institutions in the postrevolution context, Martiatu Terry offers a substantial and original history of race, revolution, and culture from below. In conversation with Ricardo Acosta, Gómez's editor Iván Arocha talks about his work with Gómez and her process. He and Luis García Mesa, her cinematographer, provide a view into the issues at ICAIC that Gómez confronted, including the final process of editing *De cierta manera*. Filmmaker Sergio Giral and *De cierta manera*'s assistant editor Rigoberto López, in interviews with María Caridad Cumaná and Víctor Fowler Calzada, respectively, offer perspectives on Gómez's life, friendship, and work that help us compose a fragmented but robust portrait.

In many of these interviews, we hear a combination of militancy and openness—a fearless speech at the edge of utopia. This is why the book begins and ends with Gómez's own words: her response to a survey about cinema published in *Pensamiento Crítico* at the beginning and an interview with the late French writer Marguerite Duras at the end. In the middle, we reproduce Gómez's illustrated article on rumba to represent her journalist's training and her deep interest in music. As her friends and colleagues interviewed in these pages attest, Gómez was deeply respected and loved both inside and outside the ICAIC. They respected her for her combination of loving loyalty and unwavering integrity, an integrity that compelled her to confront the almost exclusively white male vice ministers of government and presidents of cultural institutions, to call in the bets made on the promises of the Revolution. Her struggle to integrate art, life, and politics challenged traditional domestic relations; gender roles; the form, content, and function of art; and the shape of the social horizon.

NOTES

1. This introduction includes passages from my previously published articles (Lord 2002, 2009).

2. See the interview with Martiatu Terry and the chapter by Abd'Allah-Alvarez Ramírez for more biography.

3. For a comprehensive history of the ICAIC in English, see Chanan (2004).

4. Sources that centrally discuss Gómez's feature film include Abd'Allah-Alvarez Ramírez (2008, 2011), Amaya (2010), Baron (2011), Benamou, (1999), Burton (1997), Chanan (2004), Chijona (1977), Conte (1989), Davies (1997, 1999), Díaz López (2004), Ebrahim (1998), Fernández (2003), García Borrero (2001, 2007a, 2007b), Galiano (1978), Lesage (1979), Marquetti Torres (2015), Pick (1993), Rich, (1991), Shaw (2003), and Valdés León (2015).

5. As Benson describes in her chapter, "There remains debate about whether Gómez's documentaries were screened publicly. In an interview with me, Martiatu said the documentaries were not shown widely and that they were censored. Similarly, Ebrahim notes that Cuban censors prohibited the showing of *Crónicas de mi familia* (1966) after it was completed (2007, 111), whereas, Cuban filmmaker Rigoberto López (interviewed in this volume) says that while the documentaries did not get the circulation they deserved, he did attend a screening at ICAIC."

6. The few articles that center on her documentaries include Gerardo Fulleda-León's (1998) early essay on popular memory, García Borrero's (2007a, 2007b) blog, and Jorge Luis Sanchez González's (2010) short but thoughtful analyses of several of the documentaries.

7. There was a program at the Center for Cuban Studies in New York in 1995 with accompanying pamphlet by Jean Stubbs (1995), and a similar program showed in London in the late 1990s. Recent programming of documentaries includes Doclisboa'16 and of *Una isla para Miguel* in festivals organized around ethnographic film. *De cierta manera* has been shown regularly in various festivals in Canada, France, the United States, Mexico, and the United Kingdom since its release. More recently, Gómez's work has been taken up in the United States in terms of black screen culture and shown at festivals and events such as the Brooklyn Academy of Music's Black History Month series (http://www.bam.org/film/2017/one-way-or-another-sara-gomez). Florian Zeyfang's program from 2013 *Tears and Splices—Cuba and Europeans* (http://www.arsenal-berlin.de/en/arsenal-cinema/past-programs/single/article/4126/2804/archive/2013/june.html) included some documentaries. Ann Marie Stock's project Cuban Cinema Classics (http://www.cubancinemaclassics.org/) has issued two volumes that include Gómez's documentaries. *De cierta manera* was distributed in Canada by International Development and Education Resource Association (IDERA) and in the United States by Tricontinental. *Iré a Santiago* was distributed in the United States by Cinema Guild. Various universities hold the feature or an example or two of the documentaries. For example, Indiana University's Black Film Center Archive holds a selection; Queen's University in Kingston holds copies of all the documentaries; and IDERA's collection went to Concordia University (Montréal, QC). The distribution records of these early, pre-digital

distribution organizations have not been archived. As a result, I was constrained in my attempt to represent the publics for Gómez's films in the Americas or outside of specific festivals. This fact has inspired a new research project for the Vulnerable Media Lab on radical distribution networks in the Americas in the period 1960–1990.

8. Previous to Benson (2016) and Guerra (2012), there were few English-language accounts of Gómez's documentaries beyond those in Lord (2002) and Chanan (2004). Some analysis and description of approximately half of the documentaries, along with personal memories of friends and family, appear in the 1989 issue of *Cine Cubano*. Alessandra Müller's documentary *¿Dónde está Sara Gómez?* (2005) offers a view into Gómez's family and friendships.

9. It is important to note here that the attribution of *cine imperfecto* to *De cierta manera* is often based on the grainy, rough look of the film. However, as Arocha and Gómez's cinematographer Luis García Mesa tells us, this was an accident at the lab and not an intended aesthetic effect.

10. From 1965 to 1970, the divorce rate in Cuba doubled from 8,937 to 15,357 (Guerra 2012, 244).

11. Catherine Murphy's film *Maestra* (2011; http://www.maestrathefilm.org/) and its associated educational materials offer another source of archival documents and testimonies about the literacy campaign (Campaña Nacional de Alfabetización en Cuba). In one year (1961), more than 750,000 Cubans were taught to read by 250,000 volunteers, 100,000 of whom were young women.

12. The late Leida Oquendo, in conversation with the author, Havana, March 2004. Oquendo was an anthropologist and a close friend of Sara Gómez. She was among the group of communist youth that went to the Isla de Pinos "with the feeling that with the experiment we undertook, we carried a great burden—that of the entire future of the revolution—upon our shoulders." Also see Guerra (2012), McManus (2000), and Gloria Rolando's film *Pasajes del corazón y memoria* (Cherished island memories) (2007) about the Cayman Island immigrants who moved to the Isle of Pines in the 1920s and 1930s.

13. On Duras's visit, see García Borrero (2013).

14. See Valdés León (2015) for an insightful analysis of the profound influence of Fanon in Gómez's work.

15. In the epilogue to her book *Antiracism in Cuba: The Unfinished Revolution*, Devyn Spence Benson (2016) describes the intersectionality of the contemporary work of the *Afrocubana* project in relation to Gómez's legacy. The project, founded by Daisy Rubiera Castillo and Inés María Martiatu Terry, uses "terms like *afrodescendiente* (Afro-descended) and '*Afrocubana*' [to reflect] the group's politics of intersectionality, specifically acknowledging a black and female positionality that is often silenced in historical and contemporary narratives about race in Cuba. Inés María Martiatu Terry

explains in the prologue to the group's first published collaborative project, a 2011 book titled *Afrocubanas: Historia, pensamiento y prácticas culturales* (Afro-Cuban women: History, thought, and cultural practices), that one of the goals of the Afrocubanas movement is to 'feminize negritude and to blacken feminism'" (Benson 2016, 246; and referencing Rubiera Castillo and Martiatu Terry 2011, 2).

BIBLIOGRAPHY

Abd'Allah-Alvarez Ramírez, Sandra. 2008. *Sara Gómez: De cierta manera feminista de filmar*. Master's thesis, University of Havana.

———. 2010. "Sara Gómez in Memoriam." Teatro de Afroamérica. Accessed November 10, 2018. https://teatrodeafroamerica.wordpress.com/2010/07/06/sara-gomez-in-memoriam/.

———. 2011. "El aporte de Sara Gómez." In *Afrocubanas: Historia, pensamiento y prácticas culturales*, edited by Daisy Rubiera Castillo and Inés María Martiatu Terry. Havana: Editorial Ciencias Sociales.

Acosta, Ricardo, and David McIntosh. 1992. "*Crónicas de mi familia*: New Cuban Film and Video." Film program catalog.

Arteaga, Haydee. 1989. "Recordar a Sara." Special issue on Sara Gómez, edited by Antonio Conte. *Cine Cubano*, no. 127.

Amaya, Héctor. 2010. *Screening Cuba: Film Criticism as Political Performance During the Cold War*. Urbana: University of Illinois Press.

Baron, Guy. 2011. *Gender in Cuban Cinema: From the Modern to the Postmodern*. Oxford: Peter Lang.

Benamou, Catherine. 1999. "Cuban Cinema: On the Threshold of Gender." In *Redirecting the Gaze: Gender, Theory, and Cinema in the Third World*, edited by Diana Robin and Ira Jaffe, 67–98. Albany: State University of New York Press.

Benson, Devyn Spence. 2016. *Antiracism in Cuba: The Unfinished Revolution*. Chapel Hill: University of North Carolina Press.

Berthier, Nancy. 2008. *Cine y revolución cubana: Luces y sombras, Archivos de la filmoteca*, vol. 59. Valencia, Spain: Instituto Valenciano de Cinematografía.

Branly, Roberto. 1967. "Filmarán 5 documentales en la Isla de la Juventud." *Juventud Rebelde*, May 2, 1967.

Burton, Julianne. 1997. "Film and Revolution in Cuba: The First Twenty-Five Years." In *New Latin American Cinema, 2: Studies of National Cinemas*, edited by Michael T. Martin, 123–42. Detroit: Wayne State University Press.

Chanan, Michael. 1997. "The Changing Geography of Third Cinema." *Screen* 38, no. 4, 372–388.

———. 2004. *Cuban Cinema*. Minneapolis: University of Minnesota Press.

Chase, Michelle. 2015. *Revolution within the Revolution: Women and Gender Politics in Cuba, 1952–1962.* Chapel Hill: University of North Carolina Press.

Chijona, Gerardo. 1977. "De cierta manera." *Cine Cubano*, no. 93: 103.

Conte, Antonio, ed. 1989. Special issue on Sara Gómez, edited by Antonio Conte. *Cine Cubano*, no. 127.

Davies, Catherine. 1997. "Modernity, Masculinity and Imperfect Cinema in Cuba." *Screen* 38, no. 4: 245–59.

———. 1999. "Reply to John Hess." *Screen* 40, no. 2: 208–11.

Díaz, Marta, and Joel del Río. 2010. *Los cien caminos del cine cubano.* Havana: Ediciones ICAIC.

Díaz López, Marina. "De cierta manera." In *The Cinema of Latin America*, edited by Alberto Elena and Marina Díaz López, 141–49. London: Wallflower, 2004.

D'Lugo, Marvin. 1997. "'Transparent Women': Gender and Nation in Cuban Cinema." In *New Latin American Cinema, 2: Studies of National Cinemas*, edited by Michael T. Martin, 155–66. Detroit: Wayne State University Press.

Ebrahim, Haseenah. 1998. "Afrocuban Religions in Sara Gómez's 'One Way or Another' and Gloria Rolando's 'Oggun.'" *Western Journal of Black Studies* 22, no. 4 (1998): 239–51.

Faget, Puri, and Gisela Arandia. 1969. "El cine, los cineastas, la crítica: Una encuesta realizada." *El Mundo* (Havana), January 18, 1969.

Fernández, Antonio Eligio (Tonel). 2003. "Loss and Recovery of the City (in Cinema)." In *Pabellón Cuba: 4D—4Dimensions, 4Decades*, edited by Lisa Schmidt-Colinet, Alexander Schmoeger, Eugenio Valdés Figueroa, and Florian Zeyfang, 120–39. Berlin: b_books.

Fornet, Ambrosio. 2007. "The Five Grey Years: Revisiting the Term." Translating Cuba. Translated by Alicia Barraqué Ellison. https://translatingcuba.com/the-five-grey-years-revisiting-the-term-ambrosio-fornet/.

Fulleda León, Gerardo. 1989. "Una Reina Desoida." Special issue on Sara Gómez, edited by Alfonso Conte. *Cine Cubano*, no. 127.

———. 1998. "Sara Gómez: Una obra cinematográfica para la reflexión sobre la memoria popular." Lecture delivered at the International Symposium "Popular Memory and Changes," Ascona, Switzerland, April 1–May 1.

———. 1999. "¿Quién eres tú, Sara Gómez?" *La Gaceta de Cuba* 4 (July–August): 42–46.

Galiano, Carlos. 1978. "One Way or Another: The Revolution in Action." *Jump Cut* (December): 33.

García Borrero, Juan Antonio. 2001. *Guía crítica del cine cubano de ficción.* Havana: Editorial Arte y Literatura.

———. 2007a. "Sara Gómez (1)." *Cine cubano, la pupila insomne*, March 18, 2007. Accessed October 13, 2007. https://cinecubanolapupilainsomne.wordpress.com/2007/03/18/sara-gomez-1/.

———. 2007b. "Sara Gómez (2)." *Cine cubano, la pupila insomne*, March 18, 2007. Accessed November 13, 2011. https://cinecubanolapupilainsomne.wordpress.com/2007/03/18/sara-gomez-2/.

———. 2009. *Otras maneras de pensar el cine cubano*. Santiago de Cuba: Editorial Oriente.

———. 2010. *Intrusos en el paraíso: Los cineastas extranjeros en el cine cubano de los sesenta / Outsiders in Paradise: Foreign Filmmakers in Cuban Cinema of the 1960s*. Granada: Fundación El Legado Andalusí: Cines del Sur.

———. 2012. *Cine Cubano. La pupila insomne*. Havana: Ediciones Unión.

———. 2013. "Marguerite Duras sobre el cine Cubano y la revolución." Accessed August 3, 2020. https://cinecubanolapupilainsomne.wordpress.com/2013/09/06/marguerite-duras-sobre-el-cine-cubano-y-la-revolucion/.

García Espinosa, Julio. 1969/1979. "For an Imperfect Cinema." Translated by Juliana Burton. *Jump Cut*, no. 20: 24–26.

Gómez, Iddia. 1989. "Desde la Esperanza." Special issue on Sara Gómez, edited by Antonio Conte. *Cine Cubano*, no. 127.

Gómez Yera, Sara. 1964. "La Rumba." *Cuba* 3, no. 32: 58–67.

———. 1967. Interview with Marguerite Duras.

———. 1968. "5 documentalistas cubanos ensayan un conversatorio." *Caimán Barbudo*, no. 24: 12–17.

———. 1970. "Los documentalistas y sus concepciones." *Pensamiento Crítico*, no. 42 (July): 89–97.

Guerra, Lillian. 2012. *Visions of Power in Cuba: Revolution, Redemption and Resistance, 1959–1971*. Chapel Hill: University of North Carolina Press.

Lesage, Julia. 1979. "*One Way or Another*: Dialectical, Revolutionary, Feminist." *Jump Cut*, no. 20: 20–23.

Lord, Susan. 2002. "Temporality and Identity: Undertaking Cross-Cultural Analysis of Sara Gómez's Documentaries." In *Women Filmmakers: Refocusing*, edited by Judith Plessis, Valerie Raoul, and Jacqueline Levitin, 249–63. Vancouver: University of British Columbia Press.

———. 2009. "Acts of Affection: Cinema and Citizenship in the Work of Sara Gómez." In *Gender and Sexuality in 1968: Transformative Politics in the Cultural Imagination*, edited by L. J. Frazier and D. Cohen, 173–92. New York: Palgrave Macmillan.

Lord, Susan, Dannys Montes de Oca, and Zaira Zarza, eds. 2015. Special issue, *Public 52: Havana 26*, no. 52 (Fall).

Marquetti Torres, Rosa. 2015. "Sergio Vitier . . . *De cierta manera*," *La Gaceta de Cuba*, no. 3 (May–June): 42–43.

McManus, Jane. 2000. *Cuba's Island of Dreams: Voices from the Isle of Pines and Youth*. Gainesville: University Press of Florida.

Montes de Oca Moreda, Dannys, and Laura Dayamick Cisneros Rodríguez. 2004. "Labores domésticas." In *Labores domésticas: Versiones para otra historia de la visualidad en Cuba: Género, raza y grupos sociales*, edited by Dannys Montes de Oca and Dayamick Cisneros Rodríguez. Havana, Cuba: Galería UNEAC.

Müller, Alessandra, dir. 2005. *¿Dónde está Sara Gómez?* Savosa, Switzerland: Amka Films.

Pick, Zuzana. 1993. *The New Latin American Cinema: A Continental Project*. Austin: University of Texas Press.

Piñera, Walfredo, and María Caridad Cumaná. 1999. *Mirada el cine cubano*. Brussels, Belgium: OCIC.

Rich, B. Ruby. 1991. "An/Other View of New Latin American Cinema." *Iris: A Journal of Theory on Image and Sound* 13: 5–28.

Rubiera Castillo, Daisy, and Inés María Martiatu Terry. 2004. *Cuban Cinema*. Minneapolis: University of Minnesota Press.

———. 2011. *Afrocubanas: Historia, pensamiento y prácticas culturales*. Havana: Editorial de Ciencias Sociales.

Salkey, Andrew. 1971. *Havana Journal*. London: Pelican.

Sánchez González, Jorge Luis. 2010. *Romper la tensión del arco: Movimiento cubano de cine documental*. Havana: Ediciones ICAIC.

Schmidt-Colinet, Lisa, Alexander Schmoeger, Eugenio Valdés Figueroa, and Florian Zeyfang, eds. 2003. *Pabellón Cuba: 4D—4Dimensions, 4Decades*. Berlin: b_books.

Serra, Ana. 2007. *The "New Man" in Cuba: Culture and Identity in the Revolution*. Gainesville: University Press of Florida.

Shaw, Deborah. 2003. *Contemporary Latin American Cinema: 10 Key Films*. New York: Continuum.

Stubbs, Jean. 1995. "Images of Gender in Revolutionary Cuba." In *Cuba: A View from Inside: Short Films by/about Cuban Women*, 3–6. New York: Center for Cuban Studies.

Valdés León, Camila. 2015. "De cierta manera. Lecturas de Frantz Fanon en Sara Gómez." *Cuadernos del Caribe*, no. 19 (January–June): 45–51.

Vazquez, Alexandra. 2013. *Listening in Detail: Performances of Cuban Music*. Durham, NC: Duke University Press.

Yero, Olga García, 2017. *Sara Gómez: Un cine diferente*. Havana, Cuba: Ediciones ICAIC.

SUSAN LORD is Professor of Film and Media in the Cultural Studies Graduate Program, and Director of the Vulnerable Media Lab at Queen's University. She is co-editor of *Killing Women: The Visual Culture of Gender and Violence*; *New World Coming: The Sixties and the Shaping of Global Consciousness*; and *Fluid Screens, Expanded Cinema*. As a member of the editorial collective for the journal *Public: Art, Culture, Ideas*, she has co-edited the issues "Havana" and "Archive/Counter-Archives."

ONE

"We Have a Vast Public"
Interview for *Pensamiento Crítico* by Sara Gómez Yera

I

Didactic cinema is a necessity, not a specialty. For many of us, the vocation of filmmaker was born with that of the revolutionary—both have come to be inseparable. If we feel the necessity of a didactic cinema as revolutionaries, it will always be useful, interesting, and cinematographically valid insofar as we are filmmakers. The Cuban filmmaker expresses himself or herself in terms of the Revolution. The cinema, for us, will inevitably be biased; it will be determined by awareness [*toma de conciencia*]; it will be the result of a determined attitude when we confront our problems, when we confront the necessity of decolonizing ourselves politically and ideologically, and of freeing ourselves of traditional values whether economic, ethical, or aesthetic.

When we direct a scientific documentary as a revolutionary necessity, there is no doubt that we are expressing ourselves. We are accepting and proclaiming that it is indispensable to know and to make known, for example, the advantages of the propagation of the citrus crop by grafting plant species with characteristics that will allow them to resist typical illnesses. In a case such as this, we are using the cinema as a weapon in our multifaceted struggle. This conscious and militant contribution to new techniques and effective methods of production will constitute an authentic act of decolonization. It will have a profound significance in our own revolutionary work—by which I mean, in our case, a profound artistic significance. And this is a society whose goal is to transform everything, even the way artists express themselves and for as long as the artist reflects that desperate need. Expressing this anguish will be what is culturally valid.

Figure 1.1 Young Sara Gómez, circa 1959. © ICAIC

II

The cinema as a means of mass communication is so aggressive that I often feel my profession to be both a challenge and a privilege. When we think that millions of spectators with different levels of education and income and different backgrounds are going to receive our sound-images, and seize them in the passivity of a movie theater, guaranteeing their full attention, we feel bound to an ideological and formal rigor without limits. And in our case, the commitment multiplies when we consider that the complex technical resources needed for the realization of a film have been created by that very mass of spectators. We have a series of needs to satisfy, from a simple expansion [of the industry] to information and training. We have a vast public, including urban workers, *campesinos*, and children and adolescents whose standards expand with the increasing development of a complete education. For them and with them we have to make a cinema without making concessions. A cinema that touches the root of their interests. A cinema that is capable of expressing contradictions and with an aim to help make all of us capable of considering life as an eternal conflict against mediocrity—a conflict that we must win. Is this too ambitious? Can we do it? This must be our aim.

Translated from the original Spanish by Paul Kelley

NOTE

This was originally published in Spanish as Sara Gómez, "Los documentalistas y sus convicciones," *Pensamiento Crítico*, no. 42 (July 1970): 92–97.

TWO

"Sara Is So Very Sara!"

Inés María Martiatu Terry Interviewed by
Lourdes Martínez-Echazábal

LOURDES MARTÍNEZ-ECHAZÁBAL: *What was Sara like? How did the family environment and her social surroundings influence her film work?*

INÉS M. MARTIATU: Sara had an enormous sociological imagination, as we used to say in that period. She lived on Cerrada del Paseo Street in Guadalupe, a neighborhood in Central Havana. A lot of black and *mulato* professionals with high school and university degrees—the so-called colored middle class—lived there. For example, Nicolás Guillén lived there, on Gervasio Street between Salud Street and Zanja Street, and some of the Abreu family, who were the owners of Marcos Abreu undertakers. José Luciano Franco, the historian; Dieppa the medical doctor; and Clarita Dieppa, who was a *mulata* ballet teacher in the conservatory. And the designer Esteban Ayala's family. Interesting people who had to do with the Atenas Club, like the Ayón family, who moved in the worlds of politics and history. Juan Gualberto Gómez's family also lived there for a while, and others I don't remember right now. It was a black neighborhood, just like the Cayo Hueso and San Leopoldo neighborhoods that Zanja Street crosses.

Despite the composition of these neighborhoods, there was no segregation as such in Cuba; we didn't live in ghettos because of racism. Black professionals had fewer opportunities for work and of course a lower economic level than their white colleagues with the same qualifications. The majority of middle-class people of color lived in the same neighborhoods alongside simple working-class people. The professionals often lived in relatively modest houses, and on the same block, there were always tenements or rooming houses, but we

Figure 2.1 Young Sara Gómez, circa 1957. © ICAIC

all lived together. That was and is the reality of neighborhoods like Cayo Hueso, San Leopoldo, Pueblo Nuevo, Los Sitios, Guadalupe, and others in Central Havana and Old Havana—like in Cerro, Jesús María, and other neighborhoods farther away from the center of the city. A lot of the time we went to the same public schools or small, very modest private schools. That's the reality that should be taken into account.

As you know, the middle class of color in colonial Cuba has been studied a lot more than the same group under the republic. This history, belonging in part to the black movement, has been subsumed somewhat in the version of the Cuban Left, something that has had, and continues to have, very interesting consequences on economic, religious, and cultural levels. In addition, in all these neighborhoods and alongside both white and black inhabitants, there were immigrant populations: Spanish, Arabs, Chinese, and others. In all these neighborhoods, people practiced religions of African origin, such as Santería, Palo Monte, and Spiritism. In each neighborhood, there were sets [*juegos*] of the Abakuá secret society, and almost all of them had their groups that represented them in the carnival.

There were also music conservatories, such as the Municipal Conservatory—the most important in Cuba before 1959—which was right there in Central Havana along with other smaller, private conservatories. It was a really rich atmosphere—cults and popular culture were interwoven. It's no accident that these neighborhoods were rich in popular music. Important orchestras and groups were founded there, composers and singers lived there, and they produced an enormously fruitful scene of traditional *trova* or balladeer music, Havana-style *son* music, and rumba. *Filin* music also arose there, along with other musical expressions belonging to the Havana urban music tradition. So, this was the kind of neighborhood in which Sara lived and grew up.

LOURDES MARTÍNEZ-ECHAZÁBAL: *I also grew up on Cerrada del Paseo Street—I was Sarita's neighbor. "Sarita" was our name for her in the neighborhood. But the truth is that we didn't know the neighborhood was called Guadalupe. We thought it was called Dragones.*

INÉS M. MARTIATU: The names may have changed over the years. Central Havana is now a municipality with different divisions than the original ones. This neighborhood, Guadalupe—I think it's Guadalupe—was very near the Chinese neighborhood. Although it might have been known as Dragones, but now all that has changed and now it's all Central Havana.

LOURDES MARTÍNEZ-ECHAZÁBAL: *Who did Sara live with? I remember there being a lot of women in that house!*

INÉS M. MARTIATU: Sara's parents were married very young and then got divorced. She was born very soon afterward. She was the first grandchild, and so her paternal grandmother took charge of her. Her grandmother's house was also the home of her aunt Aleida, who is a now-retired dentist and who adored her. Another aunt was a painting teacher; Cuca was a piano teacher and also made fashionable clothes and was very linked to the music scene; and another was a housewife who looked after all of them. They all overprotected Sara because she suffered from asthma and she was a very lively child. She was also critical of her family and so had to struggle hard against that overprotection. She was very much loved by both sides of the family—the maternal side and the paternal side that brought her up. But she also suffered a lot. She talked with me about a lot of things because we're girls of the same age.

LOURDES MARTÍNEZ-ECHAZÁBAL: *What school did she go to?*

INÉS M. MARTIATU: She attended primary school in Public School No. 30, and then Upper Primary No. 1 on the corner of our street, Cerrada del Paseo and Salud Street. Afterward, she went to the Havana Institute. Sara and I met in third grade. I lived in the Cayo Hueso neighborhood, which is also in Central Havana and very close to Sara's house on the other side of Belascoaín Street. The two of us studied music at the conservatory from third grade onward, but at the time, we weren't very close. It was in eighth grade when we were enrolled in the same school, Upper Primary No. 1. They allowed us to attend class in the morning and in the afternoon go to the conservatory. Afterward, we went together to the Havana Institute and ended up in the same class as Nancy Morejón; Edelmira "Mirita" Lores, who you knew; Reynaldo García Ramos; Norma Niurka González Acevedo; Amalia Arduengo; Trini and Fernando Pérez, who are siblings; and many more people I can't recall right now. We formed a group with common activities, but no one thought about becoming an intellectual or dedicating themselves to writing.

LOURDES MARTÍNEZ-ECHAZÁBAL: *I understood that Sara lived in the United States at some point. Do you know anything about that?*

INÉS M. MARTIATU: She didn't live there. Those are things that have been exaggerated or twisted later on. The ones who lived in New York were her mother, Juana Yera; her stepfather, Margarito Baró; and her sister, Micaela. Sara was there only for a short time.

As I said, in eighth grade, Sara and I got to know each other and we attended the same school, Upper Primary No. 1. On the first day of classes, I bumped into Sara in the lineup along with two or three other classmates, and

Figure 2.2 Sara Gómez at a friend's birthday party, circa 1957. © ICAIC

the first thing she said to me was: "Hey, my mum left today for the United States, but she hasn't abandoned me." I'll never forget it. She said it just like that. In other words, on the same day she started eighth grade, her mom emigrated to the US.

Sara was fifteen years old on November 8, 1957. I remember they threw a party for her in a hotel on Prado Street, and there were fifteen couples dancing there. I was in one of the couples. Just imagine! So, because Sara couldn't go to the US at that moment, and because her mother couldn't come to Cuba, Sara took a trip to the United States in the summer holidays of 1958.

LOURDES MARTÍNEZ-ECHAZÁBAL: *With whom did her mother emigrate?*

INÉS M. MARTIATU: With Sara's sister, Micaela, and with her husband at the time, a very good person, Margarito Baró, who wasn't Sara's father. At that stage, Sara began to suffer because she thought in her little girl's mind that her grandmother was to blame for her not living with her mother. I don't know, absurd stuff, because, on the contrary, they adored her, but you know how kids are.

LOURDES MARTÍNEZ-ECHAZÁBAL: *How long did she stay in the United States?*

INÉS M. MARTIATU: Twenty-nine days, as was customary at that time. They were those kinds of trips, for tourism. So Mirita—who lived across the street from Sara's family and was a descendent of José Maceo—accompanied her to New York. I suppose their families took advantage so neither of them would have to travel alone.

LOURDES MARTÍNEZ-ECHAZÁBAL: *Did that trip have any particular influence on her? What did she tell you?*

INÉS M. MARTIATU: I think it had its influence, but it didn't mark her as much as they have wanted to exaggerate because she didn't live there—she was on holiday in New York, in the Bronx, where her family lived. When she returned, I think she talked more about music than anything else. She brought back jazz records that she'd been given and talked about the city, but I don't think that influenced her, at least at that moment, and much less in her racial awareness. She already had that in any case.

In that period, there was nothing odd about traveling to the US. Black Cubans who migrated—and they were few—didn't go to the South. They went to Harlem, to the Bronx. Even whites I knew lived in those neighborhoods. A great friend of mine who's white and now lives in Miami, Eliseo Grenet's partner, lived in Cayo Hueso, emigrated, and went to live in Harlem in that period. In our conversations, Sara and I realized the similarity between our families, who had, in fact, known each other before. Sara's family, just like mine, were professionals, and they had friends who had already emigrated—like the singer Vicentico Valdés, who was a friend of Sara's stepfather, or Giraldo Piloto, father of the composer Giraldo Piloto [Piloto y Vera], who was very good friends with my father. Sara's stepfather was related to mine through his mother, who was from the town of Limonar in Matanzas. My paternal uncle, Mariano Martiatu, volunteered in 1918 for the First World War. He went to the US but didn't manage to go to war. He traveled constantly to the US to bring back used cars but never wanted to emigrate there with his family. Several people from my family, my cousins, had gone on excursions to New York. Every year there were two or three excursions to New York made by the black societies, and they used to meet up there. I have a photo of my female cousins who used to go. I didn't get to that stage. And in New York they used to go to the Cuban Club and the American Club, which were black venues. Those excursions were cheap, and sometimes people paid for them gradually in installments.

LOURDES MARTÍNEZ-ECHAZÁBAL: *Do you think that Sara's visit to the Bronx at that moment had any influence later on the way in which she addressed a range of themes in her documentaries?*

INÉS M. MARTIATU: I don't know why there's always an insistence in relating racism in the United States and South Africa with that of Cuba. People insist on relating Sara's racial awareness with that brief trip. As if here there wasn't enough racism in all of the periods to have experienced it and be aware of it. That astonishes me, and it bothers me a bit. Perhaps at that time she was too young to be able to reflect about a world she had just discovered, but when she started to speak about the racial issue in Cuba, I think she was able to reflect on it. On top of that, in Cuba we spoke out as black people and commented about racism in the US. We did this and also traveled on those excursions, some emigrated and studied there. The black North American nuns—the Oblate Sisters of Providence—ended up having several schools in Cuba with their head school in Baltimore, and some families were able to send their daughters to study there. My mother and my youngest aunt studied in one right here in Havana. Some members of the black societies held up the development of North American blacks as an example, and they had a relationship with the NAACP.

LOURDES MARTÍNEZ-ECHAZÁBAL: *Well, at least in this case, it's not about relating racism in the United States and South Africa with Cuba, much less to establish superficial comparisons between the racism in these countries. Although, frankly, a serious study about the issue might reveal interesting connections. Rather, it's about finding out whether, in some way, it enriched her with another, more transatlantic, way of thinking about Cuba based on her experience. This experience, on the one hand, was different in Cuban reality, and in particular in daily life in Central Havana. On the other, perhaps it wasn't so different. Although I dare say that an experience like Sara's at fifteen years of age must have marked her over the medium term, whether or not she was conscious of its importance in 1958.*

INÉS M. MARTIATU: Of course. She went to the American Club and met with black Cuban families. Before the Revolution, black Cubans didn't go to Miami. They didn't go to the South. They went to New York. In fact, I had a relative, my uncle's uncle, who was the last president of the Atenas Club: engineer Félix O'Farril. He was very Americanized—he was the model of the successful professional black American. And he rose to the position of chief technician of public works. In my house, although my father was a communist, he was an English teacher and he had a lot of information about jazz and about

Afro-American culture. He always went next door to the La Rampa cinema to buy *Ebony* and *Rhythm and Blues* magazines. I always marveled to see a black woman advertising Colgate or to discover that Nat King Cole was a millionaire and that he had a swimming pool. The influence of Afro-American culture was very strong and contradictory.

LOURDES MARTÍNEZ-ECHAZÁBAL: *What do you remember about the way she worked?*

INÉS M. MARTIATU: Sara was a cultured person, and she always studied rigorously before starting a new job or project. A group of us had read Proust, Sartre, Simone de Beauvoir, Camus, Hemingway, and also the great black writers. I remember with a lot of affection the *Anthology of Black and Madagascan Poetry* with a prologue by Sartre—a revelation for the group. But also, we didn't understand Carpentier, Lydia Cabrera, and Guillén—even Lezama. A teacher who was a friend of Lezama took us to the Bellas Artes to see him, and he laughed and gave away his books to the students from the institute who approached him. Many still remember him. "A fat man who gives away books," they said. We read everything that fell into our hands. We studied in the Institute of Ethnology and Folklore, which helped her a lot—she was no idiot. Also, when she began to work at ICAIC [Instituto Cubano del Arte e Industria Cinematográficos, or Cuban Film Institute] in August 1961, Sartre and de Beauvoir had just visited Cuba and we had already started to read Nicolás Guillén.

She worked on her scripts alone much of the time, but also with Tomás González or other scriptwriters. She wanted to be a filmmaker. One of her priorities was to bring black history to the fore. We entered ICAIC together and started to work as editing assistants. That was the first job they gave us. We were very young. A lot is said about her relationship with Tomás Gutiérrez Alea, but the person who exercised the most influence on Sara becoming an assistant director, which at that time was a step toward becoming a director, was Roberto Fandiño, who died in Miami some years ago.

LOURDES MARTÍNEZ-ECHAZÁBAL: *And how did she choose the themes for her documentaries? How did she decide what she should/would work on?*

INÉS M. MARTIATU: One of the first works was *Historia de la piratería* [History of piracy], a short that she made for the *Enciclopedia* or for the *Noticiero ICAIC Latinoamericano* [Latin American news of the ICAIC, or newsreels]. She

Figure 2.3 Sara Gómez on set for the filming of Tomás Gutiérrez Alea's *Cumbite*, 1962. © ICAIC

then worked on an educational theme, a film called *Excursión a Vuelta Abajo* (Excursion to Vuelta Abajo). They were films commissioned by ICAIC but in which she tried to put a lot of herself.

LOURDES MARTÍNEZ-ECHAZÁBAL: *How did she evolve toward making documentaries about black culture in Cuba?*

INÉS M. MARTIATU: There was no evolution—she was always interested, and even in *Historia de la piratería* she introduced some element related to black culture. I remember the first work along these lines was *Crónicas de mi familia* (Chronicles of my family) (1966), a documentary that has not been well conserved but in which historic images are shown of what black families similar to hers were like, a theme that hadn't appeared anywhere—not even in literature. It focuses on a family (related to hers) of musicians, from Guanabacoa, who talked about the black societies to which they belonged, about the different families and the relationships they had among themselves, and with music, always. With this work she began to show her potential.

LOURDES MARTÍNEZ-ECHAZÁBAL: *Who were the musicians of the family?*

INÉS M. MARTIATU: The husband of one of her aunts was a musician who played in important bands. One of Sara's uncles, Roberto Sánchez, played first clarinet in the symphony, and another cousin of hers... I don't know if he still plays, but it was the funniest thing—they made him study violin and everything, but he dedicated himself to the conga drum.

LOURDES MARTÍNEZ-ECHAZÁBAL: *There's a documentary of hers called Y... tenemos sabor (And we've got flavor) (1968) that is about different musical instruments, including some that at the time the documentary was made were no longer being used. Do you know if that documentary was commissioned by ICAIC?*

INÉS M. MARTIATU: No, that was her own initiative because nobody there was interested in those themes. She was interested in a lot of issues that others in the ICAIC didn't care about—that's the truth. They didn't know about them and they didn't care. Chucho Valdés is in that documentary. He was a friend of hers, and he wrote music for several of Sara's documentaries. Chucho is a year older than us. Then there's also Rembert Egües, Tomás González as a composer, and Omara [Portuondo], who sang a very good piece. There's also a great black singer who died prematurely. The film has the only image there is of him, Amadito Barceló, called Guapachá, from Cayo Hueso. He's not remembered much, but in my opinion, he had a lot of influence on present-day Latin jazz singers.

LOURDES MARTÍNEZ-ECHAZÁBAL: *And what can you tell me about the documentary* Una isla para Miguel *(An island for Miguel) (1968)?*

INÉS M. MARTIATU: At that stage, I worked a lot with her. It's a stage when Sara developed what I call her sociological imagination—she was a great sociologist. In those times, people used to do montage film, even from the formal point of view, but Sara didn't. She did sociological film, where she herself appeared in the interviews and broke with previous paradigms. She used long shots and let people speak, express themselves. There are three "island" documentaries. She made them with a great friend, the editor Caíta Villalón, Dulce María Villalón Mesa, a good friend and excellent film editor. I was Caíta's assistant at that point. Caíta edited important documentaries by Sara and also by Nicolasito Guillén Landrián, Octavio Cortázar, Enrique Pineda Barnet, and many others. These documentaries of Sara's weren't commissioned by the ICAIC either. She proposed them, and they accepted, which meant she could use ICAIC resources. Sara didn't just make sociological, black, or feminist film—it was very political film. She was always interested in current affairs, by what might be happening at that moment. Right then, for example, important things were happening on the Island of Youth (Isla de la Juventud; originally named the Isla de los Pinos, or Isle of Pines). So she took a trip to the island to find out all about that and did three very mature documentaries that became the precedent for *De cierta manera* (One way or another) (1974).

LOURDES MARTÍNEZ-ECHAZÁBAL: *You referred before to work that Sara carried out for the* Encyclopedia popular *or the ICAIC newsreels. What were these programs?*

INÉS M. MARTIATU: The *Enciclopedia popular* (Popular encyclopedia) was like a news magazine series in which upcoming directors premiered their work. They were given short informational or news pieces, but Sara always seemed to get her way with them. She'd never put up with something superficial. For example, she did a research piece with historical data about the Plaza Vieja in Havana and another about tobacco. She could also propose subjects, and two of these subjects became documentaries because she broadened their scope (beyond that of a newsreel short). The Ministry of Public Health got her to do them. One of them, which has been lost, is called *Atención prenatal* (Prenatal care) (1972) and the other *Año uno* (The first year) (1972). They were educational documentaries for teaching women how to care for themselves during pregnancy, how to care for children, how relations with nurses should be, etc. At the time, Sara was already ill, pregnant, and a patient in the maternity ward at América Arias Hospital, so she took advantage of her own experience—as feminists do—to work on this. She used her ID card as a pregnant woman, which showed her personal details and the things she had to do in the hospital, to interview other women patients and staff at the hospital who were from her neighborhood. And they took care of her. Doctor Heredia wouldn't discharge her, and so she took maximum advantage of the experience. It's an excellent documentary. I remember the baby's head coming out and the image covering the whole screen.

LOURDES MARTÍNEZ-ECHAZÁBAL: *What is your perspective on the relationship between Sara and the ICAIC?*

INÉS M. MARTIATU: These were ambiguous times in which not everyone had the same position there. Sara was respected because she made people respect

Figure 2.4 Still of Sara Gómez's son Alfredo in the film *Año uno*, 1972. © ICAIC

her. A lot of what she achieved was due to her own persistence, because she wouldn't easily take no for an answer. The problem was that many of the things she was working on couldn't be shown. They were documentaries that challenged or refuted certain, sometimes key, political projects.[1]

LOURDES MARTÍNEZ-ECHAZÁBAL: *Would it be possible to make these documentaries today?*

INÉS M. MARTIATU: Yes—the majority of them. For example, the island documentaries such as *Una isla para Miguel, En la otra isla* (On the other island) (1968), which is perhaps the most complete one, and *Isla del tesoro* (Treasure island) (1969). At this stage, she was already doing a series of *reportajes* (reporting-style documentaries). Maybe Reynaldo González remembers, because Reynaldo was working at the *Revista Cuba* (Cuba review), where Sara found out about the news and would try to participate in journalism and propose themes. She was doing very daring documentary work for those times about overtime and voluntary work, two topics that were very—and I mean *very*—sacred. In other words, anyone who dared to question anything was taking serious risks. And she did. On top of that, Sara managed to get the protagonists to speak, and they spoke the truth about how things were. So it was tremendous, because in those documentaries she used a series of images that were already stereotypes and almost sacred, even now. With these images she demonstrated that many of the slogans were quite empty, that in the end they didn't work in practice—they weren't economically viable. She discovered this fact and said so—this is like this, that, and the other—and she sought out the main people involved, not only so they would talk about it but also so they'd say it on camera.

LOURDES MARTÍNEZ-ECHAZÁBAL: *How long did she work at the ICAIC?*

INÉS M. MARTIATU: From August 1961 until her death in June 1974.

LOURDES MARTÍNEZ-ECHAZÁBAL: *How would you say her relationship was with the ICAIC during those thirteen years?*

INÉS M. MARTIATU: At ICAIC they let her work—they knew what she was doing and they respected her. She was the first woman in everything she did—not just the first to make a feature-length film. But they didn't put her in *Cine Cubano* (Cuban cinema, a magazine) until just before her death, and the same thing occurred with *Mujeres* (the magazine of the Federation of Cuban Women). This didn't happen only with Sara, but also with many others who had a lot of talent. They asked Alfredo Guevara about this, and he never answered, simply saying that he went that way because he thought that what she was doing was important and he let her get on with it. But her work wasn't shown.

She didn't have any other privileges, like taking trips. In fact, something curious happened: They refused her maternity leave, and she had to leave ICAIC for a year around '64 or '65 because the contracts for creators in ICAIC didn't take into account the possibility that women could be directors, much less that they might give birth. They refused her maternity leave even when this had been achieved by the Cuban trade union movement before the Revolution. In a period in which this kind of leave was being promoted and there was a lot of propaganda about women's rights, they refused it to Sara Gómez—the only female film director. It's incredible that even for propaganda reasons they never promoted her as the first revolutionary black woman film director. During those years, Sara filmed *Mi aporte* (My contribution) (1972), one of her most mature documentaries about the incorporation of women into paid work, with a very interesting analysis. But this documentary was lost because someone wrongfully took it out of Cuba. Although afterward it was recovered.[2]

LOURDES MARTÍNEZ-ECHAZÁBAL: *But over the last few years, things have been changing and now a lot of people are interested in her work.*

INÉS M. MARTIATU: Yes. For example, in 2007 there was a colloquium on Sara Gómez. We met with a group of young people in my house to prepare it. Because the young people who didn't know her were very interested in her work and she's a model for them.[3] The director, Jorge Luis Sánchez, had never met her, but he promoted the screening of some of her work, studied her, and brought out her influence in his interpretation of documentary film. Now there are master's theses and other writings about her. At that moment, in the 2007 colloquium, *Mi aporte* was shown for the first time. That day, a group of about forty of us were able to see it. I have a copy of that documentary because Sandra Alvarez managed to copy it onto DVD.

LOURDES MARTÍNEZ-ECHAZÁBAL: *With what you're telling me, it seems that Sara's relationship with the ICAIC had its ups and downs—it was a changeable relationship. If Sara hadn't died, do you think they would have kicked her out of the ICAIC?*

INÉS M. MARTIATU: That would be speculation on my part. And it would have a lot to do with how Cuban cultural policy evolved during that time. It's a difficult question to answer. It would depend on so many factors, even international ones. But perhaps they wouldn't have kicked her out. In fact, around that time of the five and ten gray year periods, I don't remember anyone being kicked out of ICAIC as easily as it happened with people doing theater and in other cultural sectors. That depended a lot on the power of Alfredo Guevara, who defended many people. But that's another story.

I am sure, though, that *De cierta manera* would not have premiered as easily if Sara had been alive. Things occurred with that film that didn't come out of nowhere: the master of the film got damaged, and in Cuba, there was no way to fix something like that until years later, when it was repaired in Sweden with a new technique. It also ended up "premiering" as a play in 1976 under the title *Al duro y sin careta* (No holds barred). What happened is that *De cierta manera* was a polemical film. Tomás González worked with Sara as a scriptwriter, and for the protagonist's role he had Mario Balmaseda, a friend of ours since adolescence and a good actor with whom Sara had fought (because Sara fought with everyone)—she fought with me, too, and got me into some terrible scrapes. I still don't know what the gossip was, but Sara was like those terrorist organizations, and when something was said about Mario making some comment, she just attributed it to him even if he hadn't said it. But she had to make peace with Mario if he was going to be the film's protagonist. Since time was passing and the film still hadn't been shown, Mario performed the film with a theater group. Although by then, Sara had already died. Tomás González criticized Mario, even though the stage production was an interesting experiment and created pressure to show the film. It was strange how a play was based on a film, and not the other way around, as usually happens.

LOURDES MARTÍNEZ-ECHAZÁBAL: *What can you tell us about Sara's work in journalism?*

INÉS M. MARTIATU: That it was brief and happened after the triumph of the Revolution. When we were studying to finish secondary school, we were intellectually curious and lively. We participated in everything. We went to the theater, we read nonstop, and we were offered space to collaborate with *Mella* magazine—there were eight pages for reviewing shows. The magazine belonged to the Juventud Socialista (Socialist Youth), although we didn't belong to that group.

LOURDES MARTÍNEZ-ECHAZÁBAL: *Who directed* Mella *magazine during that period?*

INÉS M. MARTIATU: Carlos Quintela. Almost everyone who directed *Mella* is in Miami now. Eventually we were kicked out of there, of course. We were considered to be extravagant because we wore such and such clothes and because we studied at the Institute of Ethnology and Folklore of the National Theater of Cuba, which was considered contrary to scientific thinking.

LOURDES MARTÍNEZ-ECHAZÁBAL: *How long did you work at the magazine?*

INÉS M. MARTIATU: We were there for more than a year. Some of the leadership liked us—others, not at all.

LOURDES MARTÍNEZ-ECHAZÁBAL: *And what kind of work did you do?*

INÉS M. MARTIATU: We wrote all kinds of things. We did reviews of films or plays, or of records. I remember—I don't know which of the two of us wrote something about the first record Omara Portuondo did as a solo artist that she doesn't even mention now. It was called *Magia Negra* (Black magic) (1961), and on that record, she really stood out as a true Latin jazz singer. It's really good, produced with Julio Gutiérrez and his orchestra, but nobody mentions it. We had to write about the films of the year. They always tried to pressure us in lots of ways, because it was a very political magazine and every day it got more reactionary. For example, it was against rock and roll, against English music, and against lots of other things.

LOURDES MARTÍNEZ-ECHAZÁBAL: *Tell me something about* Mella *magazine: would you consider it a precursor of the* Caimán Barbudo*?*

INÉS M. MARTIATU: No, it was different. It came from the communists. It belonged to the youth wing of the Partido Socialista Popular (Popular Socialist Party). They also ran the newspaper *Hoy* (Today), led by Blas Roca and Carlos Rafael Rodríguez. We not only collaborated with the magazine but also contributed to the cultural pages of *Hoy* that came out every Sunday. I remember there were reviews of new works by the Danza Nacional (National Dance Company) and other interesting things that were happening. The cultural section was directed by Fayad Jamís and Manuel Díaz Martínez, and not by someone like Quintela, who said that all the Sistine Chapel had done for him was give him a crick in the neck! Manolo and Fayad became our friends, and we used to go out with them. They were a different kind of people, like others who also gathered there regularly, because they were poets.

LOURDES MARTÍNEZ-ECHAZÁBAL: *Apart from covering art and culture, did you both write about other themes?*

INÉS M. MARTIATU: Yes. In fact . . . when the crisis [October Crisis] happened . . . and we already knew the Americans were going to attack. It was December, and it was really cold. They sent Sara to the south to the province of Las Villas and me to Yaguajay to a place called Itabo, where I felt the worst cold in my entire life. I was accompanied by Marina Duchesne, who was the director's secretary and slightly older than me, and I'm sure they thought she was more responsible. Amalia Arduengo, who we'd brought into *Mella* around that time, was sent to the worst place: to Escambray, where she must have found out about the dangerous bandits who were raping and killing there. When Kennedy took over from Eisenhower, they confined us to headquarters, and we slept on top of the desks in the office.

I remember they put me in charge of a job to prove that Russia participated in the wars of independence, but those Russians didn't show up anywhere. They drove me crazy in the National Archives. Some adventurers appeared that had nothing to do with it. The good thing was that I got to know Conrado Massaguer, the great caricature artist, who told me some interesting anecdotes. Our last days at *Mella* came when the film *Hiroshima mi amor* premiered. Adolfo Rivero Caro was at the magazine at the time—he died not long ago in Miami. He was a very dogmatic man who was also very rude, and he offended me. I was an eighteen-year-old girl, and he told me the message of the film was "Open your legs, you I-don't-know-what." So Sara and I decided to leave. But the style was to kick people out and humiliate them. I remember, in a normal voice we told Carlos Quintela that we were leaving, and he shouted for everyone to hear that we should go, that he was kicking us out. That was their style.

LOURDES MARTÍNEZ-ECHAZÁBAL: *With respect to Sara's filmography, what do you think are the most important themes we find in her work?*

INÉS M. MARTIATU: That's not an easy question to answer. After *De cierta manera*, Sara's interest in the theme of marginality was exaggerated, using historical materialism's definition of marginality as being declassed and not belonging to either of the two fundamental classes—the proletariat or the bourgeoisie. I think that she was interested in those themes, but also in music, the presence of black culture in general, and women. If you analyze her documentaries, you find evidence of her work in political themes other than marginality. For example, how popular power functioned, voluntary work, the situation of women (whether black or white), about women's insertion into the workplace, and religion—although her interest in religion has also been exaggerated.

LOURDES MARTÍNEZ-ECHAZÁBAL: *Curious that you didn't touch on the theme of the black liberation movement in the United States given the precedent of Santiago Álvarez Román and his documentary* NOW! (1965).

INÉS M. MARTIATU: Yes, she was very interested in that theme, but perhaps she didn't have time. I know she met several figures from the Black Power movement, but right now I don't remember their names. She may have known Angela Davis because, before she was famous, Angela Davis came to Cuba several times. I do know that she met Eldridge and Kathleen Cleaver and others who came here.[4]

LOURDES MARTÍNEZ-ECHAZÁBAL: *What can you tell me about her relationship with, or influence over, other directors?*

INÉS M. MARTIATU: She used a series of documentary elements in a very different way. She knew what she was doing. Sara gave a lot of help to the Belgian-born French filmmaker Agnès Varda, who was in Cuba, and she also influenced Titón [Tomás Gutiérrez Alea].[5] Not so much on a technical level, perhaps, but in content—even though everyone thinks it was the other way around. They were very good friends, and I think that without Sara, Titón would not have made *Cumbite*, because he didn't know anything about blacks and she did.[6] Or, for example, the film *Hasta cierto punto* (To a certain point), in which Titón tried to use Sara's technique from *De cierta manera*.

LOURDES MARTÍNEZ-ECHAZÁBAL: *The version we have received of* De cierta manera *has many elements from ethnographic film. For example, among other things, the presence of the voice-over narrator. The voice-over narrator has always surprised me. It's a discourse that collides in a way and contradicts, one might say, the film's critical ethos and dramatic proposal. From my perspective, it gives it quite a didactic and officialist tone.*

INÉS M. MARTIATU: There are two narrative lines—the fictional one and the other one. But I differ from you—they don't seem to me to be contradictory. Sara and others of us who studied religion and the way it interweaves with the social don't consider religions of African origin to be perfect. In Abakuá and in Santería there are positive things, but there are other things that aren't. Especially the position of women in them. Sara, of course, had something to say about that—for example, about machismo. She had to criticize certain concepts, certain ethical issues, that you see in the workplace, or the relationship between Mario and Yolanda as a couple. I don't think they were concessions or contradictions, but a lot of truth about what we were, and still are, suffering.

LOURDES MARTÍNEZ-ECHAZÁBAL: *Yes, but that narrative line that you call "the other one" is enunciated from an officialist perspective. For example, I always remember—because it had such an impact on me—the discourse of the voice-over when referring to the Abakuá societies. These are the words that were used: "We think that their nature as secret, traditional, and exclusive societies situates them in opposition to progress and makes them incapable of inserting themselves into the values of modern life. Currently, they represent a source of marginality since they promote a parallel code for social relations, points of intransigence, and the rejection of social integration" (15:14–15:36). You can't tell me that this discourse isn't severe, because the nineteenth-century positivist ideological baggage it draws from is enough to put you off completely. Also, from my perspective, the use of concepts* such as "modern life," "exclusive nature," and "social integration" warrant serious reflection in the context of Cuban national culture. But anyway, that's another story.

INÉS M. MARTIATU: And how do you know if it's said from an officialist perspective or not? And it's true, unfortunately, that they create obstacles. It's exemplified in the workplace and in couple's relations, and the criminality of those who believe that to be Abakuá they have to kill. They're in prison. Of course, it's not always like that, and I'm not capable of putting myself on the side of those who are prejudiced about this. There are Abakuás who are professionals, white and black, doctors.... Recently there was a congress about this in the Anthropology Institute. But one can't always easily dismiss a criticism as officialism. I admire everything that the Abakuá did in the colony and its role in the workers' movement in Cuba, but nothing is perfect. Did you know about the criminal activity in certain Abakuá areas right now? So it's very debatable and you can't make abusive generalizations about it. There are Abakuás and Abakuás, and I know them at close quarters.

Sara was married to Germinal Hernández, the best sound technician at ICAIC and my brother's friend, who was a party militant, architect, and science PhD, and was like many others who weren't Abakuás but who grew up in the neighborhood. Germinal, the father of her two youngest children, was an Aberiñán of the Enforienkomó Usagaré Muñanga set (*juego*) in Cayo Hueso, my neighborhood, and for a long time its headquarters was on my block. There were many outstanding members with positions in music and in many other fields. Many of them very decent and outstanding, even in baseball. On top of that, why do you identify it with official discourse?

LOURDES MARTÍNEZ-ECHAZÁBAL: *Well, you tell me who, if not official sources, makes pronouncements with the proverbial use of we—"we believe that..."—in a film produced under the aegis of a state organization as the ICAIC was and continues to be. Of course, I might be wrong, but with what I know about Sara's visual discourse and cinematographic practice, I don't think her style manifests itself through the use of a binary and positivist language (that situates, for example, backwardness or civilization versus progress, or marginality versus social integration). I also understand that the version of the film that Sara conceived and filmed didn't have a voice-over narrator, but this was added after Sara's death [the script has narration—Ed.]. Looking at it this way, one could say that the presence of this didactic and normative voice that speaks for the Revolution, and that, according to Sergio Giral—who also worked with Sara in the ICAIC—was added to the script during the film's postproduction. If this is so, I would dare to suggest that the voice-over narrator serves as a mediating agent for, as it were, the critically imperfect character of* De cierta manera *and of Sara Gómez's work in general. In* De cierta manera, *as in most of her documentaries, Sara portrays the collision between theory and practice—between the revolutionary program and the real difficulty of its implementation. Curiously, one of the aims of* cine imperfecto *was to present stories on the screen that reveal the problems, processes, and experiences—often conflicts with which audience members could and should identify as part of their daily life. In this sense,* De cierta manera *situates itself within* cine imperfecto, *but far from offering preconceived solutions, it puts its finger in the wound and questions these things.*

INÉS M. MARTIATU: The person who would know for sure about this issue of the voice-over narrator is her editor, Iván Arocha, who lives in New York, because he was there in the editing room.[7] The film, supposedly, was finished between Iván, Julio García Espinosa—part of the leadership but a very bad film director—and Titón, trying to defend something there. They must have tried to defend the film, and, as I told you, it took years to come out.

LOURDES MARTÍNEZ-ECHAZÁBAL: *Acting now as a bit of a devil's advocate, why do you think the film was the focus of so much conflict? In the end, it's a film showing the work being done in building the Revolution in terms of getting people out of poverty and the shantytowns like Las Yaguas, and also out of mental obscurantism and counterproductive customs. So I don't understand very well what about the film was so upsetting for some people.*

INÉS M. MARTIATU: I'll start by saying that the things that upset people were not questions of taste. I don't see the film as being as inoffensive as you do. The film shows that, despite all those good intentions, it's not at all easy. Remember that at the end nothing is resolved. Also, remember that the themes Sara touches on, and the film itself, are still current. There is still racism, prejudice, violence, machismo, and prostitution. Look at the denigrating way in which official tourist material treats women alongside the phenomenon of the *jineterismo* in general, which has reached incredible levels.[8] The same with corruption and theft on every level. None of these problems that existed on a small or larger scale before has been resolved yet.

Also, Sara was alive. Is still alive. This is why many people want to disassociate themselves from her, especially people from my generation—just in case. They are afraid of her, even after she's dead. No one knew what it was that she was capable of saying or criticizing that might be seen as inconvenient. Perhaps the racial issue was what caused upset, which at that moment was said to be endangering the unity of the nation. Sara was interested in issues of race—it was one of her most important themes. In fact, Sara was summoned to meet with José Llanusa Gobel, the minister of education in that period, and she was only saved because she was in the ICAIC. Otherwise, she would have been kicked out. She told me that she was very curious to see that in the education minister's office there wasn't a single book. I'll never forget that. In any case, Sara's filmography is hardly known. The government was very aware, extremely so, that Sara was a very important figure in the black protest or black consciousness movement, together with Tomás González, Walterio Carbonell, Alberto Pedro Mendive, and Rogelio Martínez Furé. All black people, or those of us who dealt with these issues, were under suspicion even if we did nothing, you understand. Even black diplomats and Nicolasito Guillén Landrián—all of that is there.

When Llanusa summoned Sara after the Education and Culture Congress, it was for a meeting at which Tomás González, Alberto Pedro, and others I don't recall were also present. He argued with them all together, and afterward there were also separate conversations. But I know he called us "Black Power," questioned whether or not we had our hair this way or that. Some people were afraid. It was a complicated situation.

LOURDES MARTÍNEZ-ECHAZÁBAL: *It's curious—you referred to the movement, and I've been told it didn't exist, so I have to ask you: what movement?*

INÉS M. MARTIATU: Who denies it? It existed from the very moment that people manifested themselves, that artworks about black issues were created, that people dressed or arranged their hair in a certain way, etc. Even though it was outlawed in schools and the workplace, even if it was incipient and repressed, it existed. If there hadn't been a movement, the functionaries that repressed all of these expressions wouldn't have cared. They knew that certain intellectuals and other black young people shared these opinions. I remember we read books by black authors, those of [Frantz] Fanon, *The Autobiography of Malcolm X* passed from hand to hand, and other materials about black consciousness and culture from the United States and the Caribbean. Despite the criticism, the repression, and being thrown out of schools and workplaces, there was a desire—a will for self-affirmation as black people, black beauty, etc.

People shouted at me in the streets that I should comb my hair, that I had garbage on my head. Of course, I couldn't participate in a lot of things because I had an unbearable husband, my children's father, who didn't agree very much with all of this, and also my children were small. That man wasn't in a marriage *with* me but *against* me. Even so, I participated, and I was friends with all of them. And it was hard! I experienced what they did to Nicolasito Guillén Landrián and other very sad things.

Translated from the Spanish by Helen Dixon

NOTES

Published in Spanish as "¡Sara es mucha Sara!" in the *Afro-Hispanic Review*, vol. 33, no. 1, 2014.

1. It has been said that Sara's filmmaking is anthropological and sociological and that she is a feminist. She was doing all this and perhaps much more. All these angles are valid. As I have written elsewhere, I would risk supporting a thesis about political cinema based on Sara Gómez's work (Jaramillo and Lucía Ortiz 2011, 269).—Interviewer

2. Susan Lord returned a VHS copy to Cuba for the colloquium. It had been given to her by Ricardo Acosta and David McIntosh as a result of their program "*Crónicas de mi familia*: New Cuban Film and Video." See Lord's introduction to this volume for more information on that project.—Ed.

3. The group that prepared the colloquium included Sandra Álvarez, Sandra del Valle, Norma Guillard, and Danae Diéguez.—Ed.

4. Gómez was among the first black women to leave her hair in its natural state, and she received a telegram from Stokely Carmichael congratulating her as the "first free head" in Cuba.—Ed.

5. Varda made a documentary in Cuba based on animating still photos. *Salut les cubains* (1963) includes a young, dancing Sara Gómez along with other elements from Havana, which Varda could not have known about except through Gómez.—Ed.

6. *Cumbite* is an Afro-Cuban word meaning spiritual gathering.—Trans.

7. See Ricardo Acosta's interview with Arocha and Lourdes Martínez-Echazábal and María Caridad Cumaná's interview with Mesa (both in this volume) for more insight about the postproduction of *De cierta manera*.—Ed.

8. *Jineterismo* literally means "riders" and refers to those who seek out relations with foreigners to get ahead in ways that may or may not involve prostitution.—Trans.

BIBLIOGRAPHY

Jaramillo, María Mercedes, and Lucía Ortiz, eds. 2011. *Hijas del Munt: Biografías críticas de mujeres afrodescendientes de América Latina*. Bogotá, Colombia: Panamericana.

INÉS MARÍA MARTIATU TERRY (1942–2013) was a Cuban writer, theater critic, scholar, social activist, and advocate for African culture and narrative throughout Latin America. Her written legacy includes fifteen books, many articles and essays, and numerous academic and social contributions. She was a member of UNEAC (Unión Nacional de Escritores y Artistas de Cuba). She was editor with Devyn Spence Benson and Daisy Rubiera Castillo of *Afrocubanas: History, Thought, and Cultural Practices.*

LOURDES MARTÍNEZ-ECHAZÁBAL is Professor of Latin American and Latino Studies at the University of California, Santa Cruz. She is author of *Para una semiótica de la mulatez*. She is founder with Raúl Fernández of the UC-Cuba Academic Initiative, a University of California multicampus research program.

THREE

Inquisitive Gazes

Sara Gómez's Perspectives on Social Marginality from and within the Cuban Revolution

Odette Casamayor-Cisneros

For Inés María "Lalita" Martiatu, witness, memory, voice

"She could have been just a 'middle class' black female pianist" (Fulleda Léon 1999, 43). But she wasn't. Instead, Sara Gómez was, and still is decades after her death, the most important woman filmmaker in Cuban cinema. Gómez's right to this title is affirmed in her creation of more than fifteen timelessly relevant documentaries and the first feature-length film written and directed by a Cuban woman. Her work is marked by originality, high-quality cinematographic technique, and an acute poetic wit. At the same time, Gerardo Fulleda Léon, a black writer of Gómez's creative and intellectual milieu, was right: Nothing in her family history hinted at the course her professional life would take. She seemed destined to remain within the traditional sociocultural canon adopted by the Cuban middle classes until the triumph of the Cuban Revolution in 1959. She could very well have been a modest teacher or pianist, or anything else that fit with the patterns of behavior encouraged in her family. They were members of an incipient black and *mulato* urban petite bourgeoisie mostly composed of public school teachers, musicians, dedicated housewives, and businesspeople of modest means. However, instead of following the traditional path, the young Sara Gómez immersed herself in the intellectual frenzy of the first years of the Revolution (Álvarez 2008, 38) and unexpectedly became a journalist and regular collaborator on a university publication (*Revista Mella*) and a Communist Party magazine (*Hoy Domingo*).

In 1960, Gómez registered as a student at the Instituto de Etnología y Folklore (Institute of Ethnology and Folklore), where she studied popular culture, religion, and socially marginalized groups. A year later, she was working as an assistant director in the Instituto Cubano del Arte e Industria Cinematográficos (Cuban Film Institute) under the tutelage of renowned filmmakers such as Tomás Gutiérrez Alea, the Belgian-born French director Agnès Varda, and Santiago Álvarez. It was in the *Enciclopedia popular* (Popular encyclopedia; an educational documentary series supervised by Santiago Álvarez) that Gómez's first works appeared, making her Cuba's first woman director. Her trajectory was steady. From the beginning of her career, she made use of a penetrating socioethnographic gaze and demonstrated a keen interest in Cubans' daily lives, observed clearly in works such as *Plaza Vieja* (Old town square) (1962), *Solar habanero* (Havana tenement) (1962), *Historia de la piratería* (History of piracy) (1963), and *Iré a Santiago* (I'm going to Santiago) (1964). Her close collaborator, Tomás González, praised Gómez as a "natural sociologist" (1998, 113). In her cinematic productions, traditionally marginalized individuals receive particular attention.

The following pages explore Sara Gómez's unique perspective—as a black Cuban woman from the lower middle class who was committed to the revolutionary process—on marginality in postrevolutionary Cuban society.

THE NEW MAN AND THE COSMOLOGY OF THE CUBAN REVOLUTION

The transformation of the revolutionary subject is an essential concern in Gómez's work, particularly in her documentary trilogy about the lives of the young inhabitants of the Isle of Pines, which was renamed in 1978 Isla de la Juventud (Island of Youth) by the revolutionary authorities who built centers for youth reeducation there. The series is made up of *En la otra isla* (On the other island) (1968), *Una isla para Miguel* (An island for Miguel) (1968), and *Isla del tesoro* (Treasure island) (1969). The second film in the series, *Una isla para Miguel*, offers a deep analysis of the reeducation process experienced by a group of teens who are called the "Vikings" due to their violent and rebellious behavior. Gómez's voice-over explains that they had the morals of their neighborhoods, marginal environments where "being a man means being macho and being a friend." They are on the Isle of Pines, the narrator continues, to learn "the ethics of work." The documentary filmmaker not only describes these adolescents' experiences of reeducation but also researches her protagonists' social and family origins.

As the film begins, fourteen-year-old Miguel is at a disciplinary hearing—for exclusively educational purposes, according to the state authorities—accused of having "thrown stones at the birds." The film then

Figure 3.1 Still of Miguel, on the left, and his family, *Una isla para Miguel*, 1968. © ICAIC

tells Miguel's story. He comes from a poor family and is one of fourteen children. (See fig. 3.1.) In Havana, he had a marginal existence plagued by bad influences that contributed to his irresponsible and antisocial behavior. The camera shows the extremely poor and overcrowded environment of his family home, featuring a Santería shrine—a Cuban religion of Yoruba origins. Miguel's family thinks that the best way to change his disrespectful behavior is to send him away from the neighborhood and force him to comply with the harsh regime on the Isle of Pines. Subsequent images show a group of boys marching, among them Miguel. Although the filmmaker is careful not to impose a grandiloquent or triumphant tone, and nothing in her films is presented as definitive, Miguel is becoming the "New Man" necessary to the communist endeavor.

Gómez's reflections on the creation of a new subjectivity are not divorced from the debates taking place among intellectuals, ideologues, and politicians during the first years of the Revolution. In a 1965 pamphlet titled "El socialismo y el hombre en Cuba" (Socialism and man in Cuba), Ernesto Guevara asserted that, "in order to build communism, as we lay its material foundations, we must also create the New Man" (1970, 372). Gómez, however, aimed to expose both the positive and negative social, moral, cultural, and psychological particularities of each individual, while Guevara extended his description of the revolutionary subject-in-the-making to offer a uniform "product" conceived as an "actor of that strange and intense drama entailed in building socialism."[1] He examined this new subject "in its double existence as a unique being and as a member of the community" (371). To Guevara, the masses are an essential character in the configuration of the New Man, and this is his central concern. Guevara wanted to counteract critics who accused the socialist state of annulling individuality. Through his interpretation of Cuban revolutionary history, he explains how society builds a new type of individual. The guerrilla war, the popular mobilizations, and certain crucial events launch the formation of the New Man always from within the masses. Both the individual and the masses are objectified in Guevara's text. While indispensable for ensuring social transformation, the individual and the masses constitute characters that become active only after they are propelled forward by the avant-garde (the guerrilla commanded by Fidel Castro). In Guevara's perspective, Castro is the original active agent—the great maker of destinies. However, the process is complicated, as Guevara is obliged to admit. Society and its leaders are not the only agents responsible for the "direct and indirect education" of the revolutionary subject. The subject himself or herself must also be able to submit to a "conscious process of self-education" (371).

Gómez recognizes the importance of this process but draws attention to the fact that it does not occur along a linear trajectory or without accident, as if immersed in a space filled only by socialist ideology. Other factors are also responsible for problems in the formation of the heralded New Man such as erratic policy, disorganization, and dogmatism. The filmmaker is conscious of these other factors and is determined to demonstrate them in her work. If, for Guevara, young people are the "clay with which the New Man can be built without previous defects" (1970, 380), then for Gómez, the adolescents undergoing reeducation on the Isle of Pines cannot evade their pasts. What Guevara means by "defects" is not clear, but what is certain is that in Gómez's perspective, these alleged defects might be simply personal characteristics and understandable consequences of the individual's social and family contexts, which will not disappear automatically from their lives. The process of personal transformation cannot be understood as a mechanical one akin to docile clay being shaped by the hands of an expert sculptor. This was a poor metaphor employed by Guevara.

In theory, the main characteristics of the New Man exist in synergy with the cosmology of the Cuban Revolution. I have used the term *cosmology* in previous work to refer to the body of ideas conditioned by the revolutionary experience that gives logic to the world in which Cubans have been living since 1959, which rationally and emotionally sustains their existence (Casamayor 2013, 32–35). The cosmology of the Cuban Revolution justifies the continuity of the current political system based on an epic concept of an existence molded by the ideal of heroic sacrifice, resistance, and confrontation with external and internal enemies. The cosmology of the Cuban Revolution gave structure to a humanist and rationalist vision of the world. In 1961, when the revolutionary government became affiliated with the socialist system led by the Soviet Union, Marxist-Leninist precepts came to dominate the island's political and ideological landscape. As a result, starting in the early 1960s, many creative Cubans gave themselves the urgent task of exorcising the "original sin of the intellectual" (Guevara 1970, 371) of not being authentically revolutionary. For ideologues like Guevara, this "defect" resulted from not being raised within revolutionary society. Cubans who were born before 1959 were educated under capitalism (Guevara 1970, 380) and thus were obliged to improve themselves. The path to follow was that outlined by Guevara in his model of the New Man.

The Bay of Pigs battle in 1961, the Cuban Missile Crisis a year later, and then numerous counterrevolutionary attacks and threats ideologically and existentially framed the 1960s as a period dominated by a sense of confrontation and heroism. According to Tzvi Medin, this framework implies "first of all, complete identification with the guerrilla epic and with Fidel Castro, but it also implies establishing the omnipresence of a constant situation of extremity that imposes self-definition, compromise, militancy, social cohesion cemented by the indispensable national consensus, and mobilization. The alternative in a situation of confrontation is dilettantism, indifference, passivity, disintegration caused by division in the face of the enemy—in a word, betrayal" (1990, 29). Recognizing this need to establish a national consensus is crucial for understanding the racial and gender policies put in place by the Cuban Revolution. The revolutionary government saw the struggles to revalue the role of women in society and to counteract racial discrimination as key to ensuring national unity and strengthening the nation against counterrevolutionary aggression.

Such was the political and ideological context in which Sara Gómez's cinema as well as her critical gaze developed. Through her work she inquired into the ways in which those segments of Cuban society that traditionally were discriminated against, especially blacks and women, were suddenly immersed in a project of complete national reconstruction. What place, she asks, is reserved for marginalized individuals in this concept of the New Man, the ontological structure at the heart of the cosmology of the Cuban Revolution? Can marginalized people participate in this renewal of identity? Will they? These are some of the questions she raises in her polemical inquiry, which underlie my analysis here.

MARGINALITY AND REVOLUTION: SARA GÓMEZ QUESTIONS, DISTURBS, AND SURPRISES

The revolutionary subject, especially that utopian construction called the New Man, lacks racial, gender, and sexual identification. The *man* in the term *New Man* is intended to be understood to mean "human" and to specify neither man nor woman. However, a subject whose heroism is described in such ironclad terms nevertheless acquires a certain virility simply through its characterization. The New Man also does not have specific color or cultural traits. Perhaps the New Man is that "Cuban color" dreamed of by the poet Nicolás Guillén (2002) in the 1930s, and the culture of the revolutionary subject is that which the Revolution promotes.[2] The New Man belongs to just one family—the Cuban people—since Guevara stipulated that no life was possible for this subject outside the Revolution.

The Cuban Revolution adopted a model of the nation foreshadowed by the ethical structures designed by José Martí, an ideologue who was proclaimed the "apostle" of Cuban independence during the republican years (1902–58). After 1959, Martí was revered as a national hero in secular terms deemed more appropriate for the new period. Following Martí's ideals, the Cuban Revolution assumed that, for all citizens, national identity prevails over any other possible identity. A certain modern mysticism underlies the concept of *cubanidad* (Cubanness) inspired by Martí's project, in which the concept of the nation becomes sacred. From this perspective, Patria is the goddess adored, and everything is sacrificed on her altar—the only true home of Cubans. All differences must be forgotten, because what is truly important is to guide the nation along a positive path. To do so, the unity of all Cubans first must be forged and then protected. Patriotism, which for Martí represented the motor of national progress, subordinates economic, racial, sexual, gender, and cultural conditions (1963a).

Martí's celebrated statement, "Man is more than white, more than *mulato*, more than black" (1963b, 298), has dominated revolutionary ideology and structured all official thinking about racial issues from 1959 to the present. From the end of the 1960s until well into the 1980s, all pertinent discussion about the racial question in Cuba came up against implacable obstacles put in place by authorities who claimed they acted in the legitimate defense of the Revolution. They argued that in Cuba, there are no longer black Cubans or white

Cubans—only revolutionary Cubans destined to become expressions of the New Man.

According to Ernesto Guevara, the New Man had to serve as an example for the rest of society. As a result, any person taking on this exemplary role could not be perceived by other citizens as primitive or ignorant. Even when the New Man was a woman, it was important that she achieve a certain level of virility—heroic, brave, and, as a communist, atheist. Any Marxist-Leninist person must believe only, and completely, in political doctrine. Consequently, African-rooted Cuban religions and other cultural elements considered "uncivilized" could not appear in the value system of the New Man, who would lead revolutionary society toward progress and the future. As de la Fuente (2001) and Sawyer (2006) note, any racial difference became anachronistic, an expression of contrast between the past and the present, and something impossible in the contradiction-free and homogeneous future that awaited Cubans.

Consistent with the positions on Cuban racial identity stipulated by the revolutionary government, two images of black Cubans proliferated in the island's cultural production: the pre-1959 alienated black subject, exploited and marked by the "bad" influences of capitalism, and the "new black" subject. These stereotypes of black Cubans were common in the cultural production of the revolutionary period. Like other caricatures of black Cubans that populate *costumbrista* literature (a nineteenth-century genre of social types in everyday life), these new characters did not exist of their own accord. Together, the alienated black Cuban and the one "redeemed" by the new regime were created to celebrate the greatness of the Revolution. However, as stereotypes, both necessarily failed to represent the true black Cuban experience. Black people were actors playing roles assigned to them within a fiction they did not write. Their fictitious otherness resides first in the fact that they form an undeniably active part of the nation and second in that they are thought of as others and their blackness as otherness within a sociocultural context where a Eurocentric, hegemonic vision has prevailed since the inception of the Cuban nation.

In film, these stereotypes are represented through black characters who generally serve to illustrate the period of colonization, slavery, and miserable prerevolutionary life and to justify and support the solutions the new government offered to old problems. In her work, however, Sara Gómez managed to counteract such stereotypes. She offered another gaze—a black gaze on black subjects, revealing them as active participants in revolutionary society without avoiding the ethnocultural particularities of their existence. Thus, her perspective functions as the antithesis of the formation process described by Guevara in his theorization of the New Man. Gómez's gaze recognizes Cubans of any race, gender, sexual preference, or cultural identity as humans imbued with individual experiences. In this sense, her work is about bodies whose experiences and living expressions she eagerly captured with her camera.

Gómez's film *Iré a Santiago* is filled with bodies in movement. Mesmerizingly expressive, beautiful, and seductive, these bodies do not belong to isolated protagonists. They wander in rhythm with the city of Santiago de Cuba. While the narrator's voice describes some stereotypical characteristics of Cubans—and the people of Santiago in particular—as if extracted from a tourist guide, the camera follows anonymous people around the streets. Two of these people become the characters "El Santiaguero" and "La Santiaguera." (See figs. 3.2 and 3.3, respectively.) At this moment, they are presented and particularized as individuals rather than remaining part of a uniform and general portrait of what the people of Santiago de Cuba might be like. This is how Gómez gently deconstructs the myths and stereotypes of her earlier candid (though laced with subtle irony) voice-over.

There is no single mass. It is impossible for Gómez to show Cubans as a homogeneous whole. Racial identity acquires a primordial connotation in her films. She recognizes, in *Iré a Santiago*, that "there is no doubt about our condition as people of the Antilles. But all this is almost a Cuban legend built through a dream. What happens is that Santiago is there. So, it's true: Cuba is an island in the Antilles. And *mulato*? *Mulato* is a state of mind." And how is this "state of mind" re-created if not by examining the way Cuban men and women act in daily life? This is what *Iré a Santiago* is about. The documentary genre, which presupposes an attempt to portray a veracious representation of reality, spills over the boundaries of traditional technique in Gómez's creations.[3] By searching for vital expression, she extends the genre beyond the simple use of the interview and the collection of historical data. Nevertheless, the film does not evade history. In fact, Gómez uses the distinctive Haitian presence in the eastern part of the country—a consequence of the 1791 revolution in what was then the French colony of Saint-Domingue—as a way of referring to the ethnic, cultural, and racial particularities of the population of Santiago de Cuba. Under the intertitle "Santiago and the French," she shows the cultural influence of Haitian émigrés and their descendants, who have maintained the legacy of their ancestors. The director's voice reminds us that "Santiago has black people who call themselves French and do a dance-hall dance to the rhythm of a *tumba* that they call French." Gómez emphasizes that, just as Cuban society cannot be homogenized as a singular whole, its racial and ethnic groups cannot be understood without taking into account their internal specificities provoked by the diverse cultural, political, and economic dynamics of

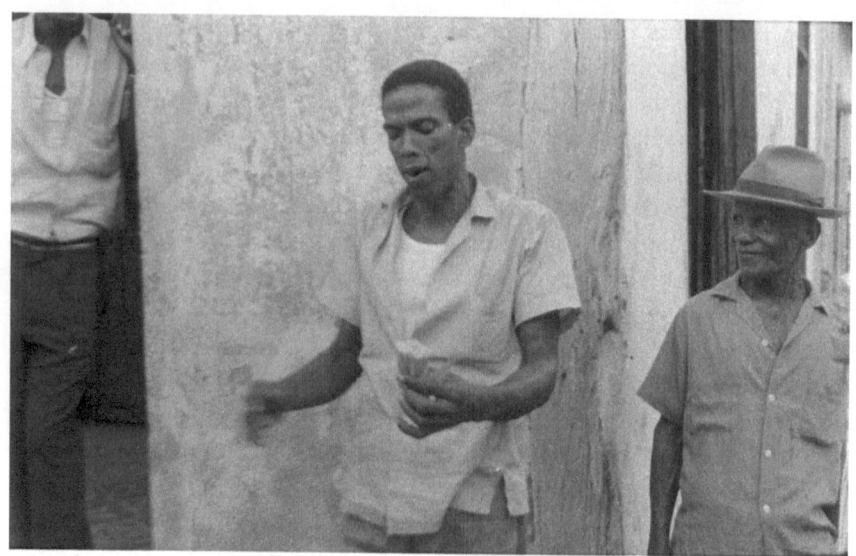

Figure 3.2 El Santiaguero in *Iré a Santiago*, 1964. © ICAIC

Figure 3.3 La Santiaguera in *Iré a Santiago*, 1964. © ICAIC

the nation. Nevertheless, it is with a certain irony that Gómez reminds us that "a century and a half later, Santiago no longer has French people... nor French coffee farms." All that survives is the *tumba*, which, the narrator emphasizes, "they call French." The traditions endure, and the new society cannot wipe them out to leave a clean slate.

From Gómez's perspective, then, Santiago de Cuba is an eccentric and colorful place full of historic and current events linked to the revolutionary experience, including people enjoying parties and carnivals and practicing various religions, superstitions, and popular traditions. Her gaze on the city seems to want to take in everything and provoke the curiosity of the spectator. Her Santiaguera and Santiaguero wend their way through the city and at the end of the day have fun and share romantic moments. Gómez's examination of the private and intimate dimensions of Cubans' lives thus deserves as much attention as the social, ideological, and political themes usually emphasized in Cuban documentary production of the Revolution's early years.

In *Iré a Santiago*, as in all of Gómez's cinematic productions, music plays an essential role (Martiatu 2007). The people of Santiago are shown dancing and drinking at parties. "Cuba works and has fun" says a poster announcing the Santiago Carnival celebrations. The Cuban people, as portrayed in this documentary, enjoy their carnivals *and* are dedicated to the production and defense tasks demanded by the revolutionary government. Gómez says as much in her "Recommendations for the Tourist": "Don't forget that Santiago also has a university. And in July, it has carnivals." The university, symbolizing conventional progress, is juxtaposed with the carnivals. The latter are filmed to the rhythm of drums, with black people dancing, sensuality overflowing, and people sharing their happiness over full glasses of beer. There is no confrontation in this contrast, simply the recognition of the complexity of Cuban reality.

Gómez's depiction of Cubans'—mostly black Cubans'—recreational activities provides an opportunity to analyze the differences and confluences between her work and similar representations in works such as the renowned documentary *P.M.* Made in 1960 by Sabá Cabrera and Orlando Jiménez Leal, this film was censored because the cultural authorities considered it inappropriate to show working people images of Cubans in nightclubs. The ban against *P.M.* became a symbol of the authoritarianism and political and cultural myopia of the new revolutionary institutions. The same sensuality portrayed in *P.M.*, along with enjoyment of dancing and recreational activities, also appears in Gómez's work. Her message, however, seems to suggest that the Cuban people can both have fun and defend the Revolution. She shows the complexity and diversity of the New Man—and Woman, Gómez would definitely insist—that the Revolution wanted to forge in the 1960s.

In Gómez's films, black people appear as individuals whose existential complexity is placed in relief, stirring up a disquieting provocation—an unexpected and sharply pointed inquiry for the spectator. To invite self-questioning among her audience seems to be a recurring strategy of the director, who is careful not to answer the questions she poses in any conclusive way. The questions that characters and narrators pose to the audience remain suspended for reflection.

Gómez's interest in the individual—usually minimized in the shadow of the Revolution's collective tasks—dominates documentaries such as *En la otra isla*, in which she interviews young people sent to the Isle of Pines. First, we meet María, a young black woman who studies and works at Granja Libertad (Freedom Farm). Although she is seventeen, she is still in sixth grade and receives training as a hairdresser. On the farm, María also has the opportunity to sing in public, and the interview ends with one of her performances. Then Fajardo "El Eléctrico" (the Electrician) appears. He is a playwright sent to the island to be "reformed" through agricultural work for writing a play considered subversive (Álvarez 2008, 50). On camera, he says that culture does not receive priority attention in the reeducation centers: "On this island I've encountered the problem that culture is not fundamental, but rather the word *work*." But El Eléctrico has decided to change this situation and promote culture on the Isle of Pines.

After this intervention, we witness Rafael's painful story. He denounces the racial prejudices still present in the socialist society, which he says he bitterly suffered while living in Havana. A tenor and graduate of the Escuela Nacional de Arte (National School of Art), in 1964 Rafael joined a lyrical arts company with whom he performed several operas and operettas. However, he began to perceive a certain "apathy" among his white female colleagues who did not feel comfortable performing romantic scenes with a black man. Rafael's uneasiness is evident in the interview. He has difficulty describing what happened and seems to feel ashamed of being the object of racial discrimination. Gómez communicates this feeling of discomfort to the spectator through the original way she films the interview. Despite Rafael's hesitation and avoidance of the camera by revealing only his profile, he is able to slowly express himself. A certain intimacy emerges between Gómez and Rafael. Their dialogue seems almost secret. Much passes between them, and the viewer's experience is like that of a voyeur to an intimate conversation.

Although Rafael's words are not intended for the public, he does face the camera in another sequence and states his hope that in the future racial prejudice might disappear from Cuban society thanks to the Revolution and to the existence of reeducation projects like the one documented in the film. At this, Gómez insists that the Revolution alone will not eliminate racism; it will require the action of young people like Rafael. This incitement to change, we might imagine, is directed at not only her interviewee but also the audience and all Cubans. Gómez demands people's awareness. By spurring on young Rafael against his inertia and the kind of resentful shame he demonstrates, the filmmaker seems to ask him to shake off his fear of exposure. She wants him to talk fearlessly about the suffering he has experienced as a subject of racial discrimination—to speak out rather than struggle against his own voice. In other words, Gómez places herself in opposition to the silence that envelops the issue of racism in postrevolutionary Cuba. Toward the end of the interview, Rafael asks Gómez if she believes that one day he could perform *La Traviata*. There is no response. Silence expands, once again reinforcing the inconclusiveness the filmmaker highlights in this and other works.

Like Rafael, the young ex-seminarian Lázaro, who appears in the next interview, is confident that his stay on the Isle of Pines will help him to fully understand the revolutionary project and to include himself within it. However, in her pursuit of uncomfortable answers, sharp-minded Gómez poses a challenging question. She asks Lázaro if he believes he could completely detach himself from his Christian convictions. The young man responds slowly, unable to fall back on fast slogans. "I am here on the island, thinking about what is to come, what we want to do," he says. And then he says that he thinks it will not be possible for him to completely abandon the beliefs with which he was raised. Finally, Lázaro recalls his girlfriend, Gladys, whom he misses. He hopes she will visit him soon. A few photos reveal that she is a young *mulata* woman. "I want her to come so she can come to the dairy farm here so she can see everything I'm doing... and fill the void that perhaps still exists in our union, or our unity, or our identity," he concludes.

"Society as a whole must become a gigantic school," Ernesto Guevara writes in "Socialism and Man in Cuba" (1970, 372), and the documentaries in this series about the Isle of Pines might be associated with this idea even though Gómez's perspective was different. Other films by Gómez are part of educational series such as the *Enciclopedia popular*, or they constituted educational notes intended to instruct the public on particular issues. In addition, these types of films were produced within the ethical-aesthetic tendencies that prevailed during the 1960s in Cuba, tendencies that were heading toward the strict regulations experienced within dominant cultural production in the next decade. If there was still some room for freedom and originality of expression during the 1960s, the infamous 1971 First National Congress on Education and Culture put a definitive end to it. The authorities reached the conclusion, for instance, that cinema and other broadcast media were "the most powerful instruments of ideological education, since they mold collective awareness, and as such their development cannot be left to spontaneity or improvisation" (Díaz and Del Río 2010, 38).

Though her work is characterized in general by an emphasis on education, Gómez's perspective challenged the state's vision of cultural production. She not only offered new information to explain particular situations and phenomena but also provoked self-reflection aimed at raising awareness. Her work's educational function was peculiar because her films raised questions that were intended to evoke reflection among viewers rather than promote the doctrinaire discourse that was all too common in Cuban cultural production of the period.

In the Isle of Pines series, the way in which Gómez interviews the young people and the answers they give inevitably raise questions about whether these reeducation farms can genuinely transform the young Cubans sent to them. In this sense, the films ask whether it is really possible to fabricate a New Man. Gómez's cinema is full of explicit and implicit questions that drive the stories in her work.

This type of latent interrogation is also essential to her important documentary, *Crónicas de mi familia* (Chronicles of my family) (1966), in which she takes up her own family history to demonstrate the socioeconomic complexity of black Cubans. In *Crónicas de mi familia*, Gómez carefully avoids the excess of textuality that would associate her message to a hegemonic epistemology. She uses few subtitles and explanatory messages about history and society, preferring instead to show cultural and religious diversity in the Havana district of Guanabacoa through visual and musical allusions. These include the impressive ceremonial practices of the Abakuá secret society, views of the Jewish cemetery in the old town center, and scenes of a classical music concert in a public park. During the filming of this concert, the camera often stops to register the concentrated and proud facial expressions of some of Gómez's family members. The musicians are men, and the audience, we discover, is mostly made up of women.

The documentary opens with the names of her family members, subtitled in stylized italic type that perhaps is an allusion to a "classical" lineage. The filmmaker's voice reinforces this impression of family pride and distinction. As her *Madrina* (godmother), Gómez's eighty-year-old great-aunt, threads together reminiscences from the past, the film reveals the value that Gómez gives to memory (fig. 3.4). Yet in no way is it an overarching historical memory about

Figure 3.4 Sara Gómez and her *Madrina* in *Guanabacoa: Crónicas de mi familia*, 1966. © ICAIC

black Cubans en masse. Rather, value is found in the story of a particular family with all its internal contradictions and with its similarities to and differences from other black families. (See fig. 3.5, a dissolve between two generations of black musicians in the family.) Individuality against the homogenization of the masses once more forms an essential element in Gómez's work. In this case, the particular sociocultural elements of sectors of the black Cuban population, to which Gómez draws the audience's attention, are distilled from a rigorous moral code practiced by many of her relatives who belonged to exclusive *Sociedades de Color* (Societies of Color), where the goal of social improvement is explicit in names such as "The Progress" and "The Future." "These were societies for black people, for certain blacks," Gómez says in *Crónicas de mi familia*, alluding to the way these institutions structured the black community. The family members presented in the first part of the documentary are examples of the black and *mulato* petite bourgeoisie who highly valued education and training as a way of escaping the poverty and constant discrimination suffered by black Cubans.

After the *Madrina*'s speech about black middle-class concepts of distinction and decency, images appear of Aunt Berta. This character seems very different from the characters described by her *Madrina*, even though she is part of the same family. Aunt Berta's daily life at home is shown silently; her voice is never heard in the film. Unlike the *Madrina*, who explains the morality of the family,

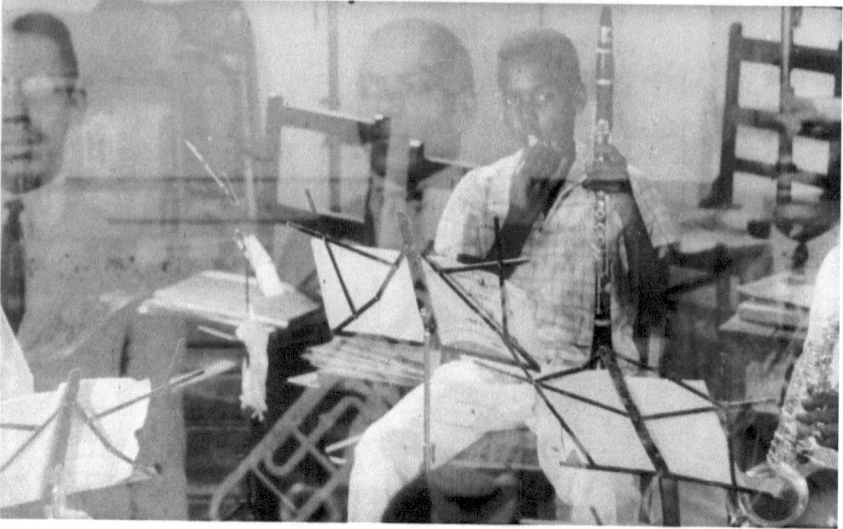

Figure 3.5 Still from *Crónicas de mi familia*—example of a cross-fade bringing different generations into the frame, 1966. © ICAIC

Aunt Berta does not speak—or if she does, no one can hear her. The audience does, however, observe the humble conditions of her bedroom—Aunt Berta drinking a beer, relaxing, and smoking. Berta belongs to another social class, and her behavior differs strikingly from *Madrina*'s. While the latter tells a story that emphasizes the strict Catholic ethics of her family, we see Aunt Berta worshipping at a shrine of the *orishas*—the gods and goddesses of the Santería. Aunt Berta's presence is silent but impressive. Gómez confesses that she is her favorite aunt because she is not ashamed of herself.

Crónicas de mi familia, the filmmaker announces near the beginning of the documentary, is dedicated to "Señorita Luisa MaríaLópez y Galaimena, whom we call Madrina, and to her sister's grandchildren." Until this point, Gómez's voice has been sweet and respectful; here she abruptly adds in a bitter tone, "but it's not good enough." What is not good enough? one might ask. But there is no reply. The audience receives only the information and the experience transmitted over the course of the film. Viewers must supply their own answers. Gómez's new way of thinking comes from her inner debate about the values of the two figures *Madrina* and Aunt Berta—a thinking that is distant and at the same time inherited from both women. Fulleda Léon calls this documentary "a filmic poem that takes its letters of authenticity out of the historic trunk, where, as black families, we have wanted to hide our false aspirations, our existing mediocrity and small human miseries, as if they were some form of unpublishable and loathsome evil" (1999, 44). In fully experiencing a radical revolutionary process, the filmmaker questions what to do with these two currents in her family—contradictions inherited from the nation's history as well as from the family's. *Crónicas de mi familia* closes with images of Aunt Berta walking out of her room in the poor tenement where she lives. With these sequences, Gómez leaves the audience with two more powerful questions: "Will we have to fight against the need to be different as black people who have improved our lot? Will we come to Guanabacoa accepting our entire history, the entireness of Guanabacoa, and be able to say this?"

These questions allude to the difficulty of determining to what extent black Cubans should transform themselves to comply with the guidelines of the new society. In improving their situation, should they abandon their traditional beliefs and popular culture? Should they recognize or deny their history as marginalized subjects? These questions prefigure the main sociological concerns that would come to dominate Gómez's oeuvre—the search for an authentic expression usually hidden behind gestures, bodies, daily experiences, and gazes.

Crónicas de mi familia offers a healthy counterimage to the utopian and nationalist project of absolute fusion in Cuban culture. Here, it is essential to recognize the Revolution's official efforts to promote an understanding of history as a monolithic wholeness around which all Cubans, black and white, can unite in harmony. Contesting such an artificial and totalizing interpretation of Cuban history, some isolated polemics emerged in that period. For instance, black Marxist Walterio Carbonell developed a powerful critique in his 1961 book, *Cómo surgió la cultura nacional* (How national culture emerged). Carbonell placed the racial question at the center of class struggle and asked readers to acknowledge the racism of some prominent figures in national history who were traditionally revered for their role in the ideological building of Cuban national identity in the nineteenth century. He argued that to build a new society based on the thinking of nationalist—and racist—ideologues such as José A. Saco, Francisco Arango y Parreño, or José de la Luz y Caballero was inconsistent with Marxist doctrine. Carbonell's words, however, were silenced by the cultural authorities. In the First National Congress on Education and Culture, the government called for increased production of historical films and documentaries to consolidate the strong links between the present and the past (Díaz and Del Río 2010, 38). In this way, the authorities wished to publicize the historic consistency of the Revolution by emphasizing its roots in the very birth of the Cuban nation in colonial times. The Revolution would consequently reinforce an image of strength and authenticity.

Once more, Gómez's art was at odds with state policies. Without directly engaging Carbonell's theoretical argument, she simply presented the historical and social diversity of a segment of the Cuban population through her own family. In doing so, she demonstrated how national history is impossible to understand in a monolithic way, and even less so from the singular point of view of the mostly white, traditionally hegemonic, classes. In her 1972 documentary *Mi aporte* (My contribution), Gómez again went beyond the immovable vision of social problems—and this time her film was censored by the revolutionary institutions, including the Federación de Mujeres Cubanas (FMC, or Federation of Cuban Women), whose history Serra recounts in this volume. The film's bold inquiry into the situation of women in the 1970s, and the way in which the government and its administrators responded—or not—to women's problems occupies an essential place in Gómez's filmography. After reproducing political slogans promoting the massive incorporation of women into the workforce and advertising the broader opportunities for personal improvement offered by the Revolution, Gómez interviews several workers who frankly discuss the real obstacles women faced in becoming fully integrated into the workplace. Their difficulties include everything from internal family problems and lack of support at home to attitudes of machismo among leaders in the workplace and the inability of governmental organizations to facilitate conditions for women as working mothers. One man interviewed, for example, does not understand that a pregnant employee needs to rest during her intense workday at the factory. It is incomprehensible to him that pregnancy produces tiredness.

Similarly, the documentary analyzes the particular situations of mothers unable to work because they lack social support and childcare. "I belong to the FMC and I want to help the Revolution. When the necessary conditions are created I will go to work," one of the interviewees says. Some women, such as single mothers who are the only economic supports for their families, have to work, but without childcare they are desperate and have no way out when state organizations do not provide appropriate solutions. In *Mi aporte*, Gómez abandons the cautious irony that characterized her previous work and openly refers to these problems. Here, without reticence she exposes the ambivalence of official discourse and the deficiencies of government institutions. She tirelessly delves into appearances to reveal the negative side of society and the need to solve problems through the implementation of effective state policies. Appearing as the interviewer in the film is Consuelo Vidal, the presenter of a popular television program of the period called *Detrás de la fachada* (Behind the facade). Evidently, Gómez chose Vidal and the musical theme from her humorous program to suggest the purpose behind *Mi aporte*: to dig deeper in search of the truth, to go *detrás de la fachada* (behind the facade) of a perfect, egalitarian society.

This documentary also includes an interesting discussion among four women professionals: Gómez, Lucía Corona, Mirta Valladares, and Gladys Egües, the girlfriend of the ex-seminarian Lázaro interviewed in the film *En la otra isla*, who is today a prestigious black Cuban intellectual. The women debate two pressing questions: Are we creating the conditions for the formation of a New Woman? And can the model traditional family subsist in the circumstances of revolutionary Cuba? With these questions as a starting point, they analyze the general lack of understanding that exists around specific problems that affect the female population—a lack of understanding also experienced by the black population, gays, and other groups that have traditionally faced discrimination in Cuban society. Social education is offered as a possible solution, but one participant in the debate proposes the idea that women need to renounce feminine roles. Gómez refuses to abandon her fight and her hopes for the construction of a better world. She expresses herself fervently, something she does rarely in her interventions in other documentaries. She declares, "One cannot make any type of concession, or accept to replace one frustration by another. I believe that if a revolution has been made, it is to make possible man's total fulfillment, in all senses. . . . I believe that it is necessary to shake consciousness, to attack, somehow."

These ideas illustrate Gómez's concept of revolution. In *Mi aporte*, the filmmaker holds nothing back from the audience. If one wants to understand her adherence to the Revolution as well as her nonconformist spirit and constant inquiry, this burst of fire contains all her answers. Revolution, in Gómez's view, is a violent and unstoppable impulse that propels the radical transformation of society and makes possible the creation of something radically new. Her concept of revolution echoes Hannah Arendt's philosophical depictions of revolution as an "irresistible movement" (2006, 38) and the revolutionaries as beings who no longer belong to themselves but to the need to change the world (48). Here is Sara Gómez the revolutionary. No institution, no power was more important than the need to transform and improve the lives of Cubans—all Cubans. But this process must include people's individual particularities as men, women, black, white, and all of Cuba's diverse cultures and religions. These complicated and diverse Cubans are the Cuban people that Gómez always sought to understand.

The conceptual proposal of her final film was an inevitable outcome of these views. The feature film *De cierta manera* (One way or another) (1974/1977) summarizes Gómez's perspectives on social education, the pervasiveness of social problems, racial and gender discrimination, and the multiple stereotypes that remained in revolutionary Cuba. Her position in this last work is consistent with that of her other productions: She does not believe in easy, general solutions; rather, she demands an understanding of individuals and their particular sets of problems. The truth remains not easily discernible, but her aesthetic procedure of mixing fiction with documentary and analytical inquiry would serve her in creating a proximity with citizens' subjectivities. In *De cierta manera*, the skillful juxtaposition of documentary scenes expressing social change and fictional scenes revealing internal transformations in individuals is outstanding.

De cierta manera recounts the love between Mario and Yolanda. Mario, a *mulato*, lives in Las Yaguas, a Havana slum whose inhabitants were slated for relocation to a new neighborhood built by the residents themselves and other workers. When given the opportunity to become a member of the strictly male, African-origin Abakuá secret society, Mario hesitates. Yolanda, a white woman and teacher, comes from a lower-middle-class background. She does not understand the mentality of the marginal enclave to which Mario belongs. She believes that such worlds as Las Yaguas "no longer existed." The misinterpretations between the two characters are determined by machismo, racism, and cultural stereotypes. Occasional voice-overs and written commentaries intervene in the narrative, offering the official point of view about marginalization: the religions of African origin were signs of underdevelopment, elements of life in marginal sectors of society, and should be eliminated. The voice-over informs us that the Abakuá society, or *ñañiguismo*, is an "expression of male chauvinism" situated in opposition to progress and to the assimilation of "modern life values." This voice states that such groups "generate marginalization and promote parallel social relations that are the antithesis of racial integration." However, when Yolanda and Mario participate in a Santería ceremony, the images do not encourage a sense of disapproval. The key combination of fiction and documentary with voice-over commentaries asks the audience to question their beliefs and assumptions—something that has by now become expected in Gómez's work.

Prejudice also comes from the people surrounding the couple—individuals belonging to Yolanda's milieu as well as to Mario's social context. Some of his friends see Yolanda as someone who will distort his masculinity and integrity. Mario himself violently accuses Yolanda of being responsible for the internal transformations that finally lead him to disclose a lie that a friend of his had told to the rest of his work brigade. Mario's denunciation is considered by his marginalized social circle as improper for a macho. This concept of maleness is debated throughout the film, as it constitutes an essential moral element in marginalized sectors of Cuban society. Likewise, a *mulato* woman friend of Yolanda discriminates against Mario, saying that, despite the Revolution and its transformations, "We are not all equal." Through this character, who is also put down by her white male partner, and other women in the film, Gómez examines the cycles that perpetuate gender inequality and the undervaluing of women. Yolanda, however, recognizes the need to create mechanisms to improve the educational level of women from poorer backgrounds. In her opinion, this task is a vital necessity if the Revolution is to interrupt the cyclical processes that reproduce social marginalization.

The neighborhood and its reconstruction form the couple's surroundings. A constant flow of images shows the demolition of old houses, which alludes to the destruction of the old and the construction of the new. However, for the men and women living within these old walls, it is not so easy to break with their pasts. The past is impervious to the wrecking ball. Occasionally, a character describes marginalization as a problem of people's "mentality." The protagonists use this word but no conclusive solution appears. A glimmer of hope is nevertheless provided by the story of a boxer who manages to change his mentality and become a singer. He says that fear stops people from abandoning their marginalization. He thinks bravery is needed to overcome this situation, because it is difficult for people who have always lived in the closed space of the ghetto to adapt to an existence outside, exposed to the totality of society. But it is a step that has to be taken.

In general, Yolanda and Mario have great difficulty understanding each other. She defends her independence as a woman, while he is tied to traditional concepts of maleness. They come from two very different social sectors that the Revolution has suddenly thrown together. However, the fact that they end up sharing the same space in society does not guarantee they will understand each other. The last images of the film show them walking away in the midst of a heated discussion in a street in the Miraflores neighborhood, where brand-new buildings now replace old shacks. There is a new material world coming, but people have still not managed to adjust to each other—they are not yet new.

Described by critic García Borrero (2007b) as "the most intense film for examining the so-called marginal areas of our society" (n.p.), *De cierta manera* offers an inconclusive end to Gómez's work. With Gómez's sudden death at age thirty-one, the final editing of the film fell to Tomás Gutiérrez Alea, Julio García Espinosa, and Rigoberto López.[4] Intentionally or not, then, the film once again reflects the inconclusiveness that is the hallmark of Gómez's creation—a constant openness to each spectator's personal interpretation. Amid this extreme openness, this permanently open interrogation, resides the contemporary relevance of her work. Still vital decades after their production, resistant even to her death, her films, along with new disseminations of her work (including documentaries such as *Mi aporte*, which was censored at the time of its release), continue to receive critical attention and powerful analysis.

Translated from the original Spanish by Helen Dixon

NOTES

1. For more on the relationship between Guevara's New Man and Gómez's work, see Serra (this volume).—Ed.
2. Guillén (2002) proposed the idea of a "Cuban color," symbol of a mixed-race nation, in the prologue to the poetry book *Sóngoro Cosongo*: "The African infusions in this land are so deep, and so many capillary currents mix and cross over in our well irrigated social hydrography, that it would be hard work for a miniaturist to untangle the hieroglyphics.... The spirit of Cuba, it seems, is *mestizo* (mixed race). And from the spirit to the skin, our definitive color will emerge. One day we will speak of Cuban color" (92).
3. See Malitsky (this volume) for more on Gómez's engagement with documentary practice.—Ed.
4. See interviews with Arocha and Mesa (this volume) for more on this process.—Ed.

BIBLIOGRAPHY

Álvarez Ramírez, Sandra. 2008. *Sara Gómez: De cierta manera feminista de filmar*. Master's thesis, University of Havana.
Arendt, Hannah. 2006. *On Revolution*. New York: Penguin.
Carbonell, Walterio. 1961. *Cómo surgió la cultura nacional*. Havana: Yaka.
Casamayor, Odette. 2013. *Utopía, distopía e ingravidez: Reconfiguraciones cosmológicas en la narrativa post-soviética cubana*. Madrid: Iberoamericana Vervuert.
de la Fuente, Alejandro. 2001. *A Nation for All: Race, Inequality, and Politics in Twentieth-Century Cuba*. Chapel Hill: University of North Carolina Press.
Díaz, Marta, and Joel del Río. 2010. *Los cien caminos del cine cubano*. Havana: Ediciones ICAIC.
Fulleda León, Gerardo. 1999. "¿Quién eres tú, Sara Gómez?" *La Gaceta de Cuba* 4 (July–August): 42–46.
García Borrero, José A. 2007a. "Sara Gómez (1)." *Cine cubano, la pupila insomne*, March 18, 2007. Accessed October 13, 2007. https://cinecubanolapupilainsomne.wordpress.com/2007/03/18/sara-gomez-1/

———. 2007b. "Sara Gómez (2)." *Cine cubano, la pupila insomne*, March 18, 2007. Accessed November 13, 2011. https://cinecubanolapupilainsomne.wordpress.com/2007/03/18/sara-gomez-2/

González Pérez, Tomás. 1998. "Memoria de cierta Sara." In *Afrocuba: Una antología de escritos cubanos sobre raza, política y cultura*, edited by Pedro Pérez Sarduy and Jean Stubbs, 109–17. San Juan: Editorial Universidad de Puerto Rico.

Guevara, Ernesto. 1970. "El socialismo y el hombre en Cuba." In *Obras (1957–1967)*, 2: 367–84. Havana: Casa de las Américas.

Guillén, Nicolás. 2002. "Prólogo a Sóngoro Cosongo." In *Obra poética I, 1922–1958*, edited by Ángel Augier, 91–92. Havana: Letras Cubanas.

Martí, José. 1963a. "El Plato de Lentejas." In *Obras completas*, 3: 26–30. Havana: Editorial nacional de Cuba.

———. 1963b. "Mi raza." In *Obras completas*, 2: 298–300. Havana: Editorial nacional de Cuba.

Martiatu, Inés María. 2007. "Con Sara Gómez a los 30 años de '*De cierta manera*.'" In *La ventana: Portal informativo de la Casa de las Américas*. Casa de las Americas, Havana, October 17, 2007. Accessed November 13, 2011. http://laventana.casa.cult.cu/modules.php?name=News&file=print&sid=3889.

Medin, Tzvi. 1990. *Cuba: The Shaping of Revolutionary Consciousness*. Boulder, CO: Lynne Rienner.

Sawyer, Mark Q. 2006. *Racial Politics in Post-Revolutionary Cuba*. New York: Cambridge University Press.

ODETTE CASAMAYOR-CISNEROS is Associate Professor of Latin American and Caribbean Cultural Studies at the University of Pennsylvania. She is author of *Utopia, Dystopia and Ethical Weightlessness: Cosmological Reconfigurations in Post-Soviet Cuban Fiction* (in Spanish) and *A House in the Catskills* (in Spanish), a collection of stories.

FOUR

Sergio Giral Interviewed by María Caridad Cumaná

MARÍA CARIDAD CUMANÁ: *From your point of view, what was the relationship between Sara Gómez and your institution, the ICAIC [Instituto Cubano del Arte e Industria Cinematográficos, or Cuban Film Institute]?*

SERGIO GIRAL: It's very curious, because the only person, I think, that had a special, unique relationship with the director's office of the ICAIC—let's start there—was Sara. She was capable of going to wherever Alfredo Guevara was with anything she thought was not working for her or was not working in the institution itself, or even outside the institution—things that had to do with culture or social development. She took liberties that none of the other filmmakers did. I once asked her how she did it, and she answered me, "Ah, very simple. I'm a woman and I'm black. I have double rights. I ask, and I have the right to receive an explanation." I consider this a very brave attitude, and it was part of her personality, definitely.

MARÍA CARIDAD CUMANÁ: *What was her working process? What was she reading?*

SERGIO GIRAL: When she was interested in Isla de Pinos (Isle of Pines)—which, after the Revolution, was called Isla de la Juventud (Isle of Youth)—Sara wanted to go and research what was going on there, and it happened to be my turn to work with her on the prescript of the documentaries about this place. She was doing sociological research, and because on the island there was a kind of social experiment, Sara put a lot of effort into understanding how this experiment was working. She wasn't a sociologist, but she had the capacity to do research as if she were. Her approach to the individual was spontaneous. She wasn't a scientist, but she managed to get the people she interviewed to tell her their life stories—the things they'd lived through, their experiences. I think she had a natural talent for that. I think her entire work shows a direct social type of relationship.

MARÍA CARIDAD CUMANÁ: *Did Sara show much concern for the mindset of the people she interviewed who weren't educated within the political discourse of the Revolution? In other words, people who hadn't been educated in schools, in the new political system, like my generation born in the 1960s?*

SERGIO GIRAL: Yes, I think so, but it wasn't only because of that. It was something very much from within her. She herself belonged to a generation in transition. Sara came from a black, middle-class family. She had the opportunity to travel to New York one time on holiday. I mean that she had a broader perspective than many others at the time. She would have been twenty or twenty-one years old—she was very young and she had, let's say, high beams [to look farther down the road]. I'm sure that's what she was looking for in others from other sectors of society. In fact, marginal sectors were something that, at the same time, were part of her own doubts, and this comes through very clearly in all her films. I can tell you that we went to Jacksonville [Cuba], which, at the time, still existed behind a military barrier. The town still existed but it was something we didn't know about—that inside Cuban territory there was a colony of people from the Cayman Islands who spoke English and were Presbyterians. This was denied for a long time. When Sara and I arrived there, there were also Cuban Caymanians, most of whom did not share the ideology of the Revolution. They were described at that time as "disaffected from the system" and were in the process of returning to the Cayman Islands. This was something that fascinated her, and she made a documentary about the Caymanians in Cuba. There's no existing copy of it—I think it wasn't even edited, but I know she filmed it. That community of Jacksonville is on what today is called the Island of Youth, on the south of the island.[1]

MARÍA CARIDAD CUMANÁ: *What themes interested Sara that you think did not end up being covered in her filmography?*

SERGIO GIRAL: Well, I don't know what to tell you, because she had two areas that she was interested in: women and the ethnological, historical, and social aspects of black Cubans. For me it was a discovery. I didn't know anything about these areas. Through them—when I say *them* I'm referring to Sara Gómez and Nicolás Guillén Landrián—I learned about a series of concerns that I had no idea about, and that's what moved me to do research as well: to read the ethnologists, the historians, and the folklorists, all of that. Because that's the theme they knew about.

MARÍA CARIDAD CUMANÁ: *Do you have any information about why the documentary* Mi aporte *(My contribution) could not be shown in Cuba?*

SERGIO GIRAL: Yes, of course. Well, that was at the time of the Zafra de los Diez Millones [Ten-million-ton harvest, a government program to improve Cuba's economy by producing a record amount of sugarcane]. To go back to the beginning, for someone like Sara, who I think belongs to a generation in transition and was mostly interested in developing work around women and black Cubans, the Zafra was a laboratory for trying to understand the process of Fidel Castro's Revolution. In her documentary, Sara was very direct. I think no Cuban filmmaker since then has achieved her degree of sincerity in relation to reality. In the documentary, among other things, a blond woman appears and says in front of the camera that she won't be going to work on the sugar harvest because her boyfriend won't let her. Sara insists and says to her, "Then you're going to leave your boyfriend." The girl answers her, "No girl, no, I'm leaving the harvest." The documentary ends with this—placing the individual over the system and the slogan. That was very brave for that period.

Vilma Espín [a Cuban revolutionary and leader of the Cuban Federation of Women, FMC] went to see the documentary, and I was present. When she finished watching the documentary, she didn't speak or comment, but it was immediately banned because it was like showing a fault in the system, in an ideology that was unable to make a young woman leave her boyfriend for a task of the Revolution—showing the individual above the slogan, underlining the right of individuality over the collective.

Another aspect of Sara's work was the way in which she reflected black culture as a culture of resistance. She emphasized those values a great deal. It's curious that she carried out experiments in her own lived experience as well, such as marrying a white man first, then a black man. She herself was a laboratory.

MARÍA CARIDAD CUMANÁ: *Her film* De cierta manera *(One way or another) was filmed by Sara but edited by another three people. To what extent do you think they respected Sara's criteria?*[2]

SERGIO GIRAL: It's very difficult to know that because their personalities are different. I mean, I have a lot of respect for Tomás Gutiérrez Alea—he was a good friend. I respect him as a filmmaker because I think he is the best Cuban filmmaker of that period, but he is nothing like Sara in the sense of how each of them focuses on reality. So I don't know what kind of interpretation he made of the material. In any case, I don't think the interpretation is totally distorted from what Sara wanted with this film, even if the discourse isn't exactly Sara's. Whatever it may be, one of Sara's most interesting aspects is her mixing of the personal and the creative. In the film, the masculine character's ethics are those of Abakuá, and this is situated in the film as something to be overcome because the Revolution is offering him solutions that perhaps he'll accept for himself. On a personal level, Sara was married to an Abakuá, Germinal Hernández, while the film reflects the development of a social process—that of the Revolution, in which the Abakuá ethic is seen as something that needs to be left in the past.

ABOUT SERGIO AND HIS FILMS AT ICAIC

MARÍA CARIDAD CUMANÁ: *It's well known that the series of films you made about slavery and the situation of the black population in Cuba for a long time was called Sergio Giral's "negrometrajes" [literally, "black-length films," a rhyme with corto- or largo-metraje, short or feature-length films]. How did you feel about this label given to your films?*

SERGIO GIRAL: It's curious. Do you know how this came about? It was because a producer [Ricardo Ávila] was a big joker and it occurred to him to say, "You're going to do another film on slavery, so you're going to do a *negrometraje*." It seemed funny to me, and that's how the label stuck. I didn't see it as a derogatory thing because at least it was a way to name it. In the 1970s here in the United States, when this kind of cinema was starting to be done, it was given the name blaxsploitation, and it's still labeled that way. I think this is pejorative for those who decide to receive it that way, people who feel offended and see it as a form of insult. Personally, it doesn't bother me at all. What the producer did in my case was to use a popular form of language to identify this type of film. He didn't write an essay theorizing this issue in particular.

MARÍA CARIDAD CUMANÁ: *At any moment did you think of doing a film about racial problems in Cuba?*

SERGIO GIRAL: Well, there's *Techo de vidrio* (Glass ceiling), a film that was a very disagreeable experience from the very beginning. I'm going to tell you an anecdote to answer your question. First of all, the argument was mine—I gave it to Manuel Cofiño, and he contributed a lot of ideas to the script. That script—when I was going into the prefilming stage, Alfredo Guevara called to see what the problem was with the script because he had received a call from the Ministry of the Interior asking why it was necessary to do that kind of film. Alfredo asked me, and I said to him, "As far as I know, the script doesn't have any problems." So Alfredo said, "Look, we're going to create a commission of three people to read the script." That commission was made up of Jorge Fraga, Pastor Vega, and Ambrosio Fornet. They read the script, took two pages out and said, "There's no problem." I began to film the movie on a very small—a minuscule—budget, and it was filmed under supervision because some people showed up who said they were inspectors from the State Labor Committee [Comité Estatal de Trabajo], which I knew was a lie. They were from state security. Well, the film was finished, Alfredo Guevara sees it, and I ask him, "What do you think?" And he says, "No, it's not okay, I'd just like to talk to you about a couple of things." After that my film disappeared from ICAIC in a matter of months. I made it in 1981. At that time, Alfredo was replaced at ICAIC, and a few months afterward I went to ask Julio García Espinosa, the new ICAIC president, about my film. First, all the negatives had disappeared from Roberto Bravo's editing room and I was given no explanation. Finally, Julio explained to me that the way in which the worker's conflict is presented is not great, because there's no strong presence of the Communist Party as the political entity in charge of dealing with these kinds of corruption problems in the workplace and so forth. I didn't say anything at that moment, and I spent five years under observation by the authorities without doing any filmmaking.

After two or three years, a friend who died recently—Eliseo Alberto Diego, better known as Lichy Diego—told me that there had been a meeting called by Fidel Castro two years before to show the film *Techo de vidrio* to a group of young communist militants. During the presentation, Fidel said to those present: "Watch this film—I already saw it. I think it's a film that damages the image of the Revolution, that it has problems. I want you to see it and tell me what you think." As you can see, the film was condemned a priori by the top leader, so there wasn't much hope for it. According to Lichy, there was a big debate there. Anyway, you must be wondering why I'm telling you this story, but I'm telling you because years later I discovered something in the film, something I hadn't taken into account when I made it, because the artist simply creates the work but isn't necessarily conscious about how the public will read it. The problem is that the black workers end up in a really bad position, because the protagonist is a black worker with a long history as part of the system, and he gives in to his principles to help a black family whose roof is caving in. In other words, he uses state resources for individual benefit. So I realized there had been a racial interpretation of the issue. I tell you in all honesty, this was not my objective.

Given what we're discussing, I want to tell you an anecdote about Sara. One day I was talking with Jorge Fraga, who took on the artistic directorship of ICAIC when Julio was made president. Jorge tells me in this conversation, "because in your case and Sara's you know a lot about this world of marginalized poor people because of your social origins, and I know something about it as well because I went to a public school." And I said to him, "Wait, wait, when I was a child living in Cuba, I went to the Lasalle [School] and I lived in a really good, middle-class neighborhood called Santo Suarez, where the only black people were my mum and me, okay, but with a domestic worker and a car, and when I was six or seven we went to the United States. All I learned about the marginalized world was after the Revolution, and Sara's experience was the same as mine. All you see in our films is the fruit of our research and our studies." He was really surprised, because he thought that because we were black, we were poor. That was inevitable.

MARÍA CARIDAD CUMANÁ: *Do you want to add anything?*

SERGIO GIRAL: Well, I'd like to let you know about the film I've just finished, whose script is by Armando [Dorrego]—my partner all these years. It's about the issue of race. I try to show what here is called the "racial profile"—the way you look is what you are. The principle of the film is that perception is not reality, and that's what it's all about in the Hispanic world.

Translated from the original Spanish by Helen Dixon

NOTES

1. Afro-descendant filmmaker Gloria Rolando made a film about the Caymanians titled *Pasajes del corazón y la memoria* (Cherished island memories) (2007)—available at http://www.afrocubaweb.com/gloriarolando/gloriarolando-ordering.htm.—Ed.

2. For more on this process, see Arocha (this volume).—Ed.

SERGIO GIRAL is a Cuban American film writer and director. He began working for the Cuban Institute of Cinematographic Art and Industry in 1961. He is director of the award-winning trilogy *El otro Francisco* (in Spanish; 1974), *El rancheador* (in Spanish; 1976), and *Maluala* (in Spanish; 1979). Most recently, he is director and writer of *Dos veces Ana* (in Spanish; 2010) and *Invisible Color: Black Is More Than a Color* (2017).

MARÍA CARIDAD CUMANÁ taught Film and Television at the University of Havana for 15 years. She was Chief Coordinator for the Audiovisual Portal for Latin American and Caribbean Cinema at the Foundation of New Latin American Cinema, co-authored *A Look at Cuban Cinema, Latitudes of the Margin: Latin American Cinema before the Third Millennium*, and co-edited *My Havana: The Musical City of Carlos Varela*. She was Field Producer in Havana for the documentary Out My Windows (NFB). She is currently an Adjunct Faculty at Miami Dade College.

FIVE

Neither Farms nor Coffee Plantations
Urban Spaces and Cultural Contours in the Script and on the Screen

Víctor Fowler Calzada

IN THE DOCUMENTATION CENTER OF the Instituto Cubano del Arte e Industria Cinematográficos (ICAIC, or Cuban Film Institute) is a mimeographed copy of a film script called *Residencial Miraflores* with argument and dialogue by Sara Gómez and Tomás González Pérez.[1] Alberto Pedro Díaz and Tomás Gutiérrez Alea also appear as advisers. Inexplicably ignored for four decades, the script is 110 pages, and although it lacks a date, a reference on the reverse of the authors' details page says it was donated to the ICAIC Documentation Center in 2006. The correspondence between this script and what is seen in the feature film *De cierta manera* is so exact that there can be no doubt that this document is the script of this film. The script is reproduced for the first time in this volume, and, as we will see, the differences between the script and the final version add richness to analyses of this film. These two quotations help us orient the breadth of meaning the script and film offer: "In short, had the 'disenfranchised' become a participating citizenry as a result of the events in Cuba between 1959 and 1969?" (Butterworth 1980, xxvi). "It's so true that illustration is the mother of all virtues, just as ignorance is the fertile source of all vice!" (Saco 2001, 293).

Residencial Miraflores, or Reparto Miraflores, is the Havana neighborhood where most of the inhabitants of the old shantytown of Las Yaguas (see fig. 5.1, a photograph of Sara Gómez in Las Yaguas during the production of *De cierta manera*) were resettled as part of the revolutionary government's struggle against urban poverty—the so-called Mutual Aid and Self-Help Plan (Plan de Ayuda Mutua y Esfuerzo Propio). This same plan is mentioned in a voice-over at the beginning of *De cierta manera*. In fact, while in the area of the old neighborhood that has been transformed according to what we see on the screen, the

Figure 5.1 Sara Gómez on set in Las Yaguas during the filming of *De cierta manera*, 1974. © ICAIC

first conversation between Mario and Yolanda takes places in front of a landscape of trees (sequence 6), along with the last words of the initial voice-over (with the text "the Revolution has not let up its actions"). This beginning is accompanied by images of new houses that, according to the narrator, are "part of a change in housing that is included in a studied strategy of integration." The first page of the script reads: "Culture exists on the deepest planes of awareness as customs, habits, norms, values, etc. that firmly resist social change. Thus, even after the socioeconomic conditions that gave rise to marginalization have been radically transformed, we can still study the culture of the sector that was shaped by those conditions" (Gómez and González n.d.).

THE ISSUE

At what moment did the idea begin to formulate in Cuba that the "dispossessed" can, because of a particular social occurrence, become "citizens" and shift from the external to the internal, from passivity to participation? Although Butterworth's question above directly addresses the space/time of Cuba's socialist revolution, it also focuses on a long-existing social category that contains an excessive concentration of negativity in defining society's poorest strata. At the same time, the question is posed from a distanced position, and in such a way that it includes a charge of both doubt and affirmation about whether the enunciation of this dream in fact led to real change. In other words, underlying the serenity of the language is the violence of history. For a question like this to have meaning, which would require the formulation of a response from society as a whole and an extensive chain of discourse from its leaders, a great distance must exist between the starting point (the marginalized—the dispossessed and socially alienated masses) and the moment of arrival (the subject integrated into the universe of citizenship).

In attempting to answer Butterworth's question, we not only put into play the pair of opposites that make up dispossession and citizenship but also—based on conditions derived from the period and the geography he studied, and in the manner of an immense prism—simultaneously encounter the mixture and interaction of issues involving race and cultural hegemony and the collision between capitalism and socialism, along with a dialogue between center and periphery, industrial modernity and underdevelopment, imperialism and liberation, and coloniality and utopia. From these angles, the question remains open to establishing connections and genealogies with moments from the past in which anxiety produces discourse, organized in the form of texts produced in the spheres of art, literature, medicine, law, politics, religion, education, and history, or simply the daily media.

In other words, the issue of the transformation of the dispossessed into citizens forms a kind of hole in the discourse that absorbs the totality of Cuban history and forces us to identify in the first place those who, in order to be considered part of the dispossessed, must have lived in conditions of deprivation continuously over a long period. Equally, given that citizenship was a universal right inscribed into the 1901 Cuban constitution, it is necessary to localize the group for whom the full enjoyment of their rights as citizens remained illusory. Having done so, the challenge then becomes determining whether a social revolution (oriented toward socialism in Cuba's case) is capable of generating a sufficient quantity, quality, and depth of transformation (of social and individual life) to incorporate the dispossessed into full citizenship.

In the deep history of nation, the will to incorporate the fragments and, in metaphorical terms, to seal off any exits from the national body, made way for *Memoria sobre la vagancia en la Isla de Cuba* (Memoir about idleness on the island of Cuba) (1830). This work by Cuban intellectual José Antonio Saco is one of the great documents of order produced by the elites of the country. It is a text that not only offers a reflection on a particular situation but also traces a map of or describes a condition, analyzes its causes and consequences, and finally proposes solutions for what the author defines during the process as "the problem." The structure of the argument establishes three vectors that orient societies within a moral discourse: the purification of customs (especially in terms of the use of free time); the utility of work as a creator of humankind's wealth and health; and a third vector that places the previous two at the service of founding prosperous, just, and morally clean nations. "Can a people be *opulent or happy* when many of its members are victims of moral disease? There is no happiness without the peace and contentment of the soul, there is no content peace without virtues, without virtues there is no love nor constancy in work, and without work there is no true wealth" (Saco 2001, 269).

By the third decade of the nineteenth century in Cuba, the sugar plantation economy had expanded to cover the whole country, thus becoming the active nucleus of national life, the clearest option for a future life of wealth, and the means for Cuba to take a place of primacy among the nations of the world. In this context, it seemed to Saco that, given that "all men are duty bound to lend" their services and that those who evade work deprive society, "society has the right to correct all idlers." He considered this argument "a point that no-one will dare to dispute" (2001, 273). The effort to correct idlers would not only force them to contribute to the common good but also prevent the negativity of nonwork from spreading throughout society. In metaphorical terms, Saco sees idlers as one of the most serious diseases, urgently in need of a cure. "They offer the other classes a pernicious example," he writes (273). To heal this disease, he prescribes a huge array of regulatory mechanisms for the production and control of ideas organized within a structure that guarantees ongoing operations for disinfection. These mechanisms should focus on the education and continuous examination of individuals who have a conscious desire to contribute to the creation of national wealth. Once these prescriptions are established and accepted by the majority who drive the "healthy" development of the country, others should be implanted to ensure surveillance and coercion for those who insist (through nonwork) in remaining outside society.

For a better understanding of Saco's text, the first factor to consider is the historical context in which it was written. The work was submitted to an 1830 competition sponsored by the Royal Patriotic Society of Havana that called on participating papers to discuss problems in Cuban society.[2] The subject of Saco's paper, the date of the prize, and the fact that publication had to be authorized by the governor general of the island all conferred on the text a special distinction. Such an assemblage of particularities acquires an even greater resonance when, in hindsight, we realize that the events that surrounded the writing, prize winning, and publication of the text sparked fundamental animosity from key sectors of the Cuban slave-owner elite against the author.

Following publication of Saco's text, a series of public confrontations culminated in the author's exile in 1834. According to the historian and essayist Eduardo Torres Cuevas (who, as well as compiling the texts for the Saco publication cited here, wrote the notes and introduction), the root cause of all national ills was to be found in slavery—the element that distorted the world of work since it served "as a pillar of these ills; especially of the idleness and disdain for work among the whites" (Torres Cuevas quoted in Saco 2001, 31). The captivating simplicity of Saco's argument enables us to engage him as a witness—the kind that emerges at the foundational moment of any country when one of its intellectuals articulates and presents a project for social improvement that happily coincides with the beginnings of nationalist sentiment across the land. In other words, Saco's is a foundational text that, when taking into account the colonial status of Cuba at that time, justifies not only the universalization of the mechanism against idleness but also its intensity and possibly, as is suggested, even violence. "These maxims can be applied without qualms to countries where the love for work has become a popular virtue and where opinion persecutes the idlers, since the law is supported with such a firm guarantee that its impositions can well be suspended, reserving punishment for those cases in which idlers commit some crime. But those peoples which find themselves in different circumstance must follow the completely opposite route" (Saco, 273). Nevertheless, the idler, from any legal perspective, does not commit any crime unless "men without a trade or occupation, nor goods with which to maintain themselves, by necessity have to gamble, steal and commit other crimes, that often remain unpunished, either due to a lack of evidence or for other motives" (304).

THE PERIOD

One hundred and forty years later, the first minutes of Sara Gómez's most recognized work—the feature film *De cierta manera* (One way or another) (1974)—begins with the staging of a workers' meeting. Humberto, one of the central characters in the story, is judged by the factory's work council, a tribunal made up of workers selected by the workers, for his unjustified absences. It is the third time his conduct as a worker has been reviewed, and he offers this explanation: "Well, I . . . I want the comrades to know that I'm willing to face whatever . . . they decide. . . . If it's a farm, then it's a farm. Now, I want the comrades to know that when I came to Santiago my mother was dying, that I spent four nights there without sleep, rushing around, helping out and accompanying the old dear . . . and if I was willing to come in now it's because I considered her to be out of danger." The tribunal of workers, and Humberto's willingness to accept work on a state farm as a sanction (work that was carried out in conditions of forced reclusion within a reeducation camp), are sufficient to imagine the environment in which this narrative sequence takes place as any moment from the passing of the "Law Against Idleness" (April 1, 1971) to the date of filming in 1973.[3]

First presented as a proposal on January 11, 1971, on the first page of *Granma*, the official newspaper of the Central Committee of the Cuban Communist Party, the "Law Against Idleness" was approved on March 17, 1971, and came into force on April 1 that same year. In the little more than sixty days that passed between approval and application, the law was discussed in workplaces, schools, and neighborhoods throughout the country. The circumstances surrounding the formulation of this law reveal the agonizing character of the discussions and tensions that take place in *De cierta manera*. The year 1971 was dubbed the "Year of Productivity" after the preceding year's failure of the Zafra de los Diez Millones (ten-million-ton harvest; a government program to improve Cuba's economy by producing a record amount of sugarcane). With the failure of that program, the dream of making an accelerated leap toward development (with profits from sales on the world market) disappeared. It is this failure that justified, or perhaps explained, the need to pass a law against idleness.

An article published on January 28, 1971, in *Granma* stated that "Cuba is an underdeveloped country, with industry mostly made of small-scale cottage industries and an economy that depends essentially on nonmechanized agriculture. Achieving an increase in production, and a rise in productivity is a transcendental necessity if we are to resolve immediate problems of supply and ultimately the country's development" (J. Oramas 1971, 3). Another article, also on the issue of applying the law, referred to "the country's unfavorable demographic structure, subjected to the double negative influence of the recession in births during the Batista tyranny and the demographic explosion at the beginnings of the century, most of whom are now of retirement age" (Pita Astudillo 1971, 4).

FROM PLACE TO SPACE

In the national imaginary, Las Yaguas embodied the image of a degraded population without hope of social integration, with a high proportion of black people and high rates of illiteracy, unemployment, prostitution, alcoholism, drug addiction, and general violence. Located in an abandoned quarry, the neighborhood began as a place of refuge for a few families in the third decade of the twentieth century and became the largest and most precarious settlement in the country. Some three thousand people lived in unsanitary conditions without possibilities for improvement. In fact, for impoverished sectors of the population, Las Yaguas offered the most minimal of conditions; the only other option for many was to live without any roof at all in the streets. Therefore, when the authorities took power in Cuba on January 1, 1959, and adopted measures to reduce poverty (either through education or improvements to housing and general living standards), they began in Las Yaguas. First, a literacy brigade was assigned to the neighborhood, but soon the entire settlement was demolished and newly constructed housing was delivered to the inhabitants, who were also incorporated into the wider workforce (A. Oramas 2011).

Despite these efforts, research carried out by Douglas Butterworth in the new settlements in 1969–70 revealed just how complex a challenge the government faced in trying to eliminate marginalization. Butterworth was a young professor from the University of Illinois who conducted field research in Cuba as a collaborator of the influential anthropologists Oscar and Ruth Lewis.[4] Oscar Lewis, the creator and principal proponent of the anthropology of poverty, reached a series of agreements with Cuban authorities (directly with Fidel Castro, the leader of the new government) to do fieldwork in Cuba's poor communities. Through his work, Lewis hoped to prove his hypothesis about the absence, in socialism, of the type of marginal behavior that he had observed in countries such as Mexico and Puerto Rico, where he had previously carried out important research projects and where the fundamental concepts of his anthropological model were born.

Although Lewis's Cuban project proved turbulent and painful, a significant part of the material he gathered remains accessible thanks to Ruth Lewis's publication of *Living the Revolution* (1977). In three volumes, she brings together testimonies recorded on the island during the several months of the research project. The work offers a rich comparative portrait of the lives of research informants from the prerevolutionary period onward, their diverse receptions of the social changes occurring around them, their different ways of involving themselves in the new way of life, the difficulties they encountered, and the changes they could not accept. The first volume of this trilogy is dedicated entirely to the testimonies of people who, before 1959, inhabited the Las Yaguas neighborhood.

Butterworth's book *The People of Buena Ventura: Relocation of Slum Dwellers in Post-Revolutionary Cuba* (1980) complements Lewis's work while transmitting Butterworth's own interest in the philosophical aspects of the problem of marginalization and its relationship with the type of social transformation that brings about a socialist revolution. In Butterworth's words, "the question of whether a social revolution can capture the attention of the poorest segments of the population and involve them in its programmes and ideologies is totally fascinating" (xiii). Although he posed his questions from a distinct perspective, they are essentially similar to the questions implicit in the first lines of Gómez's *De cierta manera*.

THE FILM

The labor tribunal scene at the beginning of *De cierta manera* takes place in the Claudio A. Camejo passenger bus assembly plant. This workshop was situated at Línea and Eighteenth Street (in the El Vedado neighborhood) of Havana, and was one of the places where those in need of work following the 1968 "Revolutionary Offensive" were offered employment.[5] Beyond the destruction of private property in the production and service spheres across the country, the Revolution caused such a total upheaval in the world of work, especially in its cultural and political sense, that its consequences are still perceptible today. If the means of production should pass definitively from individual owners to social ownership, then control over work and its products also should no longer depend on the vigilance of the boss; rather, it should become a question of ethics among workmates laboring for a common cause or the common good. According to such logic, the transformations mentioned here fueled a simultaneous effort to leave behind underdevelopment and overcome, through increased production and productivity, the country's traditional dependence on US markets (imports, exports, and financing). It is worth quoting the film's scriptwriters at length to see how they represented these issues.

SEQUENCE XX
HUMBERTO'S RETURN
INTERIOR DAY
675 to 690

Establishing shot of the Ómnibus Girón factory (Línea and 18), which is the workplace of Candito, Mario, and Humberto. Everyone is working hard, and we will re-create the atmosphere of the place, which is typical of the industrial proletariat. In this sequence we keep in mind the workshops staffed by marginalized workers who perform traditional mechanical and auto-body work. In a country where the automotive industry has never developed, this work is performed by small private shops; very few people manage to obtain a job in one of the three of four large US companies, where one has to arrive with a political recommendation from the "priests of Belén."[6] These individuals had an individualistic mentality and did not have the traditional guild to instill them with class consciousness (recall the small shops and the scene on Zanja Street in the urban Cayo Hueso neighborhood) . . .

After the triumph of the Revolution, these shops became places for commercial speculation and black market trading in car parts, and even for conspiracies. The Revolutionary Offensive of 1967 ended that illegal business. Many of the workers felt personally affected and developed openly counterrevolutionary stances, while others joined state agencies or the ranks of the Empresa de Ómnibus, where, in contact with a new force of young workers, they were integrated once and for all into the country's new way of life. With that workforce the experiments began that eventually gave rise to the Línea and 18 workshop, now the Ómnibus Girón factory. The idea is not to say all these things in the sequence, but to take them into account in its composition, how the workers are portrayed, when choosing shots of the factory and when arranging the sequences that will be filmed there. (Gómez and González n.d., 79–80)

Transport infrastructure was a crucial area of concern for the effort to draw Cuba out of underdevelopment, and so work in this area held a symbolic charge. This place, this factory, then, as well as reflecting the history of eliminating marginalization and achieving the social integration of those living in this state, points to a kind of advanced political, moral, and spiritual position within the world of work in Cuba. Because agriculture—and particularly sugar production—traditionally formed the foundation of the Cuban economy, representing the effort to modernize development in this way brings viewers of the film into the industrial universe, where the improvement of transportation occupies an important place. Indeed, the documentary filmmaker Nicolás Guillén Landrián had filmed one of his last works, *Taller de Línea y 18* (Línea and 18th Street Workshop) (1971), at the same site.

Taller de Línea y 18 is a classic film in Guillén Landrián's style, with its lucid use of montage to create signifying effects and its recourse to irony as a tool to deconstruct the discursive mechanisms of ideology seen in other works of his, especially *Coffea Arabiga* (1968). Under his treatment, something as simple, rhetorical, and tiring as a meeting to analyze production becomes a chaotic jumble of words in which the political slogans (coming from the loudspeakers) drown out the voices of those leading the meeting in such a way that no one can understand one another and the scene decays into chaos.

Both films, *Taller de Línea y 18* and *De cierta manera*, in which the respective filmmakers had to obey the aims of a political assignment, are examples of subversive behavior that end up undoing precisely what they were meant to defend.

Expected to present a vision of order, reason, and productivity aimed at social improvement and ultimately development, both films present the new world of Cuba during the first decade of the Revolution as a paradise of the incomplete, the improvised, the absurd, the irrational, the lack of productivity, and the abundance of chaos. A space/time such as this contained the potential for eternalizing, in an almost joyful way, the great terror of the new Cuba—emptied of sense and caught in the circular and schizophrenic multiplication of under/development.

The commonalities of approach between these two films allow us to compare Guillén Landrián's irony with the seriousness of the tense preface that introduces the conflict in *De cierta manera*. The story in the latter film, begins, as we have seen, just as Humberto (the absentee worker) stands up to explain to his workmates the reason he missed work for several days. The workers are open to listening, with those who lead the meeting seated at a table placed, and conceived of in the scene, as the meeting's focal point. Given that there is neither protest nor sign of nonconformity among the workers, and the humble way in which Humberto explains his absences, we can imagine that the workers are legitimate, nonprofessional authorities temporarily delegated to exercise the enormity (analysis, evaluation, sanctions, and reeducation) of the new rights model that came with the Revolution. The tribunal represents essential educational and exemplary values—we assume that the workers themselves are the ones articulating criticisms of what is considered a bad attitude at work. At the same time, however, given the spectrum of possible sanctions that include everything from the "remission to a work center under the supervision of a workers' collective and the revolutionary organizations" (the sanction finally given to Humberto) to having to leave the workplace for "production activities" carried out in conditions of internment in a reeducational establishment, we know that the tribunal has legal authority.

If the latter is true, then the first problem of interpretation comes with comparing the dates of filming, the intentions, and the content of *Taller de Línea y 18* and *De cierta manera*, respectively, since the latter functions in many ways as a rewriting of the former. On the one hand, Guillén Landrián's work aims to didactically show the Revolution's effort to increase production. Yet, as mentioned above, the assembly turns to chaos, noise, and noncommunication—not far from the madness Guillén Landrián associated with the Cuban Revolution in *Coffea Arabiga* a few years earlier in a scene in which a young foreigner, speaking a Slavic language, explains what coffee is. On the other hand, through the labor tribunal held for Humberto, that same Revolution is seen as a producer of reason.

This sort of introduction to the film is even more complex because, after Humberto justifies his absence to his workmates and the tribunal members, someone (Mario) intervenes impulsively without asking the chair for permission to speak. In contrast to the calm tone used by Humberto, Mario speaks brusquely:

> Humberto (speaking calmly, introducing pauses between words in such a way as to emphasize what he is expressing): I want to repeat to you what I said at the start... that I'm willing to accept what the assembly says.
>
> (Noise is heard. The camera abandons the medium shot on Humberto and turns quickly toward the left, looking for the source of the interruption. At that exact moment, a voice off-screen is heard that we presume is the chair of the tribunal.)
>
> Chair (OS [voice off-screen]): One moment comrade, that's no way to address the assembly.
>
> Mario: You are a barefaced liar!
>
> Humberto: Are you crazy?
>
> Mario: You are man, you are! What's wrong with you, why are you doing this? You're not respecting the comrades here! And what's worse is now you're insinuating something... that I'm a big mouth, because the only one on the *inside*, Humbertico, was me, you hear that? The only one was me. And I'm telling you, I'm gonna open my mouth here, in front of everyone. What do you make of that then? Right in front of everyone. Look guys, this stuff about his mother is a lie; he doesn't have a sick mother or anything. He was with a woman. With a woman! [This phrase is said with Mario's hands forming a loudspeaker around his mouth. The camera focuses on Humberto, who, while he contemplates how Mario is destroying his lie, smiles.] Dancing the Guaracha! Been a long time since you had a mother, *mulato*. And I'm willing to fix a time whenever you like! Whenever! (*De cierta manera*, 01:36')

This juxtaposition of calm and excitement contains within it the paradox that, in terms of absolute formal rigidity, the character who defends the truth and gives his word is the one shouting in an angry tone. Mario lacks respect for his working comrades as well as for the power represented by the chair. The collision between the serenity with which the lie is told and defended and Mario's angry, brusque outburst as he reveals the truth reveals something about the ultimate essence of the Revolution itself. The change in labor relations, particularly the abolition of every form of control and exploitation related to private property, involves the refoundation of all sociability in the realm of labor. At the same time, this process manages to take hold with greater force in cases where the ties that unite individuals—in hostility or evasion—to the procedures or goals for the common good are weaker (such as those of friendship that existed between the characters Mario and Humberto). Thus, the episode between these two characters is a condensation of the clashes between the old and the new, the individual and the collective, and the effort and the sacrifice that constitute the essence of the socialist utopia.

The elements at hand are sufficient to imagine that, in the whirlwind of a society at a historical moment when the spirit of collectivism and love for work are revered, the character of Humberto must submit to a sanction of reclusion in a reeducation camp. The construction of new worlds is a process that includes pain and ruptures, and this is the reason for Mario's raised voice and anger when he intervenes in the assembly and makes public the rupture with his friend. However, it is a process that leads to the creation and defense of a new culture, forcing individuals to take sides and to confront, in terms of values, any egotistical individualism. Mario refuses to continue in his complicity with Humberto's lie. This process, moreover, has an agonizing character (in the old sense of the word "agon"—that is, of permanent combat), because the radical transformation by which the individual also becomes new is continuously tested. It is no coincidence that in the subsequent scene an enormous wrecking ball destroys of an old building in a city neighborhood slated for demolition, while the closing sequence of the film shows Mario and his girlfriend Yolanda (whom he has treated with machismo) arguing as they walk off into a landscape of new buildings. Here, destruction and new construction impose a framework on the film's content, communicating to the viewer both the processual nature of change and the magnitude and possibility of what is really happening. (I discuss this at greater length below.)

THE DIFFERENCES: SCRIPT TO SCREEN

De cierta manera is unusual in that it is one of the most nationally and internationally recognized films and yet was not finished by its director. After Sara Gómez's death, the role of director fell to Tomás Gutiérrez Alea and Julio García Espinosa.[7] García Espinosa's participation in completing the film is understandable given his position as vice president of the ICAIC at the time. In an interview published in *Conversaciones con un cineasta incómodo* (Conversations with an uncomfortable filmmaker), he explained his approach to training:

> One of the key policies of ICAIC was the pluralist nature it gave to Cuban filmmaking. My training method for directors followed that policy. This policy was also applied to my areas of responsibility as director of artistic programming, a job similar to what in Hollywood might be the executive producer. That is to say, the analysis and discussion of scripts, casting, and editing. But of course where there were no commercial aims or single recipes for capturing audiences. Because of this, the director always had the last word in these discussions. In fact the right to decide on the last cut of the film was also their total responsibility. (Fowler 2004, 57)

Gutiérrez Alea's involvement, on the other hand, arose out of the relationship he had established with the young Sara Gómez when she worked as assistant director on *Cumbite* (1964). He had a mastery that Gómez recognized. In fact, the script for sequence 16 of *Residencial Miraflores*, titled "Conversatorio," indicates that the text should be filmed in the style of Alea's film *Memories of Underdevelopment* (1968), "and with a clear intent to invoke this film, using the same formal techniques" (Gómez and González n.d., sequence XVI). It is worth quoting this passage at length, since it reveals many of the authorial intentions:

> This sequence will play a key function in the film. Up to this point we have witnessed a dramatic progression in the relationship between Yolanda and Mario; the central issues of that relationship have also been presented, including class, their respective economic backgrounds, and their social psychology; a potential conflict with Humberto, the absentee friend, has also been raised. We think that the conditions are now in place to include a theoretical sequence with notably intellectual content, while still maintaining the didacticism that has characterized the entire film.
>
> In the style of *Memories of Underdevelopment*, and with a clear intent to invoke this film, using the same formal techniques, we will prepare and film a public discussion at the University of Havana or the National Library with the characters of Yolanda, Joe, and Migdalia in the audience.
>
> The topic of the discussion will be "The Marginalized Segment of Society, Its Participation in Popular Culture and in Contemporary Political History." (Sequence XVI)

Despite these intentions, however, the version of the film we know today astonishingly suppresses this sequence, leaving only a small imprint to suggest it. It is one thing to speculate about why this sequence is missing, but it is quite another to understand what it could have meant had it survived. Curiously, the elimination of a sequence that, with such transparency, acknowledged the impact of the teacher on the student did not erase the homage, which remains entirely recognizable in the opening of the story.[8]

Why did the scriptwriters believe that this sequence fulfilled a "key function" (the only time in the script this term is used)? The scene shows Yolanda as part of the audience in a debate on marginality among high-level experts. Does she embody in a symbolic way the relationship between the intellectual and the popular? Is Yolanda a complementary figure to Sergio in Alea's *Memorias*? And then is Mario, in his path to politicization, a possible reversal of Alea's Elena, who seems depoliticized? What relationship to continuity and rupture does this pair of films have, which, in the views of their makers—teacher and disciple—complemented each other? Why is the topic of discussion the "marginal sector of society, its participation in popular culture and in contemporary political history"? The answers to these questions might be found in addressing the three following points: the definition of marginality; the value of the potential creativity of this sector or the social stratum of popular culture; and the participation of the marginalized in contemporary political history (from progressive or reactionary positions).

One intention of the discussion forum sequence was to place the issues of marginalized Cubans into a global perspective, as is evident from the fact that they were trying to "include some foreign adversary or politician who will make a concrete contribution to the role this sector has played in national liberation movements" (Gómez and González n.d.). A parallel was aimed to reveal "the ambivalent nature of the marginalized as a political force" (ranging from members of national liberation movements in Yemen to members of the "repressive special forces" in Haiti and the Dominican Republic).

A precise notation in the script intensifies this complexity. The scriptwriters open the issue of marginalization even further by contrasting Brazil—where the military regime aimed to eliminate the marginalized, whom it considered unable "to be integrated into what is called modern society" (the "fascist solution," according to the filmmakers)—with Cuba, which they call "ours, the revolutionary humanist [solution]." They explain this solution in which "steps are taken to eliminate the socioeconomic foundations that led to the emergence of this [marginalized group], and then instituting a campaign of reeducation and sociocultural integration" (Gómez and González n.d.). Though this solution might be the more comfortable option, the internal and global project was constantly threatened by the possibility of excess delineated in two forceful tendencies that also reflected its structural components—populism or paternalism, and the rejection, superficiality, and intolerance of the petit-bourgeoisie (Gómez and González n.d.).

In this brief lesson in political sociology, one can hear the echoes of battles fought by Gutiérrez Alea as the scriptwriters of *Residencial Miraflores* amplify, complete, and respond to the doubts that Sergio, the protagonist of *Memorias*, was incapable of resolving. In contrast to Sergio's implacable baring of reality, as penetrating and sharp as it is sterile in terms of social incorporation, the *Residencial* scriptwriters took "a lucid attitude and a sincere and rational assessment of the situation, in the best sense of the term, [to] disrupt this reality" (Gómez and González n.d.) as the only means of breaking with the reality of the marginalized world and, as a warning at the same time that serves as an antidote to the excesses of revolutionary humanism in power.

The scriptwriters conclude the sequence by pointing out that, during the development of the discussion forum, "we will see Mario arrive, looking for Yolanda," and that "Mario's presence will have a symbolic function" (Gómez and González n.d.). This appears to suggest not only that Yolanda belongs to the space defined by the knowledge-sincerity-science triad but also that she has enough magnetism to draw Mario into this debate about himself and his world. In the end, in a show of ability and finesse, the script notes that Mario goes "to look for Yolanda," without telling us whether he leaves or if they remain there together listening until the debate concludes.[9]

While the elimination of sequence 16 was perhaps due to the logistical complexities involved in making the scene credible, including the foreign intellectual and staging it "in a Gutiérrez Alea style" to cover the new theme of marginal identity, the elimination of almost all the content of sequence 27 of the script (the last) appears to have been due to a desire to banish any rhetorical or cheap propagandistic element from the film. This sequence was to begin with the fulfillment of the promise to fight in Mario's explosive intervention at the workers meeting in which Humberto is judged ("we can settle this between us whenever you want"). The concept of the fight shows a first level of complexity in that the physical action, with variations associated with the spirit of both characters, was repeated with opposite results (Humberto wins in the first version and Mario in the second). A second level of complexity appears in Humberto's victory:

> Humberto walks away from the scene of the fight. The camera pans and we discover the film set. Lights, cameras, makeup artists, etc. Mario, in the middle of the set, addresses the audience.
> Balmaseda as actor: This is one possible ending for the film. (Gómez and González n.d., 106)

Here, all pretension of reality is suppressed. Showing the intestines of the cinematographic device in this way must have provoked something akin to an absolute Brechtian estrangement in the audience.

This type of technical-aesthetic procedure pushed the application of the aesthetics articulated by Julio García Espinosa in his 1969 essay-manifesto, "Por un cine imperfecto" (Toward an imperfect cinema), to a maximum. In this manifesto, García Espinosa judged Hollywood filmmaking as intrinsically colonizing because of the intention to create illusion that fed its dramaturgy in contrast to a liberating way of working aimed at stimulating critical thinking inspired by the German dramaturge Bertolt Brecht and his much-celebrated concept of estrangement. This work had broad repercussions at the time of its articulation. García Espinosa was the first to break with cinematographic illusion in the 1967 feature film *Aventuras de Juan Quin Quin* (The adventures of Juan Quin Quin) Copiously praised by national and international film critics, the film attracted the largest audiences to cinemas in Cuba. On several occasions during the film, Espinosa comments on the action through written signs and makes his character abandon the illusion of the story to speak directly to the audience.

Michael Chanan locates the rise of "imperfect film" in the final moments of the Gómez documentary *Y... tenemos sabor* (And we've got flavor) (1968), when "the musician, showing us his instruments, stresses, 'But for us we don't need all these instruments, we can also make music from pieces of iron and walking sticks'" (2004, 323).[10] The script for *De cierta manera* intensifies the elements of Brechtian estrangement in the second version of the fight, which Mario wins. At that point, the character directly addresses the audience, affirming that "it would be too easy to end by resolving the problem with Humberto" (Gómez and González n.d.). Then Humberto evaluates what has happened, giving us the basic key for understanding Mario and, in general, the meaning of the film: "But the thing is, his [Mario's] problem is not just Humberto. His fundamental problem is with himself. Also, the problem with Humberto began when Humberto confessed that he was going to Oriente Province" (Gómez and González n.d.).

The essential conflict, then, is between the values of false solidarity and extreme individualism, belonging to the "old" world (accentuated in the hostile conditions and continued survival of marginalized environments), and the models of virtuousness and comradeship proposed in the ideological, ethical, and cultural discourses of the Cuban Revolution. On his scale of things and at his social level, Mario must respond to Butterworth's question at the beginning of this chapter: "Have the 'dispossessed' become participatory citizens as a result of the events in Cuba between 1959 and 1969?"

THE DIALOGUE

In a country like Cuba, with a monoproductive, single-export economy and dependence on the United States for industrial production, financial services, tourism, and commerce, the question of development is one that causes a lot of anxiety. The complex context of great inequality between the country and the city, unbridled growth of the country's capital, low levels of industrialization, and high levels of consumerism are tied almost inevitably to the rhythms and results of the sugarcane harvest. At the same time, the largest industry in the country employs many workers, but only for about a third of the year.

By the mid-twentieth century, the combination of periods of economic crisis (that put small property owners into bankruptcy) and increasingly concentrated land ownership meant that many displaced families went to live in Havana in precarious conditions. At the time, the city already had its own history of urban poverty, which resulted in two typical housing conditions for those in the lower echelons of society: the *cuartería*, or rooming house (a large, old house subdivided into the largest possible number of rooms), and the famous Havana *solar*, or tenement (a building that contains many rooms on one or two floors, often distributed in two rows, with a common central patio, washing stand, and collective toilets, generally located at the back of the building). These buildings are located in the so-called marginal neighborhoods or shantytowns, where economic deprivation is a permanent and structural reality that generates a culture of precariousness. This culture embraces a body of values, concepts, beliefs, ideas, practices, customs, and, in general, reactions and mediations focused on surviving in ghetto conditions where people are alienated from what the hegemonic groups in society consider civilized. It was, in short, what Oscar Lewis (1967) would later describe as a "culture of poverty."

Among the works published during the first years of the Cuban Revolution that address problems of poverty and marginalization, two books of testimonies stand out: *Manuela, la mexicana* (Manuela, the Mexican) (García Alonso 1968) and *Amparo: Millo y azucenas* (Amparo: Millet and Lily) (Calderón González 1970). Both focus on life in Las Yaguas. Other outstanding works in the genre include the plays *Santa Camila de la Habana Vieja* (Saint Camila from Old Havana) by José R. Brene (1962); *Un día en el solar* (One day in the tenement) by Lisandro Otero (1985); *Las Yaguas* by Maité Vera (1964); *Medea en el espejo* (Medea in the mirror) by José Triana; *El premio flaco* (The skinny prize) by Héctor Quintero; and *María Antonia* by Eugenio Hernández Espinosa (which was made into a film by Sergio Giral in 1990). All these works deserve the recognition and praise they received from critics at the time and the plays stand out as among the most successful with audiences during the decade. Indeed, *Un día en el solar* was later performed as a ballet and adapted to film—both of which were hugely successful. Likewise, *De cierta manera* was adapted for live theater under the name *Al duro y sin careta* (No holds barred) (1976) and premiered at the Musical Theatre of Havana after the film was completed but before its release. The play was adapted and directed by Mario Balmaseda, who also acted in it and played the character of Mario in the film.[11] A brief review of these works adds elements to the context within which Gómez and González conceived the script for *Residencial Miraflores* and directed the feature film *De cierta manera*. These works establish some of the referents of dialogue that possibly influenced the script, the film, and the thinking of the authors/director. Given the importance these works held in Cuban culture at the time, Gómez must have taken them into account when she created her script and feature film.

José R. Brene, Santa Camila de la Habana Vieja *(1962)*

This play, which is set in the world of urban poverty that engulfs a neighborhood tenement house in Old Havana during the events of May 1959, was the first big success with theater audiences during the Cuban Revolution. Events envelop the lovers Ñico and Camila: She is a fanatical Santería, possessive, and very jealous; he is an individual whose ideology is born of marginality and open sexism (*machista*). The date of the action is crucial for Ñico, who had earned a living as a "notetaker" (betting agent) for *charada*, but, as a consequence of the Revolution's campaigns for social hygiene, finds himself unemployed when the story opens.[12] From the first scene of the first act, the audience encounters Ñico's ideology of marginalization—in particular, about the value of work: "Each to his own. My mother had to work like a mule while other 'very ladylike' women, heaven helped them ease their way from morning to night, very fair, right? That's why I'm proud never to have had to fight hard in my life. Let the animals and the machines do the work" (Brene 1962, 98).

Despite this declaration, Ñico—and this is the heart of the play—goes through a long process of personal change, gradually distancing himself from the person he was while adopting the values of the new reality being built by the Revolution. For example, the notes for scene four of the first act describe Camila's room "three months later," where "very visible on the backstage wall there is a plank for a bookcase with seven or eight books" (Brene 1962, 106). One of the books is about mechanics, since Ñico now wants to become a mechanic, and another book is about "political stuff." For Camila, these books "are those things he's reading now, that are eating up his brain." But bit by bit, as Ñico acquires knowledge, the hostile ghosts that haunt Camila—those that distance her from her lover—start to show up and become clearer. "The blame for all of this lies with the Revolution and the books," Camila says. Now Ñico not only spends hours reading but also, according to Camila, "he no longer uses the necklace or goes to the *toques* [Santería drumming and singing sessions]. Sometimes I think that he doesn't believe in the saints anymore" (119–20). After a diverse series of incidents that mark stages of personal growth, Ñico integrates fully into the Revolution and definitively abandons "the saints" of Afro-Cuban religious origin, moving out of the neighborhood that remind Ñico "of a past that I hate, that embarrasses me" (149).[13]

Mayté Vera, Las Yaguas *(premiered in 1964 for the Rita Montaner Group)*

This work, whose title indicates both setting and subject, was perhaps the first to establish a narrative based on a structure of temporal counterpoints between the past (identified with poverty, suffering, a lack of hope, criminal behavior, and violence); the moment of the triumph of the Revolution (a turning point after which comes a period of work security, health care, educational opportunities, and integration into the new political structure); and a future utopia toward which the present is moving, bearing the fruit of present-day efforts and sacrifices.

The work juxtaposes the destinies of Cheíto El Dulce (a marginal character from the neighborhood, head of a marijuana-selling business, collaborator with politicians, and exploiter of the poorest neighbors) and María Regla (Cheíto's lover, who has left him several times, but lacks the fortitude to break with him definitively). María Regla's dream is to leave the neighborhood and move to a better house, which she expects Cheíto to support. This expectation is in vain, however, because Cheíto's only interests are pleasure, power, and money.

Throughout the play, María Regla finds help from Pedro, a poor carpenter who quite evidently is in love with her, although he respects her too much to confess it and only lets slip a few bitter comments about the restraints tying her to Cheíto. Immediately after the triumph of the Revolution, a group of characters (Cheíto, El Nene, El Bodeguero, and Carrancho) reject the changes that have come (including measures such as the elimination of gambling), they refuse to work, and try to continue living from illegal businesses. Eventually, the police arrest them. For María Regla, however, change had already begun when she tried to stop her lover, Cheíto, from beating up Tatica, a boy of only thirteen who no longer wants to participate in distributing marijuana. Suddenly, she no longer sees violence as an attribute of virility but rather discovers its reality as abuse. When the police detain Cheíto, and Pedro finally declares his love for María Regla, María's change is complete, and the love that Pedro proposes is based on values other than base desire, as can be seen in the following exchange, which conveys the utopian energy of a world in the process of transformation:

> Pedro: (Speaking.) María Regla, come with us. Now we have a future that's just waiting for us to embrace it.
> María Regla: You really believe in all this, that they're going to get us out of here?
> Pedro: Of course. The times of the parrot councilors has gone forever and I'm sure there'll be opportunities for all honest and hardworking people.
> María Regla: (Excited.) Do you think I could work as well in building the houses?
> Pedro: But they've been saying that to you from the very beginning, woman. Come on, let's go.... (*The neighbors appear gradually carrying pickaxes and shovels*). It'll be hard work but it'll have a glorious taste to it.
> *During the following song the neighbors will sing and dance with gestures as if they're building houses.*
> CHORUS.
> Harder than our lives
> It cannot be, it cannot be;
> Harder than misfortune
> It cannot be, it cannot be, no. (Vera 1964, 325)

Aida García Alonso, Manuela, la Mexicana *(1968)*

This is the most significant work for testimony on life in Las Yaguas. Through Manuela Azcanio, known as la Mexicana, who lived for thirty-one years (1931–62) in this precarious settlement, the reader is presented with a brilliant portrait of life in marginalized conditions and a complex panorama of these spaces. Manuela is an exceptional witness, since she arrived in the neighborhood when "there were only 10 or 12 small houses" (García Alonso 1968, 170) and stayed there until after the triumph of the Revolution, when the shantytown was dismantled and the residents relocated to newly built neighborhoods.

The text is a model of its genre because it manages to avoid both victimizing and romanticizing the extremely poor while emphasizing survival strategies, interactions with the outside world, and both spiritual and moral breakdowns caused by marginalization. It also reveals a surprising event that occurred on the morning of January 1, 1959, after the announcement that Fulgencio Batista had fled and the revolutionary movement headed by Fidel Castro had triumphed. A mob hit the streets in Las Yaguas and attacked the houses of residents who belonged to Batista's political party—they even gang-raped the wife of one of them. According to Manuela, despite no one in the neighborhood having heard of Fidel Castro, "The next day everything turned green: everyone wore olive green. I don't even know where they got the clothes from, but suddenly they were all militia members" (García Alonso 1968, 415). After a few months, the shantytown was cleared and the former neighbors rehoused. The poor quality of these new houses, however, causes Manuela to comment on political loyalties: "People would spend the whole day bad-mouthing the government and the revolution" (428).

It was in such an environment of scant political awareness that the character Mario in Gómez's *De cierta manera* grew up. He tells Yolanda about moments from his past in Las Yaguas, repeating with emphasis, "I became a man in the streets, the streets!" Likewise, Manuela reveals the concrete significance of this life without control when she says of the son of one of her former neighbors, "When Celestina's son was a boy he was jailed, for stuff that boys do, like almost all the boys in the neighborhood" (García Alonso 1968, 437).

Eugenio Hernández Espinosa, Calixta Comité (1969)

Written in a popular language that centers attention on the play's title character, through novel angles *Calixta Comité* explores the conflicts that marginalized individuals experienced during their integration into the space and time of the socialist revolution. Calixta is the president of the Committee for the Defense of the Revolution (Comité de Defensa de la Revolution, or CDR) on her block in a poor neighborhood where the average educational level is low and several young people exhibit borderline precriminal behavior.[14] Aside from Calixta, who takes the protagonist's role, the play introduces Chémbalo, a young person who has served time in prison for robbery and has been rehabilitated, and El Gato, a young man who embodies the negative values of marginalized subcultures and ends up committing a chain of crimes, including theft, rape, and attempted murder. Calixta is an extremely complex character whose commitment to the Revolution comes from a political awareness sustained by the pain of being the mother of a martyr (Carlos, murdered by Batista's police). This loss, and the many years she has lived in a place where she has known all the neighbors since they were born, makes her treat others as if she were their mother. She is respected in the neighborhood as a model of wisdom for her commitment to the common good and her ability as a leader. However, her maternal treatment of others prevents her from perceiving the depths into which El Gato has fallen. Along with Hueso and Masa, two other marginalized young men in the neighborhood, El Gato steals from a warehouse, rapes Barbarita, and tries to murder Chémbalo. Calixta surprises El Gato when he is trying to get rid of stolen goods after he has been chased by neighbors. Instead of denouncing him, however, she cedes to the pleas of Charo, the boy's mother, who begs her to stay silent and give him a chance. This chain of violence shakes Calixta's revolutionary confidence.

In more than one sense, this story reveals a conflict of loyalty between old and new codes of conduct similar to the conflict experienced by Mario in *De cierta manera*. According to the unwritten laws of his marginalized subculture, Mario should have remained loyal to his friend Humberto, come what may. Calixta faces a similar choice, but she falls back on the old rules. She says, "Where I should have been intransigent I softened and let my sentimentality act. I could have avoided so many things if I had been a leader without needing to be a mother" (Hernández Espinosa 1969, 260).

Hernández Espinosa's treatment of Chémbalo, the one-time thief who has rehabilitated himself thanks to social reinsertion plans implemented by the Revolution, forms another link to Sara Gómez's feature film. Through this character, the playwright develops an in-depth discussion about the possibility of rehabilitation among those who have committed crimes—a discussion that, by extension, refers to the place and treatment of marginalized behavior in the world created by the Cuban Revolution. While Chémbalo hopes to take advantage of the opportunities he sees opening up, he reacts with unexpected violence when a neighbor proposes he take on the job of treasurer for the CDR on his block.[15] After having been in jail for theft, Chémbalo grapples with the idea that his neighbors (all of whom know his history) would trust him to control and take care of their money. This gesture speaks to the tortuous and painful path that individuals must follow if they hope to eliminate all vestiges of marginalized conduct from their daily practices. At the same time, it shines a spotlight on the psychological depth of the wounds that life inflicts on people in these environments. In words that Mario might have spoken in *De cierta manera*, a character named Iznaga says to Chémbalo, "You are afraid to face yourself. You could pick a fight with any one of us and win it. But it's not about that. Will you be able to win against yourself?" (Hernández Espinosa 1969, 99).

Jorge Calderón González, Amparo: Millo y azucenas *(1970)*

Like *Manuela, la Mexicana*, which narrates the life of a community activist with an intense vocation for service, *Amparo* tells the story of Amparo Loy Hierro, from the same neighborhood as [Manuela]. Amparo has a long history as a political activist, particularly in the struggle for the rights of women workers, and as a black woman with religious beliefs and deep political affiliations, Amparo offers perspectives that differ substantially from those of Manuela

Azcanio (although they agree on conditions of poverty). Both women, however, show clear support for the changes the Revolution has brought to the lives of the inhabitants of previously marginalized neighborhoods. Amparo's reaction to the effect of the Bay of Pigs attack, and Fidel Castro's response to it, on her neighbors reveals a moment of transition from the lack of political awareness to favor for the new powers.

> In all of the huts in Las Yaguas people were playing games and gambling when the Bay of Pigs was happening. I suffered, I cried. I said, "How can you be playing at a time like this? Haven't you heard what's going on in Cuba?" They said to me, "Oh, Amparo, take it easy. You're always going on about the same thing. You're going to be old before your time." I said, "No, guys, no, listen, listen." That's when they heard Fidel Castro say, "The militia members must come, the people must come," and the neighborhood was suddenly empty. They left me all alone with my Mama.
>
> The old people who couldn't walk were the ones who stayed. All those young men came back dressed as militia members, and I was content, because my neighborhood was put down so much, mostly by the CMQ radio station, without knowing the original reason why we were living there, so every time Las Yaguas took a step forward it was a great satisfaction for me, that's the truth. Some people put their foot in it and did bad things, they were used to living that way, but many people have got involved and channeled themselves into the Revolution. The one who has feelings for his country and heard Fidel and still stayed home, they should drag him out alive. (Calderón González 1970, 218–19)

Manuel Cofiño, Cuando la sangre se parece al fuego (When blood seems like fire) (1975)

Barely a year after *De cierta manera* was finally completed, the Cuban writer Manuel Cofiño published his novel *Cuando la sangre se parece al fuego* (1975). The result of several years of work, it contains a number of elements that complement the story told in Sara Gómez's film. Cristino Mora, the protagonist in the novel, lives in a tenement in the Regla area on the other side of Havana's bay. This area had housing typical of the poverty-stricken regions of the capital, as the novelist describes: "We were one hundred and eighty people using the other two toilets. The water went off at twelve noon and the stink spread everywhere, making the area impossible to bear. Mama burned incense to mask the smell. She was desperate to get out of that tenement" (Cofiño 1975, 65). Cristino is desperate, too. He lives in "a dark, mysterious world, made of fear, pain, and suffering" (77). The transcendent objective of the novel is to show the heart-breaking complexity of poverty revealed in characters such as Cristino's grandmother, mother, father, and neighbor. His grandmother is a Santería fanatic, believing that all human or social conflict can be both understood and resolved by the power of the *orishas* (the gods and goddesses of the Santería). Cristino's mother, a character whose story weaves across several decades, never laughs—she works without rest and continues to suffer in a situation without solution. Cristino's father struggles for the rights of his workmates and is murdered on account of it. Rosendo, a neighbor in the tenement who eats what he finds in rubbish bins, fantasizes constantly about a great past that he invents and that symbolizes the tragedy of structural poverty.

Cristino himself, who develops from political innocence and obedience to the *orishas* to political participation as a member of a group of revolutionaries, gradually becomes a recognized political leader. Like Mario in *De cierta manera*, his perspective evolves from individualism to political awareness, from complicity and false comradeship to genuine solidarity. Transcendent change comes for Cristino when he begins to help the members of a group of clandestine activists struggling against the military dictatorship of General Batista, the president of Cuba who seized power through a coup d'état in 1952. He comes to understand that the revolutionary struggle is not only about risking death but also about responding with new arguments to historical circumstances. "Revolutions don't happen by accident, but out of necessity," writes the author after Cristino's first meeting with the members of the clandestine cell. These two revelations are followed by a third big change in Cristino that occurs after the revolutionary triumph when he abandons his religious beliefs because he "glimpsed something much bigger than the gods, because the gods were not able (to make changes) but human beings were" (Cofiño 1975, 213).

What is particularly interesting is not only the close connection between Mario and Cristino's economic conditions during the years before the Revolution but also the conflict of loyalty that both characters experience between their old beliefs and the demands of participation in the new world. Where Cristino distances himself from the world of his grandmother, Mario rejects the social relation he has built with Humberto. In this sense, Cofiño's novel proposes the same answer to the conflict between dispossession and full citizenship that Gómez posed.

FEAR

If the main task of the governing political and economic elites of the nation in the first decade of the Cuban Revolution was development on the path to radicalization, then it was necessary to reorganize the economy on a massive scale (in all types of production services), to create new industry, to restructure the world of work, and, in general, to constitute a new culture and conditions for the people as citizens. The context of this task, as noted earlier, was shaped by rapidly deteriorating political, economic, and military relations with the United States and underdevelopment that became an agonizing question for the new social project. In addition to the enormous political-organizational and ideological-discursive strength needed to drive such changes in the dynamics of social mobilization, extreme anxiety pervaded each goal that was reached or project that failed. Thus, once the main political enemies were defeated and the demand for the participation of the whole of society was taken as a basis for life in the new Cuba, marginality seemed like the extreme negative to the new order—an attitude that had a massively disintegrating effect.

After Mario's words in the preface to the film and the beginning of the credits, a wrecking ball is shown hanging from a crane and demolishing old buildings. In a play on alternation that is maintained throughout this section, the scene shifts to images of precarious houses, construction workers pouring cement for new buildings, and then again to images of precarious housing. The iron ball knocks down an old wall covered with graffiti while the camera pulls back to reveal a crowded city neighborhood. In this way, the film produces meaning—we see the reason for, and magnitude of, the changes taking place while the intervention of a voice-over creates another layer of authority explaining the historical-political context in which the action takes place along with the past that conditions it. The film begins with the following:

> In Havana, at this moment, a large area of tenements and rooming houses are being transformed; they are being destroyed and the old neighborhood of Cayo Hueso is being remodeled, but during these years the Revolution has not ceased to act against the rest of marginal culture. In 1961, five new neighborhoods were built to house the inhabitants of the now nonexistent, unsanitary neighborhood of Las Yaguas. Through the Mutual Aid and Self-Help Plan areas of housing like this were built along with today's microbrigades of workers; it's all part of a change in housing that is included in a studied strategy of integration. At the same time, education is more intimately linked each day to work, and becomes our main weapon.[16]

Through this mixture of spaces and times, the past being confronted across the nation ("the now nonexistent unsanitary neighborhood of Las Yaguas") remained, from almost all angles, dialectically tied to the future that was to be built (the new city that was to be installed in "the old neighborhood of Cayo Hueso"). This context gives Mario's story (a tiny invisible dot in the huge wave of forces crashing across the country) a projection beyond itself, pointing out another, greater marginalization that is the reality of living in conditions of underdevelopment. In other words, if social marginalization is a condition derived from underdevelopment, of which it constitutes a kind of extreme deterioration, what political, social, and cultural forces need to be called together to overcome it, over how much time, and with what consequences?

If the state is responsible for offering employment opportunities, health care, educational possibilities, and improvements to housing, then the marginalized individual must take on the challenge of an even more wrenching transformation—the terrible nakedness experienced when abandoning a whole world of values, concepts, beliefs, ideals, traditions, practices, and customs that sustained the old life and gradually entering into a new cultural subsystem of rules and regulations that include the rejection of marginal behavior.[17] All this occurs inside the person. Several authors from the first decade of the Cuban Revolution focused their attention on this moment of fear, and by doing so made visible the enormous anxieties that existed about finding solutions. It is these anxieties that give the film its enigmatic title. According to sequence 2 of the *Residencial Miraflores* script:

> Candito: And what does the novice of the year have to say?
> Yolanda: Here I am, Candito, adapting little by little, but I tell you, I don't understand how it's possible that after so many years we're still facing the same struggle.
> C: They're defending themselves, teacher, I tell you they're defending themselves.
> Y: Defending themselves? But from what?
> ... From the Revolution?
> C: One way or another.
> Y: But the Revolution has given them everything, everything. New houses, a school ... everything.
> What do they have to lose?
> C: They are losing, they are losing a way of being, teacher, and they are afraid, I repeat, they are afraid. (Gómez and González n.d., 8)

The fear to which Candito refers, of losing "a way of being," forms the subject of a dialogue between Guillermo and Mario in sequence 19. Guillermo, who was born in Las Yaguas and was beginning a career as a boxer (which makes him an idol for the neighborhood boys, including Mario), saw his life truncated when, in a street fight, he killed a man who was pestering Luz, his girlfriend. Years later and now out of prison, Guillermo has become a composer and singer and invites Mario to come and hear him in his first concert.[18] The recital takes place in the concert hall of the Palacio de Bellas Artes, an unlikely place for a concert by a marginalized individual.[19] The conversation between the two occurs after the concert, in which Guillermo has sung his most recent composition, "Véndele" (Give it up). The song talks of the need to abandon the marginal world, and its lyrics echo in the words exchanged between the two friends:

> G: Thanks, Mayito, thanks. But don't forget it. You can quit the scene entirely, you have the main thing, which is that you've lost your fear, the fear of what's outside the scene. I can tell you there are many who never leave out of cowardice.
> M: Out of cowardice?
> G: Yes, Mario, one way or another, the scene is something they're already familiar with, you know, it's "the guide" for how to live, and even die there. But if they leave they don't know what can happen, so they feel more secure there; otherwise, they're scared. I'll tell you, Mario, you have to be braver to leave the scene than to stay in it. (Gómez and González n.d., 78)[20]

That fear, a reactionary force in the characters who continue to endorse the codes of marginalization in their behavior, also endures as a kind of residue in the Chémbalo character in *Calixta Comité* (Hernández Espinosa 1969), Camila in *Santa Camila de la Habana Vieja* (Brene 2010), María Regla in *Las Yaguas* (Vera 1964), Cándido Mora in *Cuando la sangre se parece al fuego* (Cofiño 1979). And it is echoed by Mario in sequence 21 of *Residencial Miraflores* as he talks to Yolanda:

> M: You want me to tell you something I've never told anyone?
> Y: Tell me?
> M: I'm scared. (Gómez and González n.d., 86)

The repetition of the same sentiment among male or female characters throughout a wide variety of works speaks of a common nucleus that generates both interest and anxiety. Faced with the modernizing machine of the Revolution (that lays bare what marginalized people lack and threatens to wipe them out, or perhaps that liberates them from the past and emancipates them), all these characters become true classical heroes in nothing short of cosmic proportions. The only solution to their conflict is to work their way through the fantasy that makes them continue to feel and act as "different," to understand how and why the Revolution is the same as a transformation in their lives—a painful process of self-recognition (what in ancient Greek drama was called *anagnorisis*). Only then can they start to fulfill the essential demand of the new world—integration. If, in their previous state of structural marginalization, the traumatic nucleus of daily life was organized around the dialectic between cloister (the protection offered by a marginal group) and a hostile exterior (objectified in the chain of repression that society offers them), the arrival of the Revolution shakes up this order. This disruption was extreme enough that knowledge and work appear as phantasmagorical enemies, thus causing the stupor and complaints of other characters who simply read of or become involved in the structures of the new world and comply with the rules of the workplace. At the last moment of this first stage, when the fantasy fades, the subjects (at last located along a pathway of disalienation) are free to understand who they are in reaching their authentic potential, and a sense of personal achievement and completion is realized.

The will toward political and social activism as well as the formidable utopian energy that animates both the script and the film is made plain in sequence 18, titled "Visita a los padres de alumnos rezagados" (Visit to the parents of students who are behind in class). This sequence, which had to be filmed like a documentary, centers on Coca, a fourteen-year-old adolescent who is Yolanda's pupil and who, in sequence 13, steals the attention of a group of neighborhood men playing dominos. She has a "provocative and adult aspect" and has participated "in several violent incidents at school" (Gómez and González n.d., 53, 73). The script's justification for the attention given to this character provides a fascinating demonstration of Gómez's ideology, which feeds into both the script and the film:

> Coca will allow us to analyze the problem of young women specifically, which to our understanding is much more precarious, as women have no legislation legally obligating them to do social service work when they reach adulthood, and neither do they have the chance to be called up for military service as a way of integrating themselves into the economic life of the country. Women in general, and especially those from this segment of society, can be marginalized from the revolutionary process and their personal goals limited to the traditional institutions of family and religious group.
>
> To truly integrate the female population, the Revolution has only the advancement of the educational system and political-ideological persuasion carried out by the task forces [*organismos de masa*]. This problem

transcends the boundaries of the formerly marginalized segment, with female dropouts from university faculties doubling those of males.

Of course, this problem is in the process of being resolved, but it is our duty to call for the appropriate changes. (Gómez and González n.d., 74–75)

Even today we are moved by the conviction of this intellectual who, faced with the disproportionate scale of a transcendent problem, was able to point out that "of course" this problem is "in the process of being resolved," and that, despite the confidence that motivates her or the issue not being at the center of the story, she feels the duty to "call for the appropriate changes."

Similarly, another "call" is made in sequence 15, titled "Cumpleaños de Isa" (Isa's birthday). The action focuses on the birthday celebration of the saint assigned to Isa (Mario's mother and Candito's wife) in the Yoruba religion in which she believes. In a note the scriptwriters made for themselves to accompany the action (a party of drumming and dancing), they write, "The *santería* as a religious phenomenon of cultural syncretism represented during our history the possibility of hope, communication, and solidarity for the lower strata of the Cuban population, since the time of the slaves of the colony up to those marginalized from the Republic" (Gómez and González n.d., 60–61). Toward the end of the sequence, Isa says to Yolanda that inviting her has been a way of making her feel part of the family and not a way to ask her for a commitment to the faith. The religious practice reveals a hidden significance even more necessary and profound for the dispossessed sectors of society. She says to Yolanda, "You know, we're not leaving ranches, or coffee plantations, none of that, just stones and shells. . . . Praise be to the spiritual energy of Obbatala" (62). The dialectic tension between the (private) notes in the script and the (public) voice of the character works as another "corresponding observation (or call for action)"—this time on the complexities of underdevelopment, the worldview of people who have developed their lives in conditions of structural marginalization, and the infinite care required for processes of social change among so many other possibilities for understanding the options for the socialist transformation of life.

The enormous ambition of this project—which proposes a fusion of documentary and fiction, questions and revises the cinematographic apparatus itself, and employs extensive textual references that feed into and interact with the project to create its own story—as well as the wealth of positions embodied by the diverse characters creates one of the most dense, lively, and disquieting works of national filmmaking and, in general, of all the culture produced during the time of the Cuban Revolution.

CONCLUSION

I turn here to what was defined previously as a "mixture of spaces and times"—that is, the moment when the story takes off and a man and woman in voice-over present the author's ideology in a completely transparent way—in the way Gómez wishes the film to be interpreted. The voices mention different political and social efforts that touch on the issue of housing and the eradication of material elements of poverty, especially the geographies of marginality, and describe a new reality that is highly utopian. The Mutual Aid and Self-Help Plan was a project in the early 1960s that built the school where Yolanda works and the houses where Mario, Candito, and Isa live (or, elsewhere, la Mexicana with her children).

Simultaneous to filming, the workers' microbrigades were creating the model socialist city, Alamar, which, it was hoped, would put into practice a pragmatic formula to resolve, once and for all, the historic housing problem and would present a consistency among architecture, construction, urban design, administration, political leadership, and new ways of living social relations under socialism. As if this were not enough, mention of the remodeling of the Cayo Hueso neighborhood directs our gaze toward the city of the future. It is no coincidence that in the same speech in which Castro announced the creation of the microbrigades as a solution to the problem of construction on a massive scale, he also referred to "the future remodeling of the City of Havana" (*Granma*, April 17, 1971).[21] Moreover, on that same occasion (a meeting with the trade union, political, and administrative representatives from 487 work centers in the capital city), the architect René Saladrigas, director of the Institute for Physical Planning, referred to the future city as, on the one hand, having taller buildings and more inhabitants per area and, on the other hand, remodeled with the most advanced urban design criteria, including more open spaces.

Although this fantasy city never appeared, all these utopian projects and their energy shaped Sara Gómez's feature film. Only in the context of these dreams can we understand the enormous strength of her work and the depth of the questions she was trying to resolve. Perhaps the only comparable film is Gutiérrez Alea's *Memorias del subdesarrollo* (1968), a film Sara Gómez admired and with which *De cierta manera* operates as an indispensable complement. Both films are documents of nonconformity, participation, a critical revision of the past, a willingness to dream about the future, and, as with all great works, a willingness to grapple with the key questions of their times.

Translated from the original Spanish by Helen Dixon

NOTES

1. The title of this chapter, "Neither Farms nor Coffee Plantations," comes from the script for *De cierta manera* or *Residencial Miraflores* (Miraflores residential complex). In sequence 15, at Isa's birthday, Isa says to Yolanda: "*Tú sabes, nosotros no dejamos ni fincas ni cafetales, nada de eso, sólo piedras y caracoles ... Maferefún Obbatalá*" (You know, we're not leaving ranches, or coffee plantations, none of that, just stones and seashells ... Praise be to the spiritual energy of Obbatala).

2. The Cuban historian María del Carmen Barcia (2008, 21) writes, "The Economic Society of Friends of the Country (Sociedad Económica de Amigos del País) convened intellectuals—each period has its ways of using 'think tanks'—to write reports proposing solutions to eliminate 'idleness' in Cuba. José Antonio Saco was the most famous of its prizewinners."

3. "*Promulgada la Ley Contra la Vagancia*" (Law Against Idleness passed), *Granma* (Havana), January 11, 1971, 3rd ed.

4. The work of Oscar Lewis had an enormous influence on anthropology in the 1960s, and he enjoyed considerable recognition in Cuba. Two of his books were published almost simultaneously in the 1960s in Cuba: Lewis (1968b, 1969c). His conceptual/methodological approach to the discipline, called the "anthropology of poverty," made a major contribution to social science at the time and provoked numerous discussions and confrontations. Lewis suggested that precarious living conditions within the same space during a long, relatively stable, and continuous period, combined with a lack of mechanisms enabling people to escape these conditions, made precariousness the only clear horizon for living and thus gave rise to a group subculture defined by specific characteristics. Lewis identified more than seventy characteristics of such subcultures, including a cult of survival at any cost, a lack of foresight, violence, a weakness in family structures, isolation, and a tendency toward practices that break the law. Lewis was a respected collaborator of the highest level on Cuban cultural publications (e.g., Lewis 1967, 1968a, 1969a, 1969b). What is distinctive and unique for our ends is that between 1969 and 1970, at the invitation of the country's highest authorities, Lewis led a research team in Havana with the aim of proving the viability of his theory in the new reality created by Cuba's socialist transformation.

5. The "Revolutionary Offensive," and the events that surrounded it, involved the decision of the political leadership of the Cuban Revolution

to eliminate by decree (accompanied by confiscations) all forms of private property throughout the country, with the exception of a small percentage of farms in rural areas. The measure affected production and services and had an enormous political, social, economic, and cultural impact because it left the state—when combined with the nationalizations of large Cuban and foreign enterprises at the beginning of the 1960s—the owner of practically 100 percent of all production and service workplaces. And with all that this control implies, also were affected were corresponding employment policies in rewarding good work performance, among many other things (*Granma* [Havana], March 15, 16, 20, 21, and 30, 1968).

6. This is a reference to the Jesuit priests who operated the most famous school in Cuba, Belen.

7. Both filmmakers appear in the final credits as those in charge of the film's dramaturgy. The issues related to the postproduction are discussed in the interviews with Mesa and Arocha (this volume).—Ed.

8. It is important to remember that it was Gutiérrez Alea who, in *Memorias del subdesarrollo*, decided to use a sequence taken from later in the film as an opening. Cutting this sequence into the beginning forms a key to understanding the essence of the conflict in the film while defying an Aristotelian temporal progression.

9. Although it was suppressed, this scene is clearly related to the last moment of the film, when Mario and Yolanda argue as they walk among the new buildings. It is also not far-fetched to connect this ending with the conclusion of the third story of the feature film *Lucía* (1969) by Humberto Solás. In both films, the lovers argue (in *Lucía*, this is a physical fight charged with eroticism), and the male character is forced to take a step forward, abandoning machismo in his transition toward definitive integration into the new world and its values. Finally, both films use an open-ended structure that stimulates the active participation of the spectator.

10. On the other hand, Iván Arocha (interviewed in this volume) claims Gómez had no interest in imperfect cinema, and any appearance to the contrary in *De cierta manera* was the result of damage the footage suffered in the lab.

11. According to the theater critic Inés María Martiatu (2008), "In the theatrical terrain we could cite *De cierta manera*, whose theater version, adapted, directed, and acted in by Mario Balmaseda, was the catalyst and background (together with *María Antonia* by Eugenio Hernández Espinosa, of course) of a whole current of enquiry into the popular world of theatre in the '70s. *Al duro y sin careta*, the title of the theatre version of the film's script, premiered first on the boards and was a precursor of works such as *Chapochachín asere* (Chapochachín, I salute you) by Tito Junco, and above all *Andoba* (So and so) by Abraham Rodríguez." See also Martiatu (this volume).

12. *Charada* is a guessing game introduced to Cuba in the mid-nineteenth century by Chinese immigrants brought in to cut sugarcane. In *charada*, a player must guess between thirty-six numbers "thrown up" by the bank. The notetakers act as betting agents in charge of going through the neighborhood, noting the bets, and paying the winners.

13. According to Martiatu (2011), "In hindsight one must value the impact of the premier of a work like *Santa Camila de la Habana Vieja* that shook up the theater scene. This was the first successful play of the Revolution that had originated precisely in the Seminary and was written by a young, previously unknown author. It was a major event in lots of ways. The subject matter, the context, the characters, the inclusion of Santería, *Santa Camila*. . . . And it is set not in a middle-class family but in a neighborhood tenement. It wiped out, with a single stroke, the most conservative theater of the time, and even some of the vanguardist works that were in fashion at that point."

14. The CDR is a political organization founded in 1961. It has a pyramidal structure from the grassroots level through its leadership, all the way up to the national directorate. This structure facilitates tasks related to the popular defense of the revolution and, in general, to mobilizing support for the same. CDR members carry out a night watch (taking care of economic installations or, simply, social property and goods belonging to neighbors), do volunteer work to beautify the neighborhood, ensure sanitation and support production, participate in health campaigns, and discuss political issues.

15. The members of a CDR voluntarily contribute a small amount of money on a monthly basis to finance activities.

16. The Mutual Aid and Self-Help Plan was the name given to the initial housing strategy by and for the inhabitants of marginal neighborhoods. The uniqueness of the project lay in the active participation of the residents of the shantytowns in building what would be their new houses, even while their old neighborhoods were still in the process of being removed. For more information, see Calderón (1970, 219–20) and García Alonso (1968, 418–19). Microbrigades refer to a construction system for housing that, although it existed from the end of 1970 onward, officially appeared only on April 16, 1971—the date on which Fidel Castro, principal leader of the Cuban Revolution, announced their implementation on a massive scale. The microbrigades were an attempt to solve the country's housing problem, and they reached their peak during this decade, at which point they became a genuine national movement with deep-seated political, social, and cultural consequences. Juan de las Cuevas Toraya describes the basic structure of the microbrigades: "The workers in the workplace selected those who could get involved in construction of housing and those who would stay in the workplace, who would work extra time to cover their absences.

The houses were then assigned in a General Assembly in the workplace, according to need and to people's social and labor merits" (2001, 285).

According to Feijóo Valdés, the remodeling of Cayo Hueso began on February 14, 1971, "with a tour carried out by our Commander-in-Chief and comrade Raquel Pérez of the Remodeling group" (1990, 62). The plan that resulted was part of a larger strategy for urban transformation, the Overall Plan for Metropolitan Havana. "The framework of the Overall Plan proposes, as well as the reorganization of the city, which implies the socialist reordering of the disorder of the capitalist city, the definition of coordinates, of parameters, of primary indicators that facilitate the transformation of the kind of temporary settlements, that this work must correspond to the new relations of production, helping to strengthen the development of production efforts" ("El esquema del Plan Director," *Arquitectura Cuba* 341, 1973, 32).

17. See Gómez's interview with Marguerite Duras (this volume) for her own thoughts on the changes brought by the Revolution.

18. West-Durán discusses the significance of this music in his contribution to this book.

19. Despite Guillermo having paid his debt to the law and firmly distancing himself from the codes of marginalized society, the script refers to the presence in him of "residues" of this type of behavior: "Guillermo comes crossing the road in a manner that makes evident the beers he has just drunk" (Gómez and González n.d., 43).

20. The song is heard again as the soundtrack of the final sequence when Mario and Yolanda argue while walking between the buildings constructed by the microbrigade, symbols of the city and the new world being built.

21. "Fidel explained the new plan for the construction of housing on a massive scale; the solution is rooted in the fundamental support, as builders, of workers from workplaces included in the plan."

BIBLIOGRAPHY

"La Arquitectura en los países en vías de desarrollo." 1963. Paper presented to the Seventh Congress of the International Union of Architects, Havana.

Barcia, María del Carmen. 2008. "La marginalidad como concepto histórico." *Revolución y Cultura* 2 (March–April): 19–23.

Brene, José R. (1962) 2010. "Santa Camila de la Habana Vieja." In *Dramaturgia de la Revolution (1959–2008): 30 obras en 50 años*, edited by Omar Valiño, 91–150. Havana: Ediciones Alarcos.

Butterworth, Douglas S. 1980. *The People of Buena Ventura: Relocation of Slum Dwellers in Post-Revolutionary Cuba.* Urbana: University of Illinois Press.

Calderón González, Jorge. 1970. *Amparo: Millo y azucenas*. Havana: Casa de las Américas.

Cárdenas, Eliana. 2003. "Valorar y rehabilitar la ciudadela habanera." *Arquitectura y Urbanismo* 34, no. 2: 7–9.
Chanan, Michael. 2004. *Cuban Cinema*. Minneapolis: University of Minnesota Press.
Cofiño, Manuel. 1979. *Cuando la sangre se parece al fuego*. Havana: Editorial Letras Cubanas.
Cuevas Toraya, Juan de las. 2000. *500 años de construcciones en Cuba*. Havana: Chavín, Servicios Gráficos y Editoriales.
Espinosa, Carlos, ed. 1985. *Comedias musicales*. Havana: Letras Cubanas.
Feijóo Valdés, Alina. 1990. *Barrio de Cayo Hueso*. Havana: Editorial Ciencias Sociales.
Fowler Calzada, Víctor. 2004. *Conversaciones con un cineasta incómodo: Julio García Espinosa*. Havana: Centro de Investigación y Desarrollo de la Cultura Cubana; Havana: Ediciones ICAIC.
García Alonso, Aida. 1968. *Manuela, la mexicana*. Havana: Casa de las Américas.
García Espinosa, Julio. 1971. "Por un cine imperfecto" (1969). *Cine cubano* 66–67: 46–53.
Gómez, Sara, and Tomás González Pérez. n.d. "Residencial Miraflores." Mimeographed film script. Havana: ICAIC Documentation Center.
González, Tomás. 1989. "Memorias de una cierta Sara." *Cine cubano* 27: 12–15.
Hernández Espinosa, Eugenio. (1964) 1979. *María Antonia*. Havana: Editorial Letras Cubanas.
———. (1969) 2006. "*Calixta Comité*." In *Teatro escogido: Eugenio Hernández Espinosa*, edited by Inés María Martiatu Terry, 23. Havana: Editorial Letras Cubanas.
Lewis, Oscar. 1967. "La cultura de la pobreza" (The culture of poverty). *Pensamiento Crítico*, no. 7 (August): 52–65.
———. 1968a. "Días con Soledad en Nueva York" (Days with Soledad in New York). *Casa de las Américas* 8, no. 48: 44–61.
———. 1968b. *Pedro Martínez: Un campesino mexicano y su familia*. Havana: Instituto del Libro.
———. 1969a. "La cultura material de los pobres" (The material culture of the poor). *Pensamiento Crítico*, no. 30 (July): 159–202.
———. 1969b. "La muerte de Dolores" (Dolores's death). *Casa de las Américas* 10, no. 57: 60–70.
———. 1969c. *Tepoztlán: Un pueblo de México*. Havana: Ciencias Sociales.
Lewis, Oscar, Ruth M. Lewis, and Susan M. Rigdon. 1977–78. *Living the Revolution: An Oral History of Contemporary Cuba*. 3 vols.: Four Men; Four Women; Neighbors. Urbana: University of Illinois Press.
López, Rigoberto. 1977. "Hablar de Sara, de cierta manera." *Cine Cubano* 93: 110–11.

Martiatu Terry, Inés María, ed. 2006. *Teatro escogido: Eugenio Hernández Espinosa*, 2 vols. Havana: Editorial Letras Cubanas.

———. 2008. "Tomás González en su definición mejor." *Cuba Literaria*. April 20. Accessed April 29, 2015. www.cubaliteraria.com/articulo.php?idarticulo=8440&idseccion=25.

———. 2011. "Novísima de teatro 45 años después." *La Jiribilla. Revista de Cultura Cubana* (November 19–25). Accessed April 29, 2015. www.lajiribilla.co.cu/2011/n550_11/550_23.html.

Oramas, Ada. 2011. "Artistas de la radio y televisión cubana en Las Yaguas." *Tribuna de la Habana*, September 22. Accessed April 29, 2015. www.tribuna.co.cu/historia/2011-10-22/mal-mayor-republica.

Oramas, Joaquín. 1971. "Las piruetas de los que no producen." *Granma* (Havana), January 28, 1971: 3.

Otero, Lisandro. 1985. *Un día en el solar*. In *Comedias musicales*, edited by Carlos Espinosa Dominguez. Havana: Letras Cubanas.

Pita Astudillo, Féix. 1971. "Un paso más hacia rumbo seguro." *Granma* (Havana), February 22, 1971: 4.

Quintero, Héctor. 1966. *El premio flaco*. Havana: Casa de las Américas.

Saco, José Antonio. 2001. *Memoria sobre la vagancia en la Isla de Cuba*. In *Obras*, edited by Eduardo Torres-Cuevas. Havana: Imagen Contemporánea.

Triana, José, 1962. "*Medea en el Espejo.*" In *El Parque de la fraternidad*. Havana: Union de Escritores y Artistas de Cuba.

Valiño, Omar, ed. 2010. *Dramaturgia de la Revolution (1959–2008): 30 obras en 50 años*. 3 vols. Havana: Ediciones Alarcos.

Vera, Mayté. (1964) 1985. "*Las Yaguas.*" In *Comedias musicales*, edited by Carlos Espinosa. Havana: Letras Cubanas.

Zardoya, María V. 2003. "La ciudadela habanera: Antecedentes históricos." *Arquitectura y Urbanismo* 34, no. 2: 10–15.

VÍCTOR FOWLER CALZADA is a Cuban poet, essayist, and writer. He is author of several award-winning books about race in Cuba and about Cuban cinema, including *Conversaciones con un cineasta incómodo: Julio García Espinosa*. He has worked as chief of publications at the International School of Cinema and Television in San Antonio de los Baños (1994–97 and 2002–7) and directed the electronic magazine *Miradas*.

Figure 6.1 Poster of *De cierta manera*. © ICAIC

SIX

Residential Miraflores
(Script for *De cierta manera* / One way or another)

Sara Gómez Yera and Tomás González

MIRAFLORES RESIDENTIAL HOUSING COMPLEX

Screenplay
Docufiction

Argument and Dialogue: SARA GÓMEZ
TOMÁS GONZÁLEZ PÉREZ

Consultants: ALBERTO PEDRO DÍAZ
TOMÁS GUTIÉRREZ ALEA

* * *

Culture exists on the deepest planes of awareness as customs, habits, norms, values, etc. that firmly resist social change. Thus, even after the socioeconomic conditions that gave rise to marginalization have been radically transformed, we can still study the culture of the sector that was shaped by those conditions.

CREDITS
1 to 10. Documentary

On top of the sequence's images of new construction—housing and social services such as schools, hospitals, etc.—we will consider superimposing shots of decrepit housing, people being relocated, etc. It may be possible to take advantage of the recently initiated plan to transform some zones of Central Havana, including the district known as Cayo Hueso.

The style of the credits will be restrained, and will clearly indicate that the figures appearing in the film are real people who are maintaining their identities and how the events depicted correspond to recent occurrences in the lives of these persons. The two fictional characters that it became necessary to include will be introduced. The viewer will be told the names of those on the technical and creative teams who will participate in making the film and the sources of the archival images in an attempt to present a coherent grouping among the respective specialties, in other words, emphasizing the teamwork that this type of film requires beyond any individual effort. We will acknowledge the collaboration of institutions and entities, as well as their respective members, on-screen.

Sequence I
Introduction to Miraflores.
11 to 31. Documentary Report

Descriptive pans of the neighborhood. Details of the residents' homes and yards. The park, the small shopping center. The bus stop, behind which stands a cluster of buildings at different stages of construction that are being erected by the microbrigade system. This neighborhood consists of small individual houses with yards and gates, and although they were similar when built (1962), now they are noticeably different from one other, whether because of their well-tended facades or their unique vegetation and improvised fenced-in yards in which all sorts of domestic animals can be found (doves, goats, chickens, sheep, bird and parrot cages, etc.). The roofs of some are also shown, sporting antennas for the occupants' newly acquired television sets.

This report will culminate with shots of activities at the school, in the classrooms, the cafeteria, the office, the hallways...

The classrooms of Yolanda and Amparo. Their students are as different as the houses of the neighborhood. Some are in full uniform and dressed neatly, others are in the most slovenly, neglected state imaginable. The scenes will be lively and busy, without direct sound, but expressive in themselves.

* * *

Sequence II
School Council. Interior at Dusk
32 to 43. Docufiction

The members of the School Council are meeting together in a classroom: The Parents' Committee, members of the CDR (Revolutionary Defense Committee), FMC (Federation of Cuban Women), and the School Workers' Collective.

> Principal: Colleagues, we are about to begin the final school term and we are worried about class attendance in general, and the possible failure of some students. The students in question are precisely the most undereducated ones, those that should already be in secondary school at their age. We have to work block by block, to inquire into the living conditions of these young people and try to encourage them to successfully complete their school year in the vocational schools and other special programs.

After this brief introduction, the meeting of the educational establishment officially comes to order, nuanced with interventions that will support and illustrate that introduction. These kinds of meetings are very common in the neighborhood and the members of the School Council are trained participants. In an improvised, spontaneous (although controlled to a certain extent) way, they participate in the discussion. This sequence cannot be set out very precisely in the script, as it will be adapted for the time, the actual situation and the individuals involved at the time of filming. It will also serve the purpose of informing the viewers, at the beginning of the film, of the problems affecting the school and of its close relationship with the community. Among the CDR officials in attendance at the meeting are Candito, a former barber in "Las Yaguas," and Yolanda, a teacher working for the first time in a classroom in the neighborhood, and one of our fictional characters. After the meeting they speak together, away from the others.

> Candito: And what does the novice of the year have to say?
>
> Yolanda: Here I am, Candito, adapting little by little, but I tell you, I don't understand how it's possible that after so many years we're still facing the same struggle.
>
> C: They're defending themselves, teacher, I tell you they're defending themselves.
>
> Y: Defending themselves? But from what?
>
> ... From the Revolution?
>
> C: One way or another.
>
> Y: But the Revolution has given them everything, everything. New houses, a school ... everything.

What do they have to lose?

C: They are losing, they are losing a way of being, teacher, and they are afraid, I repeat, they are afraid.

The participants leave the meeting en masse, talking among themselves.

* * *

Sequence III
Reconstruction (1960). Exterior. Daytime.
44 to 68. Documentary

Panoramic still photograph of the old dilapidated Cuban district of Las Yaguas. Several original still photographs. Shots of the reconstruction, showing typical scenes, with people in stationary poses, the way men used to pose for photographs in those days.

> Narrator: In 1960 the Cuban Revolution carried out a census in dilapidated districts and implemented a campaign of literacy and moral improvement in order to completely eradicate those run-down neighborhoods.

The sequence continues with the typical shots of barefoot children, but this time there are mobilizations in the streets, people shouting, talking, and a certain commotion.

> Man 1: Yeah, lots of people have come around with the same story already. All governments come up with the same scheme—to get rid of the neighborhood and the [bad] scene (*ambiente*).

Shot of a literacy tutor walking by.
(The Campaign in these neighborhoods preceded the official one of 1961)

> Woman 1: Goodbye... Tea-cher (mockingly provocative)
>
> Woman 2: (sexually aggressive) *A la rueda, dame un besito y vete pa' la escuela papi.*[1]

General shot of the neighborhood, there are some outsiders, young women with clipboards in their hands, militiamen and, among them, Adalberto, Zulueta, and Candito.

> Man 2: They'd better not ask me what I'm doing here, or anything else. No one needs to know how many people sleep and eat at my house.

Man 3: (discretely). This smells like a raid... like the police... and I'm going to bust out, they're not going to catch me red-handed.

Woman 3: As for me, my saints, who never lie to me, say that this time it's really going to happen, that these people are really going to force us out of here.

Woman 4: (showing the skin on her arms) But look at my goosebumps... look... I get that that guy has his thing, I don't know, when I see him on television speaking, *coño* [fuck], I don't know, I believe him.

During scenes from the reconstruction of 1960, Candito and Adalberto Zulueta will begin to narrate how that initial work became difficult, how mistrust and hostility created a barrier that was often very difficult to overcome. Candito and Adalberto have been key figures in the fieldwork that preceded the screenplay, and we hope to be able to do some effective film work [because of that]. They will end up talking very briefly about the work of building the new neighborhoods with the Esfuerzo Propio y Ayuda Mutua (Self-Help and Mutual Aid) program.

* * *

Sequence IV
Candito's House. Interior. Daytime.
69 to 79

Candito's house. Inside, Candito, his wife Isa and Yolanda are having lunch. The couple has invited Yolanda to see their house and to meet their children and grandchildren.

It is a typical neighborhood house, but one of the most well-tended. The furniture is in good condition and special care has been taken to make it look clean and tidy. It is not a large house. It has a foyer, a small living room, a dining area and three very small bedrooms. The bathroom and kitchen could be described as well appointed. As this is the first time in the film that we see the inside of a house in this neighborhood, the sequence will begin with purely descriptive shots of the setting, without concern that they may appear gratuitous. This will give the viewers a window into the family's domestic culture through their everyday objects and decorations.

80 to 94

C: (to the teacher) What do you think?

Y: (swallowing a mouthful) Very tasty. Who made it?

C: Well, to tell the truth, it was my old lady, but I told her exactly what to do.

Isa: (putting down a glass of beer she had been drinking) Don't be a liar.

C: Me? A liar? Who put the beans to soak? Who put them on to cook?

I: You, but that's all.

Y: (smiling) But . . . don't fight about it!

I: Look at . . . this girl . . .

C: (correcting his wife) Not this girl, no . . . "teacher."

I: (To the teacher) This girl, what's her name?

Y: Yolanda, my name is Yolanda.

I: (to Candito) What do you mean by calling the young woman "teacher," "teacher." She has a name. Look, Yolanda, my dear, let's be honest . . . he put the beans on, bought the bread, and the beer, but really, the rest of us here weren't idle. (to Candito) True or false?

C: True.

I: He came home last night and said to me, "Ay, woman, I invited the new teacher to lunch on Sunday and that's tomorrow." And me, I was exhausted, and I said to him, "Hey, don't go to bed, put the beans on." True or false?

C: True . . . but . . .

I: (angrily) But nothing, that's how it was!

95 to 101

Everyone is laughing. A girl comes into the dining room with three other children.

Girl: Teacher.

Y: Tell me, sweetheart.

Girl: When I grow up, I'm not going to be a teacher.

Y: Don't you like teaching?

N: No. I am going to be a dancer. Look how I go up en pointe.

She stands up on the tips of her big toes.

> I: (smiling at the girl's aggressiveness) Go out to play!

102 to 105

The children run out as though they had misbehaved.

> I: That's my granddaughter. Her mother studies and works in MINCIN [Domestic Trade Ministry]. We raised her.
>
> C: She's a handful.
>
> I: She wants to be like Alicia Alonso.
>
> We always have to put the dance programs on TV.
>
> Y: And who earned the television in this house?
>
> I: Mario, my son, the pride of the household.
>
> C: (acting jealous) Old lady . . . I have my good points, too.

106 to 114

Yolanda is enjoying the scene.

> I: Yes, Yolanda, my men are ahead of the game! And that includes my husband, who brought me a refrigerator. He held his own against the best of the factory. Just imagine, over there they said that the family was going to take everything.
>
> C: (standing as if to deliver a speech) "It is the duty of every man in this house to be ahead of the game."
>
> I: Now, now! (She pulls him by the pant leg) Sit down, did the drink go to your head?
>
> Y: (somewhat tipsy) Let it go, Isa!
>
> C: (squeezing Isa's arm affectionately) Look Yolanda, what she wants is for me to say that she's ahead of the game, too.
>
> I: Okay, okay, Yolanda, don't believe that I didn't earn these things, too . . .
>
> I have to wash out a lot of red dirt when they come home from the cane fields . . .

Everyone laughs.

> I: (changing the subject). Look, young woman, you don't know anything. My husband has always been ahead of the game, it's not just now . . . no

way! Before, when we all lived in a single little room that wasn't half as big as this dining room, he used to come home very late, as he was already working with the revolutionaries in those days.

…yes, Yolanda…and he even had a henchman making death threats to him, right here.

C: Not here, woman. We're in Miraflores neighborhood, created by the Revolution.

I: Excuse me…in Las Yaguas…in Las Yaguas the [rest of the] henchmen didn't want to kill him, there were all kinds of them: informers and degenerate politicians…

Cut

115 to 130

Scenes of a *charanga* or conga in the middle of the neighborhood, shots of posters and politicians moving among the neighbors distributing handouts.

The scene will be interspersed with press photographs of the violence perpetrated by the dictatorship against the revolutionaries.

INTERVIEW. José Oriol Bustamante, one of our consultants for the screenplay, will narrate his experiences working with Candito and Adalberto on the Left's attempt at political mobilization in the 1950s, and especially the idealistic project to create the Federation of Indigents.

The sequence continues in Candito's house.

131 to 147

I: One day they set a trap for her…

C: Enough, woman…you have to live in the present.

Y: Leave her alone, Candito, these things shouldn't be forgotten.

C: I'm not forgetting the past…what I don't want is for it to come back, Yolanda.

They hear footsteps in the yard, and Mario arrives, taking his shirt off as he enters.

I: My other man of the house has arrived…Hey, we have visitors.

C: (trying to button his shirt up, flustered) Good afternoon.

They make eye contact. Mario has arrived with his clothing full of dirt, obviously from working. Mario is a (fictional) son that we added to Candito's family. He is a composite of the biographical and character traits of Alfredo, Candito's real-life younger brother. Mario enters the kitchen and begins taking the lids off the pots one by one, tasting this one and that. He finishes what he is doing and returns to the dining room, unbuttoning his shirt once again.

> M: (still in the kitchen, walking out while chewing something) Tremendous feast! (to Yolanda) The teacher will have to come tomorrow so she can also try the delicious split peas [*chicharos*] that the old lady makes.

He walks through the dining room on the way to the bedroom as Yolanda smiles and watches him with interest.

> I: Oh, you're shameless! (laughing) Yolanda, don't pay him any mind.
>
> M: (pretending to scold) I bet tomorrow there'll be split peas, eh...
>
> C: Yes, so what? I'd have wanted to serve you split peas in the morning twenty years ago if I could.

Mario comes out, naked to the waist, with a towel draped around his shoulders, and walks toward the bathroom.

> M: Old days that will never come again
>
> I: (scolding) Hey, look at you.
>
> M: Well, I have to get to the bathroom, don't I? I have to wash up after work like that.
>
> I: (to the teacher) We'd better go into the living room.

They move into the living room. Candito stops in the doorway to the bathroom into which Mario has disappeared.

148 to 150

> C: And how was work?
>
> M: Picking tomatoes...
>
> C: That's a breeze.
>
> M: (shouting from the shower) Everything's a breeze to you.

The children are in the living room watching television.

It's a typical Sunday noontime scene; the neighborhood children are in the living room and the old people are sitting down to talk. Just as they finish seating themselves, Humberto arrives. He is one of Mario's and Candito's workmates, and he appears to be the typical "cool dude" on the scene. He doesn't come in. He stands in the doorway and looks provocatively at Yolanda while he talks to Isa and Candito.

151 to 164

> Humberto: (adopting a very familiar tone) Granny, has my little partner [*socio*] arrived?[2]
>
> C: I didn't know that you had gone into business with my son.
>
> H: (to Candito) And you, sir, are just as kind as always.
>
> I: (trying to head off an argument) Mario's here, but he's in the shower.
>
> H: Tell him I'm at Chino's house, "knocking over tiles."
>
> C: Doing what?
>
> H: Dominoes, old man. Tell him to come over there to see me.

He leaves. Before leaving he eyes Yolanda once again brazenly. Yolanda looks annoyed.

> C: ... That guy gets on my nerves.

165 to 180

The scene continues, with several conversations going on, the noise of the television and the children, other neighbors arriving with improvised greetings, until the noise level rises to a confusing pitch.

Meanwhile, Mario continues eating in the dining room and he and Yolanda exchange looks of mutual attraction.

* * *

Sequence V
The Pursuit. Exteriors.
181 to 206. Documentary

Shot of Yolanda leaving the school among the general crush of students. She comes across Mario, who greets her and continues on his way. This shot is the first in a sequence without dialogue, comprised of a series of shots in progression showing the developing relationship between Mario and Yolanda. We watch it progress from casual but obviously arranged encounters in different parts of the neighborhood on different days and times, to actual dates in other places—public places and recreational sites in the city proper. This will be a transitional sequence into the documentary style that shows incidentally the present-day city, the cinemas, Coppelia (ice cream parlor), stadium, etc.

* * *

Sequence VI
Mario and Yolanda. Part One. Exterior. Daytime.
207 to 227

María and Yolanda are sitting in a grove of pine trees.
Medium shot of Yolanda.

> Y: I'm 23 years old. My family had resources.
>
> M (O.S.) [off-screen]: Money?
>
> Y: Not exactly. My mom worked and so did my dad.

Medium shot of Mario, speaking more to the audience than to Yolanda.

> M: My folks did the same, and they didn't have either money or resources.
>
> Y (O.S.): Why don't you tell me about yourself?
>
> M: Are you interested?
>
> Y: Yes, very much.

Close-up of Mario that continues throughout, like a long interview. Yolanda's voice is always V.O. [voice-over]

> M: I was born here.
>
> Y: Here in The Pines?
>
> M: This would have been a really beautiful place to be born, the way it is now.
>   Before, there wasn't a single tree, and there was dirty water running between houses made of palm leaves, tin and cardboard. The houses here were built with any old thing, but in the end they were all the same . . . I became a man on the streets. Home was for sleeping.

Y: And school?

M: I went to school. The old man wanted me to be something, so I could get out of here. But the school was far away and I almost never made it there. We skipped out.

Y: And what did you do?

M: When?

Y: When you skipped school.

M: Nothing, enjoyed life.

Y: (ironically) I figured.

M: ... Until "she" arrived ...

Y: Who?

M: Who else? The Revolution. The new house. Goodbye to the barrio ... and they caught me.

Y: Arrested you?

M: No, they gave me a scholarship. In a technology institute, after I climbed Pico Turquino [Turquino Peak] five times.

Y: Were you one of those "Five Picos" boys?

M: I liked the Sierra Maestra. There, it was like being in the barrio when we skipped school. The scholarship, no way. I quit in the second year.

Y: And then?

M: Nothing, back to the street. Friends, girlfriends ... and the old man, who constantly fought with me.

Y: And ...

M: They caught me again. Military service.

Y: Just as well.

M: Nothing came on time for me, really. I was on the wrong track, the wrong track. Military service was good for me. At the time, I even thought about "leaving."

Y: You were going to leave? Leave the country?

M: No girl, I wasn't going to commit myself to that game.

Y: What?

M: Let me speak. My dream was to be Ñáñigo, Abakuá, like the best in the barrio.

CU [close-up] of Yolanda

> Y: Ñáñigo?
>
> M: I know what you're thinking. The Ñáñigos eat children on the Feast of Saint Barbara (laughs).

Close-up of Yolanda.

> Y: That's what I was told as a child.

* * *

Documentary. The Secret Society.
228 to 247

Engravings of the Port of Havana. Text (Project).
18th century.
Slave ships. Detail.

> Narrator: We are being transformed into a vast cane plantation; and the sugar cane is going to require an ever-greater number of hands, a greater number of slaves. West Africa is pillaged, and from there slaves from different cultures at different stages of development are going to arrive here.

Illustrations of the legend of SIKAN.

> Narrator: Notable among these, in the zone of Calabar, are the Efik, a semi-Bantu culture that, perceiving the need to consolidate the nascent patriarchal regime, created a myth in which the woman SIKAN betrays the great secret of the god ABASI, giving rise to a secret society from which women were excluded for being traitors.

Details of the engravings of the city of Havana. The buildings, public squares, and forts.

> Narrator: Furthermore, the colonial economy, through a House of Commerce with offices in Havana and Cadiz, paved the way for Spaniards from Seville to come to our thriving capital over a period of three centuries. Most of them were recruited as sailors and were primarily from the more marginal classes of that Spanish city. They came with the code of violence, machismo, and Marian worship typical of such adventurers and encountered a social structure in the areas around the ports of Havana

and Matanzas that they could become part of, joining the similarly marginalized local Creole population.

Engravings and drawings of blacks . . .

> Narrator: El Negro Curro
>
> In the 19th century, "El Negro Curro" appears in Havana as an authentic expression of urban Cuban folklore.

Religious attributes of Ñañiguismo. *Iremes* [dancing masked devils]. The music and its dances. The setting.

> Narrator: At the same time, in the SIKAN myth involving the slaves of Efik assembled in the governing council of the Efik Euton nation, this marginal stage will encounter a psychological motive for the creation of the Abakuá Secret Society, a cultural entity that brings together the social aspirations, norms and values of machismo in traditional Cuban ways of thinking, transcending the boundaries of ritual and myth.

An Abakuá ritual (*plante*). Emphasizing the mixed race [*mestisaje*] of the participants as well as its sordid, violent quality.

> Narrator: It may be said that the traditional and exclusive nature of this secret society situates its members against progress and incapable of satisfying the requirements of modern life. And for us, in the particular context of building a socialist project, it is going to represent a source of marginality as it encourages a parallel code of social relations, a source of resistance, a point of hardening to and rejection of social integration, as well as the last bastion of criminality owing to the marginal origins of most of its members.

* * *

Sequence VI (continued)
249 to 258

Close-up of Yolanda to the camera. Mario O.S.

> Y: My life isn't as full of things as yours is.
>
> My parents working for the Revolution, me in boarding school all the time.
>
> M: And what happened with your marriage?

> Y: Nothing. He was studying medicine, I was studying history. He was finishing up, and I wasn't.
>
> And we got married.
>
> M: Why do you say it like that?
>
> Y: It's nothing, I know you won't believe me. I was curious to know what it was like to be married.
>
> M: And?
>
> Y: We got married.

Sequence of still photographs of their engagement.

The couple on outings. Photos of the bridal shower and the wedding. The traditional photos.

Close-up of Yolanda identical to the previous one.

> Y: The first year was good. He always had exams, or night shifts at the hospital, but when we saw each other we had a good time. I was alone a lot of the time, but I am used to it.
>
> M: To being alone?
>
> Y: (firmly) To being independent.
>
> M: You're a sparrow.
>
> Y: What is that?
>
> M: A very sad bird. And how did it end?
>
> Y: I don't want to unload on you.
>
> M: Come on, girl, tell me about it.
>
> Y: It was nothing, he graduated and had to do his rural service. He wanted me to leave school and go with him. I stayed. We divorced and I began working as a teacher. I'm still in school.

Close-up of Mario to the camera.

> M: You're still single?

Close-up of Yolanda to the camera.

259 to 267

> Y: I'm still independent.

Long shot. Mario takes her hand and they come together. They kiss and begin walking.

> Y: You know something, Mario? I still don't understand this thing about being an Abakuá.
>
> M: To be Abakuá you have to be a good friend, a good son and good husband. Does that sound good?
>
> Y: It's not bad.
>
> M: But above all you have to be a man, a real man. Under no circumstances can you rat out a friend, an *ekobio*, a brother. It doesn't matter what he has done, that's the most important thing.
>
> Y: And why aren't you a Ñáñigo now?
>
> M: I don't know... my way of thinking changed.
>
> Y: Your way of thinking? Are you sure?
>
> M: Well, what do *you* think?
>
> Y: But you can't be Abakuá.
>
> M: Why Yolanda, why? (defensively)
>
> Y: Because of your way of thinking... right?

* * *

Sequence VII (Lázaro), the rabbit
Fifth-Grade Classroom. Interior. Daytime.
268 to 290

Lázaro is standing up with his head down.

His lips are pressed together and he is looking at the teacher out of the corner of his eye. Yolanda is reprimanding him as she walks toward him.

> Y: What do you think life is about? (her expression changing). The Revolution gives you everything, and you throw it into the first wastebasket you find. Why?
> Why do you think you're the wise guy of the show?

The other students laugh.

> Y: Silence! Just yesterday I gave you a notebook and pen. Today you didn't bring them to school. Today you come with your hands empty.

Yolanda is face-to-face with Lázaro. She grabs his face angrily. Lázaro is confused. He raises his hands as if to shield himself. The students laugh. Everyone takes advantage of the situation and disorder ensues.

Shot of Yolanda looking at him disconcertedly.

> Y: No... I'm not going to hit you. Where did you put the pen and notebook? Look at me!

Lázaro looks at her. All the students laugh and make fun of him.

> Student: Rabbit's a big coward!

Chorus of laughter and joking.
Rabbit! Bunny Rabbit!

Lázaro looks all around the classroom and then looks at Yolanda with as much anger as he can muster.

> Y: Where is the notebook and pencil?

Lázaro remains quiet and determined.

> Lázaro: I threw them out!

> Y: Oh no. Leave this classroom immediately!

Lázaro begins his triumphant exit. None of his classmates are mocking him now. Everyone is surprised.

> Y: Don't come back here until you bring a new notebook and pencil!

Lázaro, at the doorway of the classroom, turns to Yolanda and gesticulates.

> L: I'll never come to this dump again (exits).

> Student: Shit! Rabbit's really pissed off.

Teachers' Lunchroom at the School. Interior.
291 to 302

Yolanda is having lunch and talking to Amparo. Amparo teaches the other fifth-grade class and is a former classmate of Yolanda (Amparo is the real-life teacher).

> Amparo: It's not good that you kicked him out of class. That's precisely what they want us to do.
>
> Y: But they exasperate me. I tell you, sometimes I think about leaving this school and going to a quieter neighborhood.
>
> A: Right, where they need you less . . .

Yolanda lowers her head pensively.

> A: You have to find patience to deal with these kids, patience and a lot of love. There's no other way.
>
> Y: What upset me most was that he thought I was going to hit him.
>
> A: Don't you know Lázaro's mother?
>
> Y: No.
>
> A: (pressing her lips together)
>
> They call her La Mejicana. She has four kids, including Lázaro, who's the oldest.
>
> Y: And the father?
>
> A: "The fathers" . . . somewhere out there. Why don't we go and see her? . . .

* * *

Sequence VIII
House of La Mejicana. Interior.
303 to 325

La Mejicana's house is like any other in the Miraflores neighborhood but is quite run-down. The children's scribbles can be seen on the walls. One thing that is well kept is a very modest altar (no doubt the same one she had in Las Yaguas) in the middle of the room. The two teachers are seated while La Mejicana performs her scene. Both La Mejicana and her children are real people and the story that is told will be reconstructed from an experience they had just two months ago. While La Mejicana speaks, her daughter Orquídea is sitting on Amparo's lap and is listening casually.

> La Mejicana (to Amparo): You see, Miss, what Lazarito has done to me again. Arrested again for stealing. I don't know, this boy is going to be the death of me. I don't know what he's got in his head, just like his father.
>
> Y: And where is his father?

> LM: We'd better not talk about that, but Lázaro is going to follow in his footsteps (pauses). And you feel so ashamed, with those people from the police, that woman from Social Services, they always think that the parents are to blame, and they ask all sorts of questions. (to Yolanda) Ask Miss Amparo, she knows me from last year. I could never send my son out to steal. It's those bad friends in the neighborhood, I swear Miss, I swear...
>
> Y: I want to ask you a question...
>
> LM: ... Go ahead, Miss...
>
> Y: How is Lazarito at home?
>
> LM: Lazarito, well, I don't know... he acts very strange.
>   You never know what he is thinking...
>   The worst thing is when he goes out on the street.
>   Here, you could say he's a good boy, he's good with his younger brothers and sisters, he takes care of them, and he helps me...

Orquídea, still sitting on Amparo's lap, interrupts them.

> Orquídea: My brother is very nice. The other day he gave me a notebook and pen. My notebook was full and my pencil was too small.

Close-up of Yolanda. Looks at her colleague.
Amparo nods her head.

> LM: Yes, he is very good with his brothers and sisters. That's why I need them to let him go. The woman, the one that came, told me that they were going to let him go, but I told her to make it soon. Lázaro is the only help I have... I'm pregnant now, and if Lázaro had been here he would have got me an appointment with the doctor. And I feel bad, missy. And then I had a visit from the nurse from that clinic who comes after you if you're pregnant and haven't gone to the doctor... I'm sick and tired of her...

Yolanda interrupts La Mejicana's monologue, visibly upset.

> Y: And why do you hit him?
>
> LM: (surprised) So he doesn't become a thief.

326 to 334

Scene of La Mejicana hitting Lázaro. We can dispense with fiction entirely and do sociopsychodrama.

> L: Don't hit me, Mama!
>
> LM (hitting him): Don't you become like your father. You don't need to be a thief like him. Why do you have to be a thief, too? Tell me!
>
> LM: I never had anything. No one ever cared about me, my father sent me out to beg, he never sent me to school or anything, you have school and the food that the government gives you, if you want more then ask for it, like I did, begging isn't bad...

Lázaro looks at her with fear. Sometimes with hatred, too.

> LM: I don't want to have a son in prison, in jail, I'm alone, you're the only man in this house and you have to help me, you degenerate... son of a bitch, I've been ashamed of you so many times already.

Cut.

> LM: Teacher, (to Yolanda) you have to help me, do something for him, it's hell in this house without him.

335 to 340

Yolanda has tears in her eyes. She's about to cry. Amparo sees this and puts a hand on her shoulder. Orquídea has gone to sit beside her mother.

> Y: (with effort) I will do all I can, I promise. But promise me that you won't hit him anymore.
>
> LM: (crying) I promise, teacher. I will never hit him again.

Suddenly she stops crying and kneels in front of the altar.

> LM: As blessed Saint Bárbara is my witness, I swear that I'll never raise a hand to my son Lazarito again... or Saint Lazarus himself should cover my hand in sores... I'll never hit him again... or send him out to beg... or to steal...

Cut.

* * *

Sequence IX
The Show on the Streets. Exterior. On the street.
341 to 387

Long sequence of Mario waiting.

The clock in the ticket booth of Cine Yara shows 7:00 p.m. Mario looks at his watch, then up at the ticket booth clock. He buys two tickets, holding up two fingers. The ticket seller gives him two tickets, takes the money, then passes him five pesos change.

Mario walks around with the tickets in his hand. Mario lights a cigarette. Mario looks at his watch. He looks at the clock in the ticket booth. 7:30 p.m. Mario takes two small papers from his shirt pocket. Mario rips the papers in half at the very moment that Yolanda's hands cover his eyes [from behind]. Mario takes Yolanda's hands by the wrists and moves them apart angrily. Mario turns to her.

> M: And where have you been hiding?
>
> Y: I have serious problems at school. With a student.
>
> M: At school . . . ! Your students . . .

Mario drags her by the arm and pulls her to the ticket booth. Mario buys tickets again, takes Yolanda [by the arm] and drags her through the doorway of the theater, giving the tickets to the doorman . . .

In the vestibule, she frees herself from Mario's grasp brusquely and walks out to the street. The doorman acts surprised. Mario goes after her. He catches up with her at the corner and is forced to cross Calle 23 with her, in the direction of Hotel Habana Libre. He takes her more gently by the arm to avoid a scene among the crowds on the street.

> Y: (shaking him off). Let me go!

Mario and Yolanda stop on the sidewalk, he lets her go. They walk down L toward San Lázaro, apparently to avoid the crowds. Mario comes up to Yolanda. Mario speaks to her sarcastically.

> M: I did not know that the "educator" liked to make a scene in public!
>
> Y: The one who made a scene was you, Sir.
>   I'm far too independent to let someone come and drag me around like a rag doll.
>
> M: But you kept me waiting an hour! And I don't have to wait for anyone for an hour, (shouting). An hour!

Y: Don't yell at me (shouting). If it's a matter of shouting, I know how to shout, too.

M: (lowering his voice)
   So, what you want is to make a scene?

Y: (lying) What I want is to never see you again.

Mario, this is over.

M: You bet it's over, educator, it's over.

388 to 423

Mario makes as if to leave. They are in an alleyway. Mario goes back the way they came, while Yolanda walks toward Infanta.

Shot of Mario walking down the street trying to listen for her following him. He begins to turn his head. He turns his entire body around and sees the empty street. He surprises himself by starting to run back, to where she has supposedly gone. Yolanda has turned down Infanta. Yolanda turns around and doesn't see Mario among the people walking toward her. Yolanda changes her pace, walking somewhat hopelessly now. Suddenly she hears Mario's voice and tries to regain her former attitude of righteous indignation.

   M: Yolanda!

   Y: What?

   M: (with great effort) Forgive me, Yolanda.

Yolanda is about to say something, when she sees Guillermo calling from the pub at Infanta and San Miguel.

   Guillermo: Mario, Mario...

Mario looks across the street.

Yolanda appears confused, waits. Guillermo comes across the street, his entire "act" betraying the fact that he has just drunk several beers. He reaches Mario.

   G: Little brother. You're lost.

Guillermo hugs him. Mario waits for Yolanda, who has moved away to wait at a discreet distance.

   G: Little brother, chico, where have you been?

You don't even come 'round my house anymore. My wife said to me: "You did something to Mario." I told her, "Nothing, woman, nothing." I'm thinking of giving a concert soon. You can't miss it.

Mario looks at Yolanda.

M: (to Guillermo) Listen, let me introduce you to ... Yolanda ...

G: Nice to meet you.

Yolanda comes closer, looking serious. She finds it impossible to be spontaneous, and she doesn't think much of Guillermo. She barely holds out her hand.

Y: Nice to meet you.

G: Guillermo Díaz at your service.

Mario looks at Guillermo. Guillermo observes the situation in silence. Finally, he breaks the ice.

G: Chico, well, you know where to find me (he gestures toward the pub). You can come here or to my house, and on Monday, finally, I start working as an instructor at INDER [National Sports and Recreation Institute]. Well (to Yolanda), nice to meet you.

Yolanda mumbles a reply, moving her lips, but not speaking.

G: Goodbye, my brother, my buddies are waiting for me.

He slaps him on the shoulder. Then he puts his fists up and throws two punches, play boxing. Mario easily evades them.

G: Ha! You still remember what I taught you in my classes!

M: What's well taught is never forgot, teacher.

G: I hope so, *mulato* ...

Mario and Yolanda walk away in silence.

Guillermo watches them, looking curious but dubious about this unlikely couple.

* * *

Sequence X
Who is Guillermo? "The story of Guillermo that Yolanda doesn't know."
424 to 444

This sequence will be a reconstruction of events with Mario recalling and narrating the story, making it very obvious that his remembrance is introspective.

> M: Guillermo is a great guy and has his own story. I was a boy and Guillermo was an idol in Las Yaguas. He was a boxing champion. He came to the neighborhood after winning a fight and we followed him around, singing and running after him.
>
> Guillermo gave us money, pesos and everything.
>
> He had a beautiful, beautiful girlfriend named Luz.
>
> Guillermo loved Luz and protected her from the bad scene. There was a guy in the neighborhood who began stalking Luz, always trying to "get her," trying to see her naked. You know what I mean? Guillermo arrived one day and caught the guy. They fought, and Guillermo killed him. He went to prison. It was the end of his boxing career. That was many years ago, and now he's married to Luz and has two children, he writes songs and studies music.

This sequence will be a realistic reconstruction of Mario's narrative, with all the violence of those events, and Guillermo himself will help us. At the end we will see scenes from his current day-to-day life, in his new home, with his children and his guitar. Perhaps these scenes will have voice-overs of Mario and Yolanda talking as they walk away from the place where they encountered Guillermo.

> M: What did you think of Guillermo?
>
> Y: I didn't think much of him. What does he do?
>
> M: He sings. He's a songwriter.

* * *

Sequence XI
Yolanda Searches for Lázaro. Interior.
445 to 447

Yolanda is waiting in the waiting room of MININT [Ministry of the Interior] at Paseo and 13. It is the Center for the Control and Prevention of Juvenile Delinquency.

A woman staff member comes out and invites her to come in.

Inside the office is a lieutenant. He is friendly toward Yolanda. He has a file on top of his desk. It is Lázaro's file. This sequence will be as documentary-like as possible. Lázaro's case is recent. He is also a repeat offender. In the past two years he has been arrested three times.

> Lieutenant: You're Lázaro's teacher? I am happy you've come to show an interest, in these cases we need the collaboration of the People's Task Force and the School Council especially. This is a boy who is very behind in school; he should have started secondary school two years ago. We think it's a case of needing to be removed from the home environment. The boy himself has told us that his mother has encouraged him to commit crimes and we have confirmed this to be true. Do you know the mother's history?

Cut.

Candito (Mario's father) is sitting in the living room at home, speaking to a social worker who is investigating La Mejicana.

> Candito: I've known this boy's mother since she was a young girl. She lived in Las Yaguas neighborhood with her father and several sisters. Her father sold and repaired watches, but he was always out of work and drank quite a lot. I know them very well. I was a barber in Las Yaguas and I know everyone from there. From the time she was very young she went out begging. It was a bad scene, her sisters worked as prostitutes and she herself led a not-so-good life afterward. Lázaro's father, I think he's in prison. It's one of those situations that are difficult for the Revolution. Last year, when [we caught] Lázaro stealing in the onion fields, we went to talk to La Mejicana on behalf of the committee, but there's no talking to her...

Cut.

Lázaro is being interviewed by the lieutenant.

> Lázaro: I stole because my mom has no husband, she has no one to take care of the children so she can work. I am the man of the house. Now she's going to have another baby and she had a fight with the father...
> Lieutenant: Do you want to go home?
> L: (hopeful) Of course, Lieutenant, of course.
> My mother and my sisters are alone. I won't do it anymore, I promise I won't be back here again.

Cut.

> Lieutenant: (to Yolanda) Comrade, we believe that the school can help us. We don't want to lock Lázaro up in a prison; that young man can be saved,

but he needs help, affection, and good guidance. We're also worried about the other siblings, but imagine, Yolanda, we can't take the children away from that woman by force, the neighborhood organizations have to try to work closely with her. Perhaps the FMC [Federation of Cuban Women] can do something to get her started on the new way of life. And I know it's not easy, but we have to try. We are not responsible for her childhood, but we are responsible for her children's. We hope that you, the conscientious teachers, will help us. Take the boy.

Yolanda listens in silence. She says nothing in this sequence. Instead, it will consist of monologues that will actually be interviews about the case. There is no choice here but to give way to improvisation. In our fieldwork we have conducted interviews of this kind in one way or another, with good results.

* * *

Sequence XII
Yolanda and Lázaro. Exterior. Daytime.
448 to 468

In this sequence we see Yolanda in a news report–style scene in the area around the Carmelo de Calzada. Yolanda will take Lázaro for an ice cream as a way of building a closer relationship with him. For us, it will be a pretext for showing another type of youth, another aspect of adolescent life. Middle- and working-class high school students, perfectly integrated into urban life, full of vitality and spontaneity. The sequence will be filmed in "free" style as a microreport on the district, which we will offset with reference shots of Yolanda and Lázaro and occasionally show the perspective of this young person as someone who is discovering a world of new possibilities. FD.

* * *

Sequence XIII
Domino Game. Exterior. At dusk.
469 to 494

There is a domino table in the shared patio or courtyard of a housing complex in the Miraflores subdivision. Mario is playing dominoes with three friends. Behind Mario waits Humberto, the person from the lunch sequence in Candito's house (Sequence IV). Shot of Mario, who is smiling and putting down a tile: five and six. The next player analyzes the state of the game as he turns his head and looks at a girl walking by.

It is "Coca," a fourteen-year-old girl and a student of Yolanda's who we have seen in the classroom scenes and now appears more grown up and provocative. Player (1) comments routinely while coming back to the game, analyzing the interrupted play.

> Player (1): Look how the kid's gotten out of control. If she keeps up like this, she's gonna be a hot property before long.[3] Pass!
>
> Player (2): I doubt you'll have to wait very long, the girl's already grown out of this place. Don't be surprised if she has the starring role in the next episode. She's cheeky and then some . . . (hits the table) Can't go.
>
> Player (3): Yeah, yeah, Robertico is going around saying that he's gonna have to give her . . .
>
> M: (impatiently). Can you go?
>
> Player (3): Wait a sec . . . the best thing (points to Mario) is to do what our buddy here is doing. Go and look for a woman who's not from here (slaps his tile down on the table). Got it!
>
> Humberto: (attempting to show his annoyance) Yeah . . . sure . . .
>
> M: If you can, you can (slaps down his tile).
>
> A double for me! Double six.
>
> Mario looks at everyone, trying to get a reaction.
>
> M: No one has any more? (raises a tile threateningly).
>
> P (1): Wait youngster, wait. I have one. Careful! Don't be too quick or you'll lose!

He lays down a tile: Double three.

> P (1): A double for me!
>
> P (2): Watch your step . . . "More is always possible." (To Mario) Is it the teacher?
>
> M: Yes.
>
> P (2): Watch your step, don't throw it all away! You have a nice little piece there. A tasty morsel.

Puts down a tile: Three and five.

P (3): (sarcastically) Right, say goodbye to the neighborhood. It's got its good points, but no one [here] dies from natural causes, after all (hits the table) Can't go.

M: A double for me. (places a double five)

P (1): You have enough for everyone. Take care of what you've got! (smacks the table) Pass.

P (2): Watch out that your feet don't mess up what your head figured out! Your good head! Your turn. (to Mario). Pick this one up, you're having good luck.

P (3): (to Mario). Pick this one up, you're having good luck.

M: No one else? Then this game's over.

Everyone turns their tiles facedown on the table.

* * *

Sequence XIV
495 to 505

Mario, who has left the game of dominoes, walks along, followed by Humberto.

H: Hey, I want to talk to you about something.

M: What?

H: Me.

M: Go ahead.

H: Nothing, just that I'm "hung up" on a "piece" and I don't want to lose it. It's not something you'd want to lose.

M: And what's the problem?

H: I'm going to spend five days in Oriente Province.

M: (cutting him off) During the holidays ... right?

H: No (nodding his head in agreement).[4]
   Now.

M: Chico, but if you miss work again ... and now ... that's just more of your bullshit ...

H: ... What ... ? What's wrong with you? I know you're getting pretty full of yourself ... and what's with the *teque* [party line bullshit] ... ?

> M: Look, you're making a mistake, you're living in another world and it's going to cost you, a lot.
>
> H: Hmmm... seems like the teach is brainwashing you, buddy.
>
> M: Think whatever you want, and I'm not talking about her now (getting defensive).
>
> H: Now I understand why everyone is talking.
>
> M: (bothered) What are you insinuating?
>
> H: Nothing, buddy, let's forget it (he looks at Mario knowingly). It's just my way of talking.

Mario, who had stopped walking, now carries on, pensively. Humberto follows him and continues talking.

> H: But Mario, what am I going to do? I've got a five-day "service contract" with a chick in Oriente Province... and I've also got another little deal, you know... an exchange.
>
> M: Well... have a good trip, then.

They separate. Mario is obviously upset with the situation. Humberto stops him to give him a warning.

> H: Now, remember that I've told you what I'm going to do, and I only told you, and I believe I've spoken with a man. You know what that means?
>
> M: Is that a threat?
>
> H: No... no... just so you know, that's all.
>
> M: (sharply) And that's all.
>
> H: So...
>
> M: (firmly) Have a good trip!
>
> H: That's right, sweetheart, see you soon Mayito...

* * *

Sequence XV
Isa's Birthday. Interior. Daytime.
506 to 546

In Candito's house there is a strange religious activity going on. In the living room, a new element has appeared for the viewer. The new television is no longer the center of the room; now there is an improvised altar with colored cloths and tapestries and painted porcelain urns hung with elaborate necklaces made of beads strung together. The altar is a far cry from Western conceptions; there are no Catholic images here—once a year the traditional camouflage is set aside and the people worship Obbatalá directly. The atmosphere is very quiet and charged with religious fervor rather than with a sense of celebration. There is no *bembé* or *batá* music; the house has been invaded by an army of Iyalachas, who move around easily and respectfully, preparing sweets and floral offerings.

Several shots of the kitchen, where people are preparing the dishes traditionally served on this occasion. The sequence will attempt to create an atmosphere of female domestic activity, with the majority of the participants being women of a certain age, perhaps with small children moving among them at times.

Isa will be the perfect hostess, while Candito will appear somewhat distant from the goings-on, as though the house was not his own that day. It's the anniversary of his wife's initiation into the Santería faith. That was twenty-five years ago, when they lived in the old neighborhood (Las Yaguas), and she took ill with childbirth fever and everyone agreed that Obbatalá should be allowed to enter her mind.

The sequence will be arranged with descriptive shots of the ceremony emphasizing the essentially female environment, and will be entirely aimed at presenting a cultural and religious event that is very important among these once-marginalized groups. Throughout our history, Santería, as a religious expression of cultural syncretism, represented the potential for hope and was an expression of solidarity for the lowest segments of Cuban society, from the colonial slaves to those marginalized during the Republic.

When the sequence has unfolded enough, Mario and Yolanda will make their entrance and we will hear the first and only monologue. Yolanda arrives full of curiosity and surprise, unable to hide her avid expression. At her side, Mario appears troubled. Isa approaches the couple.

> I: Hail Mary, I thought you weren't going to come. (To Yolanda) Mario doesn't believe in these things and he's even embarrassed by them and all. But look, my dear, I myself told him to bring you. (To Mario) On a day like this I want to see all of the family. (To Yolanda) And as you are now part of the family . . .

Yolanda and Mario do not know what to say in response to Isa's words, and look at each other, perplexed. Isa continues.

> I: Come in, my dear, this is surely the only thing I have to leave you both when I die. Then you can do what you want [with it], even throw it away. Me, I have to do my duty while I am still living, and it's been 25 years now... afterward, it doesn't matter. (To Yolanda) You know we're not leaving ranches, or coffee plantations, none of that, just stones and seashells... Praise be to the spiritual energy of Obbatalá.

Panoramic shot of the altar.

Cut.

* * *

Sequence XVI
Panel Discussion—Documentary. Interior. Daytime.

This sequence will play a key function in the film. Up to this point we have witnessed a dramatic progression in the relationship between Yolanda and Mario; the central issues of that relationship have also been presented, including class, their respective economic backgrounds, and their social psychology; a potential conflict with Humberto, the absentee friend, has also been raised. We think that the conditions are now in place to include a theoretical sequence with notably intellectual content, while still maintaining the didacticism that has characterized the entire film.

In the style of *Memories of Underdevelopment*, and with a clear intent to invoke this film, using the same formal techniques, we will prepare and film a public discussion at the University of Havana or the National Library with the characters of Yolanda, Joe, and Migdalia in the audience.

The topic of the discussion will be "The Marginalized Segment of Society, Its Participation in Popular Culture and in Contemporary Political History." The participants have not been determined yet but will include historians or those who work in the social sciences who can bring some theoretical weight to the topic, although they do not necessarily have to agree. We will attempt to include some foreign adversary or politician who will make a concrete contribution to the role this sector has played in national liberation movements.

We understand that this was the case also in Yemen, for example, and we must not lose sight of the fact that in countries such as Haiti and Santo Domingo [sic], individuals from this segment have joined the ranks of the special forces of repression. A curious case that's also worth mentioning is that of Brazil, where the new system is seeking to become a great industrial and economic power and has chosen to embark on [a campaign of] genocide after having concluded that those people who neither produce nor consume can hardly be integrated into a so-called modern society. This fascist solution will be situated in opposition to our own humanist revolutionary one, in which steps are taken to eliminate the socioeconomic foundations that led to the emergence of this [marginalized group], and then instituting a campaign of reeducation and sociocultural integration.

This sequence will be enriched by a documentary with international content.

The images will be obtained from film and photographic archives and will also include excerpts from other documentary and fictional films. As much material as possible on favelas and on violence will be collected. Political material such as a shot of the Tonton Macoute and Black Muslims (Malcolm X, repressive forces, and liberation movements—Algeria, Yemen, ultimately everything that illustrates the ambivalent nature of the marginalized [population] as a political force and the socioeconomic conditions that characterize this segment of "modern" society.)

This sequence will be constructed as a didactic documentary with text, and the intent will be to make it clear, informative, and entertaining without allowing these qualities to limit its theoretical rigor. It will follow the structure outlined below.

1. Definition of the term *marginal*, in the sense of "on the margins of the economy and/or history as a consequence of the private property regime."

2. Social psychology and structure of the personality of the people who make up this segment.

3. Ambivalent nature of this segment of society as a political force, with examples.

4. The complexity and stability of the culture and its resistance to change.

The documentary will be naturally incorporated into the panel discussion to add visual interest to the scene and prevent it from becoming tedious, which would diminish its effect. It must be borne in mind that this sequence will operate as a catalyst within the film, as it contains appropriate responses to this problem, in our opinion. Above all, we hope to explain the reasons why certain norms and values have remained alive after the Revolution, and to identify where principles of traditional thinking (superstitious or otherwise) are situated and operate as a force opposing the advancement and development of a genuinely new culture. We shall also attempt to make it clear that the populist or paternalist solution will not be the most effective one, and neither will petit bourgeois rejection, superficiality, and intolerance. Only a lucid attitude and a sincere and rational assessment of the situation, in the best sense of the term, can disrupt this reality.

As the panel discussion unfolds, we will see Mario arrive, looking for Yolanda. Mario's presence will have a symbolic function.

* * *

Sequence XVII
The Dinner. Interior. Nighttime.
573 to 588

Mario and Yolanda enter the restaurant El Conejito accompanied by Joe and Migdalia, classmates of Yolanda. Their appearance indicates they are of the same social set and background [as Yolanda]. They take their seats. The maître d' lights the candle on the table.

    J: Whose birthday is it?

Everyone laughs. Migdalia makes a gesture of distaste.

    Mig: (to Joe) I don't like the smell of the candles.

Yolanda leans over the table and blows out the candle at the same time as Mario does.

    J: Hurray! Hurray for happy birthdays (clapping).

    Y: (to Joe) Joe, they'll kick us out.

Descriptive shots with details of the general setting. When we return to them, they are already eating in silence. Migdalia stares at every move Mario makes and makes no effort to hide her impression. Everyone drinks. Shots of their glasses, as though they were in a drinking competition.

J: I'm from Cienfuegos, but I don't like Cienfuegos.

Mig: But cienfuegueros are very elegant, refined, cultured people...

J: It depends. In the neighborhood where I grew up there wasn't even a drop of refinement.

(looking at Mario). Nothing, the Republic made my family tough, tough.

Bread and water, morning, noon and night. My father was a union leader, he was almost always in jail.

Mig: Well I spent quite a lot of time in Cienfuegos and I always had a great time.

J: You were lucky.

Cut.

In the ladies' restroom. The two women are fixing their hair and makeup.

Y: Are you and Joe not getting along?

Mig: No, this is the last time I'm going to go out with him. He always wants to be the poorest guy in the room.

Y: You really shouldn't let it bother you.

Mig: Things aren't working out. We [both] have a lot of reservations. It seems to me that the same thing will happen to you. That boy will never understand you, or you him.

Y: (scolding her firmly) We'll see...

Mig: Look, Yolanda, you don't have to get upset, but that doesn't make us all equal, there are different backgrounds and statuses (pedantically).

Yolanda looks at her friend curiously, as if she were seeing her for the first time.

Mig: Don't go getting too romantic. I'm just as much a revolutionary as you, but girl.

Maybe in the future, for our children there won't be differences, but now, I'm telling you that you can't block out the sun with a single finger.

Cut.

595 to 600

Mario and Joe are waiting at the bar. Both have lit cigars and are a little tipsy.

>Joe: (raising his glass) A toast, for having met you.
>
>M: (imitating him) Cheers.
>
>J: Mario, take care of the woman you have, Yolanda isn't just any girl.
>
>M: I know (pause), and Migdalia?
>
>J: She's no good. She's got a lot of baggage. Forget it. Let's make another toast. But you make the toast this time.
>
>M: A toast to . . . the process that allowed us to sit here together, you and I.

Joe and Mario look at each other seriously. Migdalia and Yolanda have come into the bar and observe the men mockingly.

>Mig: (to Yolanda) We've got to get out of here. These two are drunk.

Cut.

Exterior. Nighttime.
595 to 611

The four are walking along the Malecón. Mario and Joe walk with their arms around each other's shoulders.

Migdalia and Yolanda are walking a few steps behind them.

>J: You're my brother, Mario.
>
>M: Yes sir, I am.
>
>J: And Yolanda is my sister (to Yolanda). Come Yolanda.

Yolanda obeys. The three hug each other. And walk along together.

>M: And Migdalia?
>
>J: That one's too pretentious . . .
>
>M: I'm not getting mixed up in that.

Migdalia begins to cry. She stays far away from the group. Mario notices her absence.

>M: And Migdalia?

J: What?

M: Chico, you're treating her very badly.

Joe goes running over to where Migdalia is. He trips and almost falls down. He is tipsy. He reaches her.

J: What's wrong?

Mig: (crying) I'm no good! I'm no good!

I feel really bad.

J: Change, stop criticizing yourself.

Joe pulls her toward him. Kisses her.

Cut.

Sitting on a wall, some distance from each other, the two couples give themselves over to romance.

Cut.

* * *

Sequence XVIII
Visiting the Parents of Students Lagging Behind. Documentary.
612 to 647

Through the documentary-survey format, Yolanda and other members of the School Council will help us investigate the possible causes that turn students into habitual repeaters and therefore undereducated children. Understandably, this is another typical sequence for which we cannot provide details at this time, as we don't yet know what possible cases there are. As we hope to be filming precisely during March and April, we have tried to include within the script the typical problems teachers face in the final school term.

What we do know is that one of the cases will be Coca, a fourteen-and-a-half-year-old girl who already shows all the signs of being troubled; she has been involved in several violent incidents at school and is the one the men were speaking about during the domino game.

Coca will allow us to analyze the problem of young women specifically, which to our understanding is much more precarious, as women have no legislation legally obligating them to do social service work when they reach adulthood, and neither do they have the chance to be called up for military service as a way of integrating themselves into the economic life of the country. Women in general, and especially those from this segment of society, can be marginalized from the revolutionary process and their personal goals limited to the traditional institutions of family and religious group.

To truly integrate the female population, the Revolution has only the advancement of the educational system and political-ideological persuasion carried out by the task forces [*organismos de masa*]. This problem transcends the boundaries of the formerly marginalized segment, with female dropouts from university faculties doubling those of males.

Of course, this problem is in the process of being resolved, but it is our duty to call for the appropriate changes. We have considered creating a montage of several documentary shots of these girls, with a simple written text that will be spoken in Yolanda's voice, and including this montage within the sequence. At any rate, we believe that the specific circumstances at the time of filming will provide us with effective cinematographic solutions.

We also plan to do a montage that consists of re-creations of the violent incidents perpetrated by Coca herself in the classroom, at home and in public places. Coca, her mother, and circle of friends are willing to collaborate on the project and the improvisations.

* * *

Sequence XIX
Guillermo and his Philosophy. Interior Daytime. Nighttime.
648 to 658

At the INDER boxing club, Guillermo is watching the boys train while humming a tune.

Mario enters, unseen by Guillermo, and walks up to him.

> M: Is that your latest song?
>
> G: Did you come to train?

M: Not exactly . . .

G: Got a problem?

M: Yes, but it's nothing important.

G: She . . . ?

M: (nodding) Yup . . .

G: She doesn't get you . . .

M: She's got her hang-ups, her own ideas.

G: Do what I do. Quit it!

M: Quit her? Yolanda?

G: No man, the scene. The scene leads straight to jail.

Cut.

659 to 669

In the recital hall of the Fine Arts Museum, Guillermo is giving a concert of his own songs. Mario and Yolanda are in the audience, as well as Luz and their children.

    G: (appearing to address Mario) Look at how I am now. This really is my world, and this really is my final song.

Guillermo sings the song:

    G: *Véndele*

    Véndele

    Véndele

    a ese mundo que no te da nada

    que no tiene flor de la mañana

    solo rejas y apenas la ventana

    Véndele

    y que ella nunca sepa nada

    de aquellas cosas que por ti pasaron

    de tu bregar por esas madrugadas

    Si ella te muestra la parte vacía

    de otro mundo lleno de mentiras

Y si al mirarla buscando sus ojos

ves que te rehúye y que no te mira

véndele también a su hipocresía

véndele... véndele.

[Quit it,

quit it...

that world that gives you nothing,

that has no morning blossom,

only bars and a tiny window.

Quit it, so she never knows of those things that happened because of you

and your midnight struggles.

If she shows you the empty part

of another world full of lies,

and as you look at her, searching for her eyes, you see her pull away from you

and not look you in the eye,

quit it, too,

quit her hypocrisy,

quit it... quit it]

670 to 674

Guillermo and Mario continue their conversation at INDER.

> G: What do you think?
>
> M: Philosophy...
>
> G: Thanks, Mayito, thanks. But don't forget it. You can quit the scene entirely, you have the main thing, which is that you've lost your fear, the fear of what's outside the scene. I can tell you there are many who never leave out of cowardice.
>
> M: Out of cowardice?
>
> G: Yes, Mario, one way or another, the scene is something they're already familiar with, you know, it's "the guide" for how to live, and even die there. But if they leave they don't know what can happen, so they feel more

secure there; otherwise, they're scared. I'll tell you, Mario, you have to be braver to leave the scene than to stay in it.

* * *

Sequence XX
The Return of Humberto. Interior Daytime.
675 to 690

Establishing shot of the Ómnibus Girón factory (Línea and 18), which is the workplace of Candito, Mario, and Humberto. Everyone is working hard, and we will re-create the atmosphere of the place, which is typical of the industrial proletariat. In this sequence we keep in mind the workshops staffed by marginalized workers who perform traditional mechanical and auto-body work. In a country where the automotive industry has never developed, this work is performed by small private shops; very few people manage to obtain a job in one of the three of four large US companies, where one has to arrive with a political recommendation from the "priests of Belén."[5] These individuals had an individualistic mentality and did not have the traditional guild to instill them with class consciousness (recall the small shops and the scene on Zanja Street in the urban Cayo Hueso neighborhood) . . .

After the triumph of the Revolution, these shops became places for commercial speculation and black market trading in car parts, and even for conspiracies. The Revolutionary Offensive of 1967 ended that illegal business. Many of the workers felt personally affected and developed openly counterrevolutionary stances, while others joined state agencies or the ranks of the Empresa de Ómnibus, where, in contact with a new force of young workers, they were integrated once and for all into the country's new way of life. With that workforce the experiments began that eventually gave rise to the Línea and 18 workshop, now the Omnibus Girón factory. The idea is not to say all these things in the sequence, but to take them into account in its composition, how the workers are portrayed, when choosing shots of the factory and when arranging the sequences that will be filmed there.

The idea is to arrive on location with this information in hand and attempt to incorporate it naturally. In the midst of the report on the place we will have shots of our characters at work, as well as some of Candito taking part in union activities, distributing notices, fixing the bulletin board, etc. Mario will be working inside a bus. From the other side of the glass, Humberto will greet him, gesture to him and try to say something. Mario does not hear him but gives him an unamused look. Humberto stops talking and moves on. Mario carries on with his work.

Cut.

691 to 706

Mario is resting while having a snack.

He is covered in grease. Humberto creeps up on him from behind, taking advantage of the fact that Mario is alone.

> H: What a woman, Mayito! What an easterner!
>
> I lived like a king!
>
> M: Congratulations...
>
> H: Fuck, *mulato*, don't give me a hard time. It was a joke, and I brought my things and everything.
>
> M: Congratulations, old man, seriously, I hope it all worked out for you.
>
> H: That's your issue, I know you so well.
>
> M: That's wonderful that you know me...!
>
> H: (trying to ignore Mario's attitude), Mayito, that woman has it all... what a dish!
>
> A buffet... with beef and pork to spare...

Another coworker walks over.
Humberto exchanges his happy expression for one of false seriousness.

> Worker: What's up, Humber, when did you get here?
>
> H: Last night, just last night.
>
> W: And how were things when you left?
>
> H: (Lying) Well, the worst is over...
>
> Now there's just the waiting, you know how it is.

Mario looks at them puzzled but does not try to understand.

W: (to Mario) Listen to me, you, sir, have become rather peculiar since you got a girlfriend.

H: Eh... and you don't know the half of it...
   Have you seen her?

W: No, but people are saying great things about her.

M: Why don't they talk about... something else...

H: Listen my little brother... you're... there's just no talking to you right now...

Candito has seen Mario among the men and comes over. He looks at Humberto suspiciously. Humberto makes a gesture of displeasure then says to the other worker.

H: Look, let's get out of there, because here comes Candito, and you know he feels about me... Bye, Mayito...

Candito reaches Mario when he is alone.

C: (to Mario) Hey, remember that... (he is distracted).

M: What?

C: ... that we have to work on Sunday.

M: Here?

C: (he continues to look at Humberto, who has now joined another group) No, in the neighborhood, so don't make any commitments here.

M: Got it.

* * *

Sequence XXI
Mario and Yolanda. Part Two. Interior.
707 to 727

This scene will be constructed of sex scenes [real or implied] constantly interrupted by short dialogues.

The two are lying down naked, covered with a sheet. Mario is smoking.

M: (looking up at the ceiling) They tell me I have a rival.

Y: (smiles) Lázaro! (laughs) and he's sooo cute. If he weren't just a boy I'd marry him.

M: And not me?

Y: What's wrong?

M: Nothing.

Cut

Yolanda has a pullover on, Mario is wearing pants. Yolanda is lying down on the bed and Mario is looking at her while sitting on the floor.

M: Yolanda, what do you see in me?

Y: A man.

M: I've always been one.

Y: But I don't love the man that everyone else knows.

M: What are you implying?

Y: Nothing. You have one way of being in the neighborhood, and another for going out with me.

M: (smiles) What do you mean?

Yolanda gets up. And begins to imitate him.

Y: In the neighborhood you walk like this (Mario bursts out laughing).

M: On the street you can't fool around.

Y: You have to play the part, "so people know" (she makes fun of him).

Cut.

Close up of Mario.

M: And how am I when I'm with you?

Yolanda enters the frame with an erotic expression.

Y: Like that, there's nothing standing in the way.

He gets off the bed and kisses her breasts.

She holds him on her lap. This gesture of Yolanda's is very maternal.

Cut.

Now it is Mario who is lying down on the bed and Yolanda who is observing him while sitting on the floor.

> Y: And you, what do you see in me?
>
> M: (acting out the compliment) Just that, that you're a very fine woman.
>
> Y: Nothing else?
>
> M: (acting surprised) What else? (smiles) . . . I see a lot of things in you.
>
> Y: What?
>
> M: Sincerity. You like the truth.
>
> Y: That's why I'm very difficult sometimes.
>
> M: There's a need for that. There's a lot of fear of the truth in the scene.
>
> Y: Tell me something true.

Mario enters the frame. He kisses her.

He pulls her to him, making her stand up beside him.

He looks at her seriously.

> M: Do you want me to tell you something I've never told anyone?
>
> Y: Tell me.
>
> M: I'm scared.

Yolanda kisses him passionately.

Cut.

* * *

Sequence XXII
Revolutionary Defense Committee Work. Exterior. Daytime.
723 to 733

Members of the CDRs and workers from the school are repairing and beautifying Miraflores and their school. For this sequence we will create real working conditions and will film a real documentary report. In brief, we will do gardening work and fix the outside walls that are in the worst condition. At the school, general cleanup work will be performed along with minor carpentry repairs of the doors and furniture. If possible, we will also arrange to paint the school at the same time and add decorations.

While filming we will attempt to highlight the following action:

1. Shots of Candito and Adalberto requesting help from the workers working in the nearby microbrigades. Material aid—equipment and simple materials.

2. General festive ambience during the CDR work, with the neighbors laughing, singing and trading slogans (like a Haitian Cumbite).

3. Shots that also reflect attitudes hostile to this kind of work. Some neighbors watching the others, men leaving home dressed up on Sunday morning, avoiding the place where the others are working, some commentary related to this, etc.

All of this will be improvised and in documentary format. Two crucial scenes will occur in this sequence—scenes with La Mejicana and the teacher: During the work at the school, La Mejicana comes over to Yolanda, obviously upset:

734 to 740

>LM: Ay, teach, what a problem I've got to tell you.
>
>Y: You can tell me. What's happened now?
>
>LM: Nothing, teach. Oh, God! Now Lazarito, my Lazarito, has come up with the idea that he wants to become a fisherman. He's all excited about that Columna thing, the fishing fleet, teach . . .

Close-up of Lázaro, watching the conversation between Yolanda and his mother.

After the close-up of Lázaro, images begin to appear from the press archive of the fishermen who were kidnapped and the protests sparked by that event, as well as the newspaper headlines. These will be followed by photo-reports of Lázaro himself in a Columna camp, working, studying and finally being out at sea. Then the image of the young fishing boy who was kidnapped, speaking to the court alongside Fidel. The voices of Yolanda and La Mejicana continue.[6]

> Y: But that's the best thing that could happen to him.
>
> LM: Ay teach, I'm very afraid, that boy, alone, there. You know, my God what might happen to him?[7]
>
> Y: No, look, no matter what, Lazarito is in the most danger on the street, doing nothing; there he can continue to study, to work...
>
> LM: But teach, I'm afraid... What if something happens to him? He's never been separated from me, imagine.

Shots of Lázaro, who continues helping, integrated into the general scene, alongside the teachers, parents and students working on their communal property.

Cut.

Scene 2
741 to 747

At dusk, Mario and Candito visit the Microbrigade Construction Office to return the tools (brushes, buckets, etc.) that had been loaned to them. This action will be filmed in a long shot. On the way back, Candito and Mario talk, while we see the neighbors leaving the work area and the neighborhood appearing more attractive through their collective effort.

> C: Hey, did you know that your buddy Humbertico got written up for missing work and they are sending him before the council?
>
> M: ... No.
>
> C: This is the third time, it's not going to go well for him.
>
> M: ... So...
>
> C: Don't you care? He's your buddy, isn't he?
>
> M: Yes, but that's none of my business, that issue's between him and the council...
>
> C: No, you'll see that it's not (insinuating).
>
> M: What are you trying to say?

C: Nothing, just that it's everyone's problem.

* * *

Sequence XXIII
The Assembly. Interior. Afternoon.
748 to 780

At the headquarters of the Workers' Assembly of the Ómnibus Girón factory, the workers are in a meeting.[8]

Close-up of the president.

> P: The Labor Council of this company, at a meeting held earlier this month, decided to make this case public (Candito looks for Mario in the crowd), deeming it appropriate revolutionary practice. It deals with an absentee worker who has committed this offense for the third time.
> This is a trial of a parasite on his coworkers, as his absence is a burden on his brigade and hinders the achievement of its goals. So, the entire workforce has to take responsibility for ratifying the guilty ruling we have issued against the accused. The assembly has the floor.

Cut.

One worker stands up (we must remember that we are trying to capitalize on the workers' experience with this kind of assembly, and therefore on their ability to improvise).

> Worker 1: I work in the same brigade as comrade Humberto. (Pause). Humberto is a good worker, a little scattered, it's true; but I think we have to take into account that he's not a bad person.

Cut.

Medium shot of Worker 2.

> Worker 2: I'm not going to speak about Humberto directly. (Pause). I don't belong to his brigade.
> What I want to remind everyone is that each brigade has goals to meet, and that meeting those goals depends on the effort of each worker. Of each worker!

Close-up of the president.

> P: I will now read a telegram that the accused presented as evidence to justify his absence, which he only did once he had returned from his trip to Oriente Province, and not before. "Come. Your mother seriously ill." Dinorah.

Cut.

> Worker 3: I think that Humberto deserves another chance.

Two shot of Humberto, acting ashamed.

> Worker 3: ... Given that he had a reason for his absence, who can think of work... or anything at all when they get a message like that?

Different shots of workers, with comments in support of Humberto.

> Worker 3: ... our Revolution is human and generous above all things, comrades.

The workers applaud. Candito stands up, shaking his head. He glances at Mario, who remains with his head down. Candito interrupts the applause with a gesture.

> C: Well, does anyone have anything else to add? Any information that he can provide for or against the accused?

He looks at Mario, who shakes his head, biting his lower lip.

> C: No? (pauses) Then let's proceed to give the floor to comrade Humberto Sarrías.

Cut.

> H: Comrades, do what you want with me now, I don't care. If you send me to the farm [prison], then I'll go to work camp. When I arrived in Santiago the old lady was dying... poor thing!

Cut.

Mario is squirming in his seat.

Humberto glances over at him.

> H: I had to spend many sleepless nights running here and there, being at her side, until finally I knew she was out of danger.

He looks at Mario, who shakes his head in disapproval. Humberto becomes alarmed.

> H: And even though I know there are some in this assembly who have conspired against me...

He looks at Candito and at Mario.

> H: ...I want to tell you that if anyone doubts what I have said, if anyone dares to doubt my word, I am willing to accept any punishment, however unfair.

Mario throws his chair back as he stands up, then heads for the exit.

The president of the council notes the incident and calls out to Mario. The atmosphere begins to get tense.

> P: Hey, comrade!

Mario stops and turns around.

> P: Where are you going? You need to ask permission from the assembly to leave.

Mario gets angry.

> M: It's just that I can't stand all the theatrics. This guy is shameless (to Humberto). You're laughing at all of your coworkers and, what's more, you're trying to prevent me from telling what I know. Humberto was in Oriente Province with a woman... it's a big lie about the sick mother, because Humberto hasn't had a mother for a long time (to Humberto). And now it's up to you... we can settle this between us whenever you want.

Close-up of Humberto, whose expression changes as he realizes he's been exposed. The noise level in the hall rises as everyone begins to shout comments.

> H: Mayito! Now you've screwed yourself... (brazenly).

Cut.

The president, now standing, addresses the assembly.

> P: The Labor Council proposes to the assembly, for its ratification, the sentencing of comrade Humberto Sarrías to 6 months in prison for the crime of repeated absenteeism indicating a high probability of vagrancy, as set out in Law 1231, with the aggravating factor of proven false testimony.

Raise hands all in favor!

Everyone raises hands.

Cut.

* * *

Sequence XXIV
La Piloto. Interior-Exterior. Afternoon.
781 to 801

This sequence will explore the factory workforce. It will begin with comments by the workers themselves in the center's locker room and bathrooms.

In the pub nearby, we see workers who obviously have just left the assembly.

There we will question them about the incident, attempting to get authentic responses in the form of comments that reflect the workers' level of awareness of the Revolution and its contradictions. Obviously, we will manage the sequence so that the principles of the Revolution are conveyed very clearly and we will use the most eloquent and developed individuals as moderators or guides for the discussions. In our opinion, this is one of the most important sequences and it should be filmed with great care so that it makes a deep impression on the general public, and especially on this sociocultural minority.
The outline that will guide us will be as follows:

<u>Those in favor of Mario.</u>

> a. Because he stood up for what was right on behalf of the workers and the Revolution.
>
> b. Because Humberto provoked him by doubting his loyalty as a friend when he spoke. In other words, because he [Humberto] forced him [Mario] to defend himself against the former's blackmail.

<u>Those who are against Mario.</u>

> a. Because he never should have revealed his friend's secret, betraying his trust.
>
> b. Because, while it's fine that Mario spoke ... he was driven to do so by Humberto's words and not by his own conscience.

> c. Those who think Mario should have spoken to Humberto before the trial and told him of his intention not to be an accomplice.

As we see in this outline, the ideological situation is complicated, and its complexity arises from the contradictions between the Revolution and traditional thinking. It must be taken into account that these contradictions are not evident to this minority at this stage of their [ideological] transition.

In the midst of this sequence, Mario will enter the pub and remain apart, drinking alone. He knows they are judging him, and it will become evident that he himself has not found an ideological response to his attitude.

Upon finishing his mug of beer, he leaves the place, while all his comrades look on expectantly.

Sequence XXV
The Crisis of Mario, Yolanda, and Joe. Interior-Exterior. Daytime-Nighttime.
802 to 817

Various shots of Mario walking through the streets. Shots of streets, places, details that convey the state of the Revolution at this moment. Its economic and ideological consolidation.

Mario, now drinking somewhere else, in a bar.

818 to 824

Mario knocking on a door.
Yolanda opens it, in a bathrobe.

> M: Is anyone here?
>
> Y: No, come in.

He enters Yolanda's apartment.

> M: Did you hear?
>
> Y: Yes, the old man told me. I think it's very good . . .
>
> M: (begins to get angry) You think it's good that I'm a snitch, a piece of shit!
>> Is that the man you want to have?
>> Really?

Yolanda realizes that Mario is upset and has been drinking.

>Y: I think you'd better calm down!
>Listen . . .

>M: (interrupts her) I don't want to hear anything you have to say, I already knew that we'd never understand each other.

>Y: Well then go and ask your big friend for forgiveness, if that's what you need. I don't know what kind of man you are! (on the verge of crying)

Mario looks at her angrily. He makes a gesture as if to strike her. Yolanda notices, but doesn't shield herself, she gives him a defiant look.

Mario leaves Yolanda's apartment.

Cut.

825 to 837

Long shot of a park facing the Malecón (it could be Parque Maceo). Mario and Joe are sitting on a bench. It's around midnight.

Close-up of Mario.

>M: (finishing his story) . . . Joe, and I ratted him out like a whore, like a little queer.

>J: That's what you should have done.

>M: That's not what I should have done. He was my buddy. Fuck!

>J: Your buddy? And he got you mixed up in this, with everyone else? A buddy to you and asshole to everyone else?

>M: But I didn't act like a man, for fuck's sake! Where was my code?

>J: What code, Mario? What code are you talking about? That code went out a while ago.
>It went there. (he gestures to the sea) Mario, "I make a toast to this process that allows us to be here together" Remember?

>M: You know what, Joe? You're full of shit!

He grabs him by the shirt aggressively. Joe pulls away forcefully. Mario punches him. Joe falls back and hits the ground. He recovers quickly and strokes his jaw pensively.

J: You punch hard, Mario! But your problem isn't with me, Mayito. (Angrily, with his back turned)
   Do me the favor of going to hell with your code!

Mario is left alone in the middle of the night, disconcerted by Joe's attitude, frustrated by his pent-up aggression, full of anger and impotence.

* * *

Sequence XXVI
Candito. Interior. Dawn.
838 to 846

In Candito's house. In the bathroom, Mario is getting ready to take a shower. It's apparent that he just arrived home from a harrowing night. Mario puts his head under the sink and lets the water run over it. Candito opens the window in the bathroom. Dawn comes.
He leaves the bathroom and goes to the kitchen and begins to make coffee.

C: (yelling) It's almost 6, and if we hurry we'll catch the bus when it's empty... they say that when the apartment buildings are finished they're going to add on more buses. There's no other way, with so many people...

His words are interrupted by the rising sound of the shower.
Medium shot of Mario under the shower.

Cut.

The two are having breakfast without speaking. Isa has woken up and begins to move around the house, opening doors, dusting furniture, sweeping the entrance.

Mario doesn't look at Candito. Candito doesn't stop looking at Mario.

M: I'm fucked, old man.

C: Not really Mayo, not really... You were fucked before, when you had no problems, but now?

Close-up of Mario.

Cut.

* * *

Sequence XXVII
Mario and Humberto. Balmaseda and Limonta. Exterior. Nighttime.
847 to 859

Mario is standing on a corner.

The street appears deserted. He's waiting for someone. He knows the person is coming. He's not in a hurry. He's leaning against the wall, with one knee bent and his foot resting on the wall behind. He looks toward the end of the street and recognizes the shadow as it appears. It's Humberto. Humberto has also seen him, and walks up slowly, but guardedly and with a certain mocking expression.

Mario doesn't move. He waits. Humberto reaches Mario. Mario stands in front of him, preventing him from passing.

> M: I told you we can settle this anytime you want.

Mario says this calmly, with no special emphasis, as though he is waiting to see how Humberto reacts. Humberto begins the fight and Mario fights back. In terms of cinematographic treatment, it's a classic fight scene, but Mario's responses grow weaker until he ends up on the ground, bloody. "The Good Guy" has lost this time.

Cut.

Humberto walks away from the scene of the fight. The camera pans and we discover the film set. Lights, cameras, makeup artists, etc. Mario, in the middle of the set, addresses the audience.

> Balmaseda the actor: This is one possible ending for the film. Mario in fact has allowed Humberto, who is the bad guy, to punish him. But Mario would not assume this attitude even if he were guilty. It's false.

Cut.

860 to 872

We repeat the scene from the beginning to the moment at which Mario speaks to Humberto. But this time Mario will say the words aggressively and he will be the one to start the fight. This time the fight will have a different outcome. "The Good Guy" will use all the boxing techniques we know he learned in his childhood and will overcome Humberto quickly with rapid, confident punches in a few minutes. This time, Humberto will be the one who ends up on the ground, bloody. Mario, the good guy, has won the fight.

Cut.

Once again, on the film set, Balmaseda appears and speaks to the audience.

> B: This is another possible ending. The other way to resolve the Mario-Humberto situation. Nevertheless, it would be too easy to end the film by resolving the problem with Humberto.

873 to 878

The other actor arrives. Mario Limonta.

> L: But the thing is, his [Mario's] problem is not just Humberto. His fundamental problem is with himself. Also, the problem with Humberto began when Humberto confessed that he was going to Oriente Province.
>
> B: Right! Mario shouldn't have allowed Humberto to make him his accomplice, at that very moment he should have made it clear that Humberto could not confide that kind of thing in him.
>
> L: Yes, but that would have been too easy as well. With that level of awareness, Mario wouldn't be Mario, he'd be Joe.
>
> And it would be a different film.
>
> B: Look, the real finale is what Candito says.

Closer shot of Candito in the dining room during his conversation with Mario.

> C: You were fucked before, when you didn't have problems ... but now?

879 to 885

Shots of the Línea and 18 factory entrance, with the workers arriving in different groups and punching in at the time clock. Mario and Candito arrive, too. Main entrance. Shots of the setting.

Over these images we continue to hear the actors' voices.

> L: It's true. Mario now has problems. For him, solidarity meant with the *ekobio*, with his buddy, his friend, although he never became Abakuá.

B: Of course, he is a young man who has grown up on the margins of everything, with no regular job, only working occasionally, doing what he could to survive.

886 to 896

Shots of Miraflores, descriptive ones like at the beginning, where we see the neighborhood very briefly and pass by the school, where Yolanda appears at the end of the school day, along with the students, parents and teachers we already know, who are the real-life characters from the documentary.

L: But it's different now. Now he has the opportunity to work and become a full-fledged part of the country's destiny. He has problems, he's in crisis, it's true. Now he can transform himself, become a real man.

B: And for that he needs courage, he needs to leave behind his entire marginalized history and adopt the new values. The road is not an easy one, but at least now, Mario knows it.

897 to 900

Shot of Mario, who is waiting for Yolanda at the exit. Yolanda passes right by him and continues walking ahead of him. Mario follows her, catching up to her to speak to her, and they begin to argue. The camera will capture all of this in a long shot until they disappear, still debating, with the neighborhood as the setting and the microbrigade buildings in the background.

THE END

Translated from the original Spanish by Joan Donaghey

NOTES

1. Traditional children's song similar to "Ring Around the Rosie." Loose translation: "Ring around the rosie, give me a kiss and get to school, daddy-o."
2. *Socio* here is translated as "partner" to make Candito's response make sense. But otherwise we use "buddy" as a more appropriate English term.
3. Original: *"Como siga así, ahorita se pone de moda."*
4. Given that the word *firmación* does not exist in Spanish, we suppose that the correct expression here would be "in affirmation." In other words, Humberto affirms that he will respect the rules (travel to Oriente Province during vacation time) while negating that intention (because he is actually going to lie to his

coworkers). The original statement in the script is, "No (moviendo la cabeza en firmación) Ahora." In the film, Humberto barely nods his head, and says "Nope, now," so there is less ambiguity.

5. A reference to the Jesuit priests who operated the most famous school in Cuba, Belén.

6. There seems to be a typographical error here. The correct word would be *continúan*. [Translator's note: this endnote does not apply in English.]

7. There appears to be another error here, as the context requires an exclamation mark rather than the question mark that is used.

8. Typographical error, the article *el* is missing. [Translator's note: Not applicable in English.]

SEVEN

Luis García Mesa Interviewed by Lourdes Martínez-Echazábal and María Caridad Cumaná

LOURDES MARTÍNEZ-ECHAZÁBAL: *Well, today is the ninth of October, 2012, and we're here in Miami Beach with Luis García Mesa, María Caridad Cumaná, and me, Lourdes Martínez-Echazábal. We're taking advantage of being here together to do an interview, or rather have a conversation, with Luis García Mesa, who, as we all know, was the cinematographer on De cierta manera [One way or another], and I think you also worked on other documentaries of Sara's?*

LUIS GARCÍA MESA: On several of Sara's documentaries.

LOURDES MARTÍNEZ-ECHAZÁBAL: *Luis, why don't you tell us a bit about how your relationship was with Sara. How did you meet, how did you end up working with her?*

LUIS GARCÍA MESA: Meeting Sara . . . I don't remember. It's not one of those things where you say, we were in a meeting or a party or a place, and suddenly we saw each other, we were introduced. I have no memory of that, of the precise moment I met Sara. As soon as I knew her it was as if I had known her my whole life. She was one of those people, so Cuban in the best sense of the word: very open, very frank, very transparent. Someone you'd get to know and immediately loved her or hated her from then on. Because she was terrible, too. She spoke the truth head-on to anyone. So the opinions people working in the ICAIC [Instituto Cubano del Arte e Industria Cinematográficos, or Cuban Film Institute] had of her were terrible. And they'd say to her, "Sara, that's a hell of a tongue you have." So, it was a friendship like . . . I don't know. I have two or three best friends like her, who are men, of course. One has already died.

Rapi Diego's still around [now deceased—Ed.], so is Juan Carlos Tabío. Do you understand? Because, of course, between men it's another thing, the concept of friendship is different, but . . . women friends of mine? Just Sara. I would eat at her house. It's not like saying, "Look, this is my best friend, but I've never been to his house and his partner doesn't know my name." That is not a best friend. With Sara, I would go there and eat, and she loved inviting me because I made such a fuss when she started to eat. I would say to her, "No, wait, I'm just trying this. Oh my God, who taught you to make food like this?" [And she would say] "Luis, this is an ordinary black bean stew that has nothing else, I didn't have anything to put in it." [I'd say] "No, that's not true, you're just a great cook!" She'd say, "Oh sure, you're just saying that so I keep inviting you." So we had a lot of fun. She'd give me a drink in her house with her husband, with Germinal, who was a good friend of mine as well, and she didn't drink but she did smoke.

LOURDES MARTÍNEZ-ECHAZÁBAL: *Smoking, and with asthma—just imagine.*

LUIS GARCÍA MESA: Yes, I remember that once, because it was emotional asthma. Once we were in a film forum—I don't remember which film but it doesn't matter—I said to her, "Sara, I don't have any cigarettes right now, can I bum one?" And she says, "Yes, hang on." So we smoked right there in the cinema screening room. At that time, you could smoke everywhere, here as well. So she starts [breathing with difficulty], and I say to her, "What's the matter?" And she says, "The inhaler, I left it at home." If she hadn't opened her bag, it would have been a normal attack, but when she realized she didn't have the inhaler for her asthma, she had such a strong attack that we had to go outside with her. It was terrible. She was very emotional—she was like that. And that's what killed her, it seems—the asthma. You know the medication gradually weakens your heart.

LOURDES MARTÍNEZ-ECHAZÁBAL: *Yes, she also died. So, Luis, do you remember what the first documentary was that you did with her?*

LUIS GARCÍA MESA: I don't remember because we did . . . we did a very interesting experiment, but I don't remember if it was at the beginning or later, which was to go to the Isla de Pinos, or the Isla de Juventud [Island of Youth] as it's called now. We went with a full truck and cameras and everything on the ferry. I did the cinematography, the sound person was Germinal, there was a camera assistant, a producer, and I don't know who else. And just like that, we went to the island. And José Antonio Jorge went, who was a director. He was filming an idea that he already had scripted. We filmed it there, we gave him the film, and he grabbed the plane back to Cuba. So when he went to Havana, Sara came out. We did a documentary with Sara, and the same thing—Sara took the cans of film, and then José Antonio came, so Germinal and I ended up spending about six months on the island and they came and went. We did about three or four documentaries with each of them, including *En la otra isla* [On the other island], *Una isla para Miguel* [An island for Miguel] . . .

LOURDES MARTÍNEZ-ECHAZÁBAL: *Exactly,* Isla del tesoro *(Treasure island).*

MARÍA CARIDAD CUMANÁ: *In other words, for you, that was the first thing you did with Sara?*

LUIS GARCÍA MESA: I'm not sure I can say that. Do you have the years there?

MARÍA CARIDAD CUMANÁ: *No, I went into Cubacine [website of the ICAIC], which for me is the official place for Cuban film, although the filmographies aren't complete. It seems to me this isn't your complete filmography, but through another file I realized that the filmography of what you did with Sara Gómez isn't in Cubacine.*

LUIS GARCÍA MESA: Of course. There's a longer one than that, I'm sure it's called *Audiovisuales Luis Lacosta,* or something like that.

MARÍA CARIDAD CUMANÁ: *Ah yes, that's the Luis Lacosta file, which is different.*

LUIS GARCÍA MESA: If you put "Luis García Mesa" in there, I think you get a more extensive filmography than that. It's not all there, either—I don't know why. No one says I was in Angola for a year and a half, for example. I went because they called up a friend of ours—a cinematographer from the ICAIC. They used to conscript people through MINFAR [Ministry of Armed Forces] to do military service. They would call ICAIC people up because they didn't have cinematographers to send to Africa. So anyway, they conscripted Julio Valdés [nicknamed El Pavo, "the turkey"; who has passed away]. And El Pavo called me and said, "Luis, they've called me up to go to Africa." And I said, "And?" He says, "I can't go, I'm having an operation for cancer in my vocal chords." He ended up unable to speak. He talks with an apparatus now, and it's incredible he's still alive. They called up Anita Rodríguez, who has also passed away, another great woman friend of mine, along with El Pavo. So I said to El Pavo, "I'll go." He said to me, "You're crazy; let them send someone else." I said, "No, no, it's because I want to have that experience, because I've done . . ." I started out doing animations, then I was promoted to assistant camera, and the first year as assistant I slept two nights in the Pico Turquino [Turquino Peaks]. That was an adventure for me, an incredible thing. On top of it, I was only nineteen or twenty. I did little scientific documentaries—films for teaching.

MARÍA CARIDAD CUMANÁ: *So did you work on what was called the* Enciclopedia popular?

LUIS GARCÍA MESA: Sometimes I did the camera for them, but another department was created, which was the Popular-Scientific Department I think. That was in sixteen millimeter.

MARÍA CARIDAD CUMANÁ: *Yes, the one for scientific-technical documentaries.*

LUIS GARCÍA MESA: Yup. I worked there for a few years, and later I went over to working in thirty-five [millimeter]. Those periods were stages. They thought sixteen millimeter was less useful than thirty-five millimeter. I don't know why, it's exactly the same. But seventy millimeter would be ideal. So I worked on all of these. And I said to El Pavo, "Look, in reality, the only thing I haven't done is porn films that'll never be made here. But this is my only chance to be a war correspondent, and I'm really interested in it. It seems to me to be a passionate thing to do in cinematography." Annie Leibovitz, tons of people, Frank Capra, all those people, have made incredible images [from experiences like this]. So this was with a sixteen-millimeter film camera as well, and I went and stayed for a year and a half. What can I say? Despite getting malaria in the end. They wanted to send me back to Cuba, and I said no, because I wasn't going to tell my mother to come see me in a hospital because she would die—she'd think something had happened to me. So I'm in Angola and I've got a fever, and then eventually I get over it, and after that I was there for a while longer and then came back. But for me it was a tremendous experience.

MARÍA CARIDAD CUMANÁ: *I've also got you down here as doing Cuban ceramics and painting, and as assistant director on* Iré a Santiago *[I'm going to Santiago], which, to my mind, is a very important documentary for Sara in 1964.*

LUIS GARCÍA MESA: As assistant?

MARÍA CARIDAD CUMANÁ: *Yes, the director of photography* on Iré a Santiago *is Mayito, Mario García Joya, and it says, "Assistant Director: Luis García Mesa."*

LUIS GARCÍA MESA: Really? I don't remember that. It could be if it says so there; it's just that sometimes it's not accurate. For example, if you look for Nicolasito Guillén Landrián's *Coffea Arabiga* (1968), it says I was the director of photography and that's completely false. I filmed two or three shots. The photography was by Lupercio López, who, by the way, was in Africa. [He has passed away]. He got married there. Sometimes they put any random thing there and sometimes I've said to them, "Let's go sit down one day and correct all those things," because you can put whatever you like there and then others can erase it, like in Wikipedia and all those things.

MARÍA CARIDAD CUMANÁ: *Yes—what happened with Guillén Landrián's Coffea Arabiga is that there's a lot of archive material, very little that's been filmed, and it seems that the few shots that were filmed were filmed by you, so that's why they gave you the credit, because the rest is pure archive material.*

LUIS GARCÍA MESA: I love that documentary. I think it's great. Nicolasito was a hell of a character—he was a genius. Despite him not being able to theorize about his work. For me, he was naive, like a naive painter, who is marvelous but does what he . . . I don't know, he wasn't an academic. He didn't have schooling, he didn't have anything; he just did what he felt. When he wrote a script, he would make two scripts always—one to get approval and the other real one that he would film. And then he would keep both to one side just so he would have an idea of what he wanted to do more or less. We would go on location . . . and then you'd see the films . . . *Los del baile* [Those of the dance] [1965], for example, those kinds of sequences that are just faces, nothing more, that are like . . . they're incredible. The guy was . . . he improvised right there during filming, but he knew very well what he wanted to do. He was very clear about the overall work. I would say, "And how does this fit? Why film this?" Stuff like in *Coffea Arabiga*, when he asked the cinematographer to film the soles of his feet, and the guy said, "What for?" And he said, "Forget it, just film it." And the guy filmed it, and at that time the coffee harvest was being affected by a fungus called *pata prieta* [dark feet], and you hear his voice saying, "The *pata prieta* is terrible." Don't you remember? And they're his feet.

MARÍA CARIDAD CUMANÁ: *Now then, did he and Sara know each other? Were they friends? Were he and Sara the "negritos" of the ICAIC? I want to know about that.*

LUIS GARCÍA MESA: Yes, yes of course. You've said something very interesting now, because that's the sort of thing Sara used to say. I would say to her, "Sara, don't say those things." And she would say, "You know why I'm in ICAIC? For two reasons: first, because I'm black, and second, because I'm a woman. And for [Saul] Yelin [a producer and cofounder of ICAIC] and all those people, the directors of ICAIC, they're lacking... they need a black woman filmmaker, do you understand? Not because I might be talented, nothing like that, they don't care about that. What matters to them is when they go to festivals and things like that, when Agnès Varda comes here, they have me there to say, 'Hey look, we have a little black woman doing filmmaking!'"

LOURDES MARTÍNEZ-ECHAZÁBAL: *That's what [Iván] Arocha says.*[1]

LUIS GARCÍA MESA: Oh yeah? Arocha says that as well?

MARÍA CARIDAD CUMANÁ: *Arocha says it, sure, because she...*

LUIS GARCÍA MESA: Arocha was also very close to her, almost like me, as a friend. And she was merciless. I would say to her, "Sara, that's going to do you damage. How can you put yourself out there and say such things?" There was this young guy in Cuba—what was he called? I don't remember his name—a tall *mulato*—Jorge Luis Sánchez. He interviewed me once about Guillén Landrián and about Sara, and I talked to him about Sara, the amazing things I know about her, and at the end he said, "But can you summarize in a word what Sara is to you?" And he says, "Was Sara a revolutionary?" And I said, "Yes, yes, Sara was a revolutionary, but for me Sara was so revolutionary that if she were still alive she'd have been in prison for twenty years by now." Because she really was. She said, "The Federation [of Cuban Women], that petit bourgeois society invented by Raul's wife [Vilma Espín]? What a... whatever!" She said all those women were a bunch of Catholic ladies from the 1950s who were well dressed and starched and wouldn't go into a marginalized neighborhood. Please!

MARÍA CARIDAD CUMANÁ: *And they wore long stockings?*

LUIS GARCÍA MESA: With stockings like that, with the heat in Cuba on top of it. You'd say, "What is this? What women's federation? That's not what Cuban women are. Cuban women are cutting cane in the countryside and lining up in the... give me a break!" And Sara said it out loud, in front of anyone.

MARÍA CARIDAD CUMANÁ: *What strikes me is that you started by saying you think her work on the Isla de Juventud is the one that you feel has weight, and in* which you worked more continuously, in a more meaningful way. It's the island trilogy because at that time she made all three of them: En la otra isla, Una isla para Miguel, *and* Isla del tesoro.

LUIS GARCÍA MESA: I think so. That was in the 1960s . . .

MARÍA CARIDAD CUMANÁ: *In 1968 she made* En la otra isla *and* Una isla para Miguel, *and then in 1969 she made* Isla del tesoro.

LUIS GARCÍA MESA: Yes, in 1969 for sure, she finished editing it. They were definitely made in '68, because in '69 we made another one called *Mi aporte* [My contribution].

MARÍA CARIDAD CUMANÁ: *We'll talk about* Mi aporte *in a while, speaking of the Federation of Cuban Women. In the island trilogy, the documentary* En la otra isla *is the longest, at forty-one minutes—a really long documentary in which she interviews all those characters—but it's not clear what that place was? Was it a farm? What was it?*

LUIS GARCÍA MESA: I don't remember the term right now, but in *En la otra isla* maybe it was where the women were learning to drive tractors and all that? A women's camp, for young women?

MARÍA CARIDAD CUMANÁ: *But she interviews men there as well.*

LUIS GARCÍA MESA: Yes, of course, because they are the people in charge of the place and all that, and she always wanted to confront machismo, drive up against it, you know.

MARÍA CARIDAD CUMANÁ: *Yes, in* En la otra isla *she interviews several young women, but also a man, who evidently was a Catholic.*

LUIS GARCÍA MESA: Oh yeah—that was the husband of Richard Egües's daughter. What was her name? Gladys Egües. He had been in a seminary—now I remember. He had studied in a seminary and he was a Catholic, and with the Revolution he started to pick up on the theology of the Revolution—liberation theology and all that. In the seminary everything was peaceful and quiet, and you see him there kicking a cow and so forth because it's hard work there with the animals. And he was an intelligent young man. I don't know—I think he gave up one militancy for the other, if you get my drift.

LOURDES MARTÍNEZ-ECHAZÁBAL: *Religious militancy for political militancy?*

LUIS GARCÍA MESA: Yes, for revolutionary militancy. But that political militancy I imagine was a bit extreme. People who get a bit carried away with a theory that doesn't let them think clearly tend to take everything as the absolute truth. Any other way of thinking doesn't exist for them.

MARÍA CARIDAD CUMANÁ: *Yes. That period was like that.*

LUIS GARCÍA MESA: It was all black and white, there were no grays.

MARÍA CARIDAD CUMANÁ: *I've seen the work of film production from that period, and with the way people talked I realize that a certain way of thinking predominated. Of course, what happens when you put people in front of a camera, that's something else . . . I think Sara believed in the Revolution, in change. Of course, as you say, now she would be in prison, but at that moment she believed she could transform reality with her work.*

LUIS GARCÍA MESA: Of course, and Nicolasito too. Me too.

MARÍA CARIDAD CUMANÁ: *Everyone, absolutely everyone. So, Sara's documentary work went beyond that, regardless of the homogenizing concept that predominated at that moment—the idea of the collective, where the individual human being didn't exist. For example, you couldn't say "I am." Everyone spoke in plural, don't you remember? Ricardo Acosta tells me that one day in an ICAIC meeting he had to say, "We went to get our tooth pulled" as a way of excusing himself because he'd missed a meeting.*

LUIS GARCÍA MESA: There's a joke about that, about a guy who's proposed to join the party. Juan I-don't-know-what, who was self-taught. Everyone goes on about how Juan is magnificent, he goes on all the voluntary work brigades, he goes everywhere, he's in the militia. At the end they ask, "But does no one have anything bad to say about Juan?" So someone pipes up, "Well, can I speak? Juan goes home in the car and he sleeps with the wife." And the guy in charge says, "But what's wrong with that?" "Can I use the *tu* form, comrade?" The guy says yes. "Juan goes with *your* car, and sleeps with *your* wife in *your* house." Because everything was like that. It was we, we, we. And Fidel would always say, "*We* have made mistakes." Not *you* have made them, or *I* am sending you to cut sugarcane—none of that. Please.

MARÍA CARIDAD CUMANÁ: *It was a collective thing then?*

LUIS GARCÍA MESA: And that's how this double morality was created, by involving everyone. When people talk to me about Cuba, I tell them, "Yes, the twenty-two million Cubans." And they say to me, "Isn't it eleven?" I say, "Yes, but with the double morality we're twenty-two."

MARÍA CARIDAD CUMANÁ: *So this documentary series in particular is like a kind of frieze because it places a lot of different people before us—the young woman, that pair of men she interviews, and each one with their individuality. I can imagine it might have been a source of conflict in the ICAIC, this way of highlighting people's differences.*

LUIS GARCÍA MESA: And that's her main interest—she goes straight to the human being. To the individual. Not the number, but that particular person.

LOURDES MARTÍNEZ-ECHAZÁBAL: *Well, apart from that, there was also the contradiction between theory and practice. That was a key issue. Things can work very well on a theoretical level, on a discursive level, but at the moment they're put into practice, [one finds that] it is exactly in the space between practice and theory where life takes place. But the problem is, neither official ideologies nor most film take up the challenge of this space. But she did.*

LUIS GARCÍA MESA: Sara was interested precisely in this issue. She was interested in the conflict between humans and our environment, our society, because she loved human beings. She was a great person, a wonderful human. What she couldn't stand was dogmatism, the idea that things are that way just because they are. When people said to her, "That's just the way things are," she didn't like that idea.

MARÍA CARIDAD CUMANÁ: *There's an interview in this documentary with a black guy, in the documentary* En la otra isla, *in which Sara appears on camera and she's trying to get the young man to say why he's on the island. So he says to her that he was an opera singer, but in the opera they rejected him because he was black. The women didn't want to sing with him because who has ever seen a black guy singing opera. But there's a moment—it's not that the guy said directly, "They rejected me because I was black"—he was trying to explain around it, but Sara pokes him, pokes him and says, "Don't you think they rejected you because you were black?" And he says, "Yes Sara, of course." It's a very strong moment.*

LUIS GARCÍA MESA: It's so big, so strong, especially because it's already been self-censored by him, which is a terrible thing.

MARÍA CARIDAD CUMANÁ: *For me, it's the climax of the documentary, because she's poking him until he finally says "Yes." She was very much the provoker.*

LUIS GARCIA MESA: She always did that—she provoked. But there's another moment, too, with a blond girl who says, "If my boyfriend says I have to stop working, should I leave?" And Sara says, "Leave your boyfriend?" "No, no," the girl says, "leave my work." With that kind of thing—that's what Sara was like. Sara engages with these things [when they emerge]. Someone else would say, "No, no, no, how can the *compañera* say she'd prefer the boyfriend to her work? No, no, [it has to be] the work." But Sara said, "No, that's what she said, that's her truth. She chooses the macho, the guy." This blond girl, what would you expect her to say? She's not that famous blond German revolutionary, she's a young Cuban woman from the countryside. She's interested in finding herself a husband quickly.

MARÍA CARIDAD CUMANÁ: *So in this documentary then,* En la otra isla—

LUIS GARCÍA MESA: I think the young girl is in *Mi aporte*, the blond girl.

MARÍA CARIDAD CUMANÁ: *The blond girl is in* Mi aporte. *But in* En la otra isla, *in the part with the young black man, he stays looking at Sara and says, "Psst...." Sara says to him, "So, do you think that one day you'll be able to sing at the opera?"*

LUIS GARCÍA MESA: That's where Sara enters the image, isn't it?

MARÍA CARIDAD CUMANÁ: *Yes. Well, no. Sara is sitting like this with her back to the camera. She wasn't looking at the camera; she had her back to it with her head like this, and the young guy is the one facing the camera. So the guy says to her, "Well Sara, do you think one day I'll be able to sing at the opera?" And Sara says, "Of course you'll be able to. Of course." But laughing. So then he starts laughing, and the camera plays on his face for a little bit. I want to know if she told you how to move the camera.*

LUIS GARCÍA MESA: Yes, with her and with Nicolasito especially, we didn't cut. So what you mean is [when she says], "Do you think you'll sing?" "Yes, Sara, I think so, that I'll be singing opera." No, no, no. It was important to leave it that way, and Sara was the one who told me where to cut, because she wanted to capture that face, to see how the guy changed, how he became transformed. And Nicolasito would do the same.

MARÍA CARIDAD CUMANÁ: *And she asked you to do that?*

LUIS GARCÍA MESA: Yes. She would say to me, "Don't cut. Don't cut the interview. I'll tell you where to cut." Just to give you an idea, in Cuba we were filming *Hearts and Minds* [Peter Davis, 1974], a documentary the Americans did, that they filmed [in Cuba]. I asked them, "What proportion do you film?" They didn't understand me. I said to them, "For example, for every minute on screen, how much do you film?" It was 104 to 1 or something like that. We filmed three or four to one, because film was very expensive and [it had to be bought] with foreign currency. So the cinematographers were used to switching off the camera. She would say, "No, no. Let it run" on the people's faces and that kind of thing.

MARÍA CARIDAD CUMANÁ: *So that's her aesthetic, letting the camera run until she'd tell you to cut. Was she always the one to tell you to cut?*

LUIS GARCÍA MESA: Yes, of course.

MARÍA CARIDAD CUMANÁ: *That's something that interests me a lot.*

LUIS GARCÍA MESA: She knew the time she wanted to give things afterward in editing her documentary. Those weren't small clips of scenes, like documentaries sometimes have [sound of scissors cutting], quick flashes. But this wasn't like that. It was more meditative, more internal. Her film work was very internal, very reflective.

MARÍA CARIDAD CUMANÁ: *In other words, when she played on a face, she was doing it consciously.*

LUIS GARCÍA MESA: Of course. Completely. In thinking not only about that face but everything. In documentaries like hers, in which there are faces, you have to ensure they are presented as human beings, as people. You have to see them well.

MARÍA CARIDAD CUMANÁ: *And after this comes* Una isla para Miguel, *which is about the really difficult kids, the ones they called the Vikings, that—*

LUIS GARCÍA MESA: They were half delinquents, it looked more like a reformatory than a... I don't know what.

MARÍA CARIDAD CUMANÁ: *Didn't she have any conflicts with the ICAIC for having addressed an issue like this?*

LUIS GARCÍA MESA: I think so, but I'm not sure about that because those things weren't discussed with the cinematographers and the crew. Do you know what I mean? They called her and spoke to her, but she wasn't one to go around complaining unless she shouted it out loud in the corridor. "Who do these people think they are, treating us as I don't know what. On top of that a black woman, they want a docile black woman." I don't know. She was quite capable of doing anything like that. Sara was a huge loss to us.

MARÍA CARIDAD CUMANÁ: *Now, that was her aesthetic in the documentaries—in other words, to play around with the shots in a defined sequence in order to achieve her aim?*

LUIS GARCÍA MESA: She wasn't an aesthete, she wasn't interested in the beauty of the scene—

MARÍA CARIDAD CUMANÁ: *—but in people, each person, in a given context. Well, let's keep going with the documentaries, because later, with the feature film, we have a ton of questions to ask. There is a documentary of Sara's that few know about:* De bateyes *[The sugar workers' quarters].*

LUIS GARCÍA MESA: Yes, I made that.

MARÍA CARIDAD CUMANÁ: *You made it. Tell me what happened to it?*[2]

LUIS GARCÍA MESA: I don't know what happened to it—it was a beautiful documentary. About the *bateyes*, the sugarcane workers' communities. Both here in Havana and in Camagüey, where we went. There are a lot of workers' quarters where Haitians lived, and there is a tremendous prejudice against Haitians. In fact, I remember once Titón [Tomás Gutiérrez Alea] was in Santiago de Cuba with Ramiro Valdés, and he said to him, "Eh, what are you doing here, what's ICAIC doing here?" And Titón said, "We're doing a film called *Cumbite* [1964] about the Haitians." And he, Ramiro, said—Titón told me this, you can write that down—Ramiro said to him, "Eh, why are you doing a film about those people, they're just cheap labor?" Titón was shocked. A commander of the Revolution talking about Haitians in that way—not even about Haitians, about anyone—it was incredible. Sara was very interested in that.

MARÍA CARIDAD CUMANÁ: *It's said that Sara helped Titón a lot in researching and directing* Cumbite.

LUIS GARCÍA MESA: It's possible. I only worked on one sequence in *Cumbite*, invited by Ramón Suárez, who was the director of cinematography. At the time, I was well known for working with the handheld camera, for doing that intimist type of camerawork. So Ramón was there working with two cinematographers, of course—one operator and one camera assistant—and he called me up despite my having nothing to do with the film. It made me feel a bit embarrassed with the other two, and I said to him, "Don't you see what I'm getting at?" He said, "No, I want you to do your bit as well, just grab your handheld camera for the *Cumbite* celebration." There were two handheld cameras, Ramón's and mine, and we filmed it together. It was a marvelous experience. People went to watch the filming. Paul Leduc's daughter was there, and she fascinated me—a young woman with braids. Sara also worked on *Cumbite*, [or] I imagine she did because she knew much more about that world than Titón did. Titón was a brilliant intellectual and everything, but for the black world—the world of black people—Sara was the one.

LOURDES MARTÍNEZ-ECHAZÁBAL: *And she'd already done the documentary,* De bateyes.

LUIS GARCÍA MESA: I think so.

MARÍA CARIDAD CUMANÁ: *What do you remember about* De bateyes?

LUIS GARCÍA MESA: I remember going into sugar plantation communities in Matanzas, and I remember the legends. There were some lovely stories. For example, in Matanzas—the sugar production plant was named Conchita Baró, I think. It's a community where the cane cutters live, some of whom might come from Haiti or Jamaica or Cuba or a mixture of all these origins. In Matanzas, for example, they were Cubans more than anyone. They had been African slaves, or were descendants of African slaves. Anyway, in the area of the sugar workers' quarters there was an immense tree, this big and thick, and it had pieces of chain embedded in it. The older black people from the *batey* community [told us] that the tree had something like evil power, that's why they had to tie it with a chain. Sara said, "That chain you're seeing is around the twenty-second one, because the tree started by swallowing up the first chain." So when that happens, they wrap another one around it—it swallows it up and so on. What a crazy thing, no? The tree was full of chains inside.

Sara interviewed people and said, "So you're a descendant of slaves?" And this one old guy said, "Yes, yes, I'm a descendant of slaves." "Where from?" And he said, "Well I descended from [such and such a place] but the important ones here were the Royal Congolese." And Sara said, "Why?" "Because those guys didn't work." "What do you mean they didn't work? Didn't the overseers beat them?" "No, no, they would go to beat them, and their headman would say, 'Wait a moment, what do you want? You want us to cut cane? Put the carts there in the field and in the morning that field will be cut.' And just as he'd said, when dawn broke all the cane was cut, but they hadn't gone out to cut cane. The cane was just cut and ready to be put into the carts." Sara said, "And what happened to the Royal Congolese?" "They flew away to Angola like birds. They left because they couldn't stand slavery, they couldn't stand it." There were magic stories like that one—incredible.

Another thing I saw in Camagüey were the Haitians and the prejudice there against them. Yet theirs were the cleanest houses I've seen, with dirt floors swept like that and the sense of decoration they have with painted flowers and things on the outside of the houses. They don't paint like we do—they adorn their houses. Each house was different, depending on whoever designed it. When she was there, Sara talked to someone and asked, "So you decided to leave Haiti?" "No, I was a child, I was brought here as a child and I've cut cane all my life." "And don't you miss Haiti?" "No. How am I going to miss it when I go there every day." "What do you mean you go there every day?" "Yes, yes, when I finish work and I'm tired, I have a bath, I lie down, and I go to Haiti and see my family, except for my aunt who died two months ago." Sara was fascinated by this. "We're going to move here, to live with these people and listen to them."

There was another story, too, about a woman who had sex with a Spanish officer, but the Spanish guy covered it up because he was married to a high-society lady. I don't remember exactly how the story went, but the issue was that the black woman slept with him every night and his wife didn't know, and suddenly the officer was head over heels in love with the black woman. And the black woman said [to the officer], "If I sleep with you every night I'll keep you here forever." And he said to her, "That's a lie." "A lie? [When you get home] go have a look at your epaulette, the one from your gala uniform, the upper piece is missing because I've got it." And supposedly she had never entered his house, but her spirit had, or God knows who had gone in there, but the truth is that the guy was missing that piece from his epaulette, and she had it. These stories are like [Alejo] Carpentier's magical realist stories.[3]

. . .

MARÍA CARIDAD CUMANÁ: *How interesting, all these anecdotes that you've told me about* De bateyes *because no one else knows them.*

LUIS GARCÍA MESA: I'll tell you, too, that we filmed in Matanzas and we filmed in Camagüey. We filmed at a party in Camagüey, where they did some amazing things. There was a gigantic wooden table, and one of the dancers came—I don't know if it was a Cumbite celebration—and they took a corner of the table in their mouth and raised it like this, still dancing, and you said to yourself, "But how did they do that? I couldn't lift that table on my own!"

MARÍA CARIDAD CUMANÁ: *And you filmed that?*

LUIS GARCÍA MESA: Yes, and also a trick with a machete—swinging the machete like this—and it looked like it would land on their throats. But I don't know how, they twisted the machete around and it lands on the other side. They were very magical festivities, full of . . . it wasn't just about dancing, everything had a meaning, a language. It was beautiful, and we filmed it. We filmed all this in Camagüey and in Matanzas at the very least, which were the main *bateyes*.

. . .

LUIS GARCÍA MESA: If I'd been planning to stay in the US, I would have been careful to make a selection in Cuba and bring all the films I've worked on, those with Sara and other ones. But I couldn't; that's the thing about leaving and burning your bridges. Afterward it hurts, right now it's really painful. My wife came. We hadn't planned anything, even my wife, Susana's, university degree certificate is in Cuba, everything, everything. Later, I was able to recover some things, but mostly old family photos. It's like what we were saying about memory—if you have no memory, you are nothing. And these things are part of one's memory. Those documentaries that are lost are also a part of us that has been lost. How can they have done that? It's like burning books, like . . . I don't know.

I am more or less a free thinker, I don't have any defined ideology. I'm eclectic in that sense—I take what I want from everything.

. . .

LOURDES MARTÍNEZ-ECHAZÁBAL: *[In] the case of Nicolasito [Guillén Landrián], he wrote two scripts. One he presented and the other he put together afterward. Let's say he did what he wanted and made the one he wanted, the second one. But what happened after that? Because you'd have made the documentary, but they could say to you, "Sorry, this won't be screened, this can't be shown."*

LUIS GARCÍA MESA: Just as they said to him twenty times over. For example, *Coffea Arabiga*, that was a documentary that was made to order. It wasn't that he wanted to make a documentary about coffee. The Coffee Institute asked him for an educational documentary about coffee infestations and things like that, and he simply made an art documentary based on coffee, but with such daring things like Fidel's beard sprouting coffee flowers to the song "The Fool on the Hill." Really very risky things, incredible, very beautiful things. And Bojidara [Bojidara Kristova, now Bojidara Dent, was married to Nicolasito at the time of *Coffea*] talking about a pergola on the street. Bojidara speaking completely in Bulgarian. Things like that, that make you say, "Nicolasito, are you crazy?"

LOURDES MARTÍNEZ-ECHAZÁBAL: *But for a creator, what pleasure can be had from making something that will not be seen?*

LUIS GARCÍA MESA: Well, it was screened, at least for the Coffee Institute. I was there when they screened it for those people, with two or three functionaries—one of them was a woman. They saw it and [were dumbfounded]. When the lights were switched on again, they looked at each other and they said, "The documentary's fine. It's not what we asked for, but it's fine." But they didn't say, "The documentary's brilliant."

MARÍA CARIDAD CUMANÁ: *The thing is, it's really heavy with that last shot in which Fidel is in the Plaza de la Revolución and it says, "And now the Beatles," and he puts on "The Fool on the Hill." Come on, give me a break—that's pretty heavy.*

LUIS GARCÍA MESA: Nicolasito was also a provoker, just like Sara.

LOURDES MARTÍNEZ-ECHAZÁBAL: *What year was that documentary?*

MARÍA CARIDAD CUMANÁ: *1969. It was the famous period of the Cordón de la Habana [Greenbelt campaign in the outskirts of Havana, beginning in 1966].*

LUIS GARCÍA MESA: At the same time, Santiago Álvarez was doing news programs with Beatles music, with The Monkeys, who played like the Beatles, making fun of the Beatles, and so on. Of course, later the Beatles were officially accepted in Cuba, and now John Lennon is sitting in a park over there. So, please . . .

. . .

MARÍA CARIDAD CUMANÁ: *Anyway, someone who interviewed Nicolás before he died here in Miami told me that he said, "They didn't kick me out of ICAIC for* Coffea Arabiga; *they kicked me out of ICAIC for what I did afterward*—Taller de Línea y 18 *[Linea and 18th Street Workshop] [1971]. In other words, they said, 'Nicolás, look, you no longer fit in here. You're not allowed to come here again.'"*

LUIS GARCÍA MESA: Nicolasito said to me, "Look at the siren, look at what that siren's saying." It was a loudspeaker, in the form of a trumpet. He said, "Film that, film it with a wide angle. Now close in on it, closer, closer." And afterward he put *tock, tock, tock* over it.

MARÍA CARIDAD CUMANÁ: *And in Cuba, "trumpets" are also what we call tattletales [informants]. So that's the shot. And you say to yourself, how is it possible [so early on] that the guy realized the way things were going?*

LUIS GARCIA MESA: I was there when he was doing the sound mix. . . . Of course, sometimes there are eight tracks of sound, so you have to go along reducing them to one track to synchronize with the image until you have one single soundtrack. Nicolasito would use nineteen or twenty tracks.

MARÍA CARIDAD CUMANÁ: *They told me* Taller de Línea y 18 *has thirty-two tracks of sound.*

LUIS GARCÍA MESA: You see? So the guys upstairs would say, "Are you crazy? Thirty-two tracks? Do you know what it means to cut stuff and stick it back in, cut it out and put it back in? Just put the reel in there and hide it there."[4]

. . .

MARÍA CARIDAD CUMANÁ: *Coming back to Sara, the whole story we talked about involving* De bateyes *and what happened with it, [how it may have gotten lost]—I believe in fact that with the documentary* De bateyes *it might have been an accident, which is not the case for* Mi aporte. *We know that Sara made* Mi aporte *in homage to—I don't know what aspect of—the Federation of Cuban Women.*

LUIS GARCÍA MESA: And with the *zafra*—the ten-million-ton sugar harvest, which was the following year, the next year—that was in '69. It was "My contribution" to the ten million. Everyone was supposed to contribute something—some were sowing sugarcane seeds to harvest the next year; others were doing up their sugarcane processing plants; others were fixing locomotives. That was their contribution. Her contribution was the documentary—she was incredible.

MARÍA CARIDAD CUMANÁ: *Her contribution to the ten-million-ton sugar harvest was that documentary?*

LUIS GARCÍA MESA: Yes, to the sugar harvest. Forget about the women's federation. We showed up in Matanzas in the ICAIC's jeep, and we saw a blond guy putting on some boots, sitting on some steps, maybe to the sugar processing plant's office, and we said to him, "Hey, can we talk to the administrator?" He looked at the ICAIC logo on the jeep door and said, "Ah, so you are the ICAIC people. You'll be inflating the balloon of the ten million." You know what inflating a balloon means in Cuba? It means you're lying. And I just stood there. "Eh, are you mad? Do you know what you're saying?" So Sara got out and looked at him and said, "Who are you?" "I'm the administrator." Sara said to him, "So you think the ten million isn't going to happen?" He says, "I'm reaching my goal. I was told that I had to achieve five hundred thousand *arrobas*,[5] and I'll do it with those two small sugar mills I've got that only serve to make cane liquor. With these two, I'll reach the target. But those giant mills that they're inventing in Camagüey and in Oriente, with those new tandem mills they've just bought. Those tandems couldn't be tested in London because in London there's no cane. They do it through measurement and all that. You've got to see them to work directly in a cane field, milling cane to see how they work, why they jam, where they're going to break. Understand? They're going to stop twenty times until you correct that stuff, and they won't work smoothly until the next harvest or the one after. You can't work with brand new equipment like that." And that's what happened—exactly that. The huge sugar plants that had to mill a million a day never reached their targets. And you know what happened to that guy?

They demoted him to being a worker, and we saw him later in Cubanitro or one of those industries.

LOURDES MARTÍNEZ-ECHAZÁBAL: *He talked too much.*

LUIS GARCÍA MESA: And he spoke the truth out loud and to anybody. Because we were people working on the official propaganda—we didn't come from Hollywood; we came from ICAIC, from an official institution—the guy said, "I'm a revolutionary. I'm not involved in anything. Look, didn't you see a statue here? Oh, no, not anymore; it's been tossed into storage. There was a statue here, of Christ, that said 'Christ the Worker,' and I don't know what, so I took the decision to get rid of it because I'm a communist. I don't believe in God or Christ or anything like that. And we needed to make some parts from it, and because that kind of bronze is good to make parts. Do you understand? So I got it removed to get it melted down. [But you know what?] As soon as they took it down, it started to rain. It wouldn't stop raining, and it rained for ten days until I said, 'Okay that's enough. Just put that Christ statue back in the same place.' I don't believe any of that stuff, but I wasn't going to let it fuck up the sugarcane harvest."

LOURDES MARTÍNEZ-ECHAZÁBAL: *Yes, that's happened to other people. It's strange to me that nothing like that happened to Sara, I mean, that she was able to do everything . . . somehow, with the image, and making others say stuff, without [compromising] herself. Because [as director] you're the one that's orchestrating everything. So how did she get away with it?*

LUIS GARCÍA MESA: Because the ICAIC was something else as well. It wasn't just any institution. I'm telling you, it was an island in culture, within the Ministry of Education. In the ICAIC, the young guys from the socialist, communist youth had long hair, do you know what I mean? There was a certain amount of freedom. One time I went to lend a hand at the Ministry of Education to do a documentary, and I took a small radio with batteries and I put it on Radio W [a US radio station] to listen to American music and, ooooh . . . I could've . . . it was as if I'd tossed a grenade into the queue for food. People said, "You're crazy. Switch that off." But in ICAIC I'd put it on full volume and people would dance and knew the songs.

LOURDES MARTÍNEZ-ECHAZÁBAL: *Do you think Alfredo Guevara being there had something to do with protecting Sara?*

LUIS GARCÍA MESA: I think that . . . I don't know what to tell you. I think so—she had *ache*.[6] But apart from that, it's possible she was liked because they realized how talented she was. That's part of it, but I don't know how much. Another part is that they needed a black woman directing films, and if she was producing masterpieces, all the better. "Well, this black woman has made a documentary. No, no, it's not that she's simply a filmmaker. If she's made fifteen and a feature film, then she's a director, no?" And remember that Cuba received a lot of visits from people like Chris Marker, Agnès Varda, and I don't know who else, and she . . . they always called Sara right away.

MARÍA CARIDAD CUMANÁ: *Do you think that her relationship with Agnès Varda influenced her in terms—*

LUIS GARCÍA MESA: No, I don't think so.

MARÍA CARIDAD CUMANÁ: *Because she was a kind of guide for Agnès Varda?*

LUIS GARCÍA MESA: I think Agnès Varda was in love with her, and yes, it's possible that Agnès Varda's work may have changed after that. But the thing is, everyone was in love with Sara. She was incredible—she was a magnetic force.

LOURDES MARTÍNEZ-ECHAZÁBAL: *However, after her death?*

LUIS GARCÍA MESA: I tell you, people either loved her or hated her. There was no halfway—she didn't allow for that. She wouldn't allow for any other kind of relationship unless it was for real. Like Nicolasito, "If someone's mediocre, I don't talk to them, they don't exist and that's that."

LOURDES MARTÍNEZ-ECHAZÁBAL: *But then they passed a thick veil over her, because really it's only over the last, let's say, twenty years that people are once more, at best, interested in her work.*

LUIS GARCÍA MESA: The same thing with Nicolasito.

MARÍA CARIDAD CUMANÁ: *Nicolás's work was censored for thirty years. His work was literally shelved, but Sara's wasn't.*

. . .

MARÍA CARIDAD CUMANÁ: *We wanted to know more about* Mi aporte. *Were you also present when the documentary was screened for the* compañeras *from the Federation of Cuban Women?*

LUIS GARCÍA MESA: No. I don't remember. It's possible, but I don't recall it. I told you what Sara thought of the federation—that it was a completely bourgeois organization, that within the Revolution it was supposed to represent Cuban women, but no way. It was for the Catholic ladies from before the Revolution, like any other of those weird organizations of which there were loads. Because you realized just by looking at how they dressed, how their meetings were. "We'll be organizing a cocktail in such and such a place."

MARÍA CARIDAD CUMANÁ: *So her aim with the documentary was to show the difficulties most women faced in getting into the workplace, nothing else. But that's where the conflict arose about how that concept was handled at that moment, in Cuba at that time. Did you film* Atención prenatal *[Prenatal care] with her?*

LUIS GARCÍA MESA: She was against machismo and against . . . all the extremes, you understand. She also didn't go with extreme feminism. She has a really interesting documentary in which women are talking, friends of hers . . . that's in *Mi aporte*? Oh yeah, in *Mi aporte*. I filmed that, and I didn't remember what film that was. And they're the same, theorizing about the problems and such.

MARÍA CARIDAD CUMANÁ: *She says at the end, she closes by saying, "I refuse to declare myself powerless." That's where the documentary ends.*

LUIS GARCÍA MESA: Nice phrase. I didn't remember that.

MARÍA CARIDAD CUMANÁ: *A friend of mine, Ricardo Acosta, made a documentary about Sara in 1990 with fragments from her work, and he chose that fragment to end it. Every time he sees me, he says, "I refuse to declare myself powerless." He's constantly repeating it to me.*

LUIS GARCÍA MESA: It's really a tremendous phrase . . . and it's true—that's what her whole life was about.

MARÍA CARIDAD CUMANÁ: *She refused to declare herself powerless under any circumstances. She kept going forward in everything she did.*

LUIS GARCÍA MESA: If the Revolution wasn't working, it wasn't her fault, because she believed in the Revolution and did everything possible to improve the Revolution from within. Of course, this couldn't be done. There was such a gigantic bureaucratic apparatus so pitted against you that you couldn't do anything. But she refused to declare herself powerless and kept going.

MARÍA CARIDAD CUMANÁ: *What was her opinion about the interest in introducing socialist realism and Russian influence into Cuba?*

LUIS GARCÍA MESA: Ay, no, no.

MARÍA CARIDAD CUMANÁ: *Was she against that?*

LUIS GARCÍA MESA: Totally. The only thing that I could criticize her for—if I were to criticize something, because she was a marvelous woman, and maybe it's because it's not my world, because I've nothing to do with it—but it was at a stage of her life when she and many other black intellectuals in Cuba took up this thing about blackness and Frantz Fanon and recuperating all that—establishing respect for black people. I said to her, "It doesn't make sense, one philosophy stuck inside another." In other words, I think it can all be fixed within the existing one. I didn't understand that very well, but she was very passionate about that.

LOURDES MARTÍNEZ-ECHAZÁBAL: *Around what period was this?*

LUIS GARCÍA MESA: I don't remember well, but I think it was when Muhammad Ali was still called Cassius Clay and he said, "We're handsome, I'm handsome and what's happening with me? I'm a poet!" It's true. You had to respect him. Why not? He was a black boxer. It's like [Antonio] Maceo.[7] I was taught as a child that Maceo was a huge black guy, that he had a machete and finished off the Spanish. Later I saw posters of Maceo and discovered he was an intellectual and wrote beautiful prose with exquisite calligraphy—an educated man. So why did they sell him to me that way? Because he was black?

CARIDAD CUMANÁ: *And he loved wearing smart clothes.*

LUIS GARCÍA MESA: He was elegant, good looking, used to get all elegant to walk, they say, along the pavement by the Louvre!

. . .

LOURDES MARTÍNEZ-ECHAZÁBAL: *Do you know if before 1972, or around that time, Angela Davis was in Cuba?*

LUIS GARCÍA MESA: No, I don't remember.

LOURDES MARTÍNEZ-ECHAZÁBAL: *Do you know if Sara met her?*

LUIS GARCÍA MESA: Of course she met her, and I was there. It was on the Isle of Pines. Maybe we were doing the documentaries at the time, because I know Sara met her on the Isle of Pines in the Colony Hotel. Angela Davis—classic, with that gigantic Afro she had, really beautiful. They met each other, yes.

LOURDES MARTÍNEZ-ECHAZÁBAL: *At that time, she wasn't famous yet—she hadn't yet been imprisoned. So this was before. Angela is a good friend of mine, so she's told me some interesting stories.*

LUIS GARCÍA MESA: She'll have told you she met Sara. It was probably a question of a meeting in a hotel room one day with an interpreter, something like that. I didn't participate in the meeting. But they did meet—I was there, Sara was there, and Sara wouldn't miss out on a chance to meet Angela Davis.

LOURDES MARTÍNEZ-ECHAZÁBAL: *And is there any other person from the North American world of black politics that she might have talked to?*

LUIS GARCÍA MESA: No, no. She just read the theoreticians of blackness—Frantz Fanon and those people.

LOURDES MARTÍNEZ-ECHAZÁBAL: *Who was in that small group? I mean Sara's group.*

LUIS GARCÍA MESA: In the ICAIC?

LOURDES MARTÍNEZ-ECHAZÁBAL: *No, in terms of the people, for example, reading Fanon and all that. I imagine she was talking with some people about it.*

LUIS GARCÍA MESA: She very much respected and liked Alberto Martínez Pedro, the father—not the theater guy, but the ethnologist and folklorist.

Martínez Furé as well, from the Conjunto Folklórico Nacional (National Folklore Company). Nicolasito, of course. I don't know, at least those people.

. . .

LOURDES MARTÍNEZ-ECHAZÁBAL: *Lalita [Inés María Martiatu Terry, interviewed in this volume] also worked with Sara in the ICAIC as assistant.*

LUIS GARCÍA MESA: Yes, and it seemed to me that Lalita and Sara had a deep friendship from the time they were kids, all their lives . . .

LOURDES MARTÍNEZ-ECHAZÁBAL: *Did she never tell you about her visit to the United States?*

LUIS GARCÍA MESA: No, never. I know she had a sister there, and her mother in New York. I met her sister . . . what on earth was she called? It was something like Betty, Patty, something like that. She tried to show me how to dance one of those dances that was fashionable at the time—the mashed potato. One of those typical dances that lasts fifteen days and then is forgotten. She tried to teach me, but I don't know how to dance. I'm probably the only Cuban who doesn't dance.

. . .

LOURDES MARTÍNEZ-ECHAZÁBAL: *I don't know if you have something to sum up in terms of Sara's documentaries before we move on to the feature film?*

LUIS GARCÍA MESA: I think that Sara, despite how we all were self-taught—we had training a bit along the lines of what the New Wave proposed, learning filmmaking by doing filmmaking—and Sara learned documentary language by doing documentaries. That's why they were *her* documentaries. They were documentaries with authorship, not things done on demand that they sent you off to do them and you did them. Or filmmaking with the attitude of "I'm doing this to please. . . ."

LOURDES MARTÍNEZ-ECHAZÁBAL: *But some of her films were done for specific demands, some of them.*

LUIS GARCÍA MESA: I would imagine so, but I don't know which, and maybe the people who asked her for films may have ended up with quite the opposite of what they'd imagined. Like what happened with *Coffea Arabiga* and others—that they asked you for one thing and you do another, but another marvelous film, another that was very good. Something they couldn't attack for its artistic quality.

MARÍA CARIDAD CUMANÁ: *But how do you see Sara's work within the overall film production? Do you think her documentary film work, which is basically from the 1960s, because Sara died in the mid-1970s, do you think her work goes beyond the framework for documentaries that existed at that time in the ICAIC?*

LUIS GARCÍA MESA: I think that the Cuban documentary movement was very important, but I think—I think its importance came, among other things, from the weight that Sara's work had and also the work of Nicolasito in the movement. This is despite the fact that they didn't last long. They basically only covered the beginning, when the school of Cuban documentary making was created. Cuban documentary making isn't from the 1990s—nothing like it. It's from the 1960s and 1970s. I mean the truly groundbreaking works, the genuinely original work with authorship. I think Sara contributed a huge amount to the importance of Cuban documentary making, and Nicolasito too. Sara and Nicolasito above all. Next, Bernabé [Hernández], too, he has key works, Juan Carlos Tabío, as well.

...

LOURDES MARTÍNEZ-ECHAZÁBAL: *When we talked about the aesthetics of documentary filmmaking and especially in Sara's work, one of its particularities is that she delves into things that are not just daily life but the minutiae. They're not about great heroic acts or key dates, all that. So, to what extent—because that is what was going on during that period, I'm thinking for example of Oscar Lewis's anthropology [see Víctor Fowler's essay in this volume for more on Lewis in Cuba], the issue of ethnographic cinema, the documentary cinema that started to emerge—do you think that had something [to do with it]? They almost always attribute it to her participation in the folklore seminar, the national theater—*

MARÍA CARIDAD CUMANÁ: *Ethnology and folklore.*

LOURDES MARTÍNEZ-ECHAZÁBAL: *But to what extent are there also ... ?*

LUIS GARCÍA MESA: I think that if you have to frame it mostly around Sara's documentaries, they are ethnographic works, no? They have to do with that.

In what other way? Sociological? Of course, all this had an influence on her vision of reality. On how to transmit it in a documentary. But she had no school for making documentaries. No one taught her how to edit or focus on a reality.

MARÍA CARIDAD CUMANÁ: *No one taught her the difference between Chris Marker and Joris Ivens despite having met them.*

LUIS GARCÍA MESA: She was right there with them—she shook their hands and had a beer with them, but that was all.

LOURDES MARTÍNEZ-ECHAZÁBAL: *But remember, this was a time when, for example, testimony emerges as a literary genre.*

LUIS GARCIA MESA: *In Cold Blood* [Capote 1966].

LOURDES MARTÍNEZ-ECHAZÁBAL: *Yes, that was about giving voice to people not recognized in history to a certain extent. In this way you come closer to all these people, to the boy in* Una isla para Miguel, *or the unnamed women from the such and such factory. So that their histories ... so that they speak, they are able to speak.*

LUIS GARCÍA MESA: Like the way Nicolasito does it in *Taller de Línea y 18* as well, the bus workshop, when he gets them talking, gets the workers to speak.

MARÍA CARIDAD CUMANÁ: *Yes, yes, the woman who says that she can't be a leader, that she can't accept the post, that she doesn't want it. It was impossible for people not to accept something like that.*

LUIS GARCÍA MESA: It's a responsibility, because if they give you a trip and you say, "No, no, because of my kids...." Ah, that's okay! A responsibility that you have to accept. She couldn't say it, and Nicolasito couldn't put it on the table, that she had said that. Because if there's something in Cuba that's worse than censorship, it's self-censorship. I mean, when you were doing a script you already knew what you could say and what you couldn't.

. . .

LUIS GARCÍA MESA: Can we talk about *De cierta manera?* . . . I'm really glad you've left this until last.

LOURDES MARTÍNEZ-ECHAZÁBAL: *That's why I gave you a drink of rum. It wasn't gratuitous.*

LUIS GARCÍA MESA: Because I know it's the thing, let's say, that's going to create the most conflict in terms of what we're going to deal with. Until now it's all been very—no, in fact I think it's going to continue along the same lines.

LOURDES MARTÍNEZ-ECHAZÁBAL: *Why do you think it might be cause for conflict?*

LUIS GARCÍA MESA: Things you've told me about the Abakuá sect and all that.

LOURDES MARTÍNEZ-ECHAZÁBAL: *What you and I talked about. But that's just a small detail, isn't it?*

LUIS GARCÍA MESA: And if Sara had put that part there and...

MARÍA CARIDAD CUMANÁ: *Ah, and the voice-over...*[8]

LUIS GARCÍA MESA: The voice-over. You asked me how Sara would say that, being married to an Abakuá? I was thinking of saying to you, "Look, Sara didn't marry an Abakuá. Sara married a man, a Cuban, a black man, a sound engineer with the ICAIC, ah... who was also an Abakuá." Germinal was my friend and colleague, my brother.... I was friends with him and even went to some parties from his Abakuá set. They were *foringomó*. You know the Abakuá have several sets: *muñanga; foringomó; camaroró;* and *camaroró de fo*, depending. So, he was a *foringomó*. Their house or temple was in La Lisa. Sara was very irreverent—very herself. Well, here's something terrible about the religion, about Abakuá, that I don't know if you know, but it's not going to contribute anything.

LOURDES MARTÍNEZ-ECHAZÁBAL: *What? The thing about sacrifice?*

LUIS GARCÍA MESA: No, not that. It's that when an Abakuá has sex with his woman, they have some limitations to do with oral sex. The man can't have oral sex with his woman, with his wife. Because they say that it's like being with another man by accident, I mean, because another man had probably been there.

MARÍA CARIDAD CUMANÁ: *Well, maybe if the woman had slept with another man.*

LUIS GARCÍA MESA: That's right, because if the only partner had been him, then there's no problem. But supposing he'd not been her only partner, that she'd also been with someone else at some point in her life? If he married a virgin, there's no problem; but if not, it's like doing it with another man by accident. So their machismo goes to that extreme. The other extreme, which for me is an extreme as well, even worse, is that you never lose your membership. In other words, it's difficult to be sworn in as an Abakuá, because then you're—for example, a *padrino* [Abakuá godfather or sponsor] of mine says to me, "Hey, why don't you get involved in the *juego* [sect]?" So I say, "Okay, I'll get involved in the religion." But then I have to give them a photo and a CV with where I studied and stuff, and then they investigate me to ensure I'm a man, because to be Abakuá you have to be a man. You can't be gay—they don't admit either women or gays.... So they test you. Stuff like when you apply to be a party militant, they investigate you.

... There are no Abakuá women. As I see it, Abakuá was founded as a mutual aid society much like the Masons. The Abakuá is based on the myth of Sikán, that women discovered men's secret, that there were two earths, etc. Lydia Cabrera is brilliant on this. She has a book called *Abakuá*.

I'll tell you an amusing and interesting thing about the film. We set up an Abakuá *plante* [ceremony] in order to film it. We invited people to a place in Cubanacan I think it was. All secret societies have to register themselves in some kind of religious society, but the *plantes* had been banned for years. So they did the *plante*. They cut the goat's testicles, they cut its throat, they drink the blood, and they dance. The ones being initiated are with the *padrino*, and behind them comes the little devil. They hit him and then enter into the secret room where there's a drum and a cloth in the corner. There are several places, and the one in front is for the chief. The *nasako* is the chief of the *nasa*, or witchcraft.... I wanted to go in and film, but they say, "No, brother." But they didn't say *blanquito* [whitey], because that's very offensive—it's like saying the N-word. They just said brother. But that gave it more veracity, the fact that we couldn't go in—it was all filmed from the outside. I had the same point of view that any invited audience would have had, a friend of an Abakuá who would have seen the same thing that the camera did. I had no privilege just because we had set up the performance for us [to film it]. They took advantage and got around the government that way.

MARÍA CARIDAD CUMANÁ: *And Germinal did the sound?*

LUIS GARCÍA MESA: Yes, in the film, yes, Germinal did the sound the whole time. In terms of the voice-over, I asked Iván because I—of course, my work

Figure 7.1 Germinal Hernández, Luis García Mesa, and Sara Gómez filming *De cierta manera*, 1973. © ICAIC

finished with the cinematography, not just the filming—I have to go to the laboratory afterward and do the color correction—when it's not, it's the light correction. In other words, this is too dark, make it lighter, etc., until the copy is how I want it. And that copy was terribly mistreated.

MARÍA CARIDAD CUMANÁ: *You filmed in sixteen millimeter, didn't you?*

LUIS GARCÍA MESA: Yes, we filmed in sixteen millimeter. Ah! I'll tell you why we filmed it in sixteen millimeter. Sara said to me, "Luis, we're going to do a film where the protagonist is marginality. The Revolution has removed a group of people from Las Yaguas, one of those unhealthy neighborhoods, and they've been given some new houses." Her thesis was that it wasn't the solution. If you change a man's habitat, you're not changing the man—his mentality continues to be the same.

MARÍA CARIDAD CUMANÁ: *Of course—because the mentality doesn't change with the same speed as social processes.*

LUIS GARCÍA MESA: And she was very clear about that. It really took me some work to understand that, but then afterward I realized it was true because I also saw it there. People continued to be marginal and all that. What happens? She wanted to demonstrate that you had to change the man, not just change the house. Of course, you had to give all those people the comfort that they deserved because they were workers. They worked hard, but there needed to be much deeper societal work with them, real work, to give them information, education, train them without underestimating them and without paternalism, which is something the government tends to do a lot—it tends to be paternalistic.

MARÍA CARIDAD CUMANÁ: *I'd call it aggressive paternalism.*

LUIS GARCÍA MESA: That's true, because in the end it attacks you.

. . .

LUIS GARCÍA MESA: So then we had a great time but, well, when I talked to Iván I asked him, "Iván, when the film was finished, when Sara died I mean, you started to edit the film—did you continue the editing?" Ah, sorry, first I wanted to tell you why we filmed in sixteen millimeter and all that, I haven't told you yet. Sara said to me, "We're going to make a film about marginality, about the problem of changing people's mentality by changing their house, which is absurd." She said, "I'm going to work with professional actors, with Mario Balmaseda, with so-and-so and so-and-so, but I'm also going to work with, for example, Mario Balmaseda's father. He is going to be an older man, a worker who's not an actor, and the mother, and some other characters won't be actors, and some will be, so we're going to mix it up like that. We're going to be in their houses—nothing here will be filmed in the studio. We're going to their houses to film, so I don't want you to show up with one of those gigantic Mitchell BNCs [Blimped Newsreel Camera] and lamps and fourteen people, because we'll scare them off—they won't talk."

MARÍA CARIDAD CUMANÁ: *She did it so people wouldn't be intimidated.*

LUIS GARCÍA MESA: What she wanted was for the camera to pass unnoticed. Well, no, but as unnoticed as possible. If there'd been tiny cameras like there are now, then we would have used one of them so that it looked like we were doing an amateur job to film the family, not an ICAIC film. So I said we should do it in sixteen millimeter, which were the smallest professional cameras we had, to make sure we'd still have quality and synchronized sound with the camera. She says, "I'm okay with that, with the minimum." We went and I said to her, "Also, let's go a day early with the camera so they can see the camera and be around it, and the following day we'll film." And that's how we did it. That material then went to a laboratory and it was mistreated. I don't know how. Iván couldn't explain it either, but he said to me, "They finished it off." They ruined the film, because there was no reason it should have had the terrible quality it did. She didn't want to do an aesthetic film—beautiful, with landscapes and stuff—but neither did she want it to look like it was made forty years before. There are even films made forty years before that have better quality than that. So what did they do? They screwed it up, but well. The thing she was more interested in was the theme—the plasticity in the film didn't exist for her. On top of that, if we'd have filmed it in color—for example, you go into Las Yaguas, into the marginal neighborhoods in color—it seems to me that it sweetens the reality. Even though the reality is in color, but it gives . . . it's not the same thing to see a kid without shoes in the mud in black and white than to see it in color. It has more drama that way.

LOURDES MARTÍNEZ-ECHAZÁBAL: *You also have the precedent of Italian neorealism and all that, which was black and white.*

LUIS GARCÍA MESA: All that crude reality in black and white makes it all the more terrible. If you put in a colorful sunset in color—"Oh, how beautiful!" What a beautiful little bloated stomach of that child, all pink and full of parasites. It doesn't hit you. And she wanted that. She wanted it to be crude, hard, and dramatic. Because it's a theme like that—not a theme to applaud but to make you cry, make you think. More than anything that's what she wanted with her films. She wanted people to think and think for themselves. It's what we were saying about the individual. For her, the individual, the person, had a gigantic importance. Everything begins and ends there, in the man. One supposes that everything is done for the man and everything man does.

LOURDES MARTÍNEZ-ECHAZÁBAL: *Let me see if I can find this bit here that has always drawn my attention. It involves that voice that's so didactic and with the proverbial "we." Wow, Sara, "we?"*
   [Watching a segment of the film with the Abakuá ceremony]

. . .

LUIS GARCÍA MESA: That's very interesting—stop it there for a moment. Because you'd think that the showy dress and that stuff is from black African culture, but that comes from the Spanish dandy. In fact, that guy that you see there all dressed up—there's a pose, which for me is the most feminine thing that exists. It's that standing pose there with the hand like this. That's called Cueñón's pose, and it's considered to be the most macho thing you can do. It's the display of vanity—what's happening, man...? With the hand like this... it could easily be a queen as well. I think the two extremes end up connecting.

MARÍA CARIDAD CUMANÁ: *Yes, because I remember a scene that's filmed in a boardinghouse in* De cierta manera, *in which a young guy stands with his hand like that.*

LUIS GARCÍA MESA: Yes, that's dandyism, and [in that case] he is a queen. It seems to me so gay—I don't know [watching the video]. In the ritual, they kill the billy goat and they turn it into a nanny goat. They cut off its balls, sorry, the testicles. But I know what you're saying about the "we" she says—it doesn't seem to make sense.

MARÍA CARIDAD CUMANÁ: *She says, "We think..."*

LUIS GARCÍA MESA: In terms of a contemporary society in other words, why does the Abakuá emerge? They are black people who've come from Africa as slaves and want to maintain their culture, their customs against the Spanish who want to force them to behave like white people, Westerners. So they create the Abakuá society. With their greetings, with their way of recognizing each other, in the same way they created syncretism with the religion where, for example, Santa Barbara is Changó. And it's interesting that Saint Barbara, who is a woman, Changó is black and a man-god. But she was a woman with a sword, so they said it seemed more like that. So they believed that to ask Saint Barbara for something, they were really asking Changó. Or San Lazaro, who was Babalú Ayé, and then another and another. The Abakuá secret society was the same in defending themselves from the Spanish and the obligatory culture they wanted to impose on them along with other changes—they created the society to protect themselves. And they say it's a society in which you have to be a good man, a good father, a good son, a good brother. It's very similar to the precepts of the Masons. And people, my older Abakuá friends, have told me, "This has changed too much. Before, the Abakuá had to do with mutual support. An *ekobio* died and everyone helped the widow. Especially the *padrino*, since the *padrino* of any child substituted for the father in terms of economic obligations, their education, their maintenance, and all that. And now it's become a dandy thing, a thing about attractiveness, that's become meaningless." As I said, when it began in the time of the Spanish, the Abakuá had really important social, self-defense, and political functions. For example, you were telling me about Maceo—they say Maceo, when he went all dressed up and walked along the pavement by the Louvre, there were two or three Abakuá who accompanied him and watched his back. He wasn't an Abakuá, but the Abakuás knew how important he was as a . . . he was a distinguished Cuban, and they protected him so that the Spanish couldn't make more assassination attempts against him, taking advantage of the pause between one war and another.

LOURDES MARTÍNEZ-ECHAZÁBAL: *What surprises me is that way she speaks [in this segment of the film].*

LUIS GARCÍA MESA: It's placed there in a sort of bothersome way. Yes, I don't like it much either.

LOURDES MARTÍNEZ-ECHAZÁBAL: *For someone like her . . . almost as a mission of Sara's to underline somewhat the contradictions, emphasize those crossroads where you feel you're in some kind of predicament.*

LUIS GARCÍA MESA: I think it's done in an annoying way. But if you look at it, it's true. What function does the Abakuá have today? Something that was created in the nineteenth century to protect the slaves.

LOURDES MARTÍNEZ-ECHAZÁBAL: *Yes, but for someone trying to recuperate black roots in Cuba, for example, who's interested in black culture?*

LUIS GARCÍA MESA: But that would be the case for a scholar, not for a member of society, do you see what I mean? You'd have to be a militant in that society.

LOURDES MARTÍNEZ-ECHAZÁBAL: *But what I mean, is she saying that it's an obstacle to progress? You can say it's problematic,* machista, *but it's a bit like the state speaking, saying, "These people are backward, they're cannibals, they're . . ."*

LUIS GARCÍA MESA: I understand what you mean—it also bothers me. It seems to me not to be the best way to focus on the issue.

MARÍA CARIDAD CUMANÁ: *But what did Iván say about the voice-over?*

LUIS GARCÍA MESA: He told me, "Sara put that in." Now, something else is that Titón, when Sara died, didn't Titón take on the editing? But he said "No, Titón showed up about a month and a half later, or two months, I don't know... suddenly, for the first time, there he was in the editing room"—when they had practically finished. "In fact [said Iván], he [Titón] came with Mayito because they wanted to film some things [Mayito the cinematographer, Mario García Joya]. So I told him, 'No, no, no, Sara left me very precise instructions. She gave me them before she died, about how this had to be edited.'" Everything was there, "[Iván continued] There are even some shots that have to be filmed by Luis García, as I've agreed with him, with the same equipment and everything"—the shots of the demolition of Central Havana, the ball that knocks the walls down, the one that's in the credits, I think. So that was the only thing left to film that we hadn't filmed together.

LOURDES MARTÍNEZ-ECHAZÁBAL: *To begin with, the project was to look at the viability of those social changes that were taking place—specifically in the Las Yaguas neighborhood. That is, you changed the people's living conditions, but that was not how you changed the mentality.*

LUIS GARCÍA MESA: And we weren't there filming through to the very end of the project, because in the end you would see how people in the neighborhood ended up ripping out the doors and using them for firewood. They sold the flushable toilets and just left a hole there. That would really have been too raw.

MARÍA CARIDAD CUMANÁ: *So you filmed in the house of the woman they called La Mexicana?*

LUIS GARCÍA MESA: Yes.

MARÍA CARIDAD CUMANÁ: *Who was the one who hit the child?*

LUIS GARCÍA MESA: The child, El Conejo [The Rabbit]. El Conejo had big teeth. The little boy as well.

MARÍA CARIDAD CUMANÁ: *She'd give him a tremendous beating because he behaved badly in school. Then she got down on her knees to the teacher, who was Yolanda. I know the film by heart.*

LUIS GARCÍA MESA: Yolanda was someone else who was also incredible—an amazing actress. I went with Sara to see her in Camagüey, in a play, because she was doing theater there and had a role as a character called La Coreana, who was homeless, living on the street, and dressed in filthy rags. And I said, "Sara, is that the actress for the film?" She said, "Yes, we'll see her afterward in the dressing room." And when I finally saw her—*la china*—I said, "My God!" It was as if the roof had caved in because she was so beautiful, very pretty, and with an amazing body....

MARÍA CARIDAD CUMANÁ: *You know, it's really important that you've confirmed that Sara left precise instruction for Iván Arocha for editing the film, because there are a lot of myths surrounding what Sara said or didn't say and what she wanted. For example, it's said that the film was finished by Tomás Gutiérrez Alea, Rigoberto López, and Julio García Espinosa—that's what's in the books.*

LUIS GARCÍA MESA: Totally false. If Iván says it wasn't like that, then it wasn't. I believe in Iván. And unfortunately, Titón died. Rigoberto and Julio have more recently died as well.

...

LOURDES MARTÍNEZ-ECHAZÁBAL: *And the idea for those shots of the demolition, it seems to me—*

LUIS GARCÍA MESA: They're hers. They hadn't been filmed, but she said, "Iván . . . for the editing, I want the film to begin with a wrecking ball, one of those balls demolishing the old houses."

LOURDES MARTÍNEZ-ECHAZÁBAL: *And that was in Old Havana, or [Central] Havana.*

MARÍA CARIDAD CUMANÁ: *And that's the shot in which Mario goes to make peace with the teacher, where he's standing outside and you hear that famous song.*

LOURDES MARTÍNEZ-ECHAZÁBAL: *The one sung by the black guy's friend.*

MARÍA CARIDAD CUMANÁ: *So they are all Sara's ideas? She wanted it to be filmed like that? They were all Sara's ideas?*

LUIS GARCÍA MESA: All of it, the whole thing.

MARÍA CARIDAD CUMANÁ: *With the end like that, where he tries to get back with her, with that song in the background?*

LUIS GARCÍA MESA: *It could be that it was improvised beyond the script, but Sara was the one to create the improvisation.*

LOURDES MARTÍNEZ-ECHAZÁBAL: *Yes, because basically she finished it, except...*

LUIS GARCÍA MESA: *Look, maybe, I don't know. Maybe that language used at the end with the problem of the Abakuá and all that...*

LOURDES MARTÍNEZ-ECHAZÁBAL: *No, but that's at the beginning, where the sequence of the plante is...*

LUIS GARCÍA MESA: *That's why—it's around the part about the plante. Maybe that language in the voice-over isn't the most adequate. Maybe it was a concession she had to make because it was more important to safeguard the whole project. It was important to get the film out.*

MARÍA CARIDAD CUMANÁ: *I've been told she had to negotiate a lot to be able to.*

LUIS GARCÍA MESA: *It's quite probable.*

MARÍA CARIDAD CUMANÁ: *There's another myth in Cuba, which is that Sara died because she filmed things she wasn't supposed to film.*

LUIS GARCÍA MESA: *No, that's not true. They didn't let us film anything that we weren't allowed to film; otherwise, I would have died, too. No, no, that's not true.*

...

LOURDES MARTÍNEZ-ECHAZÁBAL: *About your participation in making this film—what are the spectacular moments you remember? Or other moments?*

LUIS GARCÍA MESA: *The hardest, most intense, most dramatic moment of the filming is obviously the Abakuá part. The rest is acting. It's more or less between acting and cinema verité—I don't know what you'd like to call it. But the Abakuá plante ritual was very intense.*

LOURDES MARTÍNEZ-ECHAZÁBAL: *And that had never been filmed before, or scarcely?*

LUIS GARCIA MESA: No.

MARÍA CARIDAD CUMANÁ: *Did Sara have any interest—for example, as a cinematographer, did she ask you to—*

LUIS GARCÍA MESA: And I don't think it's in homage to the Abakuá. A lot of people don't know about it, have never seen it.

LOURDES MARTÍNEZ-ECHAZÁBAL: *That's why I say I don't understand what's said in relation to what she did.*

LUIS GARCÍA MESA: You sometimes have to lean a little to the right in order to take a step to the left. I don't know how she was playing it because only Sara knows that—you'd have to find a medium for that. Like Rashomon [the ghost in the Japanese film of the same name by Akira Kurosawa (1950)].

MARÍA CARIDAD CUMANÁ: *Let's see—who'll channel Sara's spirit?*

LOURDES MARTÍNEZ-ECHAZÁBAL: *You see? That's why—some people have even written stuff, but it's a secret society, so really to film those things—I don't know, but I haven't seen anything else like it.*

LUIS GARCÍA MESA: I haven't seen anything before about it. I've seen—you put Abakuá into YouTube and there are dances on a stage. I myself filmed a documentary with Bernabé called *Abakuá*. That's also what I filmed—dancing on a stage. But this wasn't a stage. This was a place that could perfectly well be a place where an Abakuá *plante* took place. In any neighborhood, anywhere. But I never knew the name of the sect that was doing the *plante* ceremony or the name of the main person, who was an older white man. I never knew what those people were like, because they don't let you know. And because on top of that, I was part of the team filming . . .

. . .

LOURDES MARTÍNEZ-ECHAZÁBAL: *The rest of the film is really a . . . it seems to me to be really important. One of the things apart from marginality is how do you change someone's head [mentality]? How do you go from that Abakuá morality, or group mentality, to one that's revolutionary? And really there's no change—it's simply a change of scenery. Because the principles are the same—loyalty, fidelity with and toward your comrade, the machismo, all that.*

LUIS GARCÍA MESA: And the Abakuá are not racist. There's a sect, the *camaroró de fo*, in fact, in which white men can participate. [Earlier in an outtake, Mesa uses a pun on the rhyme of *camaroró de fo* and *camarógrafo*, or cameraman.]

MARÍA CARIDAD CUMANÁ: *Were you with Sara when she made one of her first films in 1966,* Crónicas de mi familia *[Chronicles of my family]?*

LUIS GARCÍA MESA: No.

LOURDES MARTÍNEZ-ECHAZÁBAL: *Perhaps some last words—or any afterthoughts, as they say. Is there anything you'd like to finish with, at least in terms of the interview?*

LUIS GARCÍA MESA: What was that phrase of Sara's?

LOURDES MARTÍNEZ-ECHAZÁBAL: *Which?*

LUIS GARCÍA MESA: The one that closes the documentary that...

MARÍA CARIDAD CUMANÁ: *"I refuse to declare myself powerless."*

LUIS GARCÍA MESA: It's just that it's very difficult to close it with one phrase. It seems to me that Sara's work, as I said to you a while back, Sara's documentary work has a huge weight within what later was called the school of Cuban documentary film. It seems to me that it's very important because she was someone who was very authentic, very transparent—she knew what she wanted, and what she said was always important. She didn't get lost in stupidities or adornments of any kind. She was genuinely interested in the heart, the interior, intestinal truth of things. She was a filmmaker, a sociologist, a cultured and highly intelligent young woman.

MARÍA CARIDAD CUMANÁ: *I wanted to ask you, in* De cierta manera *there is a general tendency to use medium and wide shots. Did she specifically ask you for that? And did she ask you not to film shots, let's say—*

LUIS GARCÍA MESA: Yes, no extreme close-ups.

MARÍA CARIDAD CUMANÁ: *No extreme close-ups. Just medium long shots and full shots. It's just to confirm that it was her request?*

LUIS GARCÍA MESA: All the shots, all the framing, was Sara's.

MARÍA CARIDAD CUMANÁ: *Or medium shots [planos americanos]. There are not a lot of close-ups in the film, either.*

LUIS GARCÍA MESA: No, there're not many. There are very few despite the fact we were filming in sixteen millimeter, which would suggest the opposite—you have to go a little closer in and all that.

LOURDES MARTÍNEZ-ECHAZÁBAL: *Do you think, then, that—of course this is an unfair question because Sara only managed to make one feature film, and even then, it has a lot of documentary in it—but do you think her strength was more in documentary?*

LUIS GARCÍA MESA: In terms of the work she left us, there's a lot more value in her documentary filmmaking than...

LOURDES MARTÍNEZ-ECHAZÁBAL: *And it's curious that most people don't know about it. Sara's documentary work is not very widely known.*

LUIS GARCÍA MESA: Also, the feature film is monothematic, whereas her documentaries cover a whole range of things. She dealt with a wide variety of themes.

MARÍA CARIDAD CUMANÁ: *And do you remember any theme that Sara commented to you that wasn't covered by her filmography? Do you ever remember her saying, "I would have liked to film such and such a thing but..."?*

LUIS GARCÍA MESA: I was thinking and remembering that I'd never think about this again—that the second feature film she wanted to make was with a young girl who worked in Coppelia. I have a vague idea about that. A girl that was what we call a *guaricandilla* [slut]. One of those street girls who wants to get herself a boyfriend—very superficial—but in the process a tremendous drama emerges. But I can't remember any details because she never wrote the script, I think. I think they were just ideas we talked about during the dinners she had.

MARÍA CARIDAD CUMANÁ: *When she talked about race in Cuba, was she passionate about the issue?*

LUIS GARCÍA MESA: Very passionate.

MARÍA CARIDAD CUMANÁ: *Did she think there was racism in Cuba?*

LUIS GARCÍA MESA: Yes, definitely. In other words, black people, if they had a presence, it was like her—it was to be used. Like, "We need a black man on the Central Committee. Ah, call Lazo and put him there in the Central Committee, because how can we have a Party Central Committee in Cuba without a black man, when black people make up half of the population?" She believed that or was aware of that, and she didn't shut up about it in any way whatsoever.

MARÍA CARIDAD CUMANÁ: *And she wasn't at all complacent with the official line.*

LUIS GARCÍA MESA: And she wasn't a racist. She married Héctor Veitía, who is white, and had a child with him. She had no problem about that. When she looked at a man, she looked at his mind, not his skin. The same goes for her friends—she picked people for their intelligence, or because she liked them. In my case, she liked me.

MARÍA CARIDAD CUMANÁ: *And among the Cuban filmmakers, which of them do you think were closest to her?*

LUIS GARCÍA MESA: You mean directors?

MARÍA CARIDAD CUMANÁ: *Yes, directors.*

LUIS GARCÍA MESA: Perhaps Titón. I think more than Sergio because Titón, as you know, they formed groups for creative work and he was like the head of creation in the group where she was, and so there was a feeling of mutual respect. In spite of what I told you about the end according to Iván.

MARÍA CARIDAD CUMANÁ: *And Titón treated her with respect?*

LUIS GARCÍA MESA: With a lot of respect.

MARÍA CARIDAD CUMANÁ: *Despite her being much younger than him?*

LUIS GARCÍA MESA: But Titón was a very intelligent and wise man. "That's Sara Gómez, be careful."

Translated from the original Spanish by Helen Dixon

NOTES

1. See Richard Acosta's interview with Iván Arocha in this volume.
2. With no existing print of *De bateyes*, the negatives of the sound and image have been held in the ICAIC archive. The Vulnerable Media Lab, under the direction of Susan Lord, is restoring, digitizing and subtitling all of Gómez's documentaries. The work will be completed in 2021—Ed.
3. Carpentier is a Cuban novelist, essayist, and musicologist who lived from December 26, 1904, to April 24, 1980. He is the founder of the "marvelous real," which is believed to be a significant precursor to magical realism.
4. About the thirty-two soundtracks, here is an anecdote: The technicians hid the sound effect reels, but Nicolasito always noticed when one of those was missing. When the technicians hid one of those reels, Nicolasito said, "There is a small hammer missing." For Nicolas, all the sounds had a purpose.
5. One *arroba* is the equivalent of 11.5 kilograms, or about twenty-five pounds.
6. *Ache* is a form of divine luck or strength in the Yoruba religion.
7. Afro-descendant José Antonio de la Caridad Maceo y Grajales was second in command of the Cuban Army of Independence.
8. See Malitsky's and Lord's discussions of documentary voice-over in this volume.—Ed.

LUIS GARCÍA MESA began working at the Cuban Institute of Cinematographic Art and Industry in 1960 as assistant producer for the film *Cuba Dances* (in Spanish; 1961). He is director of photography for several of Sara Gómez's films, including *One Way or Another* (in Spanish; 1977).

LOURDES MARTÍNEZ-ECHAZÁBAL is Professor of Latin American and Latino Studies at the University of California, Santa Cruz. She is author of *Para una semiótica de la mulatez*. She is founder with Raúl Fernández of the UC-Cuba Academic Initiative, a University of California multicampus research program.

MARÍA CARIDAD CUMANÁ taught Film and Television at the University of Havana for 15 years. She was Chief Coordinator for the Audiovisual Portal for Latin American and Caribbean Cinema at the Foundation of New Latin American Cinema, co-authored *A Look at Cuban Cinema, Latitudes of the Margin: Latin American Cinema before the Third Millennium,* and co-edited *My Havana: The Musical City of Carlos Varela*. She was Field Producer in Havana for the documentary Out My Windows (NFB). She is currently an Adjunct Faculty at Miami Dade College.

EIGHT

Sara Gómez
AfroCubana (Afro-Cuban Women's) Activism after 1961

Devyn Spence Benson

IN THE 1964 DOCUMENTARY *Iré a Santiago* (I'm going to Santiago), Afro-Cuban director Sara Gómez celebrated Santiago de Cuba's black history. Gómez's film employs wide shots of the eastern city's colonial streets, cathedral, and university while she explains to her audience that "the first blacks [in Cuba] were brought to Santiago and General Antonio Maceo was born here." With this film, Gómez emphasized the city's rich past and Afro-Cuban contributions to the nation.[1] However, in 1964 Gómez was not merely aware of Santiago's past. She also had a stake in its future—a future marked by the dynamic social changes of the 1959 Cuban Revolution, including both an antidiscrimination campaign and a movement to integrate women into the workforce. As the documentary's narrator, she claims that "history is beginning again in Santiago [with the Revolution]" as images of Afro-Cuban women outfitted with batons, drums, and marching band uniforms move across the screen.

As the only woman and one of just three black directors working at the Instituto Cubano del Arte e Industria Cinematográficos (ICAIC, or Cuban Film Institute) in the 1960s, Gómez routinely stood out by producing documentaries that showcased the daily experiences of blacks and *mulatos* in revolutionary Cuba. She showed blacks in neighborhoods, factories, and rural areas participating in and questioning the new government's policies. This work sat in stark contrast to the contradictory images proliferating in revolutionary visual culture that simultaneously welcomed blacks into the new nation and portrayed Afro-Cubans as in need of salvation and reform to be ideal citizens.[2] It challenged moves by state cultural institutions, the ICAIC included, to position blackness in the past—as folklore.[3] Gómez's claim that history was beginning again in Santiago mirrored statements made by revolutionary leaders who imagined 1959 as a new start for the island. However, the young filmmaker saw Cuba's renewal—its Revolution—in the lives of Afro-Cuban men and women in Santiago, Guanabacoa, and other sites far removed from the centers of white male power.

Like other Cubans, blacks and *mulatos* negotiated the changing landscape of revolutionary Cuba throughout the 1960s. New legislation such as the Agrarian and Urban Reform Laws, coupled with efforts to reduce telephone and electricity rates and provide educational scholarships and health care to working-class and rural Cubans, meant that life in Cuba had changed dramatically less than a year after the ouster of President Fulgencio Batista in 1959 (Pérez 1995; Pérez-Stable 1999). In the midst of these reforms, revolutionary leaders announced a campaign against racial discrimination in March 1959 that targeted informal segregation practices in schools, social clubs, and parks; constructed a lasting narrative that revolutionaries could not be racists; and sought to fulfill the promises of nineteenth-century patriots by creating a Cuba without blacks or whites—only Cubans. In 1960, when Fidel Castro led the Cuban delegation to the United Nations meeting in New York and met with Malcolm X in Harlem's Hotel Theresa, revolutionary leaders proclaimed the success of their antidiscrimination campaign to the world and invited African Americans to Cuba to see the island's racial paradise (Benson 2016, 153–97). Shortly afterward, public debates about lingering racism became taboo as Cuban leaders focused the national lens on defending the Revolution against US aggression, which left little public space for dissent. This silence continued until the 1990s, when economic crisis led to another wave of vocal Afro-Cuban activism against worsening inequalities and employment discrimination in the new tourism industry.

Much of the current work on race in Cuba follows this familiar arc of antiracist activism on the island. A rich body of scholarship exists about nineteenth-century slavery, slave rebellions, abolition, and Afro-Cuban participation in the Cuban wars of independence.[4] Similarly, black and *mulato* activism and national political participation during both the Cuban republic (1902–58) and the first years of the Revolution have received considerable attention (Helg 1995; de la Fuente 2001; R. Moore 1997; Bronfman 2004; Guridy 2010; Pappademos 2012; Benson 2016). Additionally, anthropologists, sociologists, and political scientists in both Cuba and the United States have analyzed racial tensions following the fall of the Soviet Union in 1989 and theorized a "return of racism" after new decentralizing economic reforms (Morales 2002, 70; 2007; de la Fuente 2008, 714; Sawyer 2006; Fernandes 2006; Roland 2010; Queeley 2015). However, there remains a gap in knowledge about revolutionary changes in the late 1960s and 1970s (Guerra 2012). In particular, more research is needed on how black and *mulato* Cubans who stayed on the island (and did not move into exile) found creative ways to have public and private debates about racial inequality despite the 1960 declaration that racial discrimination had been eliminated and repeated state attempts to silence public conversations about lingering racism in favor of national unity. Many of these Afro-Cubans, such as filmmaker Sara Gómez, found outlets for addressing discrimination and fighting for racial equality in literature and the arts (de la Fuente 2013; Barquet 2011).

Young black women—including prominent *AfroCubanas* like poets Georgina Herrera and Nancy Morejón, literary critic Inés María Martiatu Terry, and Gómez—played influential roles in these late 1960s conversations. However, the literature about the period is dominated by black men's responses. Books by and about black activists and intellectuals such as Juan R. Betancourt, Carlos Moore, Walterio Carbonell, and Pedro Pérez Sarduy are well known, in part due to the fact that international presses picked up their works and published them outside Cuba.[5] Despite this trend, as Paula Sanmartín notes in her book *Black Women as Custodians of History* (2014), the 1959 Cuban Revolution was in fact a revolution in black women's writings. After 1959, Afro-Cuban women used the education and openings provided by the new government to move from being the subjects to the objects (the creative voices) of Cuban literature and poetry. Black women of various classes, such as the former domestic worker turned poet Herrera and the middle-class documentary director Gómez, experienced and reinvented Cuba's Revolution in the late 1960s. Their lives and works illuminate tensions between opportunity and censorship in post-1959 Cuba, but they also demonstrate that, despite official government silence on domestic racism, black and *mulato* Cubans never lost sight of the Revolution's promise of racial equality.[6] Moreover, with the founding of the Federación de Mujeres Cubanas (FMC, or Federation of Cuban Women) and the rise of the state-backed women's movement in Cuba after 1959, recovering the work of black women activists who pushed an intersected agenda has become even more important. Using the case of Sara Gómez, with special attention given to her lesser-known short documentaries, this chapter reevaluates how censorship, antiracism, and feminism worked in Cuba in the late 1960s and early 1970s.

Film historian Susan Lord writes that Gómez is both simultaneously "claimed and dis-claimed" (Lord 2003, 251).[7] The history of Gómez's equivocal reception in Cuba is also discussed in Lord's introduction to this anthology as well as in the interviews with Gómez's friends and colleagues published here. While scholars both on and off the island have given more recent attention to her work, including the 2007 colloquium "Sara Gómez: Multiple Images—The Cuban Audiovisual from a Gendered Point of View," Gómez has yet to be contextualized as an extension of Afro-Cuban political activism in the republic and a response to the 1959 Revolution's antidiscrimination campaign. Importantly, the lack of public acknowledgment of Gómez's work in Cuba is not indicative of her influence during the period but rather a reflection of the limited distribution of certain types of black art and the narrowing space for public debates about race in the 1960s.

Afro-Cuban author, literary critic, and close friend of Gómez, Inés María Martiatu Terry, rightly categorizes Gómez's fifteen documentaries as a type of "political cinema" that reflected the extraordinary moment that they lived in and the political tensions of the time (Martiatu Terry in this volume). One of the ways Gómez accomplished this was by showcasing black and *mulato* neighborhoods and how they changed or remained the same as a result of revolutionary programs. Some scholars have incorrectly suggested that Gómez's attention to working-class Cubans of African descent was a result of her own background and "marginalization." However, as Martiatu explains, Gómez did not come from a poor black family. Rather, she was raised by four aunts—a piano professor, a painter, a dentist, and a dressmaker.[8] Gómez was a member of the small but highly educated black middle class, and she focused her films on how the Revolution impacted Afro-Cubans—especially black women (Martiatu 2007, 1).[9] As a part of a group of black intellectuals, Gómez, like her friend Martiatu, worked to develop a black consciousness on the island by inserting Afro-Cuban history, culture, and politics into the revolutionary narrative.[10]

Cubans of African descent faced considerable challenges to their demand to tackle lingering racism during the first decade of the Revolution. In addition to Castro's public claims that racial discrimination had been eliminated and dismissal of black critics as ungrateful, in June 1961 (two months after declaring the Marxist Leninist nature of the Revolution), the young leader declared: "Within the Revolution, everything! Outside of the Revolution, nothing!" In this speech, titled "Some Words to the Intellectuals," Castro argued that artists and intellectuals had creative freedom to do whatever work they desired but that the Revolution had the right—and its was the larger right—to review (and prohibit if necessary) any art form that would ideologically damage Cubans: "We have the responsibility to lead the people and to lead the Revolution, especially in the midst of a revolutionary struggle" (Castro 1961).

However, the speech did not mention socialism or try to validate its claims with Soviet ideology. Instead, Castro depicted the Revolution as a battle for the reeducation or decolonization of Cuban minds. In addition to attempting to unify the country after the US-backed Bay of Pigs attack in April 1961, Castro's speech took place as part of a series of meetings and public forums between intellectuals, the ICAIC, and the Consejo Nacional de Cultura (National Culture Council, or CNC) in response to the censoring of the film *P.M.* (Sabá Cabrera and Orlando Jiménez Leal, 1961). A British traveler to the island described the film as showing black and *mulato* Cubans "drinking, arguing, loving, quarrelling, [and] dreaming. A blurred negress stands in front of the lens, and the camera moves back to take in the whole jostling, sweating scene . . . the only sound is the roar of so many Cuban voices, the clink of glasses and ice from the bar, and the music" (Nicolas Wollaston quoted in Chanan 2004, 134). More pointedly, Bob Taber highlighted the difference between the Cubans portrayed in the film and the Revolution's famous literacy martyr, saying, "I didn't see a single Conrado Benítez among them, with a rifle in one hand and a book in the other" (2012, 14).

Contemporary scholars continue to dispute why the Revolution banned *P.M.* Some argue that the ICAIC and the CNC found the film's focus on black nightlife counterrevolutionary and in conflict with the celebratory rhetoric that consumed the island after the defeat of forces at the Bay of Pigs. Others see the ban as the first step in what would become a state-supported censorship campaign that only valued positive portrayals of the Cuban Revolution for both domestic and international consumption.[11] Susan Lord concludes, "The story of *P.M.* is more than a story of the censorship of a film that coincidentally has black content; it is a story about the struggle over how to tell the story about race" (2009, 184–85). Surely not coincidentally, the censoring of art featuring Afro-Cuban life, the closing of black social clubs that had existed since the late nineteenth century, and the ICAIC's later choice not to screen any of Sara Gómez's documentaries reflected Cuban conflicts over who was allowed to represent blackness and what images of blackness were considered revolutionary.[12] The state's distaste for *P.M.* centered on the fact that blacks in the film, while obviously working class (and later interviews even identified them as revolutionaries), did not accept the new government's plans to reform them. The Afro-Cubans caught on camera for *P.M.* saw little reason to give up their nightly leisure activities, nor did they fit into the parameters of appropriate revolutionary blackness, which valued clean-cut and grateful workers or *brigadistas* (Benson 2016, 198–230). Instead, these dancers were individuals who, like Gómez, dared to pursue their own destiny and definition of the Revolution.

Sara Gómez's short documentaries dialogued with many of these and other pressing questions facing Cuba in the 1960s. She explored themes related to class divisions, racial discrimination, and gender inequalities, and she used the lens of the camera and ethnographic techniques to tell stories about the realities of revolutionary life. Gómez directed her first solo documentary, *Iré a Santiago*, in 1964, three years after the *P.M.* controversy (she had previously been an assistant director on two other short documentaries).[13] *Iré a Santiago* narrates the history of Cuba's largest eastern city, Santiago, from the perspective of black and *mulato* Cubans, who composed a large percentage of the city's population at the time. The film begins with and is titled after a quotation from the Spanish author Federico García Lorca's 1930 poem, "Son de Negros en Cuba" (Blacks dancing to Cuban rhythms): "When the full moon rises, I'm going to Santiago. I'm going to Santiago in a carriage of black waters." Some years later, Compay Segundo, a member of the Buena Vista Social Club, put the poem to music (Arcos 1998)—Segundo's song resonates in the background of the film's opening scene while the camera tracks a *mulata* woman strolling into the center of the city.

Gómez frequently began her documentaries with images of Afro-Cuban women doing routine tasks such as cutting cane, cooking, walking to the market, or dancing. These panoramic moving shots, always accompanied by Cuban music, were one of the ways the director foregrounded the experiences of black and *mulata* women in her work and positioned them as central to building a new Cuba. While she does not interview any Cubans in *Iré a Santiago*, the young director achieves an intimate feeling with the protagonists in the documentary by following them with her camera into their homes and into other private moments, such as a scene in which a young black couple is out on a date.[14] Through such strategies, Gómez reveals the diversity inside Cuba's black population and highlights diasporic cultural practices. She skillfully links Cuba to Haiti by dedicating a quarter of *Iré a Santiago* to tracking a funeral procession for Esperanza, the president of a "French" society. "In Santiago, there are blacks who call themselves French," she says, "because their ancestors arrived in Cuba when white planters fled Haiti to escape the neighboring island's revolution which had freed its slaves." Even as the documentary notes that there are no longer any French people in Cuba and that the coffee plantations they owned have long disappeared, Gómez employs footage of more than fifty Afro-Cubans marching behind Esperanza's casket to demonstrate the cultural significance of black social clubs like the French society in structuring life in Santiago.

Gómez continued to draw attention to black social clubs in *Guanabacoa: Crónicas de my familia* (Guanabacoa: Chronicles of my family) (1966), this time through members of her own middle-class family who attended dances at elite Afro-Cuban societies before the Revolution.[15] The documentary offers an inside portrait of black refinement and culture through images of Gómez's uncles playing music in locales ranging from Havana's Central Park to the philharmonic orchestra. Gómez combines views of well-dressed aunts attending Catholic mass with still studio portraits of other family members at different moments in their lives, including images of babies in white christening gowns and wedding parties. One by one she introduces her family and, acting as the narrator, she remembers, "*mulato* cousins in nice suits and visiting uncles with hard collars and houses where clarinets were kept in leather cases." Watching the documentary, it is clear that the young director has fond memories of her childhood in her grandmother's home and the black cultural practices (art, music, and religion) that she learned there. Throughout the film, Gómez emphasizes her family's class status by describing how her aunts did not attend public dances because they were "decent women." Instead, she explains, they supported events and dances at El Progresso and El Provenir—two Afro-Cuban societies that Gómez says were clubs only for "certain blacks."

Combined with the scenes of the French society in *Iré a Santiago*, Gómez's accounts of Afro-Cuban associations in *Crónicas de mi familia* reflect on the controversial closing of black and *mulato* social clubs in the early 1960s. As the new government began to integrate and abolish elite white societies and recreational facilities, it faced the question of what to do with similar organizations for people of African descent. These mutual aid societies had existed since the late nineteenth century and served as spaces for middle- and upper-class Afro-Cubans, not only to gather and network but also to push for social and political change.[16] However, most private clubs—both black and white—were gone by the mid-1960s when Gómez made this documentary. Revolutionary leaders and some Afro-Cubans saw little need for these clubs after the 1959 racial integration campaign. Therefore, Gómez's mentioning of them in her films—in a positive way no less—while highlighting her own middle-class roots is likely one of the reasons her works were not screened in Cuba when they were made.

Crónicas de mi familia, however, was not a simple statement in support of Afro-Cuban clubs. While Gómez warmly remembered the dances her relatives had attended, she also acknowledged that the societies were exclusive. At the end of the short film, Gómez shows her favorite cousin, Berta, leaving her kitchen—where she had been sitting moments before surrounded by relics of the Virgin Mary and Catholic saints—and walking out of her house.[17] The documentary ends, much like *Iré a Santiago* began, following an Afro-Cuban woman down an unpopulated street. Gómez asks: "Will we have to fight against the necessity of being a better and superior black? To come to Guanabacoa and accept a complete or total history—a complete picture of Guanabacoa and to tell it all." With these words, Gómez recognizes and questions the tensions between working-class and middle-class blacks, something the Cuban Revolution's antiracist campaign often failed to do. These documentaries suggest that she saw something to be admired in the popular French society of Santiago and in the refined clubs of Guanabacoa, but she also questioned how Afro-Cuban associations perpetuated class hierarchies.

In trying to paint a complete picture of black Cuba using case studies from cities outside Havana, Gómez's work marks continuities between pre- and post-revolutionary life. She celebrated her family's history even as she felt compelled not to be a "middle-class girl who played the piano" and struggled to meld her own class background with revolutionary ideals. She insisted on using routine images of black life, including its contradictions (such as shots of Catholic religious idols sitting next to Santería *orishas* or 26th of July Movement paraphernalia in the background of a French society's funeral procession), to portray Afro-Cubans as normal humans. In doing so, Gómez built on the work of previous Afro-Cuban activists and challenged notions of grateful, simplistic, revolutionary blackness seen in other aspects of popular culture, while positioning black cultural practices as a part of present-day Cuba, not the far-off past.

By 1968, Gómez was using her camera to expose contradictions in the government's claims to have eliminated racism, and her work (in the Isle of Pines trilogy, for instance) stands out as an example of the ways Afro-Cubans continued debates about discrimination past the official end of the campaign. However, space for critiquing the Revolution continued to shrink as the decade progressed. Over four hundred intellectuals from seventy different countries gathered in January 1968 for the Havana Cultural Congress. The meeting, which celebrated the growth of a revolutionary and anti-imperialist consciousness in the developing world, was a congress of contradictions. On one hand, the Cuban government invited foreign intellectuals (often paying for their travel) and presented them with an image of cultural openness and opportunity on the island. On the other hand, the meeting served as a precursor to a five-year interlude, beginning officially in 1971, that Cuban historians now call the "gray period" in Cuban culture because of the limits placed on what was considered revolutionary art.[18] According to Martiatu, one of the topics challenged at the congress was the work of black intellectuals like Walterio Carbonell, who had fought to insert the history of Africa and blacks in Cuba into the public school curriculum. Revolutionary leaders accused Carbonell, along with other Afro-Cubans, of fomenting "black power." As a result, revolutionary leaders seized Carbonell's book *Crítica: Cómo surgió la cultura nacional* (Critique: How to build a national culture) (1961) and sent him to a reform camp to cut cane (Lord 2009, 185; Martiatu 2007, 13). Similarly, in 1968 the minister of education called Gómez and two colleagues—black playwright Tomás González and ethnologist Alberto Pedro Díaz—into his office under suspicion "of organizing activities diverging from the Revolution's ideological line and encouraging black power" (Martiatu 2007, 14). These charges point to the shrinking space for intellectual creativity in the late 1960s but also to the ways that the revolutionary government targeted some Afro-Cuban activists as counterrevolutionaries.

Race added an additional layer to the contradictions of the 1968 Havana Cultural Congress and raised the stakes for black and *mulato* intellectuals who questioned the new government. The three Afro-Cuban directors then working at the ICAIC each experienced this period in different ways. When describing a film he had made that was considered "inopportune" (and therefore not released in Cuba until years later), Sergio Giral said, "That was hard to take, because I've always felt a sense of political and social responsibility and wanted what I do to serve the revolutionary process. You exercise a form of self-censorship in not wanting to destroy the cake by sticking your fingers in it too much" (Sarduy and Stubbs 2000, 266). Giral's comment, though brief, explains why slavery and the lives of blacks in the nineteenth-century colonial period provided the content of the majority of his films. Rather than risk having his work censored, Giral chose topics that featured Afro-Cubans and educated audiences about blackness without intervening in contemporary affairs. Giral, interviewed in this volume, had a long and successful career in Cuba until the 1990s, when he moved into exile for economic reasons.

In contrast, the second black director at the ICAIC—Nicolás Guillén Landrián, nephew of national poet Nicolás Guillén—made documentaries that explicitly questioned contemporary issues by using banned Beatles music in the background of one[19] and poking fun at Castro in another. Revolutionary leaders jailed Guillén Landrián, and, after attempts to "rehabilitate" him with excessive electric shock therapy failed, the young director escaped into exile.[20]

In this high-risk environment, only Gómez directed films that showed the lingering inequalities on the island and demanded that the Cuban Revolution meet its own social justice claims. While she did not face the physical persecution that Guillén Landrián encountered, likely because she remained committed to revolutionary goals even as she highlighted their failings, the ICAIC did not screen Gómez's documentaries about youth reform camps at the time when they might have been most useful.[21]

The Isle of Pines films question why so many black and *mulato* youth were sent to reform camps. For these pieces, Gómez took on the role of ethnographer and mixed interviews with teenagers on the island with statements from revolutionary leaders describing the purpose of the reform camps. In *En la otra isla*, Gómez questions a seventeen-year-old dark-skinned girl named María about her family in Havana and her daily schedule at the camp. (See fig. 8.1.) María explains that she has seven brothers and sisters and that her mother was a prostitute before the Revolution. "But now she is no longer working on the street," María states in reference to a new program that provided former prostitutes with opportunities to attend school and obtain employment.[22] The young girl proudly describes her goal to become a hairdresser and outlines her daily routines. These include studying political culture in the morning and straightening her hair with a hot comb in the afternoon. Other than the somewhat unsettling image of a white, blonde Cuban instructing María on how to straighten black hair (there are seemingly no black female revolutionary leaders to mentor young black girls on hair care), Gómez's overall portrayal of María is hopeful, and the teenager seems genuinely happy with the education she is receiving on the island. It remains unclear, however, how María arrived on the Isle of Youth.

Martiatu notes that Gómez was interested in learning more about the island because it had featured prominently in the Cuban press as a utopian space where young people could construct a revolutionary consciousness without the bourgeois prejudices of adult Cubans. However, revolutionary authorities sent kids to the island if they got into trouble with the law, failed to show the appropriate ideological formation, or their parents could not care for them. These circumstances were often linked to socioeconomic status. Martiatu notes that Gómez encountered on the island a disproportionate number of working-class black and *mulato* youth compared with whites (Martiatu 2007, 15). By showing how social inequalities of the past were reproduced in the present and invaded the Isle of Pines, Gómez challenged the Cuban Revolution's claims to have eliminated racial discrimination and provided equal opportunities to Afro-Cubans.

In another interview in *En la otra isla*,[23] Rafael, a young, dark-skinned black man, explains to Gómez that he had studied music for two and a half years at the National Art Institute. Opera was his specialty, and he sang the tenor part. Rafael describes his love of music and the numerous concerts he had performed in Havana until "problems" began:

Rafael: Then the problems started.
Gómez: Which ones?

Figure 8.1 Still of María in *En la otra isla*, 1968. © ICAIC

Rafael: Problems with some of the *compañeras* [women] in the group. A lot of them didn't want to work with me anymore. It didn't feel right to be working in a scene with me anymore. I didn't know why that was happening to me.

Gómez: Did they not like you because you came from the National Art Institute or because of your political formation?

Rafael: No, I don't think so.

Gómez: Were they political problems? What type of problems?

Rafael: [Looking directly at Gómez] I think the problem was race.

Gómez: They were prejudiced against you? ... Weren't they revolutionaries?

Rafael: Yes ... [pause] They were revolutionaries, some not, but most were, but the fundamental problem was to tell you more concretely that the only black man was me.... [pause] Look, Sara, this wasn't about color. It was about aesthetics. They needed someone to work with a white woman in love scenes in the opera. And imagine it ... [pause] if I might have to give her a kiss? When I took this problem of race to my supervisor, they said maybe it was there before, but not now; that it must have been some error.

Gómez then cuts to images of Rafael performing agricultural work before a final close-up of him speaking again. Nodding his head affirmatively, he says:

"I have confidence in the Revolution that things will get better. So now I'm doing agriculture, I'm doing something to help the revolution... being on the island has helped me a lot, they treat me well, and it is not like there... [pause] I have a question for you, Sara, Do you think one day, a black man, could sing *La Traviata*?"

This uncomfortable exchange highlights how many of the contradictions inherent in the 1959 campaign to eliminate racial discrimination followed Cubans into the late 1960s. On one hand, Rafael benefited from the opportunity to break into the predominantly white space of opera singing, having studied and worked with the National Opera in the early 1960s—something that would likely not have been possible before 1959. On the other hand, the ongoing public silence around racism after 1961 not only left Rafael with few spaces to denounce discrimination against him but also meant that he was ashamed of what happened to his career. He had internalized it as his fault that white women did not want to sing with him. Martiatu concludes that Rafael both accepted his punishment and punished himself—the island acted as a space of "purgatory" for him (2007, 17). As Rafael completed his "reform" through agricultural work, he distanced himself from his earlier goals and hoped that the Revolution would accept him as a hard laborer since it refused to accept him as a cultural laborer—a black opera singer. However, his shy, final question to Gómez, which he poses with a small smile and without looking at her face, reveals that he still hoped he might one day sing an Italian opera for a Havana audience, even as he was hesitant to believe that such a day would come anytime soon.

In choosing to highlight the stories of youth like María and Rafael, Gómez suggests that there were things that revolutionaries could learn from the supposed deviants of society. As she told Rafael during their discussion, "The Revolution can't do everything for you. You have to make it, the Revolution, yourself." These young men and women were not delinquents to Gómez. Rather, their perseverance, commitment to revolutionary equality, and willingness to sacrifice for Cuba positioned them as potentially more revolutionary than Cuban authorities unwilling to see past their race and class status. With this understanding, it becomes clear why the opening frame of *Una isla para Miguel* (before the title and credits) quotes Frantz Fanon's *The Wretched of the Earth*: "These vagrants, these second-class citizens, find their way back to the nation thanks to their decisive, militant action."[24] Gómez's documentary reminded viewers that Afro-Cubans were not vagrants or second-class citizens. Rather, they had something significant to contribute to the nation. For her, asking tough questions about the contradictions in the Revolution's programs and documenting on film the moments when the new government benefited

Cubans and when it failed them was not a simplistic endeavor. However, it was a necessary one.

She implicitly disagreed with authorities who questioned the usefulness of art to the Revolution when she told the editors of *Pensamiento Crítico* (in an interview reproduced elsewhere in this anthology), "Didactic cinema is a necessity, not a specialty. Many of us came to this vocation with the Revolution and ... always express ourselves in revolutionary terms." Gómez saw herself as a revolutionary and imagined her craft as a space where she could use the camera as a weapon to fight against injustice. As she explained in the same 1970 interview, artists had certain responsibilities to Cubans and to the Revolution: "We [filmmakers] have a vast public, including urban workers, campesinos, children, and adolescents. ... For them and with them we have to make films without making concessions. Films that touch on their interests. Films that are capable of expressing contradictions. And that have as a goal helping all of us. ... Is this overly ambitious? Will we achieve it? This has to be the goal" (Gómez 1970). In this way, while Gómez's documentaries showed the places where revolutionary rhetoric did not meet its own expectations, especially in relation to marginalized groups such as blacks and women, Gómez also always left a space for those issues to be resolved (Martiatu 2007).

In one of the last documentaries she made before her death in 1974, Gómez assessed changes in gender roles after the Cuban Revolution. Like her other pieces, this film also paid special attention to black women. Using ethnographic techniques, *Mi aporte* (My contribution) (1972) includes interviews with men and women workers in the Camilo Cienfuegos sugar refinery and examines how they managed shifting gender roles as more women were working and more men were expected to complete household chores. Cuban women had participated in the anti-Batista coalition in the 1950s and continued to be politically active during the Revolution's earliest years.[25] This participation was centralized in August 1960 when Vilma Espín created the Federation of Cuban Women to facilitate women's organizing in response to a call from Fidel Castro for more women to join the Revolution. From an original membership of seventeen thousand in early 1961, the FMC had expanded to over two million members by 1975 and represented approximately 77 percent of women over the age of fifteen.[26]

However, it was not until the late 1960s that women joined the labor economy in larger numbers. The urgent economic needs of Cuba and the desire to mobilize Cubans for the ten-million-ton sugar harvest in 1970 pushed the government to work tirelessly to bring women into the economy. In response, almost two hundred thousand women volunteered for sugar production and other agricultural work. Women also worked part-time in factories and obtained managerial and administrative positions in small retail outlets. Of the four thousand new managers named in 1968, 90 percent were women (Lewis, Lewis, and Rigdon 1977, ix–xxxviii). Similar to the campaign to eliminate racial discrimination that resulted in the relatively quick integration of public spaces like schools and social clubs, the campaign to bring high numbers of women into factories alongside men led to anxieties that gender norms were changing too quickly or not fast enough. *Mi aporte* intervened into this highly contested social issue through interviews with workers, FMC officials, and a group of women intellectuals. The film highlighted the double duty that many working women faced, it exposed Cuban men's perceptions and stereotypes about women workers, and it examined the impact of racial and class inequality on black women workers.

Mi aporte begins by contrasting the official "positive" version of women's experiences in the workplace with a much more complicated reality. As the FMC hymn plays in the background, popular Cuban television personality Consuelo Vidal interviews a group of women about their jobs in a factory. Each one says that she enjoys her new position and has not had any trouble with her male *compañeros*. An Afro-Cuban woman named Zenaida cheerily notes that she and her husband leave for work at 3:00 a.m. and 6:00 a.m., respectively, while their children get up, eat, and dress themselves before going to state-provided childcare and school on their own. Vidal asks the woman if she is overwhelmed by cooking and cleaning for her family at the end of a long workday. The woman grins and says, "Of course not, my husband helps me with all the chores."

> Consuelo Vidal: You've never had problems with your husband?
> Zenaida: No.
> Consuelo Vidal: Because you took on a job?
> Zenaida: No.
> Consuelo Vidal: Does he help you?
> Zenaida: Yes, when I wash, he cooks.
> Consuelo Vidal: He hangs out clothes? Really?! [Laughter].

Filled with music, laughter, jokes, and positive demeanors, the opening scene of *Mi aporte* paints a utopian portrait of the lives of women workers who are fulfilled, supported, and respected by their male counterparts, just as the FMC intended.

Gómez contrasts the sheer joy pictured in this opening scene with an interview with a male worker inside the factory who is critical of what he calls women's "absenteeism" from work:

> We do not agree with what you suggest.... There are problems here and very serious problems on some occasions. The *compañeras*, because they lack the habit of tough work—work generally carried out by men—their behavior is not the best. There are cases of constant absenteeism, poor habits at work, abusing the unhappy men who work around them through paternalism, if you will, since the men do their own work and part of the work the *compañeras* should be doing, because the poor *compañeras* cannot put in the physical effort required by the task they must complete. Then, the men help them.

The unnamed man's commentary reiterates common tropes about women workers—that they are not as strong as men and they lack discipline. Oddly, he calls men doing women's jobs paternalism and implies that women are taking advantage of men's chivalry by not working as hard. At another point in the documentary, he recounts the story of a pregnant woman who sleeps during work hours:

> The problem of paternalism.... We had a very interesting case of a *compañera* who was pregnant. Then, when it was time for her shift, she made her little round. And calmly, after two or three hours, she hid in a place she had prepped with her coat and her little blanket and her pillow and to sleep she goes. Then the *compañeros* who more or less worked in the same area, in the same zone, did the work for her.... Their stance did not help her, or them or the Revolution. It helped nobody. And if this *compañera* was here, it was not because factory work was indispensable to her, but because it was a need of the Revolution, a need of the nation for women to swarm massively to work to solve all the labor force problems we have.

By contrasting these two episodes (the interviews with contented women workers and with disgruntled men workers), Gómez shows how the Cuban Revolution failed to live up to its ideals. Similarly, she juxtaposes the official narrative shown in the opening clip of the television-style interview outside the factory with the grittier daily experiences and tensions inside the building. Viewers would have left *Mi aporte* questioning the success of programs to incorporate women into the workforce and seeing the ways traditional gender norms impacted how both men and women understood and used humor to deal with anxieties about each other's new roles. For instance, that the women in the opening scene all laughed at the image of Zenaida's husband washing and hanging clothes suggests that women were not quite comfortable with men as domestic laborers. As well, not only did the male worker seem to easily accept

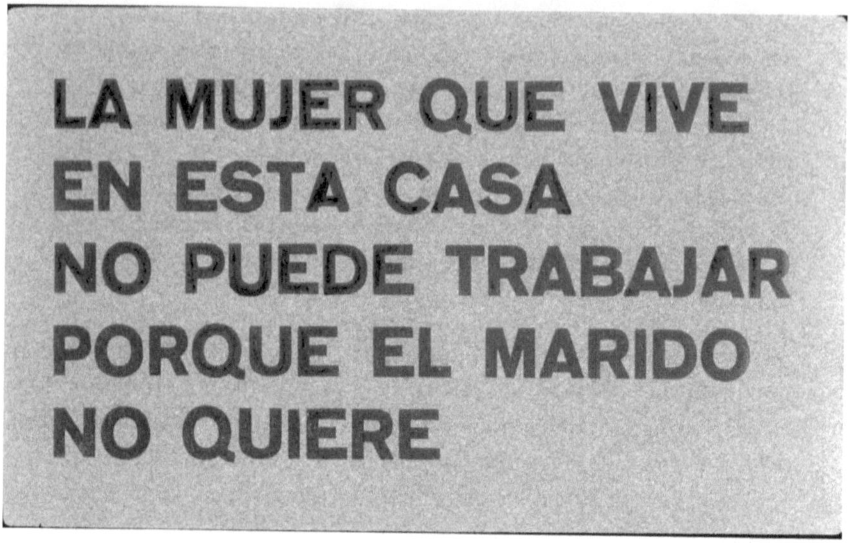

> LA MUJER QUE VIVE
> EN ESTA CASA
> NO PUEDE TRABAJAR
> PORQUE EL MARIDO
> NO QUIERE

Figure 8.2 Still of intertitles in *Mi aporte*, 1972. © ICAIC

that women were not physically capable of working in a factory because they were weaker than men, but he also chuckled while telling his story about the pregnant woman doing her "little round" and laying out her "little blanket." His laughter and use of the diminutive suggest a belief that while cute and playful, most women severely misunderstood real work. In the end, Gómez uses these scenes from *Mi aporte* to reveal that, even as revolutionary programs had altered the physical spaces inhabited by men and women, they had yet to change Cuban hearts and minds.

One of the most striking aspects of *Mi aporte*, however, is the way the documentary analyzes gender, race, and class together for an intersected critique of how revolutionary programs continued to be at odds with some working-class black women's realities. In the second half of the documentary, Gómez rides along as FMC representatives visit the homes of women who have "abandoned" their jobs to see what problems they are facing and whether they can be encouraged to return to work. The camera zooms in on a white middle-class FMC official as she converses with a dark-skinned black woman about why she has not been at work. The woman explains that she wants to work but that she cannot because the school her children are assigned to is too far away for her to drop them off and get to work on time. The mother also says that she relayed this information to officials and asked them to switch her children to a different school location, but they refused. The FMC official tries to explain that it is impossible to move the children halfway through the year and suggests that the woman accept the intern they have hired to take her kids to school and feed them lunch. However, the mother finds this option unsatisfactory, "because unless I drop him off at school, I can't go to work. Because maybe he says yes, that he's going to school. But when it comes down to it, he goes with the other kids to the river [ignoring the intern]. And one is left with the worry that maybe he drowned, or a machine killed him. I can't be calm at work, it's the truth. And I need to go work." With this example of the concerned black mother, Gómez pushes back against two notions: (1) that Afro-Cuban women do not want to work and participate in the Revolution and (2) that Afro-Cuban women are not good mothers and are lacking "culture" when it comes to raising their children. Instead, Gómez portrays the FMC official as unfeeling and unrelenting in her desire for the woman to work despite unreliable childcare options.

During an interview with another black woman, Gómez's stance on the needs of women revolutionaries becomes even clearer. This Afro-Cuban interviewee looks directly into the camera and says, "My problem is the following: I'm alone at home. I do all the household chores at home. I recognize the need that the Revolution has for labor and for all the *compañeros* to help the Revolution. I'm a member of the federation, and I would like to help the Revolution. When they generate the necessary conditions, then I will go to work."

Both of the women interviewed say that they are the "heads of household," suggesting that they are not married and do not have partners to coparent with. Nevertheless, they both have clear expectations about how they want to parent and who they trust to supervise their children. Gómez challenges stereotypes about Afro-Cubans while also pushing the Revolution to live up to its promises by showcasing women's—particularly working-class black women's—struggles to merge revolutionary needs with personal ones. Similar to the ways that Gómez represented María's and Rafael's stays on the Isle of Youth, the black and *mulata* women in *Mi aporte* are not counterrevolutionaries or women in need of reform; rather, it is the system that needs to be revolutionized to meet the needs of all its citizens. More importantly, it is clear that these Afro-Cuban women are aware of the limits of the Revolution and feel comfortable telling FMC officials and Gómez's camera about the conditions they require before they can become the contented and excited workers featured in the documentary's propaganda-like opening scene.

Gómez concludes the documentary with two focus groups that further complicate how *Mi aporte* challenges gender, racial, and class privileges to offer an inside look into continued (albeit nonpublic) debates about sexism, racism, and classism in revolutionary Cuba. The first focus group begins with a title screen asking, "Are we creating the conditions for the formation of the new woman? Some reflections on the subject." Gómez joins this conversation with three other professional young women (Lucía Corona, from the National Center of Scientific Investigations; Mirta Valladares, from the Cuban School of Industrial Design; and Gladys Egües, from the Cuban School of Journalism) as they discuss the difficulties of fulfilling the roles of mother and intellectual. Interestingly, and in a sign of changing times and an evolution in Gómez's self-presentation to the world, this is the first time she appears on camera with the Afro hairstyle that she began wearing shortly after Stokely Carmichael's 1967 visit to the island.

During the conversation, it becomes clear that these privileged, educated, professional women face many of the same problems as the working-class black women Gómez interviewed previously. However, in addition to lamenting the fact that men never miss work when their children are ill while women might have to take a month off to tend a sick child, they also debate potential solutions to these problems. One woman, Lucía, suggests that they should give up motherhood altogether. The three others disagree and debate the possibility of reeducating their sons by not raising them in a macho way. However, Mirta points out that this would lead to her son being made fun of at school: "If I educate my son in that way, taking away the prejudice of household chores, he will find, when he goes to school or with his friends on the streets, many contradictions. Because the first thing he will stumble upon is the little friend who will say: 'Oh no, no, I don't scrub, because that is a girl's thing. My mom has told me. That's a girl thing.'" Despite these limits, all the women agree that things are changing and that the Revolution gave them weapons to fight these battles: "The Revolution gives us weapons so we can grow." For the four professionals, the very fact that Gómez was making the documentary, and that they were sitting in the room having a discussion about gender norms, marked progress toward a more equitable society.

The second focus group takes place in ICAIC's private screening room with women who had just finished watching the film.[27] A heterogeneous group of Cubans (young and old, white and black, and from various classes) debate the points of the documentary, but, unlike the four professionals, it appears these women did not know each other before the screening. Despite their unfamiliarity with one another, the group has a heated conversation about the documentary and the filmed discussion between Gómez and her friends. They are especially disturbed by Lucía's comment that she only wants to work and create, to be an individual, and that she does not want to have a family or get married. The group feels that Lucía was too extreme and was closing herself off to opportunities that she might want to have later in life. They disagree with the proposition that a woman must renounce her femininity or maternal desires to be taken seriously as a worker, intellectual, or artist. They also criticize her for being selfish and for not advocating for all the other women who had children and families and needed support to work.

This interaction is telling because it marks the type of feminism that some Cuban women desired in the early 1970s. The women in this focus group want to be able to work and to be mothers, and they fully expect the Revolution and Cuban men to respect and support those goals. They also had choice words for the "unenlightened *compañero*" who thought that women used pregnancy as an "excuse" to be lazy; he is an example of men who "call themselves revolutionary but won't let their women work." Some of the women share stories with refreshing honesty about other revolutionary men who failed to accept and support women's move into the workforce, which suggests that they did not feel the need to censor their comments.

In the end, like Gómez's other documentaries, *Mi aporte* is multifaceted. Gómez applauds the Cuban Revolution for opening up a space for dialogue about gender norms and for giving women "weapons" to fight their battles—both a literal and a figurative reference, since women joined militias shortly after 1959. However, similar to her analysis of the Isle of Youth, the Revolution falls short of its promises and women still experience discrimination. In particular, she disagrees with the portrayal of poor black women as uninterested in joining the workforce as good revolutionaries, and she uses the film to draw attention to the social inequities (lack of childcare and the prevalence of women-headed households) that prevent some black women from participating. Despite the lived reality behind Gómez's evaluation of the limits of social change in Cuba, *Mi aporte* encountered strong resistance from the FMC. Martiatu recalls the response of Vilma Espín, president of the FMC:

> It was a critical documentary and the Federation thought it was going to be celebratory of the Federation and it wasn't. And when Espín saw that it was made by a black woman, she (well, here everyone is very authoritative) wanted to kill her. I'm the only one Sara told what she said: "You made this film this way because you were raised by maids and you had everything, but you don't understand the problem at all," Espín said. And she was the president of the Federation of Women, heroine of the Sierra Maestra, married to Raúl Castro, etc. And Sara was a nobody next to her. She called Sara a counterrevolutionary. She pointed the finger at her, and

like Cubans say, you know what happened next. They didn't show anything that Sara made after that. (Martiatu 2010, n.p.)[28]

That Espín thought that Gómez was critical of the Revolution's incorporation of women because of her class background (to clarify, her family did not have maids) shows just how much revolutionary authorities misunderstood the young director's feminist and antiracist project.

CONCLUSION

As described elsewhere in the volume, Gómez's funeral in 1974 was attended by her family and close circle of friends, including a collection of young people who would become some of Cuba's most famous writers, poets, and playwrights, including Inés María Martiatu, Pedro Pérez Sarduy, Georgina Herrera, Nancy Morejón, and Manulo Granados. Many of Gómez's contemporaries remember the day of her funeral in clear detail, both because of their anguish and also because of a violent rainstorm (*aguacero*) that began as Gómez was being buried. Martiatu (2005, 30) recalls,

> We were together and crying, and we all got wet when at the exact moment that they were going to bury Sara, the sky broke in a surprising rain shower. A torrential *aguacero* and there wasn't any way for us to move, no one did anything. The *aguacero* was so strong, and so much water fell in so little time that the streets of the cemetery filled up and the water ran over the gutters... a goodbye from Ochún and Yemayá, probably. When Sara was under the ground the rain stopped as quickly as it had begun.

Later, the group returned to Manolo Granados's home to console one another, cry, and say goodbye to Gómez with rum and rumba. In many ways, Martiatu's memories of that day epitomize Gómez's life—a life surrounded by friends, caught up in the storm of revolutionary change, sometimes unable to move and other times rushing forward to redefine Cuba. It seems fitting that an *aguacero* would accompany Gómez's funeral given that her work often strove to cleanse Cuba of its limitations and shine the fierce sunlight that comes after such a storm on the inconsistencies of revolutionary change.

Gómez is one of the critical missing links between Afro-Cuban activism in the early twentieth-century republic and Cuba today. Many of the new black and *mulato* antiracist organizations, especially women's groups like the Afro-Cubana Project established in 2010 by Martiatu and Daisy Rubiera, found inspiration in Gómez's documentaries and films. Despite the accepted narrative that debates about racial equality ceased after 1960 and did not begin again until the 1990s, documentaries such as *Iré a Santiago, Crónicas de mi familia, En la otra isla*, and *Mi aporte* demonstrate not only that pioneering filmmakers like Gómez were still pushing revolutionary leaders about contested social issues into the early 1970s, but so were her interviewees and postfilm discussants. That so many men and women were willing to speak candidly about their lives, struggles, dreams, and fears living in revolutionary Cuba encourages historians to take another look at how censorship worked in practice in this period and how all Cubans defined their Revolution.

In particular, Gómez's career with the ICAIC highlights how blacks and *mulatos* challenged the official declaration that racial discrimination had been eliminated and fought state attempts to silence public debates about lingering racism. Cuban conversations about racism did not end after 1961. Instead, they were reconstructed in areas outside the public sphere—in art, poetry, literature, and film. Additional research is needed on the seemingly large role black and *mulata* women artists played in this continuing struggle and on the ongoing transnational connections they invoked. Still, Gómez's work suggests that an emerging antiracist Cuban feminism was a part of the discussions taking place during this period. Her determination to feature all sorts of Afro-Cuban women on camera in respectful rather than stereotypical ways is a reminder that official discourses about blackness were not the only ones available. What other hidden transcripts, to use James C. Scott's (1990) term, might be found in the archives of 1970s revolutionary Cuba?

Gómez believed in a "perfectible Revolution" and used her art and her own intersected positionality as a black woman to push the Revolution in a more equitable direction. Martiatu notes that Gómez was not against revolutionary projects like the Isle of Youth or the FMC, but she thought "they could have been realized more coherently" (2007, 15, 18). However, as seen in how Espín reacted to *Mi aporte*, this vision of a Revolution in progress was not always looked upon favorably. Martiatu concludes, "ICAIC had a very special politics with Sara. They left her to make her documentaries, but they didn't exhibit them. They didn't show the documentaries. They didn't appear at the film festivals, but she worked, and kept working and working" (2010, n.p.).

After Gómez's death, her colleague Tomás González wrote that when he first met Gómez her hair was straight "under the neocolonial process of a relaxer," but that by 1973 she sported a small Afro. "Hers was the first natural black head in my country. A Revolution inside of a Revolution!" he claimed. This comment invokes Castro's claim that women's entrance into the workplace was a Revolution inside of the Revolution, but it does so in a way that highlights Gómez's contributions to Cuban national debates about blackness and Afro-Cubans' role in the Revolution in the late 1960s and early 1970s. Even knowing that her films would not be shown publicly for decades, Gómez continued to write and direct innovative scripts about pressing social concerns, often mixing together narratives about racism, sexism, and class hierarchies in ways that raised more questions than answers. In doing so, she captured the dynamic changes of the period and created an archive of everyday experiences of revolutionary life that existing film studies scholarship on her techniques of imperfect cinema have yet to uncover.

NOTES

Portions of this essay are reprinted with permission from the journal *Cuban Studies* and University of Pittsburgh Press. Original article: "Sara Gómez: AfroCubana (Afro-Cuban Women's) Activism after 1961," *Cuban Studies*, no. 46 (2018): 134–58.

1. Lourdes Martínez-Echazábal (this volume) discusses Gómez's influences in this film and provides a detailed overview of the entire work.

2. I discuss the contradictory nature of the 1959 Revolution's antidiscrimination campaign in *Antiracism in Cuba: The Unfinished Revolution* (Benson 2016). Portions of this chapter were previously published there.

3. For additional information on the ways revolutionary cultural institutions imagined blackness and African cultural practices as a part of Cuba's past, see de la Fuente's discussion of the creation of the Department of Ethnology and Folklore at the University of Havana in 1960 (2001, 285–96). As well, see Lord for a discussion of how, unlike those of her ICAIC colleagues, Gómez's films were not about "the 'past' of racial identity" (2009, 175).

4. For nineteenth-century slave rebellions, see Paquette (1990), García (2003), Childs (2006), and Finch (2015). For additional readings of slavery and abolition in Cuba, see R. Scott (2000), Knight (1970), Carreras (1989), and Zúñiga (2003). For the wars of independence, see Ferrer (1999), Sander (2010), Satorious (2013), and Nathan (2012).

5. As Guerra (2012) discusses, certain books (see, e.g., Betancourt 1959; Carbonell 1961) had limited circulation in Cuba and were ultimately banned by the revolutionary leadership. After leaving Cuba for exile, Moore and Betancourt continued to push revolutionary leaders to tackle lingering prejudices and racism, especially in the government. See the following works printed in the international press for examples: C. Moore (1988, 2008) and Betancourt (1961, 1964) and, more recently, Sarduy and Stubbs (2000).

6. I use the phrase "domestic racism" here because throughout the late 1960s and into the 1970s, Cuba became deeply involved and had much success in international antiracist and decolonial struggles. See Gleijeses (2002).

7. On Gómez's background, see Chanan (2004, 341–52) and Martiatu (2007). For additional information about Gómez's documentaries and their censorship, see Ebrahim (2007) as well as the interview with Iván Arocha in this volume.

8. Martiatu also discusses Gómez's family and upbringing in her interview in this anthology.

9. The Swiss film ¿Dónde está Sara Gómez? (2006) by Alessandra Müller, inappropriately portrays Gómez as someone who grew up in poverty while failing to recognize her middle-class roots and university-educated background.

10. By the late 1960s, some Afro-Cuban intellectuals had begun to form study groups such as the Seminar on Ethnology and Folklore (mentioned in this collection's introduction) to read and talk about a variety of issues, including the ways revolutionary leaders were discussing race and blackness. Frequently meeting in each other's homes or in the National Library, this group included writers, artists, filmmakers, and poets such as Nancy Morejón, Georgina Herrera, Manuel Granados, Sara Gómez, Pedro Pérez Sarduy, Rogelio Martínez Furé, Nicolasito Guillén Landrián, and Walterio Carbonell. Some of these intellectuals also published with the independent press, El Puente, until it closed in 1965 (see Alfonso 2012; Barquet 2011). Additional research is needed on how these Cuban black consciousness activists were influenced by, and had an impact on, other Caribbean notions of black consciousness/Negritude and US versions of black nationalism in the late 1960s and 1970s.

11. For additional reading on this debate, see Chanan (2004, 133–36); Guerra (2012, 162–64, 342–44); Lord (2009); Quiroga (2005, 251); and Casamayor (this volume). In particular, Guerra (2012, 343) describes how, five years later, black filmmaker Nicolás Guillén Landrián made a film resembling P.M. titled Los del baile (Those of the dance). It showed Afro-Cubans dancing and drinking in the streets of Cuba during the day. Saying "it might well have been called A.M.," she describes how revolutionary leaders also banned this film for its supposed "counterrevolutionary" content.

12. There remains debate about whether Gómez's documentaries were screened publicly. In an interview with me (May 31, 2010, Havana), Martiatu said the documentaries were not shown widely and that they were censored. Similarly, Ebrahim (2007, 111) notes that Cuban censors prohibited the showing of Crónicas de mi familia after it was completed, whereas Cuban filmmaker Rigoberto López (interviewed in this volume) says that while the documentaries did not get the circulation they deserved, he did attend a screening at the ICAIC. The truth probably lies somewhere in between. The documentaries were likely shown to small groups at the ICAIC, especially to other employees (López

worked there at the time as an assistant) since directors could host private showings to get feedback on their work. For *Mi aporte*, Gómez filmed such a postfilm discussion session and later included it in the final cut. However, there is little evidence that Gómez's documentaries interrogating revolutionary programs were screened publicly or widely in Havana or anywhere else in the late 1960s and 1970s. In his interview in this volume, Arocha comments on this issue when he describes Gómez's films as "ghosts."

13. This film is analyzed extensively by Lourdes Martínez-Echazábal in chapter 15 (this volume).

14. Casamayor-Cisneros (this volume) discusses this intimacy.

15. This film is discussed extensively in Casamayor-Cisneros (this volume).

16. For Afro-Cuban social clubs in the twentieth century, see de la Fuente (2001), Pappademos (2012), and Benson (2016).

17. Casamayor-Cisneros (this volume) elaborates on the ways that Aunt Berta occupies a particular place in this film.

18. For more on censorship in the late 1960s, see Abreu (2007), Barquet (2011), and Alvarez (this volume).

19. See the interview with Luis García Mesa (this volume).

20. See María Caridad Cumaná (chap. 9 in this volume) and Guerra (2012) for more on Guillén Landrián.

21. Martiatu also noted in my spring 2010 interview with her that Gómez had influential protectors at the ICAIC. Like other historians of 1960s Cuba, I rely heavily on oral histories and interviews to recount the experiences of revolutionary Cuba. In addition to the limited archival materials available to North American researchers for 1960s Cuba, the perspectives of blacks and *mulatos* are additionally marginalized in the written record. I met Inés María Martiatu Terry through my work with the AfroCubanas project. She was one of the cofounders of this black and *mulata* women's organization in Havana. Over a course of days, we talked about her work at the ICAIC, Gómez, and the group of young black intellectuals who met, worked, and made art during this period. The conversation between Martiatu and Lourdes Martínez-Echazábal published in this volume echoes much of what I learned in my own conversations. The interviews in this volume with Luis García Mesa and Sergio Giral also discuss Gómez's seeming ability to do and say things that others might not have been able to.

22. In 1961, the Revolution began a program to rehabilitate prostitutes. It lasted five or six years and was organized to deal with the forty thousand prostitutes on the island in 1959. See Pilar's testimony in Lewis, Lewis, and Rigdon (1977, 237–319) for an account of someone who participated in this process.

23. The interview is described in this book's introduction and by Casamayor-Cisneros.

24. The original quotation comes from the Spanish edition of Fanon (1965).

25. For women's participation in the Revolution, see Chase (2015). *Mi aporte* is discussed by various authors in this volume and is the focus of both Alvarez's and Lord's essays. It is also a topic of conversation in the interviews with Sergio Giral and Luis García Mesa.

26. See Serra's contribution (this volume) for more on the history and work of the FMC.

27. This is one of the private ICAIC screenings referred to earlier where audiences saw the documentary even though it was not widely circulated.

28. Giral has a somewhat different take on Espín's reaction in his interview in this volume.

BIBLIOGRAPHY

Abreu Arcia, Alberto. 2007. *Los juegos de la escritura o la reescritura de la historia*. Havana: Casa de las Americas.

Alfonso, María Isabel. 2012. "Ediciones El Puente y dinámicas raciales de los años 60: Un capítulo olvidado de la historia literaria cubana." *Temas* 70: 110–18.

Arcos, Betto. 1998. "Interview with Francisco Repilado aka Compay Segundo." *The Global Village*, January 1, 1998, Pacifica Radio KPFK 90.7 FM.

Barquet, Jesús J., ed. 2011. *Ediciones El Puente en la Habana de los años 60: Lecturas críticas y libros de poesía*. Chihuahua, México: Ediciones del Azar.

Benson, Devyn. 2016. *Antiracism in Cuba: The Unfinished Revolution*. Chapel Hill: University of North Carolina Press.

Betancourt, Juan René. 1959. *El Negro: Ciudadano del futuro*. Havana: Cardenas y CIA.

———. 1961. "Castro and the Cuban Negro." *The Crisis: A Record of the Darker Races* 68, no. 5 (May): 220–74.

———. 1964. *Sociología integral: La superación científica del prejuicio Racial*. Buenos Aires: Editorial Freeland.

Bronfman, Alejandra. 2004. *Measures of Equality: Social Science, Citizenship, and Race in Cuba*. Chapel Hill: University of North Carolina Press.

Carbonell, Walterio. 1961. *Crítica: Cómo surgió la cultura nacional*. Havana: Ediciones Yaka.

Carreras, Julio Ángel. 1989. *Esclavitud, abolición, y racism*. Havana: Editorial de Ciencias Sociales.

Castro, Fidel. 1961. *Palabras a los intelectuales*. Havana: National Cultural Council.

Chanan, Michael. 2004. *Cuban Cinema*. Minneapolis: University of Minnesota Press.

Chase, Michelle. 2015. *Revolution within the Revolution: Women and Gender Politics in Cuba, 1952–1962*. Chapel Hill: University of North Carolina Press.

Childs, Matt. 2006. *The 1812 Aponte Rebellion in Cuba and the Struggle against Atlantic Slavery*. Chapel Hill: University of North Carolina Press.

Ebrahim, Haseenah. 2007. "Sarita and the Revolution: Race and Cuban Cinema." *European Review of Latin American and Caribbean Studies/Revista Europea de Estudios Latinoamericanos y del Caribe* 82 (April): 107–18.

Fanon, Frantz. 1965. *Los condenados de la tierra*. Havana: Ediciones Venceremos.

Fernandes, Sujatha. 2006. *Cuba Represent! Cuban Arts, State Power, and the Making of New Revolutionary Cultures*. Durham, NC: Duke University Press.

Ferrer, Ada. 1999. *Insurgent Cuba: Race, Nation, and Revolution, 1868–1898*. Chapel Hill: University of North Carolina Press.

Finch, Aisha. 2015. *Rethinking Slave Rebellion in Cuba: La Escalera and the Insurgencies of 1841–1844*. Chapel Hill: University of North Carolina Press.

de la Fuente, Alejandro. 2001. *A Nation for All: Race, Inequality, and Politics in Twentieth-Century Cuba*. Chapel Hill: University of North Carolina Press.

———. 2008. "The New Afro-Cuban Cultural Movement and the Debate on Race in Contemporary Cuba." *Journal of Latin American Studies* 40: 697–720.

———, ed. 2013. *Grupo Antillano: The Art of Afro-Cuba*. Santiago de Cuba: Fundación Caguayo.

García, Gloria. 2003. *Conspiraciones y revueltas: La actividad de los negros en Cuba, 1790–1845*. Santiago de Cuba: Editorial Oriente.

Gleijeses, Piero. 2002. *Conflicting Missions: Havana, Washington, and Africa, 1959–1976*. Chapel Hill: University of North Carolina Press.

Gómez Yera, Sara. 1970. "Los documentalistas y sus concepciones." *Pensamiento Crítico*, no. 42 (July): 94–96.

González, Tomás. 1989. "Memoria de una cierta Sara." Special issue on Sara Gómez, edited by Antonio Conte. *Cine Cubano*, no. 127.

Guerra, Lillian. 2012. *Visions of Power in Cuba: Revolution, Redemption, and Resistance, 1959–1971*. Chapel Hill: University of North Carolina Press.

Guridy, Frank Andre. 2010. *Forging Diaspora: Afro-Cubans and African Americans in a World of Empire and Jim Crow*. Chapel Hill: University of North Carolina Press.

Helg, Aline. 1995. *Our Rightful Share: The Afro-Cuban Struggle for Equality, 1886–1912*. Chapel Hill: University of North Carolina Press.

Knight, Franklin W. 1970. *Slave Society in Cuba during the Nineteenth Century*. Madison: University of Wisconsin Press.

Lewis, Oscar, Ruth M. Lewis, and Susan M. Rigdon. 1977. *Four Women: Living the Revolution: An Oral History of Contemporary Cuba*. Urbana: University of Illinois Press.

Lord, Susan. 2003. "Temporality and Identity in Sara Gómez's Documentaries." In *Women Filmmakers: Refocusing*, edited by Jacqueline Levitin, Judith Plessis, and Valerie Raoul, 249–63. Vancouver, British Columbia: University of British Columbia Press.

———. 2009. "Acts of Affection: Cinema, Citizenship, and Race in the Work of Sara Gómez." In *Gender and Sexuality in 1968: Transformative Politics in the Cultural Imagination*, edited by Lessie Jo Frazier and Deborah Cohen, 173–92. New York: Palgrave Macmillan.

Martiatu Terry, Inés María. 2005. "Algo Bueno e interesante con Manolo Granados en el Patio del Resturante: El Patio y la ventanita del oro." *Afro-Hispanic Review* 24, no. 1 (Spring): 29–30.

———. 2007. "Una isla para Sara Gómez." Unpublished transcript of an address given at Fiesta del Caribe in Cuba. A version of this address is published in "Una isla para Sara Gómez." In *Hijas del Mwntu. Biografías críticas de mujeres afrodescendientes de América Latina*, edited by María Mercedes Jaramillo and Lucía Ortiz. Bogotá: Editorial Panamericana.

Moore, Carlos. 1988. *Castro, the Blacks, and Africa*. Los Angeles: Center for Afro-American Studies, University of California Press.

———. 2008. *Pichón, a Memoir: Race and Revolution in Castro's Cuba*. Chicago: Lawrence Hill Books.

Moore, Robin. 1997. *Nationalizing Blackness: AfroCubanismo and the Artistic Revolution in Havana, 1920–1940*. Pittsburgh: University of Pittsburgh Press.

Morales Domínguez, Esteban. 2002. "Un modelo para el análisis de la problemática racial cubana." *Catauro: Revista Cubana de Antropología* 4, no. 6: 52–93.

———. 2007. *Desafíos de la problemática racial en Cuba*. Havana: Fundación Fernando Ortiz.

Nathan, Robert C. 2012. *The Blood of Our Heroes: Race, Memory, and Iconography in Cuba, 1902–1962*. PhD diss., University of North Carolina at Chapel Hill.

Pappademos, Melina. 2012. *Black Activism in the Cuban Republic*. Chapel Hill: University of North Carolina Press.

Paquette, Robert L. 1990. *Sugar Is Made with Blood: The Conspiracy of La Escalera and the Conflict between Empires over Slavery in Cuba*. Middletown, CT: Wesleyan University Press.

Pérez, Louis A. Jr. 1995. *Cuba: Between Reform and Revolution*, 2nd ed. Oxford: Oxford University Press.

Pérez-Stable, Marifeli. 1999. *The Cuban Revolution*. New York: Oxford University Press.

Portuondo Zúñiga, Olga. 2003. *Entre esclavos y libres de Cuba colonial*. Santiago de Cuba: Editorial Oriente.

Queeley, Andrea. 2015. *Rescuing Our Roots: The African Anglo-Caribbean Diaspora in Contemporary Cuba*. Gainesville: University Press of Florida.

Quiroga, José. 2005. *Cuban Palimpsests*. Minneapolis: University of Minnesota Press.

Roland, L. Kaifa. 2010. *Cuban Color in Tourism and La Lucha*. Oxford: Oxford University Press.

Sander, Mark A. 2010. *A Black Soldier's Story: The Narrative of Ricardo Batrell and the Cuban War of Independence*. Minneapolis: University of Minnesota Press.

Sanmartín, Paula. 2014. *Black Women as Custodians of History: Unsung Rebel (M)Others in African American and Afro-Cuban Women's Writing*. Amherst, NY: Cambria Press.

Sarduy, Pedro Pérez, and Jean Stubbs, eds. 2000. *Afro-Cuban Voices: On Race and Identity in Contemporary Cuba*. Gainesville: University Press of Florida.

Satorious, David. 2013. *Ever Faithful: Race, Loyalty, and the Ends of Empire in Spanish Cuba*. Durham, NC: Duke University Press.

Sawyer, Mark Q. 2006. *Racial Politics in Post-Revolutionary Cuba*. Cambridge: Cambridge University Press.

Scott, James C. 1990. *Domination and the Arts of Resistance: Hidden Transcripts*. New Haven, CT: Yale University Press.

Scott, Rebecca J. 2000. *Slave Emancipation in Cuba: The Transition to Free Labor, 1860–1899*, 2nd ed. Pittsburgh: University of Pittsburgh Press.

Taber, Bob. 2012. "En defensa de PM." In *El Caso de PM: Cine poder, y censura*, edited by Orlando Jiménez Leal and Manual Zayas, np. Madrid: Editorial Colibrí.

DEVYN SPENCE BENSON is an Associate Professor of Africana and Latin American Studies and the Chair of the Department of Africana Studies at Davidson College. She is author of *Antiracism in Cuba: The Unfinished Revolution*. She is editor with Daisy Rubiera Castillo and Inés María Martiatu Terry of *Afrocubanas: History, Thought, and Cultural Practices*.

NINE

Racial Identity and Collisions
Gómez and Guillén Landrián

María Caridad Cumaná

SINCE THE TIMES WHEN CUBA was a colony, the island has had a tradition of struggle against racial discrimination. The abolition of slavery in 1886 did not result in the disappearance of racial prejudices. Nevertheless, this act of justice sparked a process of struggle for black rights that would not reach its full realization until 1959 with the triumph of the Cuban Revolution. In the neocolonial republic, several key figures raised their voices to denounce injustices imposed on the black Cuban population, including Juan Gualberto Gómez, Evaristo Estenoz (founder of the Partido Independiente de Color (Independent Party of Color), Jorge Mañach, José Antonio Ramos, and, especially, Doctor Fernando Ortiz. As the researcher Tomás Fernández Robaina states in his book *El negro en Cuba, 1902–1958* (Black people in Cuba), Ortiz's magazine *Estudios afrocubanos* (Afro-Cuban studies) was "a very different example of a form of struggle against discrimination and prejudice," above all due to the theoretical analysis that advanced in the magazine (1994, 141). The magazine published work dedicated to the study of Afro-Cuban roots and their contributions to the nation's cultural heritage and traditions. Intellectuals, journalists, and key figures from left-wing political circles waged diverse struggles to fight black marginalization and the disdain with which racial minorities were treated. However, the national authorities of this period acknowledged almost none of these denunciations.

With the triumph of the Revolution came the possibility of taking concrete, practical measures to eliminate racial discrimination—at least at the level of official state policy. Under these new conditions, the state created the Instituto Cubano del Arte e Industria Cinematográficos (ICAIC, or Cuban Film Institute), which started making films (news, documentary, fiction, and animation) that addressed the issue of racial discrimination and the situation of the black population in Cuba from a broad range of perspectives. Through the ICAIC, two key figures in the analysis of racial identity and the persistence of racism in Cuban society came to prominence in the 1960s. The first was Nicolás Guillén Landrián, a documentary filmmaker who had not been studied sufficiently until quite recently. The second was Sara Gómez. These two were not, of course, the only filmmakers to address these subjects, but I focus here on two particular aspects of their work: (1) their constant central concern to put black identity, religious practices, habits, and customs on screen in order to mark out the place that black people and their culture would come to occupy in the new socialist society and (2) the extraordinary aesthetic values demonstrated in their films.[1] My fundamental interest is to underline the anthropological-ethnological value of the work of these directors and to examine the ways in which they applied characteristics and styles of ethnographic cinema.

Early 1960s Cuban cinema benefited from the presence of filmmakers of great prestige and international recognition who came to the island to give workshops and teach young people how to make films. As a result, these filmmakers had a profound influence on up-and-coming artists at that time. For example, French documentary filmmaker Chris Marker (and the aesthetic proposals of cinema verité he espoused) had a significant impact on the education of the ICAIC's first generation of creators, including Tomás Gutiérrez Alea, Humberto Solas, Sergio Giral, José Massip, Manuel Octavio Gómez, and Santiago Álvarez. In Cuba, Marker's style mixed with those of other professionals, such as the Dutch filmmaker Joris Ivens, and Theodor Christensen from Denmark, who also facilitated workshops in those years of creative effervescence.

Nicolás Guillén Landrián entered the ICAIC in 1962 as a production assistant and was selected to participate in these workshops. He made his second documentary film, *En un barrio viejo* (In an old neighborhood) in 1963, in which he focused on what would later become an obsession in his work—daily life in the neighborhood and the way resistance to change threatened to violate, in one way or another, the new circumstances created by the emerging social system (with the ruptures characteristic of the revolutionary project, the call for popular participation, and the spread of a new system of values). The film's title itself points to the reality of a neighborhood whose social practices were destined to disappear over time based on the theoretical assumption that the Revolution would result in emancipation from, and the banishment of, everything that could remind people of the neocolonial past.

In hindsight, we know that social consciousness does not change at the same velocity as society at a macro level—many of the habits and customs shown in the film still exist.

En un barrio viejo begins with a freeze-frame on an elderly black man with a palm hat and a cigar; the credits appear over his face. An accelerated rhythm of drumming and singing is heard in the background, and this music both opens and closes the film. Might Guillén Landrián have intended to signal a cycle that is coming to a close? I do not think so—the final credits seem to announce that, although the film has come to its end, it is not the end: *NO ES EL FIN*. The truth of this insight is clearly revealed to us today—we know that even the religious practices to which Guillén Landrián alluded are still with us, with many nuances and new variations.

Four films compose what I call "la suite de Nicolás" (Nicolas's suite of films), referencing Fernando Pérez's well-known *Suite Habana* (Havana suite) of 2003 through the absence of dialogue and the powerful semantic charge of the image. The difference here is that African-origin religious practices have their own voice and a greater specific weight than they do in Pérez's film. Guillén Landrián's *En un barrio viejo* suggests a new ideological syncretism between politics and religion in a montage of images of Castro, Camilo Cienfuegos, and a series of revolutionary posters. The camera moves along shelves in a humble house where the portraits are placed, presided over by an enormous *prenda de palo* (a clay cauldron containing sticks and other ritual offerings). There seems to be no contradiction between religious practices and the new political system and its leaders. Rather, it would seem the latter are adored with the same devotion as the gods to whom these tributes are made.

Carolina de la Torre defines identity as "a certain awareness of the subjective self and the continuity of the I that assumes a configuration in evolution established through successive syntheses and re-syntheses, and (in speaking of social identities) the maintenance of internal solidarity, sense of belonging, and identification with the ideals of a group" (2002, 29, parentheses in original). In the four films I analyze as the suite, Guillén Landrián clearly focuses on the recurrent and not-at-all gratuitous presence of black subjects, and in some of the films he focuses on mestizos from Oriente province. We see their home life and their forms of dancing and the ways they arrange their hair, relate to one another, listen to the radio, share religious practices, and work and participate in the task of the Revolution. Guillén Landrián presents these images of faces, bodies, family environments, festivities, celebrations, and daily life with all the cultural authenticity generated by an anthropological and ethnological approach that uncovers the particularities of racial identity. Sadly, this approach will not be encountered again in Cuban cinema for forty-five years—except, of course, in the work of Sara Gómez.

Guillén Landrián's *Los del baile* (Those of the dance) (1965) calls on the internal rhythm of those who participate in a frenetic popular dance with the famous Pello el Afrokán leading the orchestra. The musical introduction announces the dancers, whose bodies, sensuality, and the abandon with which they give themselves over to the drums are intelligently portrayed by Guillén Landrián. The montage inserts the slow melody of a clavichord that reminds us of the dances and etiquette of the old societies of color.[2] The camera carries out a kind of synthetic summary of these social customs to the pleasurable cadence of the soundtrack. Through the movement of their bodies, the dancers liberate themselves from false ties and conventions, and the public square in which they are dancing becomes a carnivalesque space in the Bakhtinian sense.

According to Dean Luis Reyes (2004), the filmmaker's ethnographic vocation is clear in *Los del baile* and cannot be reduced to any sort of ethnic or political militancy. Although the black population is often the object of his gaze, Guillén Landrián gives people importance in his films as individual subjects in their own right. Guillén Landrián was a bohemian kind of person, but his preoccupation with this world did not translate into a fixation on racial labels or on specific groups. As well, his need to speak to his society compelled him to violate documentary conventions (in the strict definition of the genre): "He reveals the presence of the camera constantly and without reserve. In not a single film of his do people not look us in the eye. Who is that anonymous being? The intentions of the filmmaker are clear: human beings are history's actors—its doers—but this is never an abstract human being, but a very concrete one, with a name and a job to do" (Reyes 2004, n.p.). On this point I would take exception with Reyes. Guillén Landrián was indeed very interested in producing on-screen space for black people, which was nonexistent until that time. His interest in representing black people permits us to construct a discourse about this previously marginalized social sector, because after Guillén Landrián's and Gómez's contributions, the conflicts facing contemporary blacks disappeared from Cuban cinema.

Ociel del Toa (1965) is a major work in which Guillén Landrián examines the daily life of Ociel, a young boy, age sixteen—a rural worker and militia member who attended school only up to the third grade. The director combines almost minimalist music with cuts that go from family photos in a meager, rural house to the boy's daily work on a boat that sails the immense river. Guillén Landrián employs an economical use of typography that, between cuts, substitutes for Ociel's voice. An intertitle reads: "Now every Sunday we rural workers have our education plenary." The camera focuses on a girl behind a counter, and another intertitle appears: "The girl who sells soft drinks in the kiosk of the plenary wants to be a young communist. But she goes to church with her aunt." The girl lowers her head and looks away. Another intertitle reads: "And every day there are classes and the school is far away, but you have to go; otherwise you stay stupid."

Guillén Landrián does not economize on meaning—each intertitle exposes a different layer of significance. In this case, each phrase leads to a question. What do the education plenaries mean to these rural young people? Are they truly effective, or the beginning of a political ritual that will never be understood? To what extent could a religious faith that proclaims support for neighbors and promotes solidarity contradict communism? Could education liberate these rural people from their mystical chains and allow them to understand the new social order? More important than the several possible answers to these questions are the labyrinthine depths of the human group that Guillén Landrián examines—their world, relations, and insertion, out of conviction, into the multiple changes of the revolutionary process.

Guillén Landrián's poetics crystallize in his persistent discourse on things that are not as simple as they seem. He tells us that reality is more complicated than what appears on the surface: that transforming the consciousness of his films' protagonists will take years; catchphrases and slogans alone will not change things; and the path ahead is long. His work is not a celebration; it is about doubt and questioning. It is curious to note that people do not laugh in many of his documentaries. The camera captures skeptical faces as if they are asking, "What's this all about?"

In *Retornar a Baracoa* (Returning to Baracoa) (1966), Guillén Landrián used still photographs and photo animation for the first time in his cinematic production—techniques that he would freely apply afterward. He used these techniques as a way of disguising the narrator but also to create dialogue with images from diverse angles. The admiration he feels for Baracoa manifests through the profound anthropological and ethnological study of its inhabitants. The lyricism of the segment dedicated to "the port and a child" mixes the community's productive activity with the immobility of the people sitting in the park—and this in the context of the Revolution's job creation program in Oriente. The intercut fragments of people doing various activities in town, sitting in their houses listening to music, walking in the street, and working at their jobs may seem episodic and dispersed, but the unity of their discourse lies in their testimonial nature and the overall attempt to dig deeply into what occurs in this place in order to understand its essence.

These documentaries dealt with difference at a moment in the revolutionary process when the epic dominated cinematic discourse. Guillén Landrián preferred to direct his anthropological gaze to the more complex and contradictory aspects of social, political, and domestic contexts. As Lázara Menéndez notes in her book *Rodar el coco*, "Homogenization is important in guaranteeing a model for progress sustained by relatively univocal and global communications that engage the nation or a particular community. But it is also necessary to recognize how cultural dynamics promote heterogeneity, because they facilitate the development of personal autonomy and individual activity" (2002, 49–50). The protagonists in Guillén Landrián's films are precisely these heterogeneous subjects, and his studies of them allow us to better understand their cultural dynamics and development of both the past and the present.

The thematic spectrum of Sara Gómez's work was much greater than Guillén Landrián's. Of the sixteen documentaries she made, two express themes that enable a joint analysis of these two filmmakers: *En la otra isla* (On the other island) (1968) and *Una isla para Miguel* (An island for Miguel) (1968). Filmed in the same year, both works explore the great project of the Revolution to turn the Isle of Pines into the "island of communism"—a project that finally led to renaming the island Isla de la Juventud (Island of Youth).

En la otra isla lasts forty minutes and consists of interviews with a range of people who, for different reasons, live on an agricultural farm on the island. The people Gómez interviews provide testimonies that bring to light what I call "collisions." In each of these characters we find a confrontation of education, consciousness, and aspirations. These factors also collide with Ernesto "Che" Guevara's model of the New Man. The filmmaker's concerns regarding the human basis on which the Revolution depended to effect a definitive social transformation are made evident in the complexities of the individuals that Gómez portrays. With each case it becomes increasingly clear that these youth do not represent the perfect model of what the Revolution aspires to achieve, while the political leaders of this social project are willing to turn these young people into examples for others.

The island itself aspires to be a utopia of the Revolution, but this ambition collides with who these individuals really are. However, the optimism with which the filmmaker approaches the problem leaves the audience confident that this transformation will achieve a positive result. As Michael Chanan affirms, Gómez's purpose "is that we see those interviewed in the film as whole human beings and at the same time as representing particular social roles. [She places these together] in a mutually illuminating way: this helps the spectator make a judgment about the dialectic between the individual and the social" (1989, 29).

The most outstanding interview in this documentary is with Rafael, an opera singer. By acting and intervening in her own work, Gómez obtains one of Cuban cinema's most impactful testimonies of racial discrimination.[3] She opens a Pandora's box of prejudices that continue to exist in the new society—and there is still a long way to go to overcome these prejudices. Rarely have such themes appeared on screen in Cuba since this time, and certainly not with the impact and concern that this film and its director managed to have on the spectator.

Una isla para Miguel begins on the same island with the celebration of a disciplinary hearing in a camp for adolescents who have behavioral problems. Miguel comes from a very poor background—Gómez interviews his mother in an extremely poor house where she takes care of another seven or eight children. Miguel grew up in a marginalized environment where his mother, overwhelmed with domestic obligations, hardly had time to attend to him—a situation for which he has no respect. On the island, meanwhile, in what effectively is a youth reformatory, the audience might suppose that the Revolution would give this "rebel without a cause" something to live for, an ideal to defend, and a way of life that radically changes his path. Perhaps his volatility will become productive in the long run, and the codes he learned in the neighborhood about being a man and an unconditionally loyal friend (even if that friend was a thief or a murderer) would disappear in favor of the new political system and the Revolution.

Gómez's examination of marginality and perspectives from the edge of society repeats in her posthumous work of fiction, *De cierta manera* (One way or another) (1974/1977). This feature film engages in a deep exploration of the nature of marginalization and the difficulty of its eradication in the new circumstances of socialism.[4] Gómez places special emphasis on social awareness, ethical codes, and the difficulties of dealing with these and other aspects of the new order's system of values. Here, as elsewhere in her work, there can be no doubt about Gómez's legitimate inquiry into problematic aspects of Cuban society at the historical moment in which she is living. It is clear in her films that, rather than simply registering events, she wants to make audiences notice the importance of dealing carefully with complex humans and that the way people are treated determines not only their future but also the future of the country.

These two very distinct filmmakers brought conflicts in the social fabric inherited by the Revolution to the screen in a fresh, daring, and contemporary way. Their work transcends the limits of the historical times to which they belonged. Today, in light of new analyses presented in this book and elsewhere, the films of Guillén Landrián and Gómez enable us to better understand the history and present trajectory of Cuban society. Gómez stood on a platform that was still in the process of being built and added to it a need to explore the environment around her. Through her films, she observed the dynamics of a slow process of integration with the certainty that doing so was her contribution to social transformation and to finding a better tomorrow. Guillén Landrián, more skeptical and firmly entrenched behind his camera, was more of an observer—less participatory and more subtle. Yet he also bequeathed a wellspring of knowledge about culture and an audacious and sincere projection of his own race that has not been seen since in Cuban cinema.

Translated from the original Spanish by Helen Dixon

NOTES

1. Other filmmakers also examined the themes of interest to us in this book, both in fiction and documentary genres, and from various angles during the 1960s. However, these subjects were not as constant in their work as they were in Gómez's and Guillén Landrián's. Films of note include Manet's *El negro* (The black man) (1960); Massip's *Historia de un ballet* (History of a ballet dance) (1962) and *La decisión* (The decision) (1964); Hernández's *Abakuá* (1963); Alea's *Cumbite* (1964); Valdes's *El ring* (The ring) (1967); and Giral's *Cimarrón* (Maroon) (1967). Race is a constant throughout Giral's filmography, but he made most of his films in the 1970s and 1980s, later than the films analyzed here. In 1990, he made *María Antonia*, his last film in Cuba before he emigrated to the United States. See my interview with Giral (this volume).

2. See also Casamayor-Cisneros (this volume) and Benson (this volume).—Ed.

3. See this collection's introduction and contributions by Casamayor-Cisneros and by Benson.—Ed.

4. Víctor Fowler Calzada (this volume) provides an illuminating examination of *De cierta manera*. This film is also discussed in several other chapters. See the index for more locations.—Ed.

BIBLIOGRAPHY

Alvarado Ramos, Juan Antonio. 1996. "Relaciones raciales en Cuba: Notas de investigación." *Temas, Nueva época*, no. 7 (July–September): 37–43.

Caño Secade, María del Carmen. 1996. "Relaciones raciales: Proceso de ajuste y política social." *Temas, Nueva época*, no. 7 (July–September): 58–65.

Chanan, Michael. 1989. "Otra mirada." *Cine Cubano*, no. 127: 27–35.

Fernández Robaina, Tomás. 1994. *El negro en Cuba 1902–1958*. Havana: Editorial de Ciencias Sociales.

Fowler, Víctor. 2002. "Estrategias para cuerpos tensos: Po(li)(é)ticas del cruce interracial." *Temas, Nueva época*, no. 28 (February–March): 107–19.

Guanche Pérez, Jesús. 1996. "Etnicidad y racialidad en la Cuba actual." *Temas, Nueva época*, no. 7 (July–September): 51–57.

Hernández, Marucha. 1989. "Importancia de la obra cinematográfica de Sara Gómez dentro del cine cubano." *Cine Cubano*, no. 127: 20–23.

Menéndez, Lázara. 2002. *Rodar el coco: Proceso de cambio en la santería*. Havana: Editorial de Ciencias Sociales.

Reyes, Dean Luis. 2004. "Nicolás Guillén Landrián: El iluminado y su sombra." *Revista digital Miradas*, no. 7.

Torre, Carolina de la. 2002. "Identidad e identidades." *Temas, Nueva época*, no. 28 (February–March): 26–35.

MARÍA CARIDAD CUMANÁ taught Film and Television at the University of Havana for 15 years. She was Chief Coordinator for the Audiovisual Portal for Latin American and Caribbean Cinema at the Foundation of New Latin American Cinema, co-authored *A Look at Cuban Cinema, Latitudes of the Margin: Latin American Cinema before the Third Millennium*, and co-edited *My Havana: The Musical City of Carlos Varela*. She was Field Producer in Havana for the documentary Out My Windows (NFB). She is currently an Adjunct Faculty at Miami Dade College.

TEN

Rigoberto López Interviewed by Víctor Fowler Calzada

VÍCTOR FOWLER CALZADA: *I will ask you some questions so that you can organize your thoughts and provide answers. First, since in the end you had a different type of relationship from the one the rest of us had with Sara, how did you meet her? One of the largest mysteries about Sara Gómez is her process of finishing the film* De cierta manera. *You worked under Sara's direction on this film. How was it to work under her orders? And you ended up being a filmmaker. What sort of imprint did Sara leave on you?*

RIGOBERTO LÓPEZ: Feel free to interrupt me whenever you think I'm getting off track and referring to other things. Just before coming here I was finishing the mix of a film I'm working on.

VÍCTOR FOWLER CALZADA: *What's the name of the film?*

RIGOBERTO LÓPEZ: *Vuelos prohibidos,* about the present reality of Cuba—nothing to do with allowing people to travel or not.
    More than once I have said that if anyone has to humor my filmmaking now, to a great extent that is due to Sarita. It is her fault I developed a career as a filmmaker. I was a student at Rubén Martínez Villena secondary school in Vedado, although I lived in Cayo Hueso. I was raised there, I was born there, my parents lived there. I grew up in a *solar* [collective housing for the poor] on Hospital Street close to Parque Trillo. I bathed in the *solar*'s main room. And I think that the fact I was born there has a lot to do with not only my cultural universe, my identity, and my linkage with Cuban popular music but also my friendship with Sara. This, in a way, explains my relationship with her, perhaps

without me realizing it. So, there were times in my life, to which I will refer later, when all these things coincided and helped me grow up and helped me with my cultural orientation, a given sensitivity, and my meeting with Sara. And I think all these added force to the final result.

As I was saying, I was a student in secondary school, and I was going steady with a white middle-class girl—I was a *mulatico*, a student leader at that school. I played basketball. But then a really beautiful black girl arrived, one of those who were called *repatriados* [repatriated—those who used to live abroad and returned to Cuba after the triumph of the Revolution]. She came from the United States. She was the youngest sister of Sara Gómez Yera. She was, and still is, known as Micky. Her name is Micaela Perera Yera. So you can imagine the rest of that story. Micky was very good in math, and that was not one of my strong subjects. I was better in the humanities; I was a young poet. I wrote poems. Then we started going steady. Micky became familiar with my poems, etc. Then she mentioned her sister, Sara. At that time, Sara was assistant director to Tomás Gutiérrez Alea, who was shooting *Cumbite*. Sara came from *Mella* magazine, where she worked as a journalist and where there was a lot of cultural unrest at that time. And later on, Sara arrived at ICAIC working in the audiovisual and short documentary department. Then I started visiting Sara's home—or rather, Sara's mother's house, Juana—in Basarrate. This is important to mention—Sara used to live in Cerrada del Paseo Street, just three doors down from where [Félix] Chapottín [an extraordinary trumpet player who died in 1983] lived. Sarita taught me to dance jazz; she liked jazz.

VÍCTOR FOWLER CALZADA: *And where was that?*

RIGOBERTO LÓPEZ: This street is close to Zanja. It is a dead-end street close to a funeral home located on Zanja Street—close to that place there is Cerrada del Paseo Street, quite near Zanja Street. Sarita Gómez used to live on that street just three doors down from Chapottín and a duo of composers, Yanez and Gómez—the latter was Sara's uncle. Sara came from a black middle-class background. She was always reluctant to accept herself as a black middle-class woman who played piano. She was a piano student, just like any black middle-class girl should be. I also remember her aunt was a dentist. She is still around. I mean that people have a certain level of training and preparation—a certain cultural sophistication. She also had an uncle who composed music. She herself played piano, there was jazz, etc. So, going back to my relationship with Sara, I already mentioned I was studying at secondary school, going steady with Micky, and visiting Sara's house. There they prepared wonderful *croquetas*, specifically Juana, Sara's mother. And there you could meet Alberto Pedro, Tomás González, etc., at any time. I'm referring to 1963. I first heard about Malcom X and Martin Luther King there. They were frequently mentioned in that house, as well as [Frantz] Fanon.

VÍCTOR FOWLER CALZADA: *I was born on Basarrate Street between Valle and San José Streets.*

RIGOBERTO LÓPEZ: There is an alley from Basarrate to Infanta. I used that alley to either walk to Infanta, or, if I was coming from San Lázaro, I used it, too. Sara used to live on the first floor. I can take you there and show you the place. Micky, Juana, and Sara used to live there ... but I will go a little further since it is important for me to underline this. It really annoys me that sometimes people might have a sort of partial idea about Sara. She was a woman who went deeply into Cuban culture. She had a deep knowledge of the Cuban nineteenth century—a thorough knowledge that only a few have. I still remember never-ending conversations with her about Saco, Del Monte. But not only that, I mention this to say that I discovered the negritude movement thanks to Sara Gómez, and I learned about surrealism and Dadaism thanks to Sara Gómez. For example, [André] Breton's *Surrealist Manifesto* was yet to be published, but I read it in photocopies that circulated among this group of people. I discovered Césaire, Senghor, Diode, and more, and I became friends with René Depestre, who was close to Sara, and with whom I had a long relationship. We met him at Radio Habana Cuba, where he was working as a journalist. So I had the opportunity to be deeply influenced [by the black and radical cultural and political movements], although I have to say that I was a young man coming from a communist family, engaged in trade union work, and a young guy used to reading and thinking. One day my father took a Superman comic book from me and replaced it with *La Edad de Oro* [by José Martí], so that gives you an idea of who my father was. He read *El Quijote* three times. I read that book once and that was more than enough! He was a black worker with a strong sensitivity. Many from my generation used to visit him, to sing their songs for him, and to talk with him. A well-known poet from my generation also visited him to read his poems.

Now I will return to Sara and myself. Sara signed and gave me the book *Espejo de Paciencia* [a poem by Silvestre de Balboa published in 1608]. She also gave me *The Waste Land* by T. S. Eliot, which she also signed. Given the love we felt for each other, she was able to recognize a certain sensitivity in me and gave me those books to read. She was a woman, an intellectual—far beyond that of a filmmaker who was only interested in the "black" issue. She took on that issue because it is at the core of the essence of being Cuban. No one can understand Cuban culture and the Cuban nation without understanding that issue in full. If she worked on piracy or on musical instruments, and if she was frequently at La peña de Sirique [The Sirique Club in Havana] and a follower of the *filin* movement [US-influenced Cuban music from the 1940s to 1960s], it all resulted from the fact that she was a person moved by curiosity, by the fundamental axis of Cuban culture, of the Cuban nation. And that is why it is not possible to understand Cuba without knowledge of the popular culture that is at the core of it.

So, along this path she became interested in the marginal world. That's very important. *De cierta manera* didn't come out of the blue. That's why I said that it is a maturing process—a process of preoccupations and concerns that went hand in hand all through her personal life as well as her intellectual work. She gave me the book *Les Enfants Terribles* by Cocteau, and she told me, "You are a terrible boy." Sara was well aware of the works of Jean Cocteau. That was the time when Agnès Varda came to Cuba to shoot *Salut les cubains* (1963). And thanks to Sara, I met Varda in person. I was fifteen years old about to be sixteen, and with Sara, with Agnès, I was discovering a new world. I will always remember Sara, Agnès, and myself walking along Alameda de Paula while Sara told Agnès stories about the Cuban sugar aristocracy, about plantations in Matanzas province, and about *rumberos*. Sara asked me to cowrite a script with her for a documentary on Malanga, the well-known *rumbero* from Matanzas—a documentary that was never made and I'll explain why. And also a documentary on—which was a testimony to her particular way of seeing Cuba—underdevelopment, things that were happening under the sun in Havana. For example, how the high heels of Cuban women got stuck in the asphalt of the streets. She used to say, "What will happen when we are no longer underdeveloped? When a woman will not be touched while riding a bus?" She played with all these things. Once she asked me, "What would you say is the most sensual fruit?" I answered, "The mango." And she said, "Why not sweetsop, since you have to feel seed by seed?" That was Sara Gómez—that irreverent nature with a full mastery of Cuban custom. She had a sharp tongue. She only needed a sentence to crucify you.

I recall that Mayito García Joya, the well-known cinematographer and photographer who loved Sara, lived with his wife Marucha in a house in Vedado, and that was the headquarters of the Committee for the Defense of the Revolution on that block. They had a photo of Chano Pozo [1915–1948, Cuban percussionist, composer, singer, and dancer], since Mayito played the drums very well.

So Sara really admired that Mayito, a blue-eyed white guy, could play the drums so well. Even such a well-known person as Titón [Alea] was charmed by Sara since she was able to attract all those she met. It didn't matter if you were an intellectual or Eloy el Ambia [Afro-Cuban poet, former construction worker, director of "the yard" session at UNEAC (Unión Nacional de Escritores y Artistas de Cuba, or National Union of Writers and Artists of Cuba), who appears in *De cierta manera*]. I met all of them. Where? At the Hermanos Ameijeiras Hospital [located in Central Havana] while shooting *De cierta manera*. We had lunch there. Efigenio Ameijeiras [one of the brothers after whom the hospital is named] invited us to have our lunch there. El Ambia was the main force of the group. Just recently I was with Pablo Milanés having dinner at his house and I hadn't seen him in a long time. He surprised me by telling me he remembered that my father was the one who did El Ambia's tie for his wedding, since El Ambia didn't know how to do it and that was the first time he had ever worn one. Then El Ambia formed a bond with Sara since she was the one who introduced him to Malcom X.

I was drafted into military service. But before that, I was able to participate, led by Sara, in some of the debates held by filmmakers from the ICAIC regarding cultural policy. These took place in the 1960s, and they were something fundamental. It was 1963 or 1964 to be exact. To a certain extent, I was already starting to create bonds with the ICAIC—or rather, with people from the ICAIC. I met Titón and also an Argentinian poet who received an award at the Premio Casa and was Titón's friend. I also met some Cuban directors of that time, although I couldn't say we were friends. With some of them I had a close relationship and now we are good friends—for example, Juan Carlos Tabío. With others, I had a brief relationship: Nicolasito Guillén [Landrián]; Fausto Canel; I met [Alberto Roldan]. Those were film directors at that time, some of whom emigrated. I also worked with Sergio Giral as an assistant director. I worked on *El otro Francisco* (1974) as a first assistant director. He left some time later. Sarita, Juan Carlos, Giral, and Nicolasito Guillén were very close to Titón. The latter was like a mentor to all of them, or like a magnet to whom they were attracted. They shared perspectives and thoughts about events taking place.

Then in 1964 I was drafted into the army. I had won a scholarship to study philology in Paris, and the draft frustrated my plans. It also interrupted a moment when I was coming close to filmmaking. I have to mention the fact that my relationship with Sara, which allowed me to meet Titón and the rest, enabled me to see filmmaking as a possibility. I also should say that I had an interest in filmmaking long before I met these people. I was interested in watching films, going to film houses, and watching documentaries—especially Cuban documentary films and specifically the ICAIC newsreels directed by Santiago Álvarez. My wish was to do that as well. And this, together with films by Glauber Rocha—for example, when I watched *Dios y el Diablo en la Tierra del Sol* (1964) and later on had an opportunity to meet him in person—all these things made me think that filmmaking was possible. And my relationship with Sara increased this desire.

Then I was drafted, and the possibility of making documentary films with Sara ended as well as the scholarship to study in Paris. Overnight I was a draftee—a radio technician on the first detachment of MiG-17 planes stationed fourteen kilometers away from Santa Clara. I longed for all my usual stuff. I was a high school student in Vedado, taking the preuniversity level with Micky, Sarita's sister. I also missed my parents. I came to Havana every four months—I really regretted losing the possibility of continuing my development in that environment. While in the army, I was a sort of *avis rara* [rare bird], reading Vallejo, Hemingway, and Latrouse. People used to look at me as sort of a freak.

Something I will always remember about Sarita was shooting *Iré a Santiago*, a documentary film. She wrote me a beautiful letter. Bear in mind the fact that I'm referring to 1964. I cherish all the things Sarita either sent or gave me—the signed books, the letters. In that letter Sarita told me she was working on *Iré a Santiago* and she also mentioned another project, but I don't remember which one right now. And who could imagine that on my birthday, July 6, at the air base in Maleza, fourteen kilometers away from Santa Clara—I was told there was someone to see me. It was a Sunday. There were Sarita and Micky with a cake. She took all that trouble to travel that distance to bring me that cake. Then, when I was away on leave, Sarita told me that Titón was shooting *Memorias del Subdesarrollo* (1968) at the National Library and that he needed some extras. So she and I were extras in that film. Next time you watch *Memorias del Subdesarrollo*, you will see me sitting next to Sarita in the colloquium. This relationship during 1963–1964 gave me the opportunity to be close to the cultural polemics of the time, the debates of filmmakers, the issuing of the manifesto of Cuban filmmakers, published in the *Gazeta Oficial*.

...

When no one was talking about the black issue, Sara was. And she showed it in her aesthetics. Who were Sara's friends? Sara could introduce me to Stokely Carmichael, Ralph Brown, René Depestre, and Theodor Christensen [the Danish filmmaker], or she could introduce me to Lanza and Plátano, two buddies—both of them Abakuá—who were always together and were known by those names. And they were friends of Sara's. That allowed her to shoot *De cierta manera*. When the shooting was over and the cameras were off, she was just another member of the family. She would solve problems. She was aware of who was being initiated—she knew everything, who was selling pot....

...

Once I was discharged from the army, I wanted to work in filmmaking, as I already told you. But I forgot to mention something. Thanks to Sarita, I visited the film archive many times and had the chance to see something that has been mentioned many times—what Cuban filmmaking owes to Italian neorealism. Thanks to her, I was able to feel that this was a boiling kettle, all these ideas. And you could understand why the ICAIC was at that time in the vanguard of Cuban culture. I remember watching almost all the French New Wave, feeling the magnetic pull it had on Sara—in particular Truffaut's *The 400 Blows* (1959). I don't know how many times Sarita watched that film. Italian neorealism, Visconti, etc., *The Bicycle Thief* (1948), etc. All this helped in Sara's formation. All this mixed Sara in with the Brazilian New Cinema, basically due to her close relationship with Glauber Rocha.

I won't say much about the role I played in the making of *De cierta manera*, but I had a big part in that process. The Abakuá ceremony, the killing of the goat, who was present? [The Bolivian filmmaker] Jorge Sanjinés. Ask Mario Balmaseda about this. We were shooting and Sara was sitting on the side eating a mango. Quite calm. I was running up and down securing things. It was a little bit perturbing for an actor such as Mario Balmaseda to see a film director so relaxed. But she was fully aware of what was happening. And I understand it. If she were to borrow another style of directing, she wouldn't be able to attain the results she wanted, given the fact that you are working at the same time with professional actors and with nonactors. It would be better to avoid all the film paraphernalia. The film has some defects that were transformed into advantages since they provide an authentic nature to the film.[1] The authenticity of the film has made all these flaws into features that were almost done on purpose.

Not so long ago, I was mentioning the fact that the script of *De cierta manera* used a unique language—telling a real story, of real characters, with characters that play themselves.[2] If you take a nonprofessional actor to play a given role, there will be flaws, but since that person will be himself or herself on camera, there is no problem—they will act quite natural. So, to achieve that final result, you have to direct in a certain way. Camera in hand, no tripod, and once shooting is finished, they all will share a drink, etc.[3] Consider the example of the character Guillermo García. How did Sara discovered this character? What type of sociological knowledge did she have to find for these characters and their problems? She didn't take a stance from outside. Rather, she saw everything from within.

VÍCTOR FOWLER CALZADA: *How did you establish a link with* De cierta manera?

RIGOBERTO LÓPEZ: Before being drafted into the army, there was a guy known as "Gato." He was a member of the state security forces, and he had a crush on Sarita. . . . Castillo [Gato] was head of the film archives at the radio and TV institute [Instituto Cubano de Radio y Televisión, or ICR], so he took me to work at ICR. I started as an assistant cameraman, but I was also sort of a handyman—place the tripod there, etc. Then I became an assistant director, and I worked with Simon Escobar. I began shooting documentary films. I worked on a rather strong documentary film called *Port: Take 1*. Once I arrived at the port, I realized that we needed to make a real documentary film. For example, people were queuing to buy ice while an abandoned ice plant was covered with weeds. Streets were covered with caustic soda, an imported product—bags of it. Equipment for oil prospecting was bought in Romania, and I looked at the material of *Noticiero ICAIC* [newsreels] and found out about a huge filter for sugarcane, something like a house, brought from France. All this was covered by weeds and was rusting. And there was a character who I compared to Maceo, and he told me, "Sometimes when I get home I feel like crying." With all this evidence I went to see deputy ministers and the like, asking what they thought about all this idle material. News of this spread to the ICAIC, and Julio García Espinosa and others were told that "there is a young guy at ICR who seems to have potential." Then I had a meeting with Julio and came to work at the ICAIC. My film was shown to members of the council who directed the institution: Julio García Espinosa, Alfredo Guevara, Raúl Taladrid (the father of the journalist Reinaldo Taladrid), and Santiago Álvarez. I had to fill out forms with all my life details. Alfredo really went deep to find out whether you were really interested in filmmaking.

Then I started to work as an assistant director with Manuel Octavio Gómez on his film *Ustedes tienen la palabra* (You have the floor) (1973). There were two assistants: me and Fernando Pérez. Once I finished working on that feature film, Sara was set to start *De cierta manera*, and she called me to be her assistant director even as the script was being finished. Sara analyzed the script with many people. Titón was a sort of tutor. He visited the location with Sara only once—Tomás was the one always present. I was present during part of Sara and Iván's editing of the film, and then I traveled to Panama. Sara had a green diary, which I have. There she wrote down things she wanted to do and what not. Iván Arocha was very close to Sarita. Those who worked with her became part of her closest circle of friends. Pastor Vega traveled to Panama to shoot *La Quinta Frontera* and took me as an assistant director to compile historical information. One day after returning from Panama, I heard about Sarita's death. She suffered an asthma attack. Sergio Vitier, the musician, took Sarita down from the building, but she went into respiratory arrest. We were driving in a car and I was looking at *flamboyan* trees, and Tomás told me, "Look—when those trees look like that, something bad will happen."

In *De cierta manera*, Sara wanted to present the confrontation between the marginal world and the petite bourgeoisie in Cuban society. Mario was a man undergoing initiation at the moment of the creation of a new society and the quest for the New Man. The teacher, Yolanda, expresses the typical petite bourgeoisie opinion regarding Mario, a marginal character. In Abakuá society, ethical values flourished—machismo to its highest level—which contributed to ethical values in the popular music. There is a scene between Bobby Carcassés and Mario Balmaseda at a park. Mario was in a crisis due to what he had done: he had violated the code. This is shown again in the scene in Conejito restaurant—the dialogue with Sarita Reyes where she gives a discriminatory look. With the fight at Línea and 18, she creates a dramatic situation. El Ambia's character was a positive one, and there are some characters that simply express their own thoughts. For example, the one criticizing Mayito at the beer bar was simply voicing his thoughts. So I began encouraging El Ambia to raise the bar since the negative character was winning the argument. In the initial sequence, those present were not aware of what would happen. Once Mario denounced the other, a sort of explosion took place since an environment had been created and everyone was playing his or her own role. The scene was planned in general terms, but what would happen between the characters was not known. All this is take one. Mejicana really attacked and hit the other character, and Sarita had to interrupt the scene. Rogelito really slapped the girl while dancing. Sara made Yolanda attend the school quite often. [Sara] was able to establish an organic relationship among professional actors and nonactors.

Mario's character is a mix of several of us. There are several persons included in that character. Guillermo Díaz really loved Sarita. Mario Balmaseda and I used to visit Guillermo to listen to him telling his stories. That story of the man who has just won a boxing championship and arrives home to see a man peeping through a hole at his wife—he hits him and takes him to a gutter. Luz,

Guillermo's wife, was a real lady. Guillermo was highly respected among the Abakuás.

VÍCTOR FOWLER CALZADA: *Your filmmaking has a lot to do with Sara's work. You are always looking for the roots.*

RIGOBERTO LÓPEZ: Yes—fully influenced by her work.

Translated from the original Spanish by Miguel Ángel Pérez

NOTES

1. See the interview with Arocha (this volume) on damage to the film and on *cine imperfecto*.—Ed.
2. Fowler (this volume) discusses this as well. The script to which López refers is reproduced in chapter 6.—Ed.
3. For more on filming in sixteen millimeter, see the interview with Mesa (this volume).—Ed.

RIGOBERTO LÓPEZ was a Cuban filmmaker and president of the Traveling Caribbean Film Showcase. He was assistant director for Sara Gómez's *One Way or Another* (in Spanish; 1977). His films include *From Son to Salsa* (in Spanish; 1996), *Scent of Oak* (in Spanish; 2004), and *Forbidden Flights* (in Spanish; 2015).

VÍCTOR FOWLER CALZADA is a Cuban poet, essayist, and writer. He is author of several award-winning books about race in Cuba and about Cuban cinema. He has worked as chief of publications at the International School of Cinema and Television in San Antonio de los Baños (1994–97 and 2002–7) and directed the electronic magazine *Miradas*.

ELEVEN

Information and Education
Sara Gómez and Nonfiction Film Culture of the 1960s

Joshua Malitsky

INTRODUCTION: PRODUCING MENTALITY

One of the most noted successes of the Cuban Revolution was its education policy, and the most celebrated educational accomplishment was the National Literacy Campaign of 1961. This operation was designed to achieve the dual objectives of youth involvement in the Revolution and adult literacy, and it aimed to instill a sense of revolutionary fervor in student *brigadistas* by giving them their first real opportunity to participate in the struggle. The campaign also sought to unite urban and rural citizens, not only by joining urban-educated teachers with rural students but also by creating a situation in which people in urban areas could learn about rural daily life and work. More than 100,000, mostly urban, student volunteers lived with rural families for six months, imparting reading and writing skills as well as lessons in revolutionary politics. The campaign was hailed as a victory for the nation of Cuba, having raised the adult literacy rate from approximately 74 percent (43 percent in the countryside) to 96 percent and (Paulston 1971, 385–87).

The literacy campaign was part of a much broader education program that sought to eliminate racism and sexism, end the control of the urban over the rural, and replace a class-based system with an expanded, more egalitarian one—all to be done experimentally and with overt politicization (Bowles 1971; Richmond 1987). Abel Prieto, one of the directors of the literacy campaign—a rural schoolteacher and educational policy maker—provocatively described the ideological goals of the project: "We continue to try forming a people who reject individualism, who deny imperialism, who rebel against social injustice in any part of the world, and who have a producing, rather than consuming, mentality. Our education has an ideological character like that of the US, but on the other end of the political spectrum" (quoted in Martuza 1981, 262).

The Communist Party sought to produce this mentality by creating a work/study program where students balanced study with labor, either by splitting their daily schedules to incorporate time for labor or by devising a schedule that would enable 1.2 million students to visit the countryside to do agricultural work. The party hoped the program would counter urban/rural divisions, support the national economy, and create strong habits and a producer's mentality in students (Prieto in Martuza 1981, 263). The principles of work and study that educational leaders laid out not only required the inclusion of labor as part of students' daily lives but also the reconceptualization of the relationship with labor in a more dynamic way so that study and experience became mutually supportive. These objectives were to be achieved through curriculum design at the programmatic level and through teaching strategies at the individual class level.

This effort to transform education and the communication of information in a way that made, according to Erwin Epstein, "learning a natural part of their [Cubans'] everyday lives" (quoted in Leiner 1981, 204) also informed nonfiction film practice in Cuba. Cuban filmmakers believed that most Western nonfiction film models—newsreels, documentaries, educational and encyclopedia films—produced passive media consumers. Creating a producer's mentality required a wider range of topics, alternative narrative structures, and new approaches to narration.

Sara Gómez's encyclopedia films and documentaries came about as a part of this educational project. As a result, they likewise committed to a balance between study and labor or, perhaps more appropriately, between theory and practice. In this essay, I trace the ideas of both the educational and the informational in Gómez's films of the 1960s to explore how teaching, instructing, informing, and persuading became not only goals but objects of thought. I say "trace the ideas" rather than "follow her developments" because I hesitate to see these films as progress only. Certainly, Gómez developed both artistically and conceptually as a filmmaker throughout the decade, but such an emphasis would undervalue the degree to which she located her work within the dominant 1960s nonfiction film culture in Cuba, at times aligning with, and at other times challenging, that model. My approach, therefore, is to focus expansively on Gómez's narrational choices in these films and how she selected, organized, and rendered nonfiction film material to produce a certain effect on viewers.[1] It is at the level of narration that we can see her resonances with contemporary education policy, some of her most urgent political concerns, and where, subtly at times and at other times less so, she marked her films in relation to both Western and dominant Cuban models.

HISTORY IN PROCESS, 1961–64

In 1961, at the age of eighteen, Gómez began working on her first project for the Instituto Cubano del Arte e Industria Cinematográficos (ICAIC, or Cuban Film Institute): the *Enciclopedia popular* series (fig. 11.1). This series was inaugurated during the "Year of Education" and, like the literacy campaign, was conceived as part of a broader educational agenda. The series ran until 1963, producing thirty-eight short films. Each film, or issue, ran between seven and ten minutes and dealt with one, two, or three topics. As in her documentaries to come, Gómez was largely responsible for selecting the topics of her films. Single-topic issues were most often categorized as "special" and were more experimental in form.[2] María Eulalia Douglas, Sara Vega, and Ivo Sarría of the *Cinemateca de Cuba* describe issues as "informational-didactic" films. Topics ranged widely and included biographies of famous political and cultural figures (Chaplin, Da Vinci, Villena); the science of vision diseases or the solar system; tourist depictions of Cuban cities, regions, and national institutions; and process films about factory production. The *Enciclopedia popular* series served as a training ground for people who would become some of the leading filmmakers of the 1960s and 1970s—in addition to Gómez, Octavio Cortázar, Nicolás Guillén Landrián, Oscar Valdés, Humberto Solás, and even Tomás Gutiérrez Alea directed issues or sections of issues.[3]

The *Enciclopedia popular* series formed one part of an ICAIC-produced, postrevolutionary Cuban nonfiction film project that included newsreels and documentaries intended to project models (both materially and psychologically) through on-screen examples and instill a socialist revolutionary mode of thought and being through the emotional and visceral dimension. Although these institutional homes were seen in part as training grounds for feature fiction filmmaking, the ICAIC privileged nonfiction film production for its economic efficiency and attention to material reality. The immediacy and authenticity of nonfiction film could expose the falsity of fiction film in the same way that Marxism could bring to light the ideological deceptiveness of Western capitalism, and it could do so by means of an affordable, entertaining practice. The series embraced the principle of comprehensiveness, covering a wide range of educational topics and branches of knowledge.[4] However, just as the *Latin American Weekly Newsreel* borrowed from and ultimately challenged the Western newsreel tradition, the *Enciclopedia popular* reworked established

Figure 11.1 Title for the *Enciclopedia popular* series, 1961. © ICAIC

models of educational filmmaking.[5] Gómez's work for the series embodies this effort.

Gómez made five films for the series, three of which are currently available: *Plaza Vieja* (1962), *Fábrica de tabacos* (1962), and *Historia de la piratería* (1963).[6] In these films, as well as in her films *Iré a Santiago* (1964) and *Crónicas de mi familia* (1966), we see her early efforts to instill historical imaginations in Cuban viewers, and to do so while calling into question established conventions of how to speak about history. For Gómez, everyday objects must become worthy of historical thought, and the means by which viewers commonly encounter everyday objects—including, but not limited to, audiovisual examples—must be reworked for this to occur. Doing so not only raises the stakes for types of media associated with the "informational" but also transforms the meaning of the term by removing its association with positivist neutrality.

Plaza Vieja runs just over four and a half minutes and consists of a single female voice-over narrator describing key historical events that have taken place in one Havana square over the last four centuries. The narrator begins by noting the founding of the square in 1587 as a place for bullfights and public festivals.

She concludes at the contemporary moment, explaining that revolutionary historians and urban planners have decided to study and preserve the history of this and other Havana plazas. Along the way, she pays considerable attention to the architectural history of the square—doorways, facades, building levels, and even underground parking lots—pointing to both the social and political history of the location.

The image track consists of contemporary footage of the square that frequently emphasizes present activity. Sometimes images align fairly directly with the voice-over; at other times, the relation is more oblique. The tightest shots, and the ones that focus most on individual faces (often with direct looks back at the camera), come in the last minute of the film, when the narrator concentrates on the contemporary moment. Overall, the film presents neither an exhaustive history of the present nor a detailed analysis. Instead, it is organized more thematically than chronologically, offering an approach to seeing and describing the world as more than a digested, bundled package of information.

The square itself offers no shocking or even remarkable details—nothing that, at first glance, would seem to explain why a film about it was made. Rather, we get a hint at the purpose of the film in its emphasis on preservation and study that comes at the conclusion. The film aims to model and instill an approach to seeing Cuba anew in such a way that everyday objects and spaces—ones that initially seem not to have obvious or necessary historical value—become worthy of historical and cultural consideration. The gaps between the voice-over narration and the image selection as well as the loose narrative structure create spaces for audience intervention. The object of the film is thus historical thought itself, with the recognition that Cuban history is multinational, multiethnic, multiracial, and shaped by class conflict.

Fábrica de tabacos, the second film Gómez made as part of the *Enciclopedia popular* series, speaks in related ways about history, everyday objects, and the process of thought. The film demonstrates the process of cigar production, beginning with a man buying a cigar at a store and then moving on to the process of making the cigar. We see the initial selection of tobacco leaves, the de-stemmers, the process of drying, and the rollers. Eventually, we end up back at the same store. Now, however, we see the object differently—because we have seen the laborious process embedded in it, we see it as an object of labor. The cigar itself is now akin to Plaza Vieja, an object open to historical thought—in this case, the process of its production. According to the logic of *Plaza Vieja* and *Fábrica de tabacos*, nonfiction film organizes audiovisual material in a way that allows the audience to see objects anew—to see the previously hidden relationships in them, whether the object in question is a lived space or a single box of cigars.

The process of production-made-visible is not limited to objects on-screen. The films themselves, in fact, double this effort. Like the ICAIC's *Latin American Weekly Newsreel* and many other documentary projects, the *Enciclopedia popular* series served as a training ground for filmmakers. Some imagined themselves preparing to make better nonfiction films, while others imagined moving on to feature fiction filmmaking. Indeed, the ICAIC certainly believed that nonfiction filmmaking would prepare filmmakers, socially and politically, to make fiction films; like the cigar workers in *Fábrica de tabacos*, Gómez and her team learn their craft. Although not as presentational as films made later in the decade, *Fábrica* evinces a self-conscious playfulness that celebrates both crafts. We see experiments with lighting, an extended tracking shot through the factory, and a beautiful-but-brief visual metaphor comparing rolling cigars to making music. Gómez and her team are workers like any other—they are productive, skilled, and precise. They work to become more professional.

Learning new processes of communicating information was part of their education. Doing so effectively was their practice, their applied education. In modeling and aiming to instill a historical imagination attentive to the process of production while functioning as productive citizens in their own right, Gómez and her team embraced broader Cuban educational goals. They balanced the conceptual with the literally productive—study with work—while keeping political concerns at the fore. In most ways, Gómez's work with the *Enciclopedia popular* series aligned with dominant approaches to nonfiction filmmaking in Cuba at the time. For example, in the early 1960s, the ICAIC's *Latin American Weekly Newsreel* tended to focus on collectives or on individuals as representatives of collectives, whereas its documentaries concentrated on personalizing narratives.[7] Likewise, Gómez's encyclopedia films addressed and sought to build the nation as a whole, as a collective, while her documentaries such as *Iré a Santiago* and *Crónicas de mi familia* offered more personal accounts—even if they frequently lacked significant personal testimony.[8]

Despite such superficial similarities, Gómez's work differed in two significant ways from the dominant model. First, her films were much more attentive to race and gender as topics of concern in Cuba. As others in this book explain, Gómez was committed to presenting images of black Cubans and women as developed and differentiated subjects by consistently addressing Afro-Cuban issues and themes in her work.[9] In contrast, Álvarez's *Now!* (1965), for example, addressed race in Cuba only indirectly by showing support for the US civil rights movement and its historical antecedents. The second and related point of difference is in Gómez's explicitness about the role of the articulating self, which takes many forms in her work. In *Plaza Vieja*, she employs a female voice-over narrator, and in *Historia de la piratería* (1963), another *Enciclopedia popular* film, she alternates between male and female voice-over narrators.[10] Neither of these conventions was common for the time, as singular male voice-over narrators dominated Cuban nonfiction film. In *Iré a Santiago*, as I discuss below, the opening title sequence playfully inserts a young black woman as Gómez's avatar,[11] and throughout the film she physically inserts her camera, and at times herself, into the space of the event, becoming part of the crowd and sparking both reflective and reactive moments in social actors. She sustains and develops these reflexive, disruptive moments, refusing to cut once the immediate effect of authorial recognition is achieved. Álvarez's reflexivity, on the other hand, was of a different type. He called attention to the fact of enunciation, to a voice speaking through film without calling attention to an articulating self. Álvarez was a voice of the Revolution—white, male, and empowered to speak for and to the collective. That is not to deny his attention to issues of race and gender but rather to point out that his authority precluded his need to speak as a specific self.

FIRST-PERSON, (MULTI)CULTURAL HISTORIES

The connection between form and theme that Gómez began to explore in her *Enciclopedia popular* films took new shape in two documentaries from the mid-1960s—*Iré a Santiago* and *Crónicas de mi familia*. Like the *Enciclopedia popular* films, these documentaries responded in part to a generic tradition—in this case, the travel genre. Yet in both cases, Gómez traveled to a city in Cuba (Santiago and Guanabacoa) to make a film about each place. As in her earlier films, she again asserts an alternative approach to understanding the primary objects of thought, openly challenging traditional answers to the question, What does it mean to make a film about a place?

Iré a Santiago opens with a playful title sequence that hints at Gómez's role as an authorial voice. A young black woman walks in front of a wall on which a quotation from Federico García Lorca is painted. The camera picks her up and follows her down the sidewalk until she turns and walks up a staircase where the film's credits are painted on the steps. The young woman returns to view as Sarita's writer and director credits appear. It is now clear that the young woman is Sarita's stand-in—she announces, however obliquely, Sarita's identity and authorial presence.

The body of the film opens with a series of street scenes of Santiago. Some synchronized sound runs below the guajira music. A woman's voice-over, speaking in first-person plural, characterizes street life and connects it to a larger Cuban personality. "We laugh and talk loudly, aggressively, and with pride," she asserts. The images, especially the gestures of the people, seem to confirm her statements. The only element that potentially disrupts the narrative is a series of direct looks at the camera, which harken back to the end of *Plaza Vieja*. We see friendly gestures, aggressive stares, playful performances, and outright escapes from the frame. The camera pushes those who appear within its frame for a response, often pursuing the subject by panning, tracking, or zooming. As in the opening authorial gesture, once again the film asserts itself as an authored piece. If an observational element remains, it is an aggressive version. Gómez accompanies this challenge to a traditional observational vision with a fascinating questioning of her own voice-over authority.[12] After describing the Cuban personality, the Antillean personality, and seemingly establishing its truthfulness through the image track, the voice-over suddenly questions the viability of its own claims: "All this is almost a legend. This is the myth of Cuba." What follows then is her alternative to stereotypical history.

The critical section of the film arrives about four minutes in, marked by an audio title, "Santiago and the French." The sequence opens with a well-attended funeral of the leader of French society. The narrator explains that Santiago has black people who are called "French" and who dance to the rhythm of a drum called the French *tumba*. She then explains the roots of this cultural connection: These are the descendants of slaves who came to Cuba with French settlers fleeing the Haitian Revolution. These settlers established "French" coffee plantations worked by their slaves—this last piece of information is communicated only through visuals of chains and cuffs. The narrator then explains that whereas Santiago no longer has "the French" or the coffee plantations, what is left is the drum that everyone calls "French." We hear people play the drum for almost a minute—about as long as the rest of the sequence.

In *Plaza Vieja*, Gómez had transformed traditional objects of historical thought by moving from singular, iconic moments and their representative objects to everyday objects and spaces with their layered, multiply inflected archaeological structures. In *Fábrica de tabacos*, she focused on a single object and its process of production: the cigar. In *Iré a Santiago*, Gómez offers another example of a traditional cultural object through which we can understand history. Instead of a city square or a cigar, we have a drum. Moreover, she gives us time—almost a full minute—to listen to and reflect on the meaning of the drum. If *Plaza Vieja* encouraged us to see history in everyday objects and spaces, and *Fábrica de tabacos* helped us understand the labor value of products, then *Iré a Santiago* invites us to hear history, binding the intellectual and the sensorial into a new process for engaging with the past through objects. In so doing, Gómez continues to build the foundation for an audiovisual, multicultural history—one that encourages a range of audience engagements, including the questioning of voice-over narration as the authoritative means of conveying information.

Crónicas de mi familia (1966), Gómez's follow-up film, was her most personal to this point in her career and more defiant of a certain kind of revolutionary ideology than her previous work. As in her earlier films, Gómez highlights the centrality of culture in Cuban life and history while reminding the audience how multinational, multiethnic, and multicultural Cuba in fact is. In addition, she expands her earlier subtle critiques of dominant voice-over narration by opting for an even less authoritative approach to the communication of information while never failing to recognize, and take responsibility for, her own role in shaping the film.

The film runs thirteen and a half minutes and focuses on Guanabacoa, the township in eastern Havana from which she comes. The area has rich African, indigenous, and Jewish traditions, to which Gómez visually alludes in the opening sections of the film. She establishes the personal element right away by dedicating the film to her godmother, who died at age eighty just prior to Gómez receiving the final film prints. The opening credits run almost a minute and a half and sustain the personal, familial theme through historical still photographs of family members. The next six minutes consist of an array of musical performances and rehearsals occasionally interrupted by street scenes or Guanabacoan landmarks. Family members are identified by title as they play or listen. Musical styles vary throughout, with European, African, and indigenous traditions and instruments all appearing periodically. This section establishes the centrality of music in Gómez's family life and personal history in Guanabacoa and, by extension, in Cuba as a whole. It does so in two interesting ways. First, it proceeds without the aid of voice-over narration—we do not hear Gómez's voice until almost eight minutes into the film. Second, the section attends not only to public performances but also to rehearsals, thus emphasizing the role of music in everyday life and establishing a theme to which she returns at the end of the film.

At about the eight-minute mark, the film changes tone when, after the introduction of family members via still photographs and Gómez's voice-over, we meet Gómez's eighty-year-old godmother. *Madrina* tells stories about going to church as a child, not for religious reasons but because the priests gave out bread and guava paste. She explains that there were social clubs that she did not attend as a young woman because they were not appropriate for "certain blacks." It is the combination of *Madrina*'s commitment to certain social codes and her honesty about them that so impresses Gómez the filmmaker.[13] She sustains this theme in the final section of the film about her "favorite cousin," Berta. The sequence consists of Berta and Gómez talking and drinking beer in Berta's kitchen. However, because there is no synchronized sound, we attend not to what Berta says but to her gestures and her environment. In comparison to the honesty Gómez values in *Madrina*, Berta communicates another quality—defiance.

It is the combination of honesty and defiance, and their realization in Gómez's formal choices, that opens the politics of the film to analysis. The film's final sequence consists of Berta walking out of her apartment and down the stairs into the world as Gómez, in voice-over, poses a compelling, yet rhetorical, question.[14] She asks whether showing an honest and "total history" must necessarily challenge the idea of racial uplift. In other words, although she acknowledges the value of presenting positive representations of Afro-Cubans to some degree, she more strongly questions what constitutes such positive representations. For Gómez, the film as history needs to live up to the honesty of her interlocutors, not deny or purify the past. Film is about showing diversity, personalities, and stories, and doing so in a way that does not speak for social actors but, as Trinh T. Minh-ha suggests in an interview with Nancy Chen, "speaks alongside" them (Chen 1992, 82–91). *Crónicas de mi familia* demonstrates Gómez's effort to show history visually and aurally—that is, less logocentrically—by highlighting details of gesture and cultural performance (shows as well as rehearsals) while intervening less authoritatively through overt narration.

For Gómez, the defiance and honesty of her family members are not just true but are preferable (Berta is "her favorite" cousin). Confrontational, combative people are the most interesting and, possibly, the most revolutionary. Moreover, a total audiovisual history of Guanabacoa—realized here as method and aesthetic, not as fact—must account for social and personal divisions and differences. Erasing the messiness of life creates a false and ultimately less interesting national collective. For Gómez in *Crónicas de mi familia*—and, as we will see, in the Isle of Pines trilogy—embracing multinationalism, multiethnicism, and multiculturalism need not override unity. Rather, in these films she aims to reshape the terms of the debate in favor of what Susan Lord describes as a "society based upon cultural difference and expressed through popular democracy" (2002, 253). In *Crónicas de mi familia*, the personal serves a larger political agenda.

To be sure, Gómez was not alone in challenging the dominance of voice-over narration during this period (1965–70) in Cuban film history—a period that

John Mraz describes as dominated by "dramatic form" (1990, 147). Santiago Álvarez's films were artistically experimental and his formal choices likewise reflected his political and ethical commitments. However, whereas Álvarez's viscerally and emotionally intense affective aesthetic—which by no means sought to reduce narrational authority—aimed to include a diverse constituency and be international in reach, he addressed and imagined a Cuban public that was much more singular and unified than the one Gómez addressed at the same historical moment.[15] Gómez's narrational choices during this period were not observationally naive—they were subtly inventive. She did not claim to merely "capture" the world; her authorial stamp on her films makes this point clear. Indeed, it is the combination of her authorial stamp and her effort to reduce a logocentric narrational authority in her films of the period that demonstrates her commitment to communicating a Cuban history of multiple voices.

AN AESTHETICS OF INCLUSIVITY

Between 1967 and 1969, Gómez, Luis García (camera), and Jesús Pascau (producer) made three films on and about the Isle of Pines, now known as the Island of Youth—an island south of Havana used at the time to educate Cuban youth and train them in agricultural work. However, the three films are stylistically and structurally distinct. *En la otra isla* (1968) consists largely of solo and group interviews with the youth living and working on the island. *Una isla para Miguel* (1968) offers an exploration of male youth culture focused on how a rebellious urban group interacts with the authoritarianism and discipline of the island and its militant leaders. Yet neither of these films presents any definitive conclusions about proper youth behavior on the island, nor whether the island's leaders serve the Revolution in an exemplary way. The final film, *Isla del tesoro* (1969), is the most expository of the trilogy. Employing multiple voice-over narrators (again both male and female), the film is structured according to a now-familiar old/new logic: Spanish and American imperialists exploited the island and imprisoned its people/we produce for the people and liberate the citizens. Other than the location, these films are united only in the multiplicity of their narrational forms, both in the individual films and across all three. The variation and constant shifts in address call attention to a dynamic between filmmaking method and the performance of the social actors that serves to celebrate multiple voices as a revolutionary model of speech. This dynamic is achieved most forcefully in the first two films of the trilogy.

En la otra isla is Gómez's longest film to that date, running over forty minutes. It begins with the island's anthem, which tells the story of the Isle of Pines ("the other island," where people under twenty "who don't fear life" work and "where the flag of a new youth is born"). The introduction contains images of young women laboring in the fields. The body of the film opens with direct testimony from a young woman talking about her schedule, school, and work training as a hairstylist. The narration is tight but not staid, as there is a playful self-consciousness to it. María is asked to describe herself, and the resulting sequence is neither naturalistic nor traditionally formal. María first appears in front of work activity, speaking rather formally about responsibilities. Second, she appears in her bunkroom, where she speaks more personally and where we hear Gómez's voice as well. Partway through this brief sequence is an early sound bridge and then a cut to the source of it—María singing a song with two young male accompanists. The performance shows the variety of María's daily schedule; after hairdressing, she goes to "cultural rehearsals." The end of the song marks the end of the sequence. But just prior to the cut, María confirms with Gómez that her performance is acceptable. Immediately thereafter the tone changes and another, and highly unexpected, narrational form of address begins as a title card indicates "A discourse by Fajardo: We hope the audience will enjoy." We thus witness various forms of narration—a musical anthem over women laboring; interview material; a musical performance; self-conscious commentary from the interviewee that directly addresses the filmmaker; and a title card—all in the first four and a half minutes of the film. Gómez sustains this striking array of narrational forms throughout the film.

The last section of the film includes three interview types: interviews with two very different young women; an interview with their group leader; and a secretly filmed interview with the camp leader who responds to the other interviews. This constant variation in narrational form, including direct interaction with the camera, shifts the mode of address from what Thomas Waugh (2011) would describe as the representational to the presentational—a model that makes explicit its terms of engagement. For Waugh, the presentational is a "convention of performing an awareness of the camera rather than a nonawareness, of presenting oneself explicitly for the camera" (76). In *En la otra isla*, the presentational allows Gómez to "authorize" the performances by giving the participants, as Waugh states, the "right to play" themselves, here in a doubled condition of social construction—the experiment that is the Isle of Pines and the one that is the documentary itself (92).

Likewise, *Una isla para Miguel* employs a presentational mode of address but one that Gómez now achieves through different formal means. The film examines the attempt to "neocolonize" the "Vikings," a group of boys age thirteen to seventeen who have come to the island and who "represent the morale and life of the barrios." In many ways, the film is about a confrontation of forces—the rebelliousness of the Vikings versus the rational political arguments of the militants. We hear the attitude of the militants toward the boys and see the boys' response in their defiant looks toward the camera, aggressive actions toward each other, and willful avoidance of labor. The structure alternates between testimony from militants and visuals of the boys, but the images do much more than confirm the testimony. In fact, there is never a sense that the militants are simply correct and the boys are in need of total behavioral and attitudinal overhauls. The film is more an exploration of male, bad-boy youth culture. The camera is curious, interested in the violence, competitiveness, playfulness, energy, and defiance of (this kind of) masculinity and youth.

The film's final scene exemplifies its resistance to definitive conclusions. Following the snap of the clapboard, we see Miguel, the boy who is the film's main focus, sitting with César, a model militant youth. They sit close to each other on steps, facing the camera more than each other. César does all the talking, explaining to Miguel what it takes to become a militant. Miguel sits passively, sometimes with his head in his hands. At the end of César's "inspirational" speech, the film jump-cuts across three shots of Miguel posing around the island, looking directly at the camera. The clapboard prompts a cut back to César, who confidently remarks, "Miguel. As a friend of mine and as a man, I know he'll behave." Despite the remark, the film presents neither youth as entirely confident or assured that Miguel will do so. Rather, its formal self-consciousness (realized primarily through jump cuts, scene marking with the clapboard, and the interview format), playfulness, and interest in defiance encourages viewers to question the purity of what the narrator herself describes as "neocolonization." *Una isla para Miguel* does not deny the value of the practical and theoretical educations the youth receive on the island, but it does question the method by which these are achieved and the standardization of the message. In this way, Gómez manages to reiterate one of Castro's earlier revolutionary themes—that students should not be allowed to lose their "combativeness."[16] Moreover, she does so at the level of form as well as by refusing to definitively "complete" the film by celebrating one side or the other.[17] The ambiguity of the film's ideology thus aligns with the continuing open-endedness of Miguel's situation at the end of the film—each case requires the viewer to actively engage rather than to passively digest.[18]

These twin efforts offer ways of diffusing narrational authority even more thoroughly than we saw in *Iré a Santiago* and *Crónicas de mi familia*. As in the earlier films, Gómez remains committed to reconceiving the relationship between study and work, theory and practice, thought and labor. However, in the trilogy she is more pointed in her effort to transform the process by which information gets communicated. Here, Gómez radically challenges the singular, dominant, narrational voice of the ICAIC's *Latin American Weekly Newsreel* and its implicit singular "voice of the Revolution." In their place, she asserts a more democratic vision—a society that accepts and celebrates cultural difference and multiplicity. Gómez creates spaces at the table for those who confront revolutionary conformity.

Elsewhere, I have described Santiago Álvarez's documentaries of the mid- to late 1960s as governed by an aesthetics of mobilizability (Malitsky 2013, esp. 150–52). His films exhibit a persistent and varied juxtaposition at the level of the singular image between sound and image as well as across sequence, reel, and documentaries of the same period. Combined with the films' declared foci on productivity and collective effort, the range of juxtapositions, their effort to jar, and their intensity aim to create a subject uniquely responsive to the shifting economic and social conditions then facing Cuban citizens. Álvarez worked to critically and sensorially prepare citizens for the likelihood of mobilization, be it economic or military.

Gómez's films likewise demonstrate a reflexive aesthetic eclecticism that highlights juxtaposition across sequence, film, and nonfiction genres. The structural shifts and the multiplicity of narrational strategies Gómez deploys challenge the assertion of a singular authorial or authoritarian voice, pointing to the need for multiple revolutionary voices. If the goal of Cuban education at the time was to create a "producer's mentality," Gómez seems to warn against the dangers of creating citizens who only "consume ideology" articulated elsewhere.

NOTES

1. For a comprehensive consideration of narration as it functions in fiction film, see Bordwell (1985).

2. This is also true for newsreels produced during the period. Santiago Álvarez made some of his best-known and internationally renowned early documentaries, *Ciclón* (1963) and *Now!* (1965), as special issue newsreels.

3. For details on the series, see Douglas, Vega, and Sarría (2004, 188–195, quotation from 188).

4. For a fascinating and utopian example of a filmed encyclopedia of the world, see Paula Amad's (2010) discussion of Albert Kahn's *Archives de la Planète*.

5. For more on the Cuban newsreel, see Chanan (2004), Johnson (2013), and Malitsky (2013).

6. I have been unable to locate a copy of *Solar Habanero* (1962), a short film about popular Cuban folk dance and music and part of issue 31 of *Enciclopedia popular*.

7. See Malitsky (2013, 58–88).

8. Both Casamayor (this volume) and Benson (this volume) discuss these films and the audio title "Santiago and the French" from *Iré a Santiago* referred to later in this essay.

9. As Anna Serra (this volume) notes, Gómez and other intellectuals interested in carving out spaces for black identities in revolutionary Cuba participated in an ethnology and folklore seminar led by the Haitian negritude philosopher René Depestre during the 1960s. The seminar was shut down by the regime for its promotion of ethnic and gender difference over national unity.

10. See the interview with Martiatu (this volume) for a discussion of voice-over narration in Gómez's nonfiction film.

11. Serra (this volume) develops this theme more fully.

12. Martínez-Echazábal (this volume) and Lord (this volume) highlight this questioning.

13. Likewise, Casamayor (this volume) notes this narrative focus.

14. Benson (this volume) also discusses this final sequence.

15. For more, see Malitsky (2013, 117–54).

16. Prieto tells of an interesting example that speaks to Castro's commitment to this principle: "The school-in-the-country-side can be traced back to 1962. After the literacy campaign was over, all of the students who participated were told that, henceforth, they should dedicate themselves to study. A scholarship program was established, and beautiful houses owned by rich people were converted into schools for them. But Fidel said that we could not allow our children to lose their combativeness by living in the houses of the rich. So all of the scholarship students (about 50,000) were sent to pick coffee in Oriente province" (in Martuza 1981, 262, parentheses in original).

17. For more on the political implications of "completing" the documentary by means of a problem/solution narrative structure, see Winston (1995, 40–48) and Casamayor (this volume).

18. On Gómez's strategy of open-ended questioning, see also Casamayor (this volume).

BIBLIOGRAPHY

Amad, Paula. 2010. *Counter-Archive: Film, the Everyday, and Albert Kahn's Archives de la Planète*. New York: Columbia University Press.

Bordwell, David. 1985. *Narration in the Fiction Film*. Madison: University of Wisconsin Press.

Bowles, Samuel. 1971. "Cuban Education and the Revolutionary Ideology." *Harvard Educational Review* 41, no. 4: 472–500.

Chanan, Michael. 2004. *Cuban Cinema*. Minneapolis: University of Minnesota Press.

Chen, Nancy. 1992. "Speaking Nearby: A Conversation with Trinh T. Minh-ha." *Visual Anthropology Review* 8, no. 1: 82–91.

Douglas, María Eulalia, Sara Vega, and Ivo Sarría. 2004. *Producciones del Instituto Cubano del Arte e Industria Cinematográficos: 1959–2004*. Havana: Cinemateca de Cuba Press.

Johnson, Mariana. 2013. "The Revolution Will Be Archived: Cuba's *Noticiero ICAIC Latinoamericano*." *Moving Image* 13, no. 2: 1–21.

Leiner, Marvin. 1981. "Two Decades of Educational Change in Cuba." In "Education in Cuba: 1961–1981." Special issue commemorating the twentieth anniversary of Cuba's National Literacy Campaign, *Journal of Reading* 25, no. 3: 202–14.

Lord, Susan. 2002. "Temporality and Identity: Undertaking Cross-Cultural Analysis of Sara Gómez's Documentaries." In *Women Filmmakers: Refocusing*, edited by Jacqueline Levitin, Judith Plessis, and Valerie Raoul, 249–63. Vancouver: University of British Columbia Press.

Malitsky, Joshua. 2013. *Post-Revolution Nonfiction Film: Building the Soviet and Cuban Nations*. Bloomington: Indiana University Press.

Martuza, Víctor. 1981. "A Conversation with Abel Prieto." In "Education in Cuba: 1961–1981." Special issue commemorating the twentieth anniversary of Cuba's National Literacy Campaign, *Journal of Reading* 25, no. 3: 261–69.

Mraz, John. 1990. "Santiago Álvarez: From Dramatic Form to Direct Cinema." In *The Social Documentary in Latin America*, edited by Julianne Burton, 131–50. Pittsburgh: University of Pittsburgh Press.

Paulston, Richard G. 1971. "Education." In *Revolutionary Change in Cuba*, edited by Carmelo Mesa-Lago, 375–97. Pittsburgh: University of Pittsburgh Press.

Richmond, Mark. 1987. "Educational Change in Post-Revolutionary Cuba: A Critical Assessment." *International Journal of Educational Development* 7, no. 1: 191–204.

Waugh, Thomas. 2011. *The Right to Play Oneself: Looking Back on Documentary Film*. Minneapolis: University of Minnesota Press.

Winston, Brian. 1995. *Claiming the Real: The Documentary Film Revisited*. London: BFI Press.

JOSHUA MALITSKY is Associate Professor of Cinema and Media Studies and Director of the Center for Documentary Research and Practice at Indiana University. He is also adjunct faculty in the Russian and East European Institute, the Department of Slavic Languages and Literatures, and the Center for Latin American and Caribbean Studies. He is author of *Post-Revolution Nonfiction Film: Building the Soviet and Cuban Nations* (2013) and *A Companion to Documentary History* (2020).

TWELVE

Virtual Heroes in the Midst of Shortage
Sara Gómez Confronts the New Man

Ana Serra

THE 1960S IN CUBA WAS an exhilarating and turbulent decade—when extraordinary people espoused beliefs in heroic ideals. Ernesto "Che" Guevara has rightfully been called "the century's first Latin American," because his ideals galvanized a continent and his exceptional qualities made him world renowned (Guillermoprieto 2001, 76). The Cuban filmmaker Sara Gómez was another powerful figure of the 1960s, although she received little recognition until after the 1990s despite her being both a product and a maker of the era. In fact, Che Guevara and Sara Gómez had a great deal in common: both had asthma; both died young; both were ardent revolutionaries; and both bore an existential affinity with the liberating currents of the 1960s. Despite these commonalities, however, Guevara and Gómez represent two very different discourses of the many that found expression in the 1960s. My task in this essay is to unveil the implicit dialogue between Guevara and Gómez as well as to explain the dominance of Che Guevara's legacy compared to the silence that has surrounded Sara Gómez from the 1960s until recently.

Between Gómez and Guevara stands a third figure whose stature and power would nowadays be equivalent to that of an avatar or action figure—the "New Man." As with all avatars, the New Man was a persona of his creator, Che Guevara, who fashioned him with attributes drawn from his own life, his own mind, and his own textual obsessions, strongly influenced by ideologies in vogue in the 1960s. The 1959 Cuban Revolution espoused a radical break with the previous era and introduced a virtual reality in the form of a new society in which all Cubans were to picture themselves. "Socialism and Man in Cuba," Guevara's foundational document on the Cuban Revolution, stressed the idea of a "new man," "a new society," and a "new consciousness" with "new values"

(1989, 6). As with any action figure, the New Man was designed to play in a virtual world—in his case, a communist existence whose success projected into the future through the unlikely realization of a utopia. As a textual and fictional construct, the New Man became overused, oversaturated, reified, and ultimately rendered empty over the years. After Guevara's death, he himself came to be identified with the New Man ideal and turned into a more perfect human being than he had ever been in life.

An examination of Che Guevara's essay and Sara Gómez's documentaries in the context of the lives of both authors reveals examples of what Damián Fernández (2000) calls "the politics of passion." Both figures were propelled by a personal, affective relationship to ideology inspired by the moral crusade that dominated 1960s Cuba. Yet, while some have characterized Gómez's work as representing a "New Woman"—a suitable counterpart to Guevara's New Man—in her life and works Gómez herself resisted the model of a woman fashioned out of, or in relation to, a male figure. Gómez's works, specifically three of her lesser-known documentaries, demonstrate that even those who paid allegiance to the Revolution in its early years might question the strategically motivated ideal of the New Man. In the midst of the dominance of the New Man avatar, Gómez tested the powers, limits, and glitches of Guevara's virtual life, and in so doing, she challenged the politics of masculinity, womanhood, and personhood implicit in the concept of the New Man.

"SOCIALISM AND MAN IN CUBA": GUEVARA'S REVOLUTIONARY TESTAMENT

Guevara wrote "Socialism and Man in Cuba" while on a trip to Africa in 1965 during a low point in his tenure as minister of finance in Cuba. After Guevara's return from Africa, Fidel Castro expressed discomfort with an anti-Soviet speech Guevara had given in Algeria. Other disagreements with Guevara's economic policies underpinned a mutual understanding that Guevara's days as a politician were over and he could turn to his aspirations as a guerrilla in the Congo. "Socialism and Man in Cuba" had previously appeared as a letter to the editor in the Uruguayan journal *Marcha*. However, Guevara's imminent departure from the Cuban government, in addition to his request to republish the article in Cuba, gave the text the value of a farewell or final testament. In "Socialism and Man in Cuba," Guevara attempted to solidify ideas that he had mulled over in previous writings: the individual versus the masses; direct and indirect education; the law of duty versus the law of value; moral incentives versus material incentives; artistic creation; consciousness; and sacrifice. Most importantly, Guevara articulated the idea of the New Man for the first time as a counterfigure to the "old man" of capitalism, which the new Cuba was leaving behind.

As a testament, the letter (later published as an article) bears the trace of Guevara's own life. Argentine writer Ricardo Piglia states that Guevara had originally dreamed of devoting himself fully to writing, but his life took a different path. Guevara, Piglia argues, represents the epitome of the occasional writer who evolves into a politician. Isolated and stubborn, he promoted a kind of personal politics based on his own experience (2005, 114). In addition, it is safe to assume that Guevara was exposed to the popular music and literature at the time, which proclaimed the wish to escape convention, acquire life experience, live frugally, and seek the extreme. Just as the Beat generation took youth as its banner, Guevara associated youth with strength and renewal. Though the anticapitalist mood of the times and his extensive trip through Latin America had transformed Guevara's rebellious impulse into a desire to fight inequality and injustice, numerous tenets of 1960s counterculture remained at the base of his beliefs.

Contrary to Walter Salles's view of Guevara in the film *The Motorcycle Diaries* (2004), which sentimentalizes Guevara's trip around Latin America as an encounter with "the oppressed peoples of the world" in a grand sense, Piglia argues that Guevara chose radical politics as a means of escape—a way to transcend the domestic and predictable life of a middle-class student in Buenos Aires—and a channel for his creative energy. To Piglia, Guevara perceived a tension between his own cloistered, exhausted reality and the sphere of politics as a means of passage to a different reality (2005, 126). Thus, the metaphor of the avatar is relevant because the New Man allowed Guevara to entertain a different way of operating—one based on his own standards of steadfast commitment to the Revolution but otherwise unencumbered by human needs.

In Guevara's virtual world, the New Man is forged in the fire of guerrilla war and is destined to return to it after lending himself as a vanguard leader to the revolution for a short time. As his *Episodes of the Cuban Revolutionary War* (1996, originally written in 1963) attest, Guevara's experience in Sierra Maestra was foundational for the bellicose articulation of his discourse and his military understanding of politics. In fact, Guevara saw his work as president of the national bank and minister of finance in Cuba as interim positions before he resumed his true calling to spread the Revolution worldwide. In his farewell letter to Castro before leaving for the Congo, Guevara wrote: "I feel I have accomplished the task that committed me to the revolution in Cuban territory.... Other countries of the world reclaim the fruits of my modest efforts" (quoted in

Taibo 2005, 567).[1] When preliminary attempts at revolution in Latin American countries failed, Guevara set out to support the revolution in the Congo, where he believed the true spark of world revolution could be ignited.

The avatar that Guevara created in "Socialism and Man in Cuba" (1965/1989 edition) displays his own attributes as a fighter in the context of a civilian life conceived as a constant struggle. The New Man fittingly appears as part of a mass of people resembling an army ready for combat: "Thus we *march on*. At the head of the *immense column* . . . is Fidel. After him come the best cadres of the party, and immediately behind him comes the people in its entirety, a solid structure of individualities moving toward a common goal, individuals who have attained consciousness of *what must be done*, men who *fight* to escape from the realm of necessity and enter that of *freedom*" (1989, 16; emphasis added). In describing the political structure of the Revolution, Guevara describes a squadron—a highly hierarchical and solid structure that would be challenged in later years with initiatives such as the Asamblea del poder popular (Popular power assembly) that Sara Gómez celebrated in her documentaries.

In "Socialism and Man in Cuba," the New Man "embodies the highest virtues and aspirations of the people and does not wander from the path" (Guevara 1989, 17). Women, on the other hand, appear only as "wives who must be part of the general sacrifice of their [men's] lives in order to take the revolution to its destiny" (15). The revolutionary is moved "by great feelings of love" for the masses, but Guevara regards personal affect as "ridiculous." He interjects a great deal of emotion into his political rhetoric but paradoxically associates love with a weak, feminine sentiment in which a true revolutionary could not indulge. In Guevara's virtual world, male emotion is expressed only in the context of leadership and mentorship, in what he calls *la guerra de guerrillas* (guerrilla war) "the mother hive" (2004, 15). Expanding the role of the *foco*, or guerrilla group, the mother hive is formed by a group of cadres who bring their leadership to another location once they have accomplished their mission in a given area. As the head of a mother hive, Guevara sees himself as an example of a radical transformation of personhood in those at his command.

Revolutionary activity allowed men, according to Guevara, to become "the highest rank in the human species" and to "graduate as men" (quoted in Guillermoprieto 2001, 85). The ultimate expression of masculinity was thus achieved in combat. In the framework of the traditional bourgeois ideal of a heterosexual family, Guevara calls for total dedication to revolutionary duties, which, among other things, results in women having to shoulder the responsibilities of home and children.

As a member of this exemplary cohort of men, Guevara drew on a pedagogy of personal example founded on his ethical, political, and military code, in which "leaders must constantly offer the examples of a life of purity and sacrifice" (2004, 40). Indeed, Guevara's probity as a revolutionary is not just the base of a mythology; according to his biographers, he showed a flawless commitment to the Revolution at all times. The repudiation of material rewards in favor of moral incentives was a constant point of contention during Guevara's tenure as minister of finance. He articulated his belief that work should be considered "a pleasant duty" rather than "a painful necessity" in an emphasis on volunteer labor for all Cubans (Guevara 1967, 586). Moreover, he preached through example: Several documentaries from the first five years of the Revolution show Guevara digging ditches or cutting cane every weekend, breaking records for numbers of tons (Castañeda 1997, 238). On Guevara's initiative, the government began to regulate volunteer labor in 1960, which became the cornerstone of collective stimulus. The workplace was to be the primary location for adult socialization, promoting the development of a *conciencia*—a workers' consciousness—and a social duty (Guevara 1967, 600). The negative effects of volunteer labor manifested years later, however, when overtime was shown to cost more than achieving work goals during standard work hours (Castañeda 1997, 238). In 1971, the failure of the massive campaign to harvest ten million tons of sugarcane demonstrated that the overwhelming transfer of labor to one particular task would have severe consequences for the national economy.

"Socialism and Man in Cuba" thus highlighted three ideas that are integral to the legacy of Guevara's thought and his definition of the New Man: the central role of the vanguard; the masculine traits of the New Man; and the notion of moral incentives tied to volunteer labor. The New Man–as–avatar had few of the functions of avatars in most contemporary video games. Although the New Man had powers of endurance and dedication that were far superior to those of any human —avatars are godlike creatures after all—he was severely restricted in the ways he could realize his subjectivity. The next section explores how Sara Gómez, as a filmmaker, juxtaposed real-life problems to the virtual life of the New Man, and in so doing challenged the concepts of the vanguard, masculinity, and labor that Guevara espoused.

SARA GÓMEZ AND A LIFE OF VIBRANT CONTRADICTIONS

Sara Gómez's documentary and film production (1962–74) spans arguably the most fertile and exciting years of the 1960s and the transition to the period of the *quinquenio gris* (five gray years, 1971–76)—the first significant crackdown on intellectuals and artists.[2] As Rogelio Martínez Furé notes, "Looking at Sara's life is to look at the way we were in the 60s, and those of us who survived the decade think of what she would be like today" (quoted in Padrón 1989, 41). Gómez's outlook was a product of the 1960s in a much wider sense than Che Guevara's, not only in her engagement with the Revolution in Cuba but also in regard to trends of liberation and transgression that were sweeping most of the world at the time. As Fredric Jameson famously argued, "the Third World began" in the 1960s through the waves of independence and decolonization (including the triumph of the Cuban Revolution) that swept the world—it was then that ethnic, racial, and gender "minorities" appeared as "subjects of history," no longer subsumed under the all-encompassing category of class (1984, 180). A constant concern of Gómez's, as evidenced by documentaries such as En la otra isla (1968), was what remained marginal to the institutional revolutionary project and what was not contemplated specifically in institutional discourse, such as the interests of blacks or women.

More intriguingly, Gómez aligned herself with some elements of the counterculture that were quite foreign to Cuba at the time. According to her contemporaries, Sara was a true transgressor. She poked fun at the most revered subjects and public figures, and her lifestyle did not conform to the restrictive mores of the time (Gladys Egües, interview with the author, January 2011).[3] As the first woman and Afro-Cuban documentary filmmaker of her time, and a middle-class intellectual, Gómez was aware of expectations to behave properly.[4] In her documentary Crónicas de mi familia (1966), for instance, Gómez wondered whether she would yield to the pressure: "Will we have to comply with the need to be a distinguished black person?" Nevertheless, she did not fear the cost of leading an alternative lifestyle. Her public love affairs and the fact that she left her husband, renowned filmmaker Héctor Veitía, for the sound technician and Abakuá Germinal Hernández, violated the rules of decorum held by an intellectual class that was striving to establish itself in the new cultural arena.[5] Her disregard for the standards of decency held by most of her peers explains why, despite Alfredo Guevara's support as director of the Instituto Cubano del Arte e Industria Cinematográficos (ICAIC, or Cuban Film Institute), the administration delayed the exhibition of her documentaries and kept her opinions outside public forums.[6] It is thus not surprising that the post-Special period, after the crisis of the 1990s, interest in marginal identities, at least in the arts, has brought Gómez back to the pantheon of Cuban film directors.

While the ideal of a new Africa animated the fledgling revolutionary consciousness in Cuba, as illustrated by Castro's call to join the Organization of

African Unity as an "overseas African country" (quoted in Lord 2009, 182), the regime resisted expressions of black identities as divisive and distracting from the revolutionary national project at the time. Despite this bias, Gómez made Afro-Cuban issues central to her work and actively cultivated an Afro-Cuban persona. For instance, she was one of the first Cuban intellectuals to wear her hair in an Afro. Furthermore, the ethnology and folklore seminar series conducted by Argeliers León that she attended also included among its participants such prestigious intellectuals as Manuel Moreno Fraginals, Rogelio Martínez Furé, and Miguel Barnet. Under the influence of René Depestre, the Haitian poet and critic of negritude, the group of intellectuals attending the seminars thought of themselves as trying to carve out a space for black identities in the emergent Cuba. However, these seminars were stopped at the end of the 1960s due to the regime's demand for unity at the expense of ethnic and gender differences. The *parametración*, or investigation into supposedly subversive tendencies among artists and writers, questioned Gómez and the other seminar participants. Her interrogation was but one piece of evidence that in her short career as a filmmaker she had provoked the suspicion of the regime by seeking ways of expressing identity that did not correspond to the "color-blind" New Man.

Aside from her transgressive lifestyle, Gómez was an enthusiastic supporter of the young Revolution. According to John Mraz (n.d.), her work differed fundamentally from that of Tomás Gutiérrez Alea, her mentor. Alea's position toward the ideology of the Revolution was inevitably that of an outsider, since his formative years came before 1959, and while Alea portrayed a "critical bourgeois realism," Gómez steeped herself in the Revolution and deployed a "critical socialist realism" as she reasoned within the demands for a more equal society. Unlike the classic practitioners of socialist realism in the Soviet Union, however, who blindly agreed to serve the interests of the state, Gómez strongly believed that Cuban filmmakers had a mission (see her interview in *Pensamiento Crítico* in chap. 1 of this volume).

Gómez was keenly aware that a new era was dawning in Cuba (as Guevara himself said in "Socialism and Man in Cuba") and that film offered a powerful instrument to shape the new socialist consciousness. In addition, she worried about the habitual passivity of audiences and so dispensed with aestheticizing techniques to focus instead on confronting the problems of the Revolution as directly as possible. Rather than telling a story, her interest lay in trying to understand her characters' different lifestyles and removing obstacles to individuals' commitment to the Revolution. As Juan Antonio García Borrero (2007) noted, Gómez's way of filming had such spiritual nakedness that it was almost "pornographic." Some critics were disturbed by the direct style of her filming, which attempted to give a sense of lack of mediation. In addition, the word *pornographic* points to her penchant for uncovering controversial issues and revealing what, for most people at the time, must remain private. She knew no limits in probing the depths—even those that might expose the regime's own flaws—and her films that question the New Man offer a case in point.

The immediacy and urgency of Gómez's style does not make her films less nuanced, however. In fact, she thrived in exploring contradiction and ambivalence—for instance, in documentaries such as *En la otra isla* (1968) and *Una isla para Miguel* (1968). As she stated in an interview, "Those I trust the most are the controversial youths in every classroom, in every farm, in every factory. [I trust] those who ask questions that nobody had asked, demand an answer and make others think" (quoted in García Borrero 2007). In *En la otra isla*, Gómez explores how issues such as religious conviction, rebellious counterculture, motherhood, and artistic aspiration can get in the way of youths expressing their commitment to the Revolution. Her filming technique, which contemporaries such as Nicolás Guillén Landrián also used in documentaries such as *Reportaje* (1966) and *Taller de Línea y 18* (1971), among others, highlights individual stories revealed to the viewer in what appears to be informal conversations.[7] In her filming, as much as in Guillén Landrián's productions, characters stand out against the narrative of the Revolution: their close-ups reveal their uniqueness and their personal struggles over and above their commitment to the larger project.[8] Further, in *En la otra isla*, the narrative perspective shows that understanding people's inherent contradictions involves listening without assigning guilt.

ICAIC leaders at the time believed that "documentary training was essential to develop filmmakers' understanding of their social role" and that documentaries allowed new filmmakers to slowly familiarize themselves with techniques employed in feature films (Amaya 2010, 146; see also Malitsky, this volume). In the first decade of the Revolution, moreover, documentary filmmakers were encouraged to use social science modes of inquiry in interviews that elicited people's personal experiences. As a young filmmaker, Gómez was advised to focus on documentaries before making a feature film. Three of her least known documentaries, *Poder local, poder popular* (Local power, popular power) (1970), *Sobre horas extras y trabajo voluntario* (Extra hours and voluntary work) (1973), and *Mi aporte* (My contribution) (1972), use interviews to explore contradictions inherent to the political structures, labor, and gender at the heart of Che Guevara's legacy and the New Man.

PEOPLE IN FLESH AND BONE: GRASSROOTS POLITICS CONTEST GUEVARA'S AVATAR

The documentary *Poder local, poder popular* reports on the atmosphere before a momentous event in the life of a community: the election of a local assembly representative in a sugar factory in central Cuba. While the film educates the viewer about the meaning of the election, it also sets up expectations about how the election should be conducted. The elections are presented as necessary and democratic, serving the interests of the community. Further, in exploring suitable types of leaders, the people interviewed consider the possibility of a woman representative. At a time when the local assembly was still an informal body with little representation in the larger structure of the Revolution—when the idea of democracy was an undesirable remnant of a capitalist past and the regime had not yet taken up the "woman question"—these were highly controversial and urgent topics.

In the mid-1960s, *juntas de coordinación, ejecución e inspección* (coordination, execution, and inspection boards), which had been created to mediate between the state and individuals, were replaced by *poder local* assemblies meant to incorporate ordinary citizens into state administration. By 1970, when Gómez made this documentary, the *poder local* was an administrative unit with few real powers. Delegate elections had been repeatedly postponed, semiannual meetings between delegates and citizens had not been held as scheduled, the promised congress between the Partido Comunista de Cuba (Communist Party of Cuba) and the *poder local* assemblies had been canceled, and, once it was confirmed that the sugar harvest had not achieved its objective, *poder local* delegate elections were canceled altogether (Roman 2004, 67). The system of *poder local* assemblies never really succeeded, and they were replaced in the mid-1970s by the *Órganos del poder popular*—a more reliable system of representation.

The fact that Gómez ignores the unfortunate history of the *poder local* and highlights instead the momentousness of a delegate election at a sugar factory gives the documentary a forceful impact as a representation of the way *poder local* "should" work. Rather than the hierarchical power structure that Guevara offered, with Castro and the vanguard leading the mass of New Men as one, Gómez represents the need for a democratic and inclusive revolution. Unlike Guevara, Gómez chooses to foreground a civilian structure, not a military one. Revolutionary leadership would come to recognize this need for representation over time, though the organs of popular power remain a work in progress to this day. Whereas Guevara and the leadership of the 1960s were convinced that creating mechanisms to represent a wide variety of interests entailed a risk of division and bureaucratization (Bengelsdorf 1994, 106), the documentary stresses the need for a democratic election. The word *democratic*, shown in separate titles on the screen, does not appear in an abstract or theoretical sense, as was often the case at that time during the Revolution; the objective of the elections is to choose a delegate who will truly represent the very concrete demands of community members.

The main issue in this community involved food shortage. In the style of ICAIC newsreels, which were familiar to Cuban audiences at the time, *Poder local, poder popular* informs the viewer in a seemingly objective manner. However, the narrative perspective makes it clear that the problems in food distribution are the fault of the administration, not the workers at the sugar factory. The workers, who perform various roles in the process of food distribution, are all given a voice. Some of them speak individually to what appear to be military officers, while others address the camera confidently. Even passersby are asked to offer suggestions. The documentary starts from the collective perspective of the sugar factory but emphasizes that every individual is affected by faulty distribution and every opinion matters.

A key scene shows an assembly meeting as members discuss the consequences of unequal food distribution. In the background, perhaps to emphasize the irony, a picture of Che Guevara presides. In fact, Guevara's biographers attest that he was very sympathetic to people affected by food shortages and advocated strongly for the equal distribution of goods in the provinces as well as in the capital city. However, in his speeches—particularly in his definition of the New Man—Guevara emphasized a degree of asceticism that was hard to maintain in daily life. According to Guevara, the New Man "should not be distracted by such worries as that his child lacks certain things, that his children's shoes are worn out, that his family lacks some necessity" (1989, 16). By contrast, women in the documentary are quite vocal about the consequences of food shortages for their families. These women show starkly that shortages of basic products cause anxiety among women and children, and ultimately paralyze entire communities.

Gómez devotes much of the documentary to delineating the characteristics of the ideal delegate of the *poder local* assembly. It becomes clear that she is unconcerned with the identification of the ideal leader with the New Man. Instead, she probes whether the community would consider a woman to be the right candidate. All the people she interviews agree that the new delegate should be a committed revolutionary, but they part ways when it comes to gender—men are doubtful that a woman representative could meet the demands of the job. The documentary thus identifies the high cost of Guevara's cavalier injunction that men focus on their revolutionary duties at the expense of caring for children at home. In fact, in the first election of the *poder popular* assemblies, which succeeded the *poder local* assemblies, 13.5 percent of nominated delegates were women, but only 8.7 percent of elected representatives were women (Bengelsdorf 1994, 109). To this day, few women occupy positions of leadership in Cuba (Luciak 2007, 33, 65). *Poder local, poder popular* preceded and anticipated Gómez's documentary *Mi aporte*, in which she directly tackled the problem of women's lack of participation in leadership and the workforce.

Meanwhile, *Sobre horas extras y trabajo voluntario* spoke directly to one of Guevara's strongest commitments as minister of finance. Gómez forcefully identifies the central problem of volunteer labor through numerous interruptions of the film with written messages that emphasize particular points. The use of these interruptions in the film and the frequent disconnect between the written messages and the stories the characters tell situate Gómez in line with French director Guy Debord, who had visited Cuba at the time and was tremendously influential on several Cuban directors. The opening titles simulate typed notes from the twelfth congress of the Central de Trabajadores de Cuba and emphasize the importance of volunteer labor to the regime. However, the rest of the documentary systematically questions the efficacy of this type of work. For instance, a worker with whom many viewers would no doubt identify appears on the screen and states that he has worked 240 hours of overtime in the past six months. A brief conversation between this man and Gómez, who appears in the frame, reveals that the worker never inquired whether these hours were necessary. Rather, he did them out of duty. Gómez proceeds to ask the questions that most supervisors apparently were not asking: "Are workers coming to work on time and every day?" "Has there been an increase in productivity?" The voice-over then calls volunteer hours "a vice" and the product of "self-deception" because they do not offset the cost of keeping the buildings open longer and the general decrease in productivity due to tiredness. Thus, by exposing the gaps between ideals and practice, Gómez openly questions the national regulations that leaders had declared to be good. Women turn out to be Gómez's most forthcoming interviewees—one openly states that overtime takes time away from families and that volunteer labor often entails empty effort. She gives a telling example: volunteers were asked to haul some rocks from one place to another over several days, until the rocks ended up back in their original place.

In a voice-over, Gómez lays out a list of preliminary tasks that need to be accomplished before sending a group of people on a volunteer mission, such as organizing the work to be done, deciding how many people are necessary to achieve it, estimating workers' level of productivity, making sure that the area is ready for the intervention, and that the results justify the investment. No leader had stated such preconditions; they were Gómez's own policy recipe. As the documentary draws to an end, Gómez proleptically introduces quotations by Guevara and Castro on the importance of volunteer labor to create *conciencia* (awareness) and includes footage of both leaders doing volunteer work at different locations alongside a crowd of citizens. However, Gómez herself has the last word, stressing once again that overtime or volunteer labor must be judged on the basis of "quality, productivity, and cost." The written messages that interrupt the documentary deliver the point even more forcefully, illustrating the gap between ideals of political discourse and citizens' sentiments. Often, the gap between official recommendations and what the interviewees propose is marked by the insertion of *"PERO"* (but) in a written message. In effect, the documentary makes clear that while people committed to the Revolution may be willing to follow official directives in doing volunteer work, the consequences of this work may be detrimental to their lives and the overall progress of the Revolution.

Research on Cuban women has repeatedly shown that the Revolution did not specifically struggle against gender inequalities.[9] Although Cuban women received education, health care, and reproductive rights that they had not enjoyed before, changes in gender policy were not far reaching because of persistent patriarchal notions and the fact that the needs of the Revolution superseded women's emancipation. Vilma Espín, president of the Federación de Mujeres Cubanas (FMC, or Federation of Cuban Women) (created in 1960), stated from the beginning that the purpose of the FMC was intricately connected to the larger context of the Revolution: "The problems women face cannot be seen in isolation from other social problems, and they cannot be analyzed outside of their economic context" (1991, 55). The theory of the New Man who replaced the old man of the capitalist era failed to consider that, if not addressed specifically, many of the patriarchal preconceptions of the former era would carry over to the new society. To give one example, Tomás Gutiérrez Alea's film *Memorias del subdesarrollo* (Memories of underdevelopment) (1968) critically represented many bourgeois male attitudes against women, such as objectification. As well, Rolando Díaz's *Si me comprendieras* (I wish you would understand me)(1999) brazenly displays the same stereotypes of women. By not addressing the specific demands of women, the regime hindered women's potential and reined in their ambition. Men's development was also hindered, as aptly shown in Gómez's film *De cierta manera* (One way or another) (1974).

The first decade of the Revolution saw little activity among the FMC—just one congress in September 1962 and a few small meetings before a second congress in November 1974. It was not until the 1970s that legislation was passed that could be considered directly relevant to women's rights, including the Ley de la Infancia (Law of Childhood) in 1971, Reglamento de Círculos (Rules of Daycare Centers) in 1973, Ley de Maternidad (Maternity Law) in 1974, and the Ley de Familia (Family Code) in 1975. In the early 1970s, as the need to incorporate women into the workforce became more pressing, the regime adopted an increasingly negative rhetoric toward household chores and the lives of housewives. For example, after the devastating failure of the ten-million-ton sugar harvest campaign, housewives were blamed for their supposed lack of commitment. In reality, many housewives had to stay home with their families or fill the jobs that their husbands left vacant to work in the harvest. After a short period, many of these women were forced to abandon their husbands' jobs to care for their children. The labor minister, Jorge Risquet, called housewives "a dense layer of idle women" at a moment when laws against idleness, also discussed by Fowler (this volume), interpreted idleness as disaffection with the Revolution (Padula and Smith 1996, 100). A "feminine front" was created for the Cuban trade unions to keep track of women's attendance and performance at work as well as their family duties (101).

In contrast to their "unimportant" home duties, the regime presented work outside the house, including volunteer tasks, as more suitable challenges for women.[10] In response, the FMC reacted to the stress that resulted from the coexistence of old and new attitudes toward women and women's triple schedule of home, work, and volunteer labor. The organization's magazine, *Mujeres*, began to suggest ways for women to use their time effectively at home so that they could be more productive at a job outside the house. This magazine and films such as Pastor Vega's *Retrato de Teresa* (Portrait of Teresa) (1979) represented the gap between the official discourse on idle housewives and the experience of many women with triple schedules. The 1975 Family Code declared that men and women should share household duties, which only began the process of changing people's minds about what types of work are suitable for women and men—a struggle that continues to this day.

In this context, Gómez made the documentary *Mi aporte*, which she started in 1969 and released in 1972 (also discussed by Casamayor, Abd'Allah-Alvarez Ramírez, Lord, and Benson, all in this volume). Filmed at the request of the FMC, the documentary made two concessions to the women's organization: inclusion of the opening song ("*Las mujeres cubanas, adelante, adelante*") and the final cine-debate session meant to mitigate the impact of a conversation shown earlier in the film between Gómez and three women professionals (Gladys Egües, interview with author, January 2011). Nevertheless, the FMC considered the documentary too controversial, and, as a result, following its debut at the Dúplex, the film was not exhibited again until 1978. Most Cubans critics today cannot believe that anything in this documentary could be considered objectionable; in fact, it is often shown in retrospectives and tributes to Gómez. Still, the film relentlessly questioned the gender discourse of the time and aired issues that had not been discussed in public forums before. In offering a tribute to women's contributions to the ten-million-ton sugar harvest, one of the movie's first images is of a sack of sugar, and the legend "Mi aporte" refers both to the outstanding participation of women in the campaign and to Gómez's personal attempt to advocate for women.

The beginning of the film follows the model of *Poder local, poder popular* by quoting an established idea only to question it and expose its weaknesses throughout the rest of the documentary: "You who bring in a new day whenever you come back home. New ideas, new thoughts to share with the husband and the children when you reunite [after the workday]. Respected and loved by her husband and children, firm and determined at work, a woman is one more worker for this Revolution."

This perfect picture of a woman worker and mother would have been familiar to documentary viewers at the time because official discourse stressed the self-enrichment possibilities for women working outside the home. Thus, the quote speaks to the heart of the objective of the women's movement to make women "one more worker for the Revolution." Over the course of the film, however, interviews with workers at the factory reveal the obstacles to fully integrating women into the labor force. One man recognizes that his paternalistic attitude toward women gets in the way of his productivity because women's problems with pregnancy or family make him feel obliged to take over their work. A woman reveals that if her husband did not allow her to work, then she would immediately have to quit her job.

In the style of an ethnographic investigation, Gómez follows women to their homes and witnesses their commitments to their families as well as the attempts of the FMC and Comités de Defensa de la Revolución to fully engage these women in work outside the home. Each visit makes clear that the women raise children largely by themselves. The film stresses that fundamental ideological biases as well as practical matters hinder both men's and women's progress. By the time the question "Are we creating the conditions for the new woman?" appears on-screen, the irony is clear: Having *la mujer nueva* "be part of the sacrifice of the Revolution," as Guevara put it, means that women will have to yield to patriarchal biases.

The heart of the documentary, which tellingly takes place at home, is a conversation among four professional women: Sara Gómez; Lucía Corona (from the Centro Nacional de Investigación Científica, or National Center of Scientific Investigations); Mirta Valladares (from the Escuela de Diseño Industrial, or School of Industrial Design); and Gladys Egües (journalist and personal friend of the author). Each participant presents a different point of view in her analysis of motherhood, career plans, education of men, and gender bias, but all share a strongly critical attitude toward the dominant gender discourse. They agree that education is essential to challenge gender stereotypes in the family environment. In addition, they discuss the role of motherhood in perpetuating women's career difficulties and the possibility of not marrying in order to reach professional and personal fulfillment. Implicit in all their reflections is the idea that the strict division of labor between home and street that Guevara embraced is an obstacle to women's advancement.

The FMC's cine-debate that ends the film, however, dilutes the impact of the preceding discussion and presents a more hopeful perspective. Cine-debates were instituted in the 1960s following the screening of films in theaters. They were meant to teach critical viewing skills in order to extract the correct revolutionary message from a film. In *Mi aporte*, the debate was included in the documentary as a means of reframing the problem of women's fulfillment in relation to motherhood. During the debate, some members of the all-female audience enthusiastically participate in the conversation with the director while others yawn or look completely disinterested and detached. Still others deny that they have ever had problems reconciling demands at home and at work. Yet, over the course of the debate, the audience is led to assume that women are frustrated and incomplete if they do not become mothers. Thus, the cine-debate reflects the difficulty of shattering gender stereotypes and educating an audience about gender roles. The emphasis on motherhood recalls Espín's key observations made at the first congress of the FMC: "The ideal of the new woman . . . is that of a healthy woman, full of the joy of life, future mothers of the generations who will make Communism a reality" (Espín 1990b, 22). The song that ends the documentary, "*Ser comunista para triunfar*" (To be a communist is to win victory), stresses the importance of women in the workforce and the contradictions, challenges, and goals facing the movement for women's rights in Cuba. As a result, the issues discussed in the earlier conversation among Gómez and the three women resonate once again at the end of the movie despite the cine-debate. It is this discussion that reveals the critical intention of the film, even as the cine-debate gives FMC members a chance to speak as well.

Gómez's fervent commitment to the Cuban Revolution from its inception cannot be denied. In a previously unpublished 1970 interview with Marguerite Duras that now appears in this anthology, Gómez confessed that she did not understand the French writer's work, which is pervaded by sadness, melancholy, and an inability to comprehend or face life's challenges. Gómez states without a shade of irony that she is, on the contrary, "exhilarated, immensely happy with the time she is experiencing" and thrilled with her role as a filmmaker (Gómez 1972). Her commitment to a new society based on the ethics of solidarity pushed her to puzzle out the fundamental aporia of an official discourse that projected itself onto the future yet offered models of identity to individuals whose situation was less than ideal in their present.

The New Man as a superhero avatar took on different guises over the course of the Revolution.[11] It was no doubt a powerful figure, but one that functioned only in a virtual reality. As the enthusiasm of the 1960s waned and Guevara became the hallmark of a nostalgic ethical ideal, he became the only New Man ever seen. Gómez's documentaries of the first half of the 1970s show that the "sublime and improbable" rhetoric of the "political religion" (Fernández 2000, 56) that dominated official revolutionary discourse in 1960s Cuba crumbled when tested against food shortages, the need to be heard, and the desire to channel one's creative energy through pursuits other than work. Gómez proves that Cubans were critical of the gap between official constructions of identity in political discourse and their daily routines, and while they might have been persuaded to become better, they had no desire to become new men.

NOTES

1. Translations from Spanish originals are my own unless otherwise noted.
2. Benson (this volume) argues that the *quinquenio gris* started in 1968 with the first Cultural Congress in Havana.
3. For a description of the changes and continuities of social mores in prerevolutionary Cuba, the 1960s, and beyond, see Lumsden (1996, 28–80).
4. See Martiatu Terry (2011; this volume) for the account of a personal friend on Gómez's background.
5. In Alexandra Müller's documentary, *¿Dónde está Sara Gómez?* (2005), Julio Machado, a good friend of Sara and of her husband, claims that Germinal Hernández was "a marginal man himself" because of his lifestyle and peculiar temper.

6. Benson (this volume) discusses this further.
7. Lord discusses this in her introduction to this book.
8. See Casamayor's (this volume) discussion of this.
9. See Bunck (1992), Randall (1992), Molyneux (2000), and Hamilton (2012), among others.
10. For instance, Castro stated that projects where mainly women worked, and where the leaders were also women, did away with the prejudice "that women are only capable of washing dishes, doing laundry, ironing, cooking, cleaning the house, and bearing children" (1981, 50).
11. See Kapcia (1997) for an overview of the New Man's appearances and transformations over the decades.

BIBLIOGRAPHY

Amaya, Héctor. 2010. *Screening Cuba: Film Criticism as Political Performance during the Cold War.* Urbana: University of Illinois Press.
Bengelsdorf, Carollee. 1994. *The Problem of Democracy in Cuba: Between Vision and Reality.* Oxford: Oxford University Press.
Bunck, Julie Marie. 1995. "Women's Rights and the Cuban Revolution." In *Cuban Communism (1959–1995),* edited by Irving L. Horowitz, 427–49. New York: Transaction.
Castañeda, Jorge. 1997. *Compañero: Vida y muerte de Che Guevara.* New York: Vintage.
Castro, Fidel. 1981. "Revolution within the Revolution." In *Women and the Cuban Revolution,* edited by Elizabeth Stone, 48–54. New York: Pathfinder.
Díaz, Rolando. 1999. *Si me comprendieras.* Havana: ICAIC.
Duchesne, Juan. 2010. *La guerrilla narrada: Acción, acontecimiento, sujeto.* San Juan, Puerto Rico: Callejón.
Espín Guillois, Vilma. 1990a. "Discurso en el acto de constitución de la Federación de Mujeres Cubanas." In *La mujer en Cuba,* 1–27. Havana: Editora política.
———. 1990b. "Informe central del congreso de la Federación de Mujeres Cubanas (1962)." In *Informes centrales de los congresos de la FMC,* 5–39. Havana: Imprenta Central de las FAR.
———. 1991. *Cuban Women Confront the Future.* Melbourne: Ocean Press.
Fernández, Damián. 2000. *Cuba and the Politics of Passion.* Austin: University of Texas Press.
García Borrero, José A. 2007. "Sara Gómez (1)." *Cine cubano, la pupila insomne,* March 18, 2007. Accessed April 14, 2015. https://cinecubanolapupilainsomne.wordpress.com/2007/03/18/sara-gomez-1/.

Gómez, Sara. 1970. "Los documentalistas y sus convicciones." *Pensamiento Crítico*, no. 42 (July): 92–97.

———. 1972. "Interview with Marguerite Duras." Havana: ICAIC Cinemateca archive.

Guevara, Ernesto "Che." 1967. "Sobre el sistema presupuestario de financiamiento." *Obra revolucionaria*, 577–601. Mexico City: Ediciones Era.

———. 1989. "Socialism and Man in Cuba." In *Socialism and Man in Cuba*, edited by Che Guevara and Fidel Castro, 1–19. New York: Pathfinder.

———. 1996. *Episodes of the Cuban Revolutionary War*. New York: Pathfinder.

———. 2004. *La guerra de guerrillas, obras escogidas*. Santiago de Chile: Digital por Resma.

Guillermoprieto, Alma. 2001. "Ernesto Che Guevara: The Harsh Angel." In *Looking for History: Dispatches from Latin America*, 73–86. New York: Vintage.

Gutiérrez Alea, Tomás. 1968. *Memorias del subdesarrollo*. Havana: ICAIC.

Hamilton, Carrie. 2012. *Sexual Revolutions in Cuba: Passion, Politics and Memory*. Chapel Hill: University of North Carolina Press.

Jameson, Fredric. 1984. "Periodizing the Sixties." In "The Sixties without Apology." Special issue, *Social Text* 9/10 (Spring/Summer): 178–209.

Kapcia, Antoni. 1997. "Political and Economic Reform in Cuba: The Significance of Che Guevara." In *La situación actual en Cuba: Desafíos y alternativas*, edited by Mona Rosendahl. Stockholm: Institute of Latin American Studies.

Lord, Susan. 2009. "Acts of Affection: Cinema, Citizenship, and Race in the Work of Sara Gómez." In *Gender and Sexuality in 1968: Transformative Politics in the Cultural Imagination*, edited by Lessie Jo Frazier and Deborah Cohen, 173–92. New York: Palgrave.

Luciak, Ilja A. 2007. *Gender and Democracy in Cuba*. Gainesville: University Press of Florida.

Lumsden, Ian. 1996. *Machos, Maricones and Gays: Cuba and Homosexuality*. Philadelphia: Temple University Press.

Martiatu Terry, Inés María. 2011. "Una isla para Sara Gómez." In *Hijas del Muntu: Biografías críticas de mujeres afrodescendientes de América Latina*, edited by María Mercedes Jaramillo y Lucía Ortiz, 269–92. Bogota, Colombia: Panamericana.

Molyneux, Maxine. 2000. "State, Gender and Institutional Change: The Federación de Mujeres Cubanas." In *Hidden Histories of Gender in Latin America*, edited by Elizabeth Dore and Maxine Molyneux, 291–21. Durham, NC: Duke University Press.

Mraz, John. n.d. "Sara Gómez—Director." *Film Reference*. Accessed April 14, 2015. http://www.filmreference.com/Directors-Fr-Ha/G-mez-Sara.html.

Müller, Alessandra, dir. 2005. *¿Dónde está Sara Gómez?* Savosa, Switzerland: Amka Films.
Padrón, Frank. 1989. "Retrato múltiple de Sara." *Cine Cubano* 127: 36–44.
Padula, Alfred, and Lois M. Smith. 1996. *Sex and Revolution: Women in Socialist Cuba*. Oxford: Oxford University Press.
Piglia, Ricardo. 2005. "Ernesto Guevara, rastros de lectura." In *El último lector*, 103–38. Barcelona: Anagrama.
Randall, Margaret. 1992. *Gathering Rage: The Failure of Twentieth Century Revolutions to Develop a Feminist Agenda*. New York: Monthly Review.
Roman, Peter. 2004. *People's Power: Cubans' Experience with Representative Government*. Oxford: Rowman and Littlefield.
Salles, Walter, dir. 2004. *The Motorcycle Diaries*. Los Angeles: Universal.
Taibo, Paco Ignacio. 2005. *Ernesto Che Guevara también conocido como el Che*. México City: Planeta.
Vega, Pastor. 1979. *Retrato de Teresa*. Havana: ICAIC.

ANA SERRA is Associate Professor Emerita of Spanish and Latin American Studies at American University in Washington DC. Her book, *The New Man in Cuba: Culture and Identity in the Revolution* (2008), examines the construction of a new Cuban identity in literary representations of political campaigns during the formative decade of the Cuban Revolution. She has also published on Cuban film and popular culture in peer-reviewed journals such as *Journal of Latin American Studies*, *Journal of Latin American and Caribbean Studies*, *Hispanic Journal*, *Revista de estudios hispánicos*, and *Journal of Gender Studies*, among others. In 2019, Ana Serra retired to pursue a second career in clinical social work, and she is serving Latinx and Latin American patients as a therapist.

THIRTEEN

Iván Arocha Montes de Oca Interviewed by Ricardo Acosta

IVÁN AROCHA MONTES DE OCA: I'm Iván Arocha. I was born in 1942. The first thing I wanted to do in life was to be a painter. I've more or less kept up the discipline of painting all my life. For more than thirty years I worked, I stayed in the ICAIC [Instituto Cubano del Arte e Industria Cinematográficos, or Cuban Film Institute] working as a film editor, but right now I'm not connected with film anymore. I'm focusing on painting.

RICARDO ACOSTA: *So, Iván, we could say that you were part of the first generation of filmmakers—of what's known as* cine cubano *(Cuban film)?*

IVÁN AROCHA MONTES DE OCA: I'm practically part of that generation, the first generation of cine cubano, from the sixties. The institute was one of the first things the Revolution founded, together with the agrarian reform. The film institute was created in 1960, and in 1961 I started working with the ICAIC.

RICARDO ACOSTA: *Could you tell me who your friends were from this generation? Who were those creators and friends with whom you found a community as an artist?*

IVÁN AROCHA MONTES DE OCA: When I began at the ICAIC, I wasn't trained, I wasn't prepared. As a student I jumped into a professional world for which I wasn't trained, and I established relationships with certain people beyond professional relationships—human relationships. With Raúl Molina, Miguelito Ordoqui—some of the people's names don't come to mind now. But there was someone who always fascinated me, who was exceptional, and that was Sara Gómez. And I was scared of Sara Gómez. One day Sara Gómez came up to me and said, "You know something? We have something in common, we came into ICAIC in the same way." I was stunned. "Eh?!" I didn't know Sara was talking to me. And it turned out Sara didn't try to enter the ICAIC, in exactly the same way that I didn't try to enter. We were recruited to work at the ICAIC. The Cuban Institute for Cinematic Art and Industry created a strategy to capture talented young people, and both Sara and I belonged to the Union of Rebel Youth, although we didn't know each other—she was from one sector and I was from another. I was in the Institute of El Vedado studying to finish secondary school, and she was working at *Mella* magazine. Somehow we were recruited, and we came to work at the ICAIC. She was from one generation—the graduating class before mine, one or two before mine. When I started, she knew how these talent recruitments were done in different sectors of young people, and she knew that I had been recruited. This was ... so that's why she approached me, and we established a relationship that lasted for the remainder of Sara's life.

RICARDO ACOSTA: *And your life.*

IVÁN AROCHA MONTES DE OCA: Well, our relationship—when Sara died, the relationship couldn't continue between us.

RICARDO ACOSTA: *Iván, there's something I've always wanted to ask you. For you, who was Sara as an artist and as a person?*

IVÁN AROCHA MONTES DE OCA: As an artist, Sara was a human being, and that's the best definition you can give of an artist or talented person in any area of art—a human being. Sara was a very talented, very analytical, very irreverent human being, and among her friends she was unconditional. Sara wasn't easy to get close to because she was very selective about her friendships, but when she allowed you to enter her world of human relationships and the environment around her friends, she was very loyal. For her, friendship was a very valuable thing. What can I say? Analytical, deeply human, and honest, with very rigorous principles—in every sense an incalculably human being.

RICARDO ACOSTA: *Lovely. Another question for me is very important. How was the creative process between the two of you? There is always a very intimate, particular relationship between an editor and a director, especially when it has to do with documentary films because of the way they are created in the montage process. You weren't just colleagues, but friends. You were also part of Sara's life, because you also had a role to play in her children's lives. So, how was that mixture, the personal-artistic relationship between you? And how did you journey from that personal relationship to the editor-director relationship and into the creative process? Did you leave the friendship out? I would imagine not. You left it in the mix? How did you do this?*

IVÁN AROCHA MONTES DE OCA: Look, look, as I said, Sara was an exceptional person as a human being and also as a filmmaker. I can illustrate with some examples. Sara was interested in working on film without so much rigidity as tends to be established on filmmaking teams—you are the editor, you the cinematographer, your responsibilities as editor are these. She was interested in a more integrated team approach. She was interested, for example, in the editor forming part of her film, in the cinematographer being part of her film. We would meet in her house when she was just beginning to conceive of the film, and we talked about the project and shared ideas that fed into it that could be applied later on. That was the system that Sara established. For her, being a film director never meant a hierarchy. She didn't take it on with arrogance, she didn't take it on... Sara gave equal importance to being a mother, being a woman, and being a director.

RICARDO ACOSTA: *Filmmaker?*

IVÁN AROCHA MONTES DE OCA: When this happened, she... sought to integrate her role as a woman, as a mother, and as a filmmaker, in an atmosphere—she had to create a nucleus.

RICARDO ACOSTA: *And in that nucleus there were several artists that were also her friends. Who were they? Can you tell me who was in this creative group, this group of friends? I think that in Sara's case, her relationships with artists, friends, and collaborators were very much intertwined.*

IVÁN AROCHA MONTES DE OCA: Yes. And, look, you know that Sara studied ethnology and folklore. In that process she established very close relationships with Alberto Pedro and Tomás González, with the cinematographer Luis García [Mesa; see interview with Mesa in this volume], who was the cinematographer on many of her films. In my case, I started to work with her after she had done a great piece of work with another editor, Dulce María Villalón. These teams were part of her daily, domestic world, and we met in her house so it was a friendly and professional relationship—very rich and very solid.

RICARDO ACOSTA: *Germinal?*

IVÁN AROCHA MONTES DE OCA: Of course, Germinal [Hernández], who was her husband and did the sound on almost all her films. So, in this way, Sara's domestic and professional worlds were one and the same—they were totally connected. Sara created social gatherings (*tertulias*) in her house with intellectuals, as I said, like Tomás González, Alberto Pedro, and all of us, and she would be cooking and feeding her children, and at the same time we'd all be talking about film, philosophy, the project, the next project, or perhaps another one that would happen after that. And it was a very closed-in, narrow world, and yet very wide open at the same time. Sara's domestic world overflowed to reach into the infinite.

RICARDO ACOSTA: What were the works, the films you edited with Sara? Please mention some of them and tell me, for you, which are the ones that to some extent—as an editor I also have my memories of particular projects that I've done and I feel affection for all of them, and I have a very specific relationship with all, but there are some that are like prodigal sons, more adored than others. Which, do you think, is the most relevant work that you and Sara did together?

IVÁN AROCHA MONTES DE OCA: Without a doubt the most important film I worked on with Sara was her first feature film, *De cierta manera*. *De cierta manera*, because it was her first feature film, and not only that but also because of all the implications of the film's theme. It was the most important work of Sara's in which I participated. All the rest were like commercials, even the documentaries. She felt the need to start with a series of somewhat light, trivial documentaries as a strategy. Sara was always a very critical woman, very severe in her criticism, very intransigent, and that's how she was in her filmmaking—severe, intransigent, and rigorous. As much about sexual themes as about political or racial issues. Sara came to the conclusion that, as a strategy, she needed to make films that would reach out to the public, so that she could begin to be known in Cuba as a film director.

RICARDO ACOSTA: Wait a moment. Just to understand—this was a survival strategy, like a kind of culture, cultural resistance we might say? A filmmaker's survival strategy or cultural resistance, since her most important work had been censored and she was a kind of ghost filmmaker at the beginning?

IVÁN AROCHA MONTES DE OCA: Practically all Sara's work was like a ghost, as you say. Her work lived in the archives permanently.... All filmmakers make work to be shown, and she was interested in getting her audience—that was, Cuba, the people to whom she directed her work—to see her films, but they weren't seeing them because all of her work was shelved. As a strategy to get beyond the boundaries of the archive and onto cinema screens, she decided to start making a series of more trivial films so she could move forward and get her films shown.

RICARDO ACOSTA: *For example?*

IVÁN AROCHA MONTES DE OCA: That's how she made *Parqueando el carro* (Parking the car). I don't know, now I can't remember the series or title of these lighter documentaries. In the meantime, she was working on the script for her first feature film that would eventually be *De cierta manera*. Once Sara began to mature, once she began to work conscientiously on *De cierta manera*, she took an interest in making sure all of her team—the cinematographer, sound recorder, and editor—participated in the development of the work from the very beginning. Whenever I could, she would ask me to go see the research she was doing so that I could get to know that world, so that I connected with it. This way, when I was working in the editing room, I wouldn't be like a stranger who receives a quantity of money and then spends it without thinking and ends up cutting indiscriminately looking for a rhythm and trying to—no! This way I would be emotionally involved like her, like the camera operator and sound person, in the world we were addressing in the work. For her, that was really important.

At that time, the ICAIC had a shortage of film materials, and this was resolved when several agreements were established with Germany, Czechoslovakia, and the Soviet Union to do an exchange and receive film material from those countries. Until that moment, color and thirty-five-millimeter film were a bit like luxuries for many directors.

RICARDO ACOSTA: *For fiction they were fundamental?*

IVÁN AROCHA MONTES DE OCA: For fiction, yes. When Sara presented a project to do her first feature and she said she wants to do it in sixteen millimeter, it was a scandal. Even Tomás Gutiérrez Alea told her, "But you have to do your film in color and in thirty-five millimeter!" And she said, "No, I don't want to do it in thirty-five millimeter or in color. I want to shoot it in sixteen millimeter and in black and white." Everyone was [stunned]. Something else happened in that period. . . .

RICARDO ACOSTA: *What?*

IVÁN AROCHA MONTES DE OCA: I'll tell you later on. In that period, I was working with Nicolás Guillén [Landrián]. We'd finished Nicolás's film *Coffea Arabiga* (1968), and *Coffea Arabiga* ended up being a film that was considered to be troublesome both in terms of the film as a product and in the production process. We were accused of having taken too much time, of having wasted time and having wasted materials, and both Nicolás and I were sanctioned and fired from our jobs. Then, Sara is doing her project and she says that she wants to do a sixteen-millimeter film—and on top of it she wants me as the editor. And they tell her, "No, but there are a lot of editors available who haven't been punished or are in other work." She says, "But I want to work with Iván Arocha, and he's the editor I need." She piled on the pressure, and they took me out of the work they'd given me as an editor. I was restoring films that had been damaged in commercial cinemas. They took me out of there and brought me back to my job as an editor to work with Sara. Thanks to Sara, I returned to my job as an editor.

Sara was very respectful of religious themes because she respected her ancestors, respected their religion. The film *De cierta manera* was going to have certain sequences with religious material, and she didn't want these sequences to be commercialized by the color of the film. She said, "I don't want these images to be seen like prints in a calendar . . . that are put there like adornments, to be pretty." When Sara selected her team, she asked for me, Iván Arocha, as editor, Luis García Mesa as cinematographer, and Germinal as the sound person. They said to her—ah, yes!—they said to Sara, "Why Iván Arocha? Iván Arocha has no experience in feature films, as well as being sanctioned. Luis García Mesa doesn't have feature film experience either. We propose you edit with Nelson or with another editor. And that you use Livio Delgado." And she said, "No, no, no, wait a minute, I'm not interested in Livio, or in Nelson, I'm interested in Iván and Luis." She had a reason—not only because of the friendship we had. This was going to be her first fiction feature. She wanted, in terms of internal balance, for it to be her first fiction feature, my first fiction feature, and Luis García's first fiction feature. It was a question of balance and strength. She said, "I don't want Nelson Rodríguez or Livio Delgado's experiences in feature film. I'm interested in the professionalism of Iván and Luis, and in working together on their first feature film with me. I don't want a relationship in which the editor, because of his experience, imposes himself on the work, or that a camera operator imposes his experience on the work." Do you understand what she was saying? She was looking for this balance.

RICARDO ACOSTA: *That's very interesting because, in my personal experience, in general I'm the more experienced person when I work with first-time directors or first-time producers, and someone has to tell me, and know how [to do certain things]. But in this case, we're talking about a filmmaker who knew what she wanted, and that's the difference.*

IVÁN AROCHA MONTES DE OCA: Who knew what she wanted and had her own personal criteria.

RICARDO ACOSTA: *She had her own very defined criteria, and she was working with a team of people who were artists and her friends—her creative group?*

IVÁN AROCHA MONTES DE OCA: On a film that was sui generis.

RICARDO ACOSTA: *It was sui generis?*

IVÁN AROCHA MONTES DE OCA: It wasn't going to be a fiction feature like any other. And that's why she didn't want any imposition of traditional criteria that other potential members of the team might have. She defended this with a lot of…

RICARDO ACOSTA: *It seems to me very beautiful.*

IVÁN AROCHA MONTES DE OCA: And she was more interested in people's professionalism, creativity, and analytical sense than their experience and, let's say, discipline within a specialty.

RICARDO ACOSTA: *In other words, we're returning here to the point about her moral integrity and her commitment, her faithfulness, her loyalty?*

IVÁN AROCHA MONTES DE OCA: To human beings.

RICARDO ACOSTA: *Her compassion—there's a very clear sense of respect for others. At a time when there was a lot of jostling for position, to be able to occupy that small space that there was for glory.*

IVÁN AROCHA MONTES DE OCA: Yes. Look, when we were talking about Sara in terms of her films that were shelved and the need, the strategy of hers of having—she said something so… that reflects the moment, the circumstance, everything. Sara said, "It's just that I feel like the little black woman that they have in the ICAIC to show to the foreigners. And they only keep me there for that reason, because I'm a woman, I'm black, and I have that role—more as a diplomat than a filmmaker." She defined herself that way—like the little black woman that the ICAIC had to show to foreigners who visited the institute. She was the first film director—woman film director—that the ICAIC had, and on top of that black, and she felt she was being used like so many others because of that.

RICARDO ACOSTA: *For me, there's a very important point that people rarely talk about, and it's that, as an editor, relationships are an important part of the creative process and the validity of the work. The achievement of the work is in the strength of the collaboration and in the fluidity of and respect for that collaboration. I don't make a film by myself; I make a film with a director.*

IVÁN AROCHA MONTES DE OCA: It's the work of a team.

RICARDO ACOSTA: *It's teamwork and collaboration, then. So, what happens? How does that process suddenly, without wanting it, without anticipating or imagining it, turn into something that feels for an editor like being an orphan, being abandoned? With a film so important, so troublesome?*

IVÁN AROCHA MONTES DE OCA: When Sara died, the film was practically finished in terms of the structure, the whole concept—it was finished. There were sequences yet to be filmed, but they were already marked out in the main framework of the film—this sequence is going to have this length, this dub will be this long. Conceptually, the work was concluded when Sara died, but there's a problem. The work wasn't abandoned, it wasn't orphaned because its mother died. It was orphaned because everyone abandoned it, which is sadder. The assistant director never showed up again, the adviser, Titón [Tomás Gutiérrez Alea], never reappeared—the work was abandoned. Only Luis and I took care of filming the sequences that remained, which were shots of the demolition of the Cayo Hueso neighborhood, where the film was developed [and set].

Worse than that, the orphan tried to get adopted. One day, Titón appeared in the editing room with Mario García Joya, who, as is known, wasn't the film's camera operator, and he asked me to pass the film on to him—saying that he was the adviser. I gave him the film, of course, but during the process of passing the film through the Moviola [film editing and viewing apparatus], Titón and Mayito [Mario García Joya] start to talk about the shots they were going to film and changes they were going to make in the structure and concept. When I finished showing them the copy, I asked Titón, "Titón, what...?" "No...we're going to make some changes in the film." I said, "No, look, forgive me, the film is finished just as Sara wanted it to be finished, and in terms of the only things left to do Sara decided what was missing and we know what else there is and we're doing it. The film is not going to change." Titón respected my attitude; I don't know why, but he respected it. He never again insisted on making any changes, but he didn't take responsibility for doing anything either.

RICARDO ACOSTA: *In his advisory role?*

IVÁN AROCHA MONTES DE OCA: As the adviser. The only thing he said to me was, "This is a very sloppy film and the only thing I'm trying to do is save it." Because he didn't think—from the moment Sara asked to film it in black and white, he began to underestimate the film. He remained as adviser because of the circumstances and relationships and, well, it was his role. But after Sara's death, and after his attempt to change the film with another, unrelated camera operator as he saw fit, he was frustrated. He never again appeared in the editing room.

RICARDO ACOSTA: *And the film was finished?*

IVÁN AROCHA MONTES DE OCA: Eventually the film was finished, but a lot of things happened in trying to do this. When you are shooting a sixteen-millimeter black-and-white film, there are distinct materials to select and work with: the stock, the storage, and the rewinds. The stock we used was standard sixteen-millimeter, reversible sixteen-millimeter, and Super sixteen-millimeter. This had consequences when the film editing was being finished. Well, I had to edit it, and I took it to the laboratory. I went to the lab to talk with the person who was to direct the work—responsible for cutting the negatives—and I explained about the different material because some of the material was reversible—it has emulsion on one side, and in this case it was not on the normal side. And there was sixteen-millimeter material that had an anti-halo coating that also, at the moment of splicing the material, had to be scraped on both sides so that the glue would stick. I don't know if the people in the lab took into account all these factors, but obviously something happened so that when the film entered the developing machines it broke into multiple pieces. I had to go to the lab and restore the negatives. I had to substitute shots...some of the shots were destroyed. So I had to find other shots to substitute for them. That is, out of shots one, two, and three, shot three was the best, but I ended up having to choose shot one, which was not great. And like this, in many cases the film began to undergo changes after it had been in the lab.

And this also has to do with the abandonment—the film being orphaned, as you said. This history was repeated so many times that it was apparent that the film was pretty much discarded, and it was never talked about again. Sara's film suffered such destruction in the lab that it was abandoned, until it was produced, I don't know in what year, at the International Women's Congress held in Havana. Some of Sara's friends who knew about her professional history in depth intervened in the conference and denounced the way Sara's existence had been ignored in the magazine *Cine Cubano*. To clean up its image, the institute decided to produce a special edition dedicated to Sara's memory.

RICARDO ACOSTA: *A special edition of the film magazine?*

IVÁN AROCHA MONTES DE OCA: A special edition of *Cine Cubano* dedicated to Sara's work. The curious thing about this magazine is that it reprints articles from different film history articles, and an article can be found about Sara's film as an example of *cine imperfecto* [imperfect cinema]. Sara was never interested in imperfect film, nor did she share the criteria of Julio García Espinosa of *cine imperfecto*. The imperfection of the film was the destruction it suffered in the lab. It was black and white and sixteen millimeter precisely because of a perfection, not because of an imperfection—a perfection of Sara's criteria and concept. And everything—jump cuts, deterioration, and textures—are the result of the film having been so damaged in the laboratory. That was not part of the ethic, aesthetic, or concept of Sara's. There is also an article that mentions the work as an example of sabotage, as if the film had been sabotaged. I never agreed with this opinion, but with the passage of time I think it could be that the negligence that caused the destruction and deterioration of the film in the laboratory process could have been an implicit and discreet sabotage of the film. Although at the beginning it seemed absurd to me, I am now careful about this point of view. There's something else that can be found in this magazine that tells you—articles that say, "After Sara's death, the film was finished by Tomás Gutiérrez Alea," or "It was finished by Julio García Espinosa," or it was finished by the assistant director, what was he called?

RICARDO ACOSTA: *Rigoberto López.*

IVÁN AROCHA MONTES DE OCA: Rigoberto López. None of these people finished the film; none of them continued to be concerned enough to ensure someone finished the film. The film was finished by Sara after her death, and Luis García and I executed her plan in concluding the film. It's that simple. Let me tell you, when Sara was dying, I had a lot of work. I was working on five different productions at the same time in addition to hers, three of which were documentaries. I worked morning, noon, and night. I was in superproduction, and she was trying to communicate with me. For a whole week I received two or three messages saying that Sara wanted to speak with me, and because I had no time, I couldn't. She even sent me the message, through some of her neighbors who worked in ICAIC, that I should go to her house because she needed to talk to me. But because of work pressures, I couldn't go. Early one morning there was a knock on my door. It was a colleague from the ICAIC, at around two in the morning, to tell me, that same week, that Sara had died. That stuck with me always, you know. When you know someone insists that they want to speak with you because they have something important to tell you, and you don't speak with them and that person physically disappears, because they die, and you get stuck with such a strange sensation for the rest of your life.

There's something lovely that happened at Sara's funeral. Sara was the daughter of Yemayá, and the day of the funeral was beautiful, sunny. All her friends and colleagues, all of us were there. When they lowered her coffin so it could be buried, the sky suddenly darkened, a tremendous thunderclap sounded and it broke open the sky and an impressively heavy rain fell. When the rainstorm was over and we left the cemetery, the sun was shining just as it had been when we had entered. It was that moment.

Translated from the original Spanish by Helen Dixon

IVÁN AROCHA MONTES DE OCA is a Cuban film editor and visual artist. He was editor of several of Sara Gómez's films, including *One Way or Another* (in Spanish) (1977), and of Nicolás Guillén Landrián's *Coffea Arábiga* (1968). His art exhibitions have appeared in the Metropolitan Art Museum and the Soft Art House Gallery.

RICARDO ACOSTA, CCE, is a film editor, story editor, and creative/editorial consultant who has been working in the film industry since the early 1990s. He has studied and worked at the Cuban Institute of Cinematographic Art and Industry. He is curator with David McIntosh of the series *Chronicles of My Family* (in Spanish; 1992). He has contributed to several award-winning and award-nominated films, including *Herman's House* (2012), *Marmato* (2014), *Sembene!* (2015), and *The Silence of Others* (2018).

Illustrated Essay: Rumba by Sara Gomez

450 becarios se hacen TECNICOS EN ALIMENTACION en un Instituto donde estudian desde las desviaciones de los electrones hasta la elaboración del yogurt

Reportaje de SANTIAGO CARDOSA ARIAS con fotos de CARLOS NUÑEZ
Páginas 4 a 13

INDICE DE LA REVISTA CUBA AÑO 1964
PAGINAS 70 A 73

EL ILUSTRE SABIO ATOMICO EL DIBUJANTE GUERRERO CUENTA UNA HISTORIA DE NAVIDAD
PAGINAS 74 Y 75

LAS "MAKARENKO": historia de las muchachas que se iniciaron como alfabetizadoras y hoy son alumnas universitarias y profesoras al mismo tiempo

Escribe ALEJANDRO VERBITSKY
Fotos CARLOS NUÑEZ
Páginas 16 a 23

UN DIQUE SOVIETICO CUENTA SU VIAJE POR CLARA VELAZQUEZ FOTOS CARLOS NUÑEZ
PAGINAS 26 A 31

MUSEO "FELIPE POEY"
En el antiguo Capitolio Nacional la Revolución creó dos kilómetros de Museo de Ciencias Naturales. Junto a la belleza de las mariposas del trópico, de sus peces, caracolas, pájaros, flores, las creaciones del hombre cubano

Escribe JOSE LORENZO FUENTES
Fotos de ORLANDO GARCIA y NICOLAS DELGADO
Páginas 36 a 55

DISEÑARON LAS PORTADAS
1RA. GUERRERO
2DA. VILLAVERDE
4TA. GUERRERO

TRANSITO
Una semana de lucha contra los accidentes estimulada por el color y la imaginación de CARTELES Y DIBUJOS
Páginas 32 a 35

CUBA SE RECREA
INFORMAN: OSWALDO QUINTANS Y GARCIA SUAREZ
PAGINA 14

CUBA EN LA CULTURA
INFORMA: RINE LEAL
PAGINA 24

CUBA EN EL TIEMPO
INFORMA: GONZALEZ BERMEJO
PAGINA 56

CUBA EN LA ECONOMIA
INFORMA: JOSE VAZQUEZ
PAGINA 68

VIÑETAS DE OSCAR ENERAL

LA RUMBA nacida hace cerca de dos siglos, creada por los negros esclavos que trabajaban en el azúcar. Su ritmo sigue aún vibrando en el mundo entero. Crónica de SARA GOMEZ. Imágenes de MAYITO. Páginas 58 a 67

ACOGIDA A LA FRANQUICIA POSTAL E INSCRITA COMO CORRESPONDENCIA DE SEGUNDA CLASE EN LA ADMINISTRACION DE CORREOS DE LA HABANA. AL NUMERO 20-006/F. I. DIRECCION Y ADMINISTRACION. EDIFICIO SIERRA MAESTRA, AVENIDA RANCHO BOYEROS Y GENERAL SUAREZ, LA HABANA, CUBA. EDITADA EN LA IMPRENTA DEL INRA Y EN LA EMPRESA CONSOLIDADA DE ARTES GRAFICAS; UNIDAD No. 205-01. TELEFONOS: REDACCION. 70-9975; ADMINISTRACION, 70-0071; FOTOGRAFIA. 70-0010. DISEÑO. 7-4181. SUSCRIPCION A 12 EDICIONES: CUBA $2.40. EXTRANJERO $3.50

LA HABANA, DICIEMBRE 1964
AÑO III   NO. 32

DIRECTOR/LISANDRO OTERO ▶ JEFE DE REDACCION/DARIO CARMONA ▶ DIRECTOR DE DISEÑO/JOSE GOMEZ FRESQUET ▶ DIRECTOR DE FOTOGRAFIA/FEDERICO MORALES ▶ JEFE DE REDACCION DE LA EDICION EN RUSO/SERGIO F. ALPIZAR ▶ ADMINISTRADOR/ROBERTO PEREZ GONZALEZ ▶ JEFE DE CIRCULACION/RAIMUNDO PEREZ ▶ REDACCION/JOSE LORENZO FUENTES, SANTIAGO CARDOSA ARIAS, BALTASAR ENERO, DULCILA CAÑIZARES, RAFAEL ESCOBAR LINARES, NORBERTO FUENTES Y THEUDIS IRAETA (hijo) ▶ DISEÑO/RAFAEL MORANTE (PARA LA EDICION EN RUSO) ▶ ARMANDO NAVARRO, ALEXIS DURAN, ROBERTO H. GUERRERO, ALFREDO ROSTGAARD Y JORGE CHINIQUE ▶ FOTOGRAFIA/ROBERTO SALAS, CARLOS NUÑEZ, MARIO GARCIA JOYA, ORLANDO GARCIA Y NICOLAS DELGADO ▶ ARCHIVO/MYRNA DE ZAYAS ▶ ADMINISTRACION/CARLOS LOPEZ, MELBA LOBAINA, JOSE SENDE, ELOY PANEQUE, ARQUIMEDES ALDANA, HERIBERTO LEON, RAMON CLEMENTE Y CELESTE GARCIA ▶

El Yambú es cosa de negro viejo

Quiero aprovechar esta oportunidad para decirles a ustedes como una pequeña historia del Guaguancó, que a través de los años, el que les habla a ustedes, un servidor, Agustín Pina, que desde muy pequeño me dicen mis amigos, cariñosamente, Flor de Amor.

Flor vive en el barrio de Luyanó. En una de las casas a la entrada del solar que forma la esquina de Municipio y Atarés. Allí Flor escribe sus memorias.

Como primer punto de partida para conocimiento de todos ustedes, soy Rumbero de Fundamento, y digo esto porque desde pequeño no he hecho otra cosa que cantar y tocar Rumbas y Guaguancós y Claves. Por mi casa han desfilado todos los grandes Rumberos de la República.

En el Yambú no se "vacuna"

Su ritmo es lento

y acompasado

LA RUMBA

POR SARA GOMEZ YERA

FOTOS MAYITO

La Rumba es la música que crea el negro para divertirse, es música no ritual, música profana. El negro deja a un lado sus dioses, siente la necesidad de expresarse como individuo dentro de una sociedad, necesita reunirse y hacer su fiesta, hacer su música. Entonces es cuando crea, cuando "arma" la Rumba.

Ya desde el siglo XVII aparecen en América una serie de vocablos emparentados fonéticamente con la palabra Rumba. Samba, Tumba, Macumba, Tango, Tambó, se integran en el vocabulario americano y designan a las fiestas con carácter urbano creadas por el negro. Sobre esto ha escrito Alejo Carpentier en su libro "La Música en Cuba".

A fines del siglo XVIII se inicia un proceso de urbanización en la región occidental de la Isla como consecuencia de la naciente expansión azucarera. Estos centros urbanos son los pequeños caseríos y bateyes cerca de los ingenios. El azúcar reúne gran cantidad de negros esclavos y mano de obra asalariada. En estos centros urbanos, más tarde unidos por la línea del ferrocarril a los puertos de La Habana y Matanzas, surge la Rumba, que ya no es música de campesinos ni música ritual. "La Rumba es el género o especie folklórica capaz de agrupar a todos los sectores de la población", dice Argeliers León.

En la mansión residencial de algún potentado le pagaban a unos cuantos Rumberos, que la mayor parte de las veces los buscaba José Benito Serna. Pepe Serna, que era artista del Alhambra y como blanco era gran bailador de Guaguancó y Columbia. Y una de las Rumbas a la que fuimos con Pepe, fuimos los Rumberos siguientes: Tumbador, Dionisio el tabaquero del coro de Paso Franco; Repiqueteadores y cantantes. Cafuanda el albañil de Pueblo Nuevo y Fermín Reyes, que fue el que sacó a una niñita que se estaba ahogando en uno de los muelles, no sé exactamente qué muelle era. Y esta Rumba fue en las faldas del Castillo del Príncipe, en una finquita de Pepe el Isleño y era la fiesta de los Señores Magistrados de la Audiencia de La Habana.

El negro para poder divertirse, para poder "rumbear" se armó de los instrumentos que tenía a su alcance. Una madera percusiva cualquiera: una vieja silla, una gaveta de un escaparate, el costado del mismo escaparate, y un par de cucharas bastaban en la habitación del solar; o quizás un simple cajón de bacalao y una pequeña cajita de velas "Sabatés". Luego se utilizaron tambores del tipo tumbadora en dos tamaños diferentes.

La verdadera Rumba, como el Guaguancó, se tocaba y se tiene que tocar con cajón, que es como antes.

Entonces todo está listo para asimilar elementos de música occidental. En contradicción a la música ritual traída del África, el plano sonoro grave se mantendrá con figuras rítmicas constantes y el plano agudo se transformará en rico, segmentado y variable. A semejanza de las orquestas occidentales, por su sonido agudo, el cajoncito de velas, la gaveta o el tambor más pequeño se llamará **quinto**. En el canto el negro no abandonará la relación dialogada, alternando coro y solista sin dejar de incluir una parte narrativa en décimas, cuartetas o prosa.

Estudiosos como Argeliers León y Odilio Urfé sitúan dentro del llamado **Complejo Folklórico de la Rumba** a los géneros Guaguancó, Columbia y Yambú. Sin embargo algunos informantes, el mismo Flor de Amor, se empeñan en llamar Rumba solamente a esa parte dialogada, bailable, un poco "por la libre" que se inicia al solista en un momento de la fiesta. Gonzalo, Rumbero viejo como Flor, me pone un ejemplo:

—¿Qué le gusta a la negra prieta?

—El ñame con manteca —respondería el coro.

El Guaguancó, se dice, es cosa de La Habana. Comienza en un lalaleo[1] que continúa con la parte narrativa hasta culminar en la Rumba, donde la pareja puede salir a bailar. El baile es mimético; ella tratará de protegerse —moviendo su amplia falda, el pañuelo o sus manos— de la persecución sexual del macho. La habilidad de él consistirá en lograr "vacunarla", gesto simbólico de la pelvis.

El Yambú es cosa de negro viejo. En el Yambú no se "vacuna". Su ritmo es lento y acompasado. Un conocido Yambú es ése que dice: **"Ave María morena"**.

La Columbia es cosa de gente de campo, no tiene lalaleo. El cantante emite unos gritos o lamentos al que llaman **"lloras"**.

La Columbia suele tener un texto elegíaco o disparatado, absurdo, simplemente por aquello de vivir el disparate y nada más.

Una Columbia puede hablar de una vieja en esquina empinando un papalote.

La Columbia es un baile para hombres, no por casualidad sus pasos suelen recordar a los del **Iremé Abakuá**[2] de los ñáñigos.

Hace algunos años una mujer, Andrea Baró, bailó Columbia. Desde entonces no es raro escuchar a algunas mujeres que argumentan que "hace ya años que las mujeres tienen derecho al voto" y que Andrea Baró bailó la Columbia".

Se conocen como **Rumbas del Tiempo de España** a una categoría más mimética de la Rumba en la que podemos imitar desde los quehaceres del hogar hasta un desfile militar.

Durante la inspiración el solista a veces repite textos de origen Congo, Lucumí o Abakuá. En la Columbia es común escuchar alusiones a los dioses Sarabanda y Chola. A esto le llaman **"virar pa' Rumba un canto"**. Estos y otros elementos son los que hacen pensar en la influen-

Mario canta: "Unión de Reyes llora a su rumbero mayor... que vino regando flores desde La Habana... a Morón"

cia de la Columbia en figuras como la del desaparecido cantante Benny Moré. Quizás sólo baste con recordar su **lloreo**, sus conocidos gritos interrumpiendo un Son.

Muchas veces, cuando presenciamos en el espectáculo de un cabaret habanero a una pareja de Rumberos no podemos menos que entristecernos y pensar que es un género que va perdiendo fuerza en nuestro Folklore, que está degenerando en simples movimientos convulsivos acompañados de percusión. Pero entonces recordamos la Rumba que arman los niños del barrio golpeando sobre los guardafangos de los autos estacionados en la cuadra. Entonces recuerdo que entre las Columbias elegíacas hay una dedicada a "Malanga", Rumbero de Unión de Reyes y otra dedicada a la memoria de Chano Pozo y también una parr Patricio Lumumba:

*Que se pare mi cuero,
que no suene mi Rumba,
que no bailen el mambo
porque allá en Katanga
mataron a Lumumba.*

Hace apenas un año en un café cerca de los muelles se armó una Rumba sobre este motivo:

—¿Qué le pasa a los cambios cuantitativos?

—Se convierten en cambios cualitativos —respondía el coro.

Y Flor, en su pequeña casa de la esquina de Municipio y Atarés, continúa sus memorias.

En ese tiempo yo tenía 18 años y de ese tiempo a la fecha actual todavía rumbeo en mi casa y trabajo en el Consejo Provincial de Cultura y tengo 75 años.

(1) **Lalaleo**: Forma cubana parecida al tarareo. El cantante expresa una melodía con un la, la, la.

(2) La secta secreta **Abakuá** sólo admite hombres. Tienen un danzante llamado **Ireme** o **diablito**.

El aire se quiebra: un rumbero entona La Clave de Martí

LA RUMBA

Empieza como Guaguancó y culmina en la Rumba

Primero baila el hombre solo mientras ella acompasa la Rumba

Se formó la pareja de Rumba. Ella trata d protegerse del hombre

Hace cerca de 200 años nació
la Rumba. Brotó en torno
al azúcar: la crearon los negros esclavos
y los trabajadores asalariados. Su ritmo
se contagió desde los bateyes próximos a los
ingenios, hasta las ciudades como
La Habana y Matanzas

Dos cucharas y una caja. Total: brota el ritmo de la Rumba

La pantomima de la Rumba tiene pasajes de danza arrebatada

LA RUMBA

"¿Qué le gusta a la negra prieta?... el ñame con manteca"   El diálogo, tradición de la Rumba

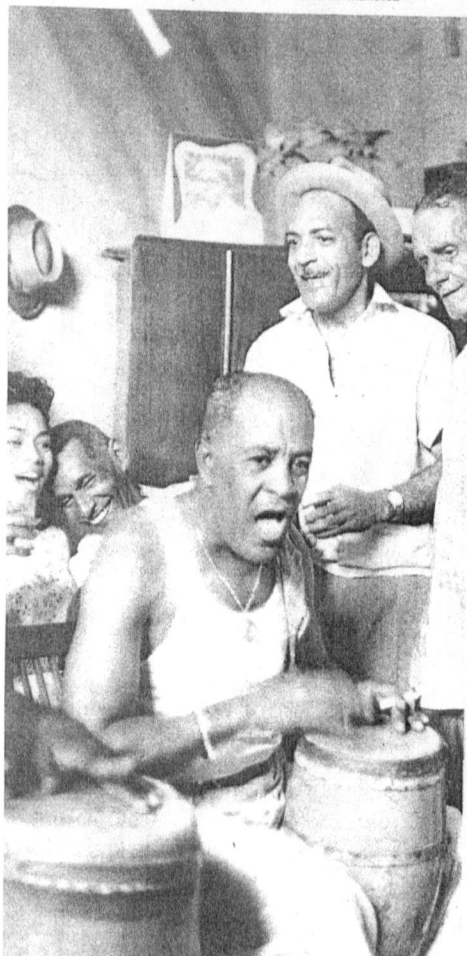
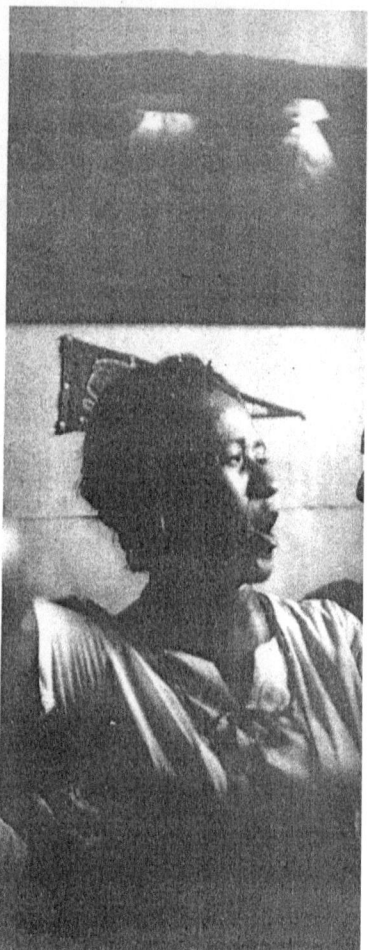

Los "bongoes", las "tumbadoras" levantan la Rumba

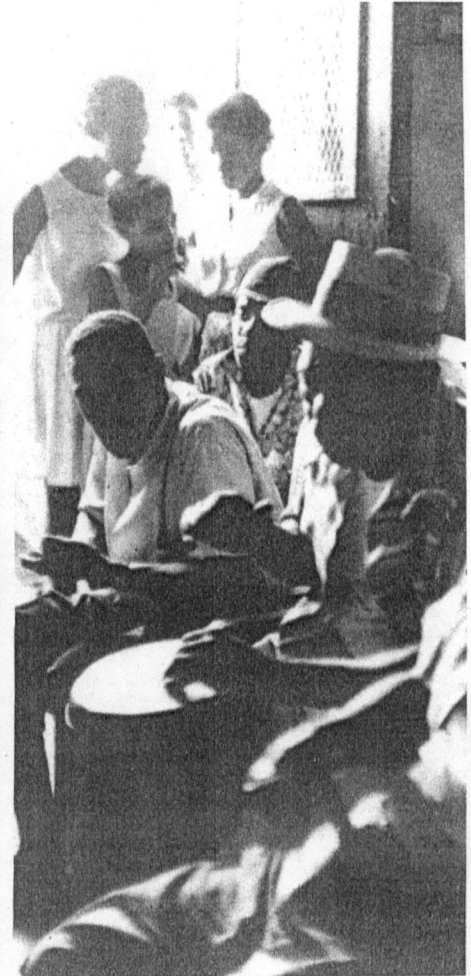

La Rumba es profana,
no es ritual.
El negro deja a un
lado a sus dioses,
quiere hacer su música,
vivir su fiesta.
Quiere divertirse:
inventa la Rumba

Terminó la rumba en casa de Flor de Amor

LA RUMBA

"Ave María morena, cuánto tienes cuánto vales..."

En la verdadera rumba un cajón se usa como instrumento de percusión

Un objeto cualquiera se convierte en instrumento musical cuando el negro quiere rumbear

"Soy Rumbero de Fundamento; me llamo Agustín Pina, pero desde muy pequeño mis amigos me dicen Flor de Amor..."

La Columbia es una clase de Rumba.
Su letra es disparatada y la bailan sólo
los hombres. Pero hace años una mujer,
Andrea Baró, bailó Columbia.
Aún se recuerda su gesto de rebeldía

FOURTEEN

Sabor and *Punctum*
Music in Sara Gómez's Films

Alan West-Durán

AN INDELIBLE IMAGE OF SARA GÓMEZ from a thirty-minute short by Agnès Varda titled *Salut les cubains* (1963) and reprised in a documentary by Alessandra Müller titled *¿Dónde está Sara Gómez?* (2005) shows Gómez dancing cha-cha in a *miliciana* (military) uniform with vivacious charm and joy. To create the sequence, Varda took still shots, pieced them together set to a cha-cha, and then "animated" them to simulate the movement of the dancers—all of them students at the Instituto Cubano del Arte e Industria Cinematográficos (ICAIC, or Cuban Film Institute). Gómez's smile is more than an expression of joy—it is a burst of sheer energy, a visual foregrounding of the boundless creativity she would exhibit in her short but prolific career as a filmmaker. Sara Gómez, who had studied piano, was a keen lover of music and used it skillfully in her films, whether the subject matter was music itself, as in *Y... tenemos sabor* (And we've got flavor) (1967), or as part of the soundtrack in her only featurelength film, *De cierta manera* (One way or another) (1974/1977).

As a documentary filmmaker in post-1959 Cuba, Gómez was deeply influenced by the revolutionary aesthetics of Santiago Álvarez (1919–98), who eschewed some of the more traditional methods of the documentary genre (voice-over narration; the appearance of objectivity; linear narrative; overreliance on statistics; creative use of still images such as photos, magazines, newspapers, and art; and creative use of text). He used music just as creatively—for example, his use of Lena Horne's "Now!" in his famous short about the civil rights movement in the United States (1965), the juxtaposing of Iron Butterfly's "In-A-Gadda-Da Vida" with images of the funeral of Ho Chi Minh in *79 Springtimes* (1969), not to mention his Brechtian distancing effect in *Hasta la Victoria Siempre* (1967), where he uses a syrupy, over-the-top number by Pérez Prado over images of rural poverty in Bolivia along with snippets of Che Guevara, the subject of the film.[1]

Álvarez's work points to a different approach to film music that shuns total subordination to the image and tries to avoid what Adorno and Eisler ([1947] 2007) warn about in the first chapter of their *Composing for the Films*, aptly titled "Prejudices and Bad Habits." Among the pitfalls they outline are the abuse of leitmotifs, melody and euphony (tunefulness), unobtrusiveness, visual justification, illustration, geography and history, stock music, clichés, and standardized interpretations (1–12). In summing up melody and euphony, Adorno and Eisler state, "All music in the motion picture is under the sign of utility, rather than lyric expressiveness" (4). On unobtrusiveness, they flatly say, "One of the most widespread prejudices in the motion picture industry is the premise that the spectator should not be conscious of the music" (5). Finally, they argue for a cinematic music that attains autonomy and holds its own in terms of artistic integrity. In the following analysis of five Sara Gómez films, I examine her use of music in different contexts and how it intersects with her view of a revolutionary cinema.[2]

Gómez's only film that deals directly with music, *Y . . . tenemos sabor*, is a twenty-four-minute documentary that examines popular dance music. In it, Gómez takes a didactic approach, examining certain musical genres such as the *son*, rumba, and guajira music as well as some important instruments: clave; *quijada* (jawbone); *bongó* (bongos); guitar; maracas; guiro; *guayo* (metal scraper); *botija* (a hollowed-out clay jug that functions as a wind instrument); *marímbula* (a wooden box with metal strips, now replaced by the bass); *cencerro* (cowbell); *tumbadoras* (conga drums); *timbales*; and the *corneta china* (the Chinese cornet). Musician Alberto Zayas (1908–83) provides the film's guiding thread, explaining the different instruments and musical genres and carefully giving his views on Cuban musical history. A noted singer and composer born in Matanzas, Zayas was a member of the Septeto Habanero and later directed a folkloric ensemble called Lulú Yonkori.

Zayas begins with the simplest but perhaps most emblematic instrument of the Cuban repertoire, the clave—two highly resonant wooden sticks used to play the fundamental beat of most Cuban dance music, which is also known as *clave*. Zayas refers to the clave's sound as *"sensual y ensoñadora"* (sensual and dreamy), essential to Cuban music's *sabor*, its flavor. *Sabor*, as a term, is a little hard to pin down, though. In his delightful and often funny book, *From Afro-Cuban Rhythms to Latin Jazz*, Raúl Fernández includes a chapter on the aesthetics of *sabor* (2006, 42–57). *Sabor* can refer to certain inflections in a musician's playing (Lilí Martínez's vamps, Chucho Valdés's crashing clusters)

Figure 14.1 Still of Alberto Zayas from the opening credits of *Y... tenemos sabor,* 1967. © ICAIC

or the way a player embellishes a rhythm, melody, or even a vocal trait (Pérez Prado's famous grunts and Celia Cruz's delicious way of saying *"Azúcar!"*). Or, think of a performer's movements on stage, such as Benny Moré's strut with his hat and cane or La Lupe's melodramatic gesturings. Chucho Valdés explains *sabor* in terms of identity: "Our music is our identity" (quoted in Fernández 2006, 56). A recent concert at the Roldán Theater in Havana illustrates this point: A Korean pianist performed the work of Ernesto Lecuona and did an admirable job as she played famous works such as "Alhambra," "Malagueña," "Danza lucumí," and "La comparsa," the latter one of Lecuona's most beloved compositions. She played all the notes, but the *sabor* was missing.[3]

Fernández, drawing on Radamés Giro, claims that *sabor* inheres also in the Cuban ability to draw on so many different traditions and yet come up with something uniquely Cuban. Among those traditions that Zayas points out in the film are Spanish romance, flamenco, *pasacallo*, *punto*, and West African rumba and ritual music, to which we must add German lied, French *contredanse* and the congó minuet, Italian romanza, song and opera, American jazz and ragtime, and Austrian waltz traditions. Zayas also refers to instruments in pairs (male and female) and to musical genres as *mulato* (mixed-race, combined), or, in the words of Fernando Ortiz, transculturated. In this sense, Zayas does not depart from how most Cubans describe the country's culture in general or its musical culture in particular—a perfect union (marriage or love affair—take your pick) between strings (guitar, *tres*) and percussion (maracas, bongos, conga drums). Zayas eloquently praises the *son*, perhaps the most emblematic of Cuban musical genres, which took center stage in the 1920s when it finally arrived in Havana from the eastern part of Cuba. Gómez's film claims to investigate Cuban dance music, perhaps evoking Emilio Grenet's quip that "Cubans are a people who dance" (Fernández 2006, 49). As Zayas takes us through some of the instruments in the *son* (the *cencerro*, the *marímbula*), we begin to understand the importance of instrumentation. As Fernández so correctly points out, "As with the *marímbula*, the acoustic bass in the son plays a prominent rhythmic role and provides the main cues for the dancers. Some of the great innovators of the son in the twentieth century were bass players, notably Ignacio Piñeiro, Israel 'Cachao' López and Juan Formell" (2006, 31).

Of course, the film treats us to rumba as well (a *guaguancó*), perhaps Cuba's other most popular musical genre and also made for dancing, although the skills for rumba are more exacting than they are for *son*. As the film advances, Zayas's explanations become less frequent, although he does emphasize the central role of the *tumbadoras*: "Without the tumbadora there is no cha-cha-chá, nor conga lines, nor Cuban music." After also quickly mentioning that Italian opera companies brought the *pailas* (or timbales) to Cuba in the nineteenth century, the rest of the film becomes less didactic and we witness a beautifully played cha-cha as an example of *charanga francesa*, the unique blend of violin, flute, and piano (that was also part of the *contradanza* tradition). Irrepressibly, the music takes over.

The film closes with a *guapachá* rhythm from after the Revolution featuring electric guitar and an amazing female voice doing a kind of scatting. The closing number suggests that the rich musical tradition of Cuba will continue to combine elements in new ways to generate new genres (like *nueva trova*, the Mozambique, timba, and rap). Though the film does not have the artistic, free-floating form of Rogelio París's *Nosotros la música* (We are the music) (1964)—after all its purpose is far more didactic—*Y... tenemos sabor* emphatically reaffirms Valdés's and Grenet's assessment that Cubans listen with our feet and taste with our hips. Fernández writes, "*Para bailar bien el son / hay que tener la cintura / dulce como raspadura y caliente como el ron*" (To dance the son well / you have to have a waist / as sweet as crude sugar and as hot as rum) (2006, 26).

Gómez's nine-minute short from 1969, *Isla del tesoro* (Treasure island), features some of her most creative use of music. As the film begins, we see a map of the Isle of Pines with a musical accompaniment of percussion, maybe *marímbula* and an oboe (or clarinet). Interestingly, the credits appear in blocs, not all at once, which echoes the building of notes into chords. The first shot is of a boat on water with beautiful scenery set to guitar and flute music. The music reinforces the calm nature scene—trees, river, and boats. Then there is an abrupt cut to an iron grate crashing from a window, hitting the ground to the sound of electronic music. Although this image is repeats throughout the film, it is not really a leitmotif because its meaning does not become clear until the end. It is rather a temporal narrative, a sound jolt—highly effective, if not a little disorienting in that we are unsure how to interpret it. In some ways, the image plays a similar role to the wrecking ball in *De cierta manera*, except that in the latter film, the referent (and symbolism) is clear throughout. Only at the end of *Isla del tesoro* will this image become "readable."

A narration accompanied by piano and flute music relates some of the history of the island on which political prisoners were held, the most famous being José Martí. Other prominent prisoners included Evangelina Cossío Cisneros, Raimundo Cabrera, and Pablo de la Torriente Brau as well as members of the 26th of July Movement such as Raúl Castro, Juan Almeida, and Fidel Castro himself. During colonial times, the island saw pirate activity, and several landmarks and geographical sites reflect this, such as la Laguna de los Bucaneros (the Buccaneer Lagoon). In her anti-imperialist analysis, Gómez ties this buccaneering activity to US attempts after 1898 to try to annex the Isle of Pines, but the US Supreme Court ruled in 1907 that the United States had no legal right to the island, and the Hay-Quesada Treaty in 1925 further ratified Cuban sovereignty over the island. During the Machado regime (1925–33), a panoptic prison based on the ideas of Jeremy Bentham was built with the purpose of holding five thousand prisoners.

The Martí segments of the film are very effective, using some of his poetry, a shot of a ceiba tree and some of Martí's objects as well as the cell where he was imprisoned. The ceiba tree is sacred in Afro-Cuban religions and, therefore, symbolically charged. Offerings are deposited beneath it, and among the poetry recited is Martí's *"cultiva una rosa blanca"* (from his *Versos Sencillos*) (1891), which, linked to the ceiba, gives the sequence of images a kind of Santería undercurrent (white is often used in ritual ceremonies).

In Gómez's shots from inside the prison we see the devastating power of the all-seeing panopticon, here edited with a reverb electronic music and voices. The voices are distorted, giving the scene a truly hallucinatory quality, which, combined with shots of prisoners, captures their dreary plight. The next shot very briefly shows Castro and other July 26th members when they were amnestied in 1955. Then Gómez repeats the falling grate with the same electronic musical accompaniment. This shot blends into an industrial plant that makes bricks (with sounds of the factory), more shots of the factory (now with a droning sound), and an outdoor shot of a quarry (with sounds of equipment and trucks), followed by an aerial shot of water and sand. We hear a woman's voice singing:

> *Tierra de mármol y arena*
> *donde los de la bandera*
> *crean una nueva juventud*
> *tierra para el hombre por venir*
> *de un nuevo siglo*
> *tierra para la aurora*
> *para borrar la noche de ayer,*
> *¡Tierra!*
> *Juventud de apenas veinte*
> *y que no le temen a la vida,*
> *¡Tierra! ¡Tierra!*

> (Land of marble and sand,
> where those who uphold the flag
> create a new youth
> land of men of the future
> of a new century,
> land of the dawn
> that wipes away the dismal night of the past
> Land!
> Youth of barely twenty
> And not afraid of life
> Land! Land!)

The imagery in the song is of young people doing volunteer work—black and white youth together planting and harvesting—of camaraderie and joy. A more cynical perspective, or a cursory glance at the scene, might see socialist realism with a tropical beat, but that is too simplistic a reading. First, the images of youthful joy are too sincere to have been faked, staged, or forced. Second, the beauty of the music does not evoke heroic workers marching into the future as in Soviet poster art from the 1930s. Third, the word *tierra* (land, earth) would be an odd choice for a dreary proletarian hymn. The logical word choice in such a case would be *patria* (homeland or, more accurately, fatherland), and yet the song eschews this narrowly nationalistic term. Gómez has captured revolutionary fervor with great aesthetic beauty. As a historical note, these images might reflect the efforts of the Centennial Youth Column (linked to the

Union of Communist Youth) created in 1968, and the Army of Working Youth (with closer links to the Cuban army) to increase production through moral incentives directly linked to Che Guevara's idea of the New Man.[4] If so, then Gómez's film shows great prescience, because the island would be renamed the Island of Youth in 1978.

Next, we see the results of the youth's work as conveyor belts carry boxes (marked "Treasure Island") of grapefruits for export. Again, the shot of the grate falling from the window appears accompanied by electronic music echoing on the soundtrack. Shots of the prison walls follow, on which we see a map, graffiti, written words, and religious imagery. An exterior shot reveals workers removing iron bars from windows with blowtorches. Finally, the falling window grate image makes sense—we are witnessing the dismantling of the Presidio Modelo in 1967 when it stopped being the National Penitentiary for Crimes against the Safety of the State (its name from 1959 to 1967). In 1973, the prison was converted into a museum, and in 1978, it was named a national monument.

For *Una isla para Miguel* (An island for Miguel) (1968), a very young Chucho Valdés (only twenty-five at the time) provided the soundtrack. Dave Brubeck's "Take Five," performed by Valdés, provides one of the more intriguing uses of music in the film. It appears only in a brief citation, maybe two bars at most, but it is clearly identifiable and repeated. The first time it is used is in a shot of a barbershop; the second time, in an interview with Mario Monzón, a regional committee leader of the Union of Communist Youth of the Isle of Pines; the third time, when Miguel, a boy who has been accused of throwing rocks, speaks about his life. Miguel, of course, is the "star" of the film, and we learn about his life of poverty and the beatings he received from his father. We hear his sister say, "Miguel is strong willed, pig-headed if you will, he doesn't heed anyone," followed by Miguel declaring, "It's the way I am."

Gómez uses Brubeck in three different contexts, and so not as a leitmotif. The first time, the music accompanies ordinary activities (kids playing baseball, flying kites, and getting haircuts). The second time, it underlines comments by Monzón, who says, "They were rebels without a cause—our commitment as militants was to give them a cause." The innovative use of the music links his comment to a political insight that goes back to a quote by Frantz Fanon at the beginning of the film: "Those classless idlers will, by decisive and militant action, discover the path that leads to nationhood" (1963, 130). The third instance, during Miguel's testimony, links the personal and the political, the individual and the collective, by building on the first two instances where the music is used in the film. Perhaps Gómez meant to draw attention to Brubeck's title—taking five minutes, stopping the ordinary flow of things to reflect on what is happening. Although this connection may have been lost on many Cuban viewers at that time who did not know the name of the song or what it meant, the film is structured in ways that support this interpretation. Gómez skillfully used music, interview, commentary, titles, and written text to create pauses that make the audience think about the social and personal causes of social ills.

In *De cierta manera*, her only feature-length production, Gómez uses music to highlight some of the social agents in the film but also some of the ideological tensions that are present. Sergio Vitier, the gifted guitarist and composer and lesser-known brother of José María Vitier, did the soundtrack in collaboration with the Grupo de Experimentación Sonora del ICAIC. To a degree, Abakuá music and a composition by former boxer turned songwriter, Guillermo Díaz, accentuates old ways of seeing and feeling in contrast with a revolutionary consciousness. Mario's struggles are highlighted by his closeness to the male-only Abakuá society that draws on the religious traditions of the Cross River of southeastern Nigeria and southwestern Cameroon. The Abakuá tradition is associated with a hypermasculinity characteristic of Cuban *guapería*, an association Gómez draws on to depict Mario's link to tradition (though he never becomes an initiate) as chauvinistic and regressive. The film even shows documentary footage of the Abakuá in a way that seems to emphasize their "otherness" (Ebrahim 1998, 243), especially when contrasted with how the film depicts Regla de Ocha (Santería). Despite the male-centric aspects of the religion, members are expected to adhere to a strict code of conduct as good sons, fathers, and husbands. Abakuá have been expelled or rigorously disciplined for failing to do so.

Nonetheless, attitudes in general toward Afro-Cuban religious traditions at the time the film was made were not exactly supportive (or respectful), and Gómez's views were consistent with the times—up to a point. Her depictions of Ocha seem more benevolent than how the Abakuá were generally portrayed. However, Tomás González, who helped with the script and direction, states that the final version of the film, a presumed two-hour project, was cut almost in half by Tomás Gutiérrez Alea and Julio García Espinosa (González in Müller 2004), so we do not know what material was left out.[5] In the final version, certainly, the song "Véndele" (or "Ríndele") and Abakuá drumming provide audio and ideological signposts that accompany Gómez's examination of marginality. Gómez's work shows respect for Afro-Cuban religions, going against the trend within the cultural establishment at the time of seeing these religions as backward or superstitious, or at best a remnant from pre-1959 Cuba that would eventually disappear with the advent of socialism.

In an analysis of *De cierta manera,* Hector Amaya mentions the influence of Althusser on the Cuban intellectual and cultural milieu of the time and that Gómez's embrace of scientific methodology squared with the French philosopher's notion of an antihumanist Marxism founded on the twin scientific endeavors of dialectical and historical materialism (Amaya 2010, 146). Althusser and Balibar's *Reading Capital* ([1968] 1970) was devoured on the island, and subsequently Althusser's much discussed essay "Ideology and Ideological State Apparatuses" ([1971] 2001, 85–126), provided a significant contribution to the conceptualization of ideology as material practice (embedded in institutions) and as something that was not merely imaginary or an example of false consciousness.[6]

These insights provide a key context to Gómez's explorations in *De cierta manera.* The film examines attitudes that persisted despite the radical changes enacted by the Revolution. Humberto (Mario Limonta), is a factory worker who asks his *socio* (buddy) Mario (Mario Balmaseda) to cover for him while he spends four days with a lover in Santiago—a classic Cuban dichotomy between *sociolismo* (social relations) and *socialismo* (socialist ideology). Mario grew up poor and had considered becoming an Abakuá initiate. He meets Yolanda (Yolanda Cuéllar), a young teacher from a well-to-do family who has embraced the Revolution and teaches in a school where many of the children come from broken or marginalized families. The film shows her struggling with, and trying to discipline, the children and her colleagues trying to help her understand the class dynamics that underline their attitudes and her own blindness to a kind of revolutionary paternalism in handling them. Gómez's film explores the gaps between material realities and how humans situate themselves in relation to these realities in their consciousness. Or, in Althusser's famous statement, "Ideology is a 'representation' of the imaginary relationships of individuals to their real conditions of existence" ([1971] 2001, 109). This is not the place to tease out all the implications of this statement (including Lacanian ones) but rather to appreciate how Gómez engaged in a documentary approach that tried both to examine Cuban realities as scientifically as possible and to show and seek to explain the supple (and stubborn) nature of ideology in a rapidly changing society.

Perhaps the crudest symbol in the film is the wrecking ball tearing down old, defective housing and clearing a path to a new urban and social environment free of conditions of marginality, violence, and sexism. At one point, the following title appears on screen: "With the triumph of the Revolution, all marginal sectors of the population were integrated into the society"—more a revolutionary goal than a statement of fact. Gómez's film seems to contradict this claim in an interview with Yolanda, who states, "I thought this [the old world] was a world that no longer existed." Through music, Gómez adds dimension to the images on-screen. For example, the first time the wrecking ball appears, a woman's voice (singer Sara González, it turns out) accompanies it, vocalizing *lei-lo-lei*-type sounds. The effect is powerful. The soundtrack offsets the destructive and harsh image of the wrecking ball with a lyrical and lovely voice, and the combination reveals the "creative destruction" of revolutionary change. Elsewhere, we hear the musical equivalent of the wrecking ball—a song by Guillermo Díaz (the ex-boxer turned songwriter) that openly addresses the changes needed to make a new life and leave his old world of marginality and violence behind (Guillermo has done jail time for accidentally killing a man). In the song, Guillermo describes himself as a phoenix rising from the ashes of an old world of degradation, violence, alcohol, and drugs. At one point, he tells Mario that "people don't leave their environment out of cowardice." It is a telling statement, and it contains an undeniable truth—but perhaps only a half truth. We admire Guillermo for being able to transcend his former life of violence and marginality, but that does not mean thousands of others will be able to do so. Even so, it is precisely the post-1959 changes (in housing, literacy and education, employment, and health care) that allowed for the collective possibility of lifting disenfranchised Cubans out of poverty and despair.

Toward the end of the film, the opening scene repeats, with Humberto appearing before the workers assembly, saying, "He who is not a good son, is not a good worker, nor a good man." Interestingly, these words seem to echo the creed of the Abakuá and certainly carry the weight of truth, but the fact that Humberto utters them to disguise a lie makes his statement almost farcical.[7] His utterance would, in fact, be an act of self-condemnation if the assembly knew that he had already betrayed his own words. One person in the assembly—Mario—knows the truth, and he denounces Humberto in no uncertain terms. Later, when Mario tells Yolanda about the incident, he is still tormented by self-doubt and concern over betraying the trust of his *socio* and blurts out, "I acted like a woman." In the next scene, the men of the factory talk about the events that have just transpired and criticize Humberto for using his mother as a pretext for inexcusable behavior, for being a *descarado* (someone with a shameless lack of work ethic), and for lack of principles. In a discussion that highlights issues of individual desire and collective responsibility, one of the men says, "The Revolution is bigger than us." The entire scene thus plays out beautifully as a response to Mario's previous self-assessment of acting "like a woman" (see Díaz Lopez 2003 for further analysis).

The film ends with Mario and Yolanda speaking as they walk toward some new housing that has gone up, as the Guillermo Díaz song plays again. The song, which resituates a love song, giving it a social and political meaning, suggests hope. But the accompanying image suggests that the issue of marginality (as well as racism and sexism) will form a long dialogue in Cuban society. Issues of sexism and machismo come up again in the films *Portrait of Teresa* (Pastor Vega 1979), *Up to a Certain Point* (Tomás Gutiérrez Alea 1983), and, of course, *Strawberry and Chocolate* (Gutiérrez Alea 1993), but Sara Gómez's pioneering film raised the issue first and in an aesthetically and more politically challenging way than any of these films.

Finally, Gómez's nine-minute short *Excursión a Vuelta Abajo* (Excursion to Vuelta Abajo) (1965) uses guajiro music and tobacco as emblematic of a certain Cuban *sabor*, opening with shots of Pinar del Río and the *mogotes* (hills) of Viñales. She alternates between using guajiro music featuring the *tres* with vigorous string music classically inflected with pizzicato. At one point, she interviews a tobacco worker who talks about the new machinery that allows a more efficient harvest but also requires more maintenance. The worker says the hoe and the *guataca* (spade) were easier. Gómez ends the film saying—in a bit of Ortician enthusiasm—we continue to be the island of palm trees, maracas, sugar, and tobacco, "but that does not mean agrarian underdevelopment." As the film ended, I could not help thinking about the hoe and the *guataca*. Were they more related to *sabor* than *saber* (to know)?

En route to a conclusion, I would like to discuss the notion of *sabor* (and *saber*) with Barthes's notion of *punctum*. In a recent concert in Boston, Cuban pianist Elio Villafranca played a series of duets with guitarist Spiros Exaras. By any standard, it was an extraordinary tour de force, combining Cuban standards such as Sánchez de Fuentes's "Tú" with freer compositions that delved into Cuban and Greek folk traditions with equal ease. Villafranca, a lanky figure with long flowing dreads, was seated at a Steinway, and next to the piano was a *guataca*, the metallic part of a hoe often used as a percussion instrument in Cuban music. For most of the time, the *guataca* remained at his side, until the two performers played a melody based on the Arará tradition. Villafranca picked up the *guataca* and played it, chanting the lyrics. The haunting melody, buttressed by the *guataca*, reminded me of Barthes's distinction in photography, the *punctum*—which is something in the photo that is "lightning like . . . [with] a power of expansion" that radically alters your perception of what the photo captures (1981, 45). The *punctum* is a moment in time, but it has a ripple effect that never ceases. In effect, the *guataca* became a *punctum*. The *guataca* is used in Arará religious ceremonies (*toque de santos*), and it introduced an eerie yet completely familiar rhythmic intimacy to the composition. For over an hour, the rough, metallic sound of the *guataca* was still resonating in the fluid and sometimes jagged piano of Villafranca and the flowing lines of Exaras's guitar. Even though Villafranca only played the *guataca* for a couple of minutes, it left a lingering, sonorous *sabor* for the rest of the evening—like a haunting memory. This was reinforced by the appearance of the *guataca* itself—weathered and slightly rusty in stark contrast to the shiny, sleek colors of the piano and the guitar. I wonder: Is Barthes's notion of *punctum* similar to the Cuban notion of *sabor*? If so, then the bolt of lightning, "the power of expansion," alerts us to a wider understanding of Sara Gómez's use of music in her films as the use of *sabor* on the journey toward *saber*, the complex grappling with Cuban social realities that has not abated since her death in 1974.

NOTES

1. For more on Álvarez and Sara Gómez, see Malitsky (this volume).—Ed.
2. Lourdes Martínez-Echazábal (this volume) also discusses the importance of music, specifically in the film *Iré a Santiago*.—Ed.
3. Even the excellent five-CD collection of Lecuona's piano works, with some 140 compositions by Thomas Tirino, and an excellent recording by BIS still lack the *sabor* Fernández (2006) refers to.
4. Serra (this volume) provides an in-depth analysis of Guevara's "New Man."
5. See the interviews with Iván Arocha and Luis García Mesa in this volume for more about the process on the postproduction of *De cierta manera*.—Ed.
6. Not everyone agrees with Althusser's claims, and still others say that despite these distinctions he never really dispensed with the notion that science is the opposite of ideology. As a result, he reintroduced metaphysical abstractions into a Marxist view of ideology. See Rancière (2011, 125–54), and Thompson (1978, 1–205).
7. The words also bear an eerie resemblance to the Olofi story during the banquet sequence of "The Last Supper," where a character imitates the Truth that walks around with the body of Truth but the head of a Lie.

BIBLIOGRAPHY

Adorno, T. W., and Hanns Eisler. (1947) 2007. *Composing for the Films*. New York: Continuum.

Althusser, Louis. (1971) 2001. *Lenin and Philosophy and Other Essays*. Introduction by Frederic Jameson. Translated by Ben Brewster. New York: Monthly Review Press.

Althusser, Louis, and Etienne Balibar. (1968) 1970. *Reading Capital*. Translated by Ben Brewster. London: New Left Books.

Amaya, Hector. 2010. *Screening Cuba: Film Criticism as Political Performance during the Cold War*. Urbana: University of Illinois Press.

Barthes, Roland. (1964) 1973. *Elements of Semiology*. New York: Hill and Wang.

———. 1981. *Camera Lucida: Reflections on Photography*. New York: Hill and Wang.

Davies, Stephen. 1994. *Musical Meaning and Expression*. Ithaca, NY: Cornell University Press.

Díaz Lopez, Marina. 2003. "De cierta manera." In *The Cinema of Latin America*, edited by Alberto Elena and Marina Díaz López, 141–49. London: Wallflower.

Ebrahim, Haseenah. 1998. "Afrocuban Religions in Sara Gómez's *One Way or Another* and Gloria Rolando's *Oggún*." *Western Journal of Black Studies* 22, no. 4: 239–51.

Fanon, Frantz. 1963. *The Wretched of the Earth*. Translated by Constance Farrington. New York: Grove.

Fernández, Raúl. 2006. *From Afro-Cuban Rhythms to Latin Jazz*. Berkeley: University of California Press.

Kalinak, Kathryn. 2010. *Film Music: A Very Short Introduction*. New York: Oxford University Press.

Müller, Alessandra. 2004. *¿Dónde está Sara Gómez*. Film. Switzerland: AMKA Films Production.

Nattiez, Jean-Jacques. 1990. *Music and Discourse: Towards a Semiology of Music*. Translated by Caroline Abbate. Princeton, NJ: Princeton University Press.

Rancière, Jacques. 2011. *Althusser's Lesson*. Translated by Emiliano Battista. London: Continuum.

Thompson, E. P. 1978. *The Poverty of Theory and Other Essays*. New York: Monthly Review Press.

ALAN WEST-DURÁN is Associate Professor of Cultures, Societies, and Global Studies at Northeastern University. He is author of *Cuba: A Cultural History*, of *African Caribbeans: A Reference Guide*, and of *Tropics of History: Cuba Imagined*. He is editor of the two-volume *Cuba: People, Culture, History* and of *Latino and Latina Writers*.

FIFTEEN

The Santiago of Two Pilgrims
F. G. Lorca and Sara Gómez in Search of Eastern Cuba

Lourdes Martínez-Echazábal

PILGRIMS

The *peregrinos* (pilgrims) we follow in this chapter, Federico García Lorca (1898–1936) and Sara Gómez (1942–74), journey not to Santiago de Compostela but to another Santiago—Santiago de Cuba.[1] Guided by poetic devotion, both made their way to the epicenter of Cuban nationality and spirituality, where they enshrined the memories of their journeys in a poem-*son* and a poetic documentary, respectively.[2] As García Lorca wrote: "*Siempre dije que yo iría a Santiago*" (I always said I'd go to Santiago) (2008). In the following pages, I embark on my own journey in the footsteps of Lorca and Gómez. I observe their conversation across time about the same place and watch as Lorca appears in Gómez's film, how she inscribes him on the city, and how she turns different corners than he did.

Voilà!

Federico García Lorca

On March 7, 1930, Federico García Lorca arrived in Havana after spending nearly nine months in New York, where the poet had already confessed his deep fascination with black culture and black people. This is an important detail because it suggests the presence of a certain negrophilia typical of Western artistic vanguards in the interwar period.[3] Referring to Lorca's New York phase and his great admiration for blacks and all things black (*lo negro*), Ian Gibson, one of Lorca's primary biographers, comments that "the blacks, whose 'primitive drive' and 'incorruptible spiritual foundation' the poet wasted no time in recognizing and deeply admiring, in addition to their spontaneity, energy, music and carefree sexuality, served to prolong the symbolism of the Gypsies depicted in his 'romancero' (collection of ballads), but in a much wider context" (2009, 204–5). Presumably, Gibson is referring to the US context or, more specifically, to that of New York and the Cuban one that followed.

With mixed feelings, Lorca left his much-admired Harlem—where "obscenity has an accent of innocence that turns it into something disturbing and religious" (García Lorca 1996, 3:166–67)—and the desolate, industrial, dehumanized, and heartless megalopolis of modern New York City. That megalopolis is where "not even one person has time to look at a cloud or dialogue with one of those delicate breezes which the nearby sea obstinately sends" (165), where "the dawn comes, and no one receives it in his mouth / because no morning or hope is possible there" (2008, 72), and the stock market crash delivers "suicide cadavers on the pavement" and "the groans of unemployed workers" (1996, 1:525; 2008, 42). Lorca disembarked at the port of Havana, Cuba, and gave himself over to a city by the sea that opened its doors, bodies, and hearts to him.

In Havana, the imaginary, hidden city of Lorca's childhood begins to take shape, and the poet finally begins to feel "at home" (quoted in González Esteva 2000, 16), not only because he finds in Havana "the yellow of Cádiz in a higher degree, the rose of Seville stretching to carmine, and the green of Granada with the subtle phosphorescence of fish" (15) but also because—as Gibson tells us—Lorca "already carried much of Cuba within himself before disembarking" (2009, 231). As a child, the poet "had listened, spellbound, to the *habaneras* who sang in Fuente Vaqueros . . . [and had seen] the exotic labels pasted inside the cigar boxes his father received directly from the island" (231). In other words, as a citizen of the metropole, a certain vision of Cuba already inhabited Lorca's dreams and fantasies. Now, added to those dreams and fantasies, all that rich, poetic imagery, were the blacks and US black culture. Indeed, there is no doubt that Lorca found in the blacks—and Cuban blacks in particular—a counterpart to the Gypsies. In his own words, Lorca encountered in Cuban blacks "*negritos* without drama, who roll their eyes and say 'we are Latinos,'" and in their rhythms, the poet confesses, is "the typical one of the great Andalusian people" (1996, 3:173). In contrast to his New York experience—in which depression, joy, and anxiety all intermingled—the poet was simply happy in Cuba. So pleasant was his time on the island, in fact, that in a letter to his parents, he wrote, "This island is a paradise. If I *lose myself*, come and find me in . . . Cuba" (1997, 686; emphasis added).[4]

Curiously, during his three-month stay in that island paradise, Lorca wrote but a single poem—though that poem is no less important for standing alone.[5] The poem, "Son de negros en Cuba," begins with the promise of a journey: "*Cuando llegue la luna llena iré a Santiago de Cuba, iré a Santiago*" (When the full moon rises, I'm going to Santiago, Cuba, I'm going to Santiago).[6] This is precisely what happened: on the last day of May 1930, the poet from Granada fulfilled his promise and "in a wagon of black water" embarked on his journey-pilgrimage to Santiago de Cuba, the island's political capital and the center of the Cuban national myth and island spirituality.[7] Nevertheless, as Manuel Iturria Savón (2006, 24) comments, "Lorca's visit to Santiago, to which he dedicates his celebrated *son*, was unknown to the Cuban people, including the *Santiagueros* themselves." It is therefore worth asking—Why was the poet so interested in Santiago de Cuba?

We know that Lorca went to Santiago de Cuba in response to an invitation from Dominican writer and critic Max Henríquez Ureña, who at the time was living in the city, where he worked as professor of literature at the Escuela Normal para Maestros de Santiago (Teachers Training College) and served as president of the city's branch of the Institución Hispano-Cubana de Cultura (Cuban-Hispanic Cultural Institute). Lorca accepted the invitation and while there delivered a talk at the college titled "The Mechanics of the New Poetry." However, there is more. Let us recall that Max Henríquez Ureña had lived in New York for three years and, like Lorca, had come to Cuba from there. As a result, we can make certain conjectures about the emotional bond forged by their shared experience and feelings, especially given their mutual love of poetry and the fact that both played the role of pilgrim with the same New York–to–Cuba trajectory. Viewing the situation from this speculative angle may clarify, at least in part, the question that many have posed about why Lorca went to Santiago de Cuba.

Lorca's poem "Son de negros en Cuba"—better known as "Iré a Santiago" (I'm going to Santiago) because of the refrain that repeats several times throughout the poem in typical *son* style—is an ode to the island written in the *negrista* style of the times. It is a poem that, as Cabrera Infante correctly points out, provides "a vision of the poetic possibilities of blackness and its somewhat foreign, alien dialects. Exotic would be the word" (2006, 96–97). Through the use of metonymy, Lorca creates this ode to the island in which Santiago, its first capital, becomes Cuba, and Cuba becomes Santiago. This metonymical relation is enabled by certain images that remind us of the island's colonial and postcolonial contexts. These images are expressed, among other means, by evoking the memory of the labels found inside Lorca's father's Cuban cigar boxes—the stamps and the identifying rings wrapped around the cigars. What do the phrases "the blond head of Fonseca" and "the rose of Romeo and Juliette" refer to if not to brands of cigars?[8] The invocation of this colonial product, coupled with images that evoke natural rhythms and music in natural surroundings on the margins of industrial modernity, reaffirm what Cabrera Infante (2006) would call Lorca's exotic, fetishizing vision of (Santiago de) Cuba, the blacks, and their culture.

"Son de negros en Cuba" follows a child-poet who carries his imagination with him as he embarks on a journey across the sea and translates into poetry the imaginary forged in the metropole of his youth. This imaginary is one driven by the vanguardist gaze that, in its most acute form, forces one to flee from civilization and to embrace naive life and exotic nature. For this reason, "Son de negros en Cuba" can provide only a partial representation of (Santiago de) Cuba and black culture. In this light, one can perhaps comprehend the anticipated remembrance of Andalusia—"I always said I'd be going to Santiago"—and the journey to Santiago in 1930 as the fulfillment of a dream or premonition. Into this imagination—and we know that Lorca's was boundless—the poet incorporates blacks and their music.

With "Son de negros en Cuba," Lorca flees from a dismal island (Manhattan) to one that is spellbinding (Cuba), "full of noises, sounds, and sweet airs that give delight and hurt not."[9] Thus, to the rhythm of a *son* Lorca closes his book *Poet in New York*, written in 1929–30 and published for the first time in 1940, four years after his death. According to Cedeño Pineda and Castañeda (2003), "'Son de negros en Cuba'... with its air of fantasy, would have remained in obscurity if [the poet's] genius had not ignited the music." Yet how could Lorca's words not set fire to the music and the other arts—those pulsing verses created by the poet of flamenco—who is enchanted by, indeed "loses" himself in, the Cuban *son*?

Federico García Lorca's poem has inspired composers and singers ranging from Roberto Valera to Ana Belén and Compay Segundo. However, as far as I know, the significance that the Granada native's poem held for Havana filmmaker Sara Gómez—who made her eponymous documentary five years before Valera debuted the first highly popular musical rendition (a choral arrangement) of "Son de negros en Cuba" in 1969, has never been studied.

Sara Gómez and Iré a Santiago

Sara Gómez is the other pilgrim referred to in the title of this chapter. I will focus on the documentary in which Gómez pays tribute to Lorca and to Santiago (de Cuba) and the young filmmaker embarks on her own pilgrimage. I am referring to her 1964 documentary *Iré a Santiago*. According to Gerardo Fulleda León, "*Iré a Santiago* is one of the most remarkable documentaries filmed in Cuba during that time, given its quality, rigor and rich creativity" (1999, 43). Michael Chanan considers the film "perhaps the most striking 'free cinema' documentary ever produced in Cuba" (2004, 341).

Each time I watch *Iré a Santiago*, I say to myself, "Sara must have had a ball making that film!" To be clear, I do not mean that it is a slipshod or unsubstantial documentary—one in which the integral components of the filmmaker's art (images, script, and music) are not extremely well thought out, selected, and joyfully articulated throughout the entire production, direction, and editing process. On the contrary. When I point out the playful character of the documentary, I am referring specifically to two components that encode that aspect of the work: the parodic discourse (both visually and of the commentator) and the tone. The parodic discourse of *Iré a Santiago* is simultaneously self-referential and critical—it is nuanced by a gesture that I label deconstructionist. Although since the Derridean notion dates from the late 1960s, after Gómez made the documentary, perhaps we should speak instead of a Barthian influence and refer to a demystifying gesture. For its part, the tone is without a doubt sarcastic and incisive, even bordering on mockery at times, and through it Gómez seeks to delve into the hidden, unobserved side of the most everyday truths. By means of these two devices, Gómez makes an intervention into three very important registers—the historic, the revolutionary triumphalist (of 1959 and the early 1960s), and the touristic. With the latter, she pulls Lorca through the historic and the revolutionary times and spaces of this place. The documentary also carries out an implicit examination of certain foundational ideas of Cubanness (such as the notion of transculturation, for example) deployed by the mythologizing—and necessarily mystifying—tradition endemic to all three of the abovementioned discourses.

As described below, *Iré a Santiago* clearly establishes the young filmmaker's marked interest in the history and identity of the African diaspora in the Caribbean, and particularly in Cuba. By focusing on the cultural and religious expressions of this diaspora and bringing them to the screen, Gómez performs a valuable documentary and archival task while bringing into play a theoretical reflection supported by the subliminal impulse afforded by the seventh art.

IRÉ A SANTIAGO: A DOCUMENTARY IN SIX ACTS

For the purpose of my analysis, I have organized the documentary into six parts, or acts, divided into two segments by a mixed intermission. The structure is as follows.

Act 1: Identity
Act 2: "Santiago and the French"
Act 3: The Historic Santiago Palimpsest
   a. History before Castro (and after Columbus!)

"Mixed Intermission"
  b. History after Castro
Act 4: "The Men and Women of Santiago"
Act 5: "Recommendations for the Tourist"
Act 6: July Is Also Carnival Month

The acts set in quotation marks are structured around observations provided by the documentary's commentator; the others I formulated by taking into account the mise-en-scène and—as is only right—the music.

It is the music, with its rhythm, tonality, and accent, that structures the theme of identity and thus plays an important role in *Iré a Santiago*. From the very beginning—as the chords of "Son de la loma" (sung by quintessential Santiago natives Trío Matamoros) emerge to accompany a close-up shot of a verse from Lorca's poem graffitied on a wall (see fig. 15.1) in the eastern capital (including the refrain "Iré a Santiago" that will serve as the title of Gómez's documentary)—to the very end—when alternating medium shots and tracking shots invite the viewer to savor a performance of then famous Pello el Afrokán and his contagious "Mozambique" rhythms—the music joins script and image in a joyful, all-embracing synergy.[10]

ACT 1: IDENTITY

In *Iré a Santiago*, Lorca's "Son de negros" first arises as a *mulato son*, "Son de la loma," and this in turn is followed by an Ernesto Grenet song, "Drume negrita," performed by the Quinteto Instrumental de Música Moderna, with Frank Emilio on piano and Tata Güines on the large conga drum. This first sequence closes with the classic *danzón* tune "Tres lindas cubanas" by Antonio María Romeu. The first song—"Son de la loma"—accompanies the film credits (editor, cameraman, sound editor, commentator, production supervisor, photographer, and, last, writer and director), which are handwritten, graffiti-style, like the verse from Lorca's poem, scrawled either on a wall or on the steps of the celebrated stone staircase of Calle Padre Pico in Santiago de Cuba. The signature of the film's writer and director—*Sarita*—is inscribed on a post rising from the base of the same Calle Pico staircase.

Beyond this rather unconventional arrangement of the credits, there is another important aspect here that alludes to the rebellious avant la lettre nature of Gómez's work as a director in the ICAIC—a female voice-over narrator, or, more accurately, commentator.[11] By giving this figure the title "commentator" rather than voice-over narrator—the latter being the title that any man would

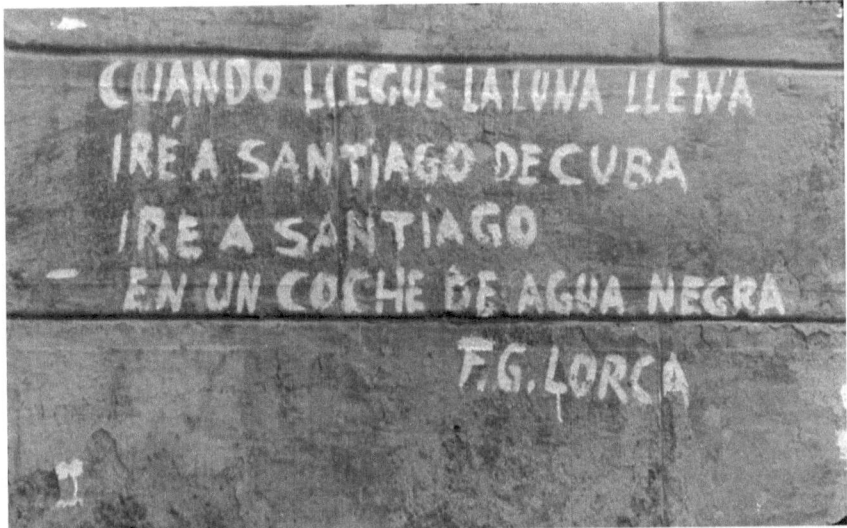

Figure 15.1 Still of Federico García Lorca's poem from the credit sequence in *Iré a Santiago*, 1964. © ICAIC

a priori assume within the epistemological regime—Gómez broke with the established tradition of the disembodied figure far removed from the subjects he presents or the situation he describes and who, for the same reason and within a classical patriarchal framework, inscribes his ethnographic authority on the visual narrative. It should also be noted that the director signs the documentary as "Sarita," and not Sarita Gómez or Sara Gómez, as she signs most of her other work. This gesture, not in the least gratuitous, and the unconventional way of presenting the credits (graffiti as a feminist resignification of the conventional terms and titles of documentaries of the time, an intimate, informal signature, perhaps) affirm from the very beginning the rebellious, vanguardist, and playful character of Gómez's filmmaking.

Along with the script, the music lends a strong identifying touch to the documentary. *Sones* and *danzónes* accompany crowd scenes that act as parentheses, bracketing the documentary's first "act," in which viewers witness people working, taking the bus, moving through the streets and experience the open-air market and the sellers with their ubiquitous carts of fruit and meat who occupy the street corners or wheel their wares around the city. Drawn in by the images, gestures, and music, we become part of the audience gathered around a wandering magician who, like a modern minstrel, entertains those who encircle him in Parque Céspedes. We see them, and they look at us—the Santiagueros look at the camera, some recognize it with surprise, others dodge it, many ignore it, while still others do not notice it at all. The audience, mostly non-Santiagueros from Havana—like the filmmakers, I daresay—watch these scenes and recognize ourselves, and, as though pulled along by our own duende, we join in the pilgrim's eager journey to meet those people and that land of Santiago de Cuba, as familiar as it is foreign to those who dwell elsewhere on the island but most especially to the men and women of Havana.

One minute and fifty-three seconds into the film, the music ("Son de la loma") gives way to the voice of the female commentator. "What are the people of Santiago like?" is the unvoiced question to which the commentator, like a ventriloquist for the myth of Santiago de Cuba, responds, "Yes, they say we are from an island where the land quakes and the *mulatos* smell of fresh herbs. Here we adapt to the heat by drinking the fermented juice of roots."[12] These words are spoken as the camera follows a young man carrying a case full of soda bottles that might be *pru*, a typical Santiago de Cuba beverage made of a fermented herb-and-root juice that is meant to combat the heat, if not quench the thirst. Though it might be a case of commercial soda pop, and the shot might be intended to precisely underline the gap between word and deed.

As this first act of *Iré a Santiago* continues, the commentator continues her description of what *they*—the Santiagueros—are like. Yet, at some point, she begins speaking about *we* the Santiagueros and how *we* see ourselves, first assigning the identity and then assuming it. "We laugh and speak in loud voices, aggressively and proudly, our body language is exaggerated and graceful . . . there's no doubt we are people of the Antilles [that is, *mulato*]."[13]

From its representation of the boisterous collective space of the street, the *son* relinquishes its lively sound and gives way to the more intimate space of the elders, of tradition, of the family, and of the home, where there always is—and always must be—a rocking chair, also known as the *sillón* (big chair). A sequence follows of several shots of men and women of different ages rocking in their chairs. The rocking chair rules the household, and, indeed, as the commentator tells us to the accompaniment of the first verses of the song "Drume negrita" (a lullaby) by composer Ernesto Grenet, "On my island, the siesta is a rocking chair of wicker and wood" (emphasis added).

As in Lorca's poem, the narration that accompanies the documentary's early sequences establishes a metonymic relationship that governs the bond between the part and the whole—between the city of Santiago (first capital of the island, cradle of Cuban nationalism and the island's spirituality), the island of Cuba (symbolic national-space), and the Antilles archipelago (the island arc that shelters and contains Cuba.¹⁴ In this cartography of island space, Santiago is both perceived and presents itself as a uterus that self-engenders, that engenders and contains (the island), while being contained by it and by the group of islands known in English as the West Indies and in Spanish as Las Antillas (Guillén 1980, 62–71). The commentator notes, "There is no doubt about our Antillean identity. But all of this is virtually a legend, it's the myth of Cuba constructed in a *son* [in a *black son*?]. The thing is, Santiago is there, and so, yes, it's true: Cuba is an island of the Antilles."

From the rocking chair, or *sillón*, in a long shot the camera takes us inside a house, the family space, which in this case is a black home. For the first time in Cuban cinema (the second will occur a couple of years later in Gómez's 1966 documentary *Crónicas de mi familia*), the black family—the black home—appears in a dignified role within a frame from which it has always been excluded.¹⁵ Of course, I am referring to the frame of the scene—whether in film, television, the theater, or even the limited frame of literature and, above all, in the interwar period—that was envisioned and presented as the exaltation and appreciation of blackness and black people and their culture, within which Lorca's poem "Son de negros en Cuba" stands as an example worth considering. In fact, the narrator uses the word *home* instead of *house* to refer to the place where we live as a family and, once again through the first-person plural, tells us that "our homes are welcoming to our compadres, our brothers." It is worth asking whether the possessive adjective qualifying the word *homes* offers the part—in this case, the black home—for the whole, meaning the Santiaguero or even Cuban home, or whether, on the contrary, the Cuban home is constituted and presented through the black Santiaguero home. If so, the scene would seem to bring to light the importance that Gómez places on the black home as the cornerstone not only of the Santiagan family but of the Cuban family, too. Whatever the case, the fact is that in this scene—which lasts a mere thirty-five seconds—image, discourse, and music(ality) are presented in perfect harmony to create a singular scene, the likes of which had not been seen before in Cuban film.

However, near the end of this first act, the commentator turns on her own discourse to refute all those things that musicians, poets, narrators, and tourist guides say time and again about *us* (and ourselves), affirming, "But this is almost a legend. This is the myth of Cuba constructed from a *son*." She then corrects herself once more, falling back on a gesture that is always unfolding between the yes and the no, as Santiago itself seems to be rocking back and forth in tenuous equilibrium on this myth, trying to recover it and to affirm that which assuredly underlies all myths, all legends. The commentator explains in a playful tone, "The thing is that Santiago is there, and so, yes it is true—Cuba is an island of the Antilles... and *mulato*... *mulato* is a state of mind." Once again, through the commentator's intervention, the fundamental importance of Santiago in the construction of the island-national-Antillean identity is affirmed, as it is Santiago—and not Havana or any other region of the country—that provides the Caribbean accent to that otherwise hispanophilic, orientophobic island.[16]

ACT 2: "SANTIAGO AND THE FRENCH"

The film's voice-over tells us: "A century and a half later [after the Haitian Revolution, and the subsequent migration of French colonists and their slaves to Santiago de Cuba], Santiago no longer has French people in Calle del Gallo, nor French cafés, but Santiago still has the tomb of the one they call *"la francesa"* (Iré a Santiago, 1964).

Despite the absence of French people (both black and White) that the commentator highlights in this quotation, this segment of the documentary opens with the camera following the funeral procession of Esperanza, the president of a local French society. In this segment, the filmmaker continues her exploration of the historic French identity as well as the current French-Santiagan-Cuban-Antillean cultural identity. By focusing on the funeral rite and other cultural expressions derived from slaves who arrived from Haiti with their masters, Sarita seems to circumvent the French identity.

It is common knowledge that during the Saint Domingue rebellion, later known as the Haitian Revolution, thousands of White French colonists and their *mulato* descendants came to eastern Cuba and brought their slaves along with them. In the area around Santiago, they installed a system of coffee plantations that the people called *franceses*. They also brought their family names, food, music, dance, and other cultural and religious practices to Santiago, which over the years were vernacularized. They were ultimately Cubanized, although they were still called French. This segment of the documentary makes clear that, for Gómez, identity is not a unitary, preconceived concept; rather, identity allows for movement and adaptation. It is continually being created, elaborated, and changed. Being is naming. Being is a process of singularization and differentiation through which identity is constructed by naming (including of oneself). Thus, naming is being. Seen in this way, then, although the script affirms that by 1964 there were no "French" people left, "not even on Calle del Gallo," the descendants of those slaves still maintain some societies and dances that they name—that is, characterize—as French.

This sequence of *Iré a Santiago* makes very clear that the young director was extremely interested in the history and identity of the African diaspora in the Caribbean, particularly in Cuba. She was also interested in the myths and rituals that endured among that diaspora and were expressed as creole culture, whether in Esperanza's funeral or in Gómez's later, spectacular footage of an Abakuá initiation in *De cierta manera* (1974). Other cultural expressions that Gómez explored include the Santiago conga with its singular inclusion of the so-called *trompeta china* (Chinese horn), the French tomb, and even (the Santiago) Carnival itself. By bringing these cultural and religious expressions of the African diaspora in Cuba to the screen, Gómez carries out valuable documentary and archival work at the same time as she brings into play a theoretical reflection on the process of creolization or transculturation. Whether forced or not, the myths, rituals, and other cultural expressions of the African diaspora have undergone this process over time as the result of the various historical processes that have shaped the societies of the Caribbean Basin and its islands.

ACT 3: THE HISTORIC SANTIAGO PALIMPSEST

a. History before Castro (and after Columbus!)

"The story always begins in the bay," the film tells us. In other words, it is in the bay, with its palimpsest-like surface, that the history of Santiago (and therefore of Cuba) has been written since the "discovery" and subsequent founding of the first settlement on the island by Diego Velázquez de Cuéllar in 1514. In the first part of this third act, Gómez reviews the history of Santiago before the triumph of the Revolution in 1959. Parading across the waters of the bay are conquistadors and pirates, slave ships and warships, writers and musicians, uprisings and wars, until one day...

"MIXED INTERMISSION"

This scene, or *intermedio mixto* as the commentator calls it, interrupts the historic narrative with a mysterious tone that situates it within the realm of the supernatural or mystical. There is a shift from the real to the magical. The scene begins with a shot of a boat with the name *Virgen de la Caridad* clearly visible. A shot of a beach follows, where, thanks to some fancy film editing, a woman appears and disappears among the remains of a time-battered breakwater. In the final shot of this sequence, she walks into the sea.[17] The commentator, in full charge of this scene, tells us in a tone that accentuates the suspenseful, mythical (nonempirical) nature of the story, "There's a rumor, which has yet to be confirmed, that every afternoon in Las Múcaras a woman in a bathing suit and with a striped scarf tied around her head appears and wants to communicate." After this brief intervention, this mixed intermission that interrupts the historic with the magical and seems to signify the spirituality of the inhabitants of Santiago (and of Cuba in general)—their alleged propensity for myth and legend—Gómez takes us back to the historical discourse, this time with an air of triumphalist grandeur.

b. History after Castro

Part two of the third act opens with a panoramic shot of some mountains that we assume are part of the Sierra Maestra range. In a grandiloquent tone, the commentator's voice comes in on top of the sound of a marching band and states: "But history has begun once again in Santiago." Immediately the camera offers a medium shot of a parade led by a military band playing a march. Following the band is a contingent of nurses and then another of students carrying two floral wreaths. I think I can make out the name Frank País on one of the ribbons adorning the wreaths, from which I deduce that these wreaths were offerings destined for the martyr's tomb during the commemoration marking the anniversary of his assassination, which occurred in Santiago on July 30, 1957. Notwithstanding the affirmation that the story begins with the failed attack on the Moncada barracks on July 26, 1953, the reference to País and the use of the adverbial clause "once again" seem to indicate that, underneath this new history, Santiago still bears the marks of past histories.

At this point in the documentary (8:50), it is clear that Santiago is preparing to celebrate July 26 and the beginning of the new history—the marching tunes accompanying the parade images are suited to the occasion. However, one should recall that the month of July hosts celebrations not only of the Castro-led insurgency but also the feast day of the city's patron saint, Santiago (on July 25). Also, unlike the traditional carnival, this pagan festival is celebrated here in summer and thus escapes religious and political mythology [because it is not associated with a religious holiday or a revolutionary "victory"].[18] The marching music gives way to a *changüí* song with the lyrics, "Santiago was full, Santiago was full of *guajiros*, Santiago was full."[19] Thus, from its untamed mountains and that myth of Cuba "built upon a *son*" (or upon a *changüí*), the history of Santiago and of Cuba begins again. Nevertheless, Gómez makes sure that those other histories are not erased by the overwhelming tide of the triumphalist discourse of the Revolution with its messianic pretentions. On the contrary, they remain legible and in place—albeit *sous rature*—upon the silvery waters of the bay, or, more fittingly, in celluloid.

ACT 4: "THE MEN AND WOMEN OF SANTIAGO"

Two figures, a woman and a man, walk separately along the streets of Santiago de Cuba and, intentionally or not, meet up in one of the city's cafés. They begin flirting, and in the next scene, we see them sitting together at an outside table. These scenes are accompanied by another *changüí* tune with lyrics that repeat, "Now, yes ... because he's had a taste of the honey of the women of Santiago." With their fresh images, these sequences capture aspects of the human heritage of Santiago de Cuba—the spontaneity, joyfulness, self-assurance, and sensuality. They also present what, for the Cuban people and especially Cubans in the eastern region of the island, are the typical types of Santiago de Cuba. At the same time, they place the city's human heritage on par with its architectural, physical, and cultural-religious heritage.

ACT 5: "RECOMMENDATIONS FOR THE TOURIST"

This part of the film begins with a low-angle shot of El Morro castle accompanied by the *son* "Tres lindas cubanas." The rest of the act alternates high- and low-angle shots of unique tourist attractions in and around Santiago de Cuba, including Puerto Boniato, La Gran Piedra, the cathedral, and Calle Pico. The mountainous geography of Santiago and its environs means that each of these places is situated at the top of a hill or on a rock, so the visitor has to climb up to reach them. With freshness and humor, the commentator emphasizes that any scenic tour of Santiago should include the human, intellectual, and popular heritage as well.[20] She recommends that tourists who go to Santiago should make sure to visit one of the local residents at home and reminds them that "Santiago also has a university and Carnival in July." Notably, this reminder is accompanied by a frontal shot of the main building of the Universidad de Santiago de Cuba followed by another frontal shot of a person dressed up in a very sui generis costume that includes a hood with two antennae, each topped with a bell. In stark contrast to the outfit is the pair of white sunglasses worn by the reveler as well as the fried roll this person eats while walking along and staring unabashedly at the camera. The shot ends with a comment that seems out of place: "If you want to know something about Lilith, call 30-5566." However, this comment is not out of place given the Carnival-esque context as well as the generally playful tone of *Iré a Santiago*.

In her "recommendations," Gómez visits common tourist sites such as El Morro, Gran Piedra, and the cathedral, and then she includes places such as the typical Santiago home (an intimate space not usually considered a tourist attraction), the university (a place where specialized knowledge and information is produced), and Carnival (a ritual through which the people of Santiago de Cuba display their traditions and popular culture). Gómez positions these sites within the local (and national) heritage as worthwhile for visitors to know, explore, and appreciate on par with historical and physical-ecological heritage. Thus, in 1964, Gómez intervenes in the register of the tourism industry by expanding on the notion of what can and should be considered areas of interest for tourists and travelers visiting Santiago.

ACT 6: JULY IS ALSO CARNIVAL MONTH

"Cuba works hard and has fun." This quotation, which appears on a banner in one of the shots in this act, should read, "Cuba works hard but also has fun." Indeed, in our modern society, work and fun are presented as opposed activities, or at least activities belonging to two different registers. However, this is not the case in (Santiago de) Cuba during Carnival—or at least that is what Gómez seems to imply with this shot.

The final act opens with a street shot of a group of musicians playing Haitian rhythms. This is followed by a self-referential shot of the cameraman Mario García Joya (Mayito) reflected in a small mirror adorning a blanket or cape inscribed with the words *"Los vikings"* (the use of Spanglish here is curious), perhaps referring to one of the troupes or groups participating in the Santiago Carnival. What comes next is a series of street scenes, still in daytime, of people dancing, being social, and having fun. The transition from daytime to nighttime festivities is marked by a clip of a cartoon in which we see the 1950s–60s character Mr. Magoo (known in Cuba as El Señor Magú) opening a bottle of *champán añeja* ("aged champagne," a takeoff on aged rum) to the sound of a typical Santiago conga rhythm (not even this cartoon character can escape creolization!). Immediately the camera offers a couple of short takes of people "rolling" along the street to a conga beat. The next shot is accompanied by another musical cut in which the conga gives way to Pello el Afrokán and his cast of blond *mulato* and dark-haired White women who take to the stage dancing to the recently released (in 1963) song "Mozambique." This song also accompanies shots of a parade float carrying a group of musicians and dancers in the midst of whom is a *mulato* woman of Santiago (perhaps she's the woman from Act 4) dancing at the center of the float. After a brief journey through the crowd

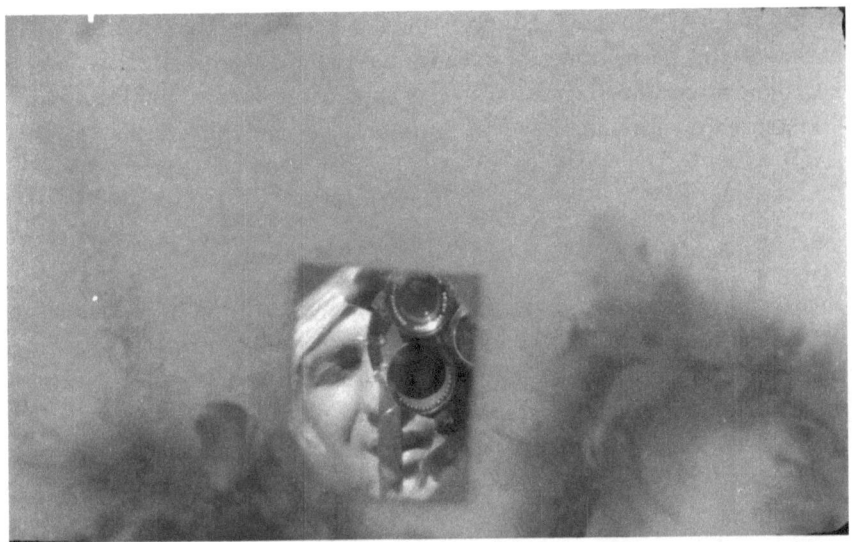

Figure 15.2 Still of the cinematographer Mario Garcia Joya from *Iré a Santiago*, 1964. © ICAIC

Figure 15.3 Still of Sara Gómez, highlighted, captured from a street scene in *Iré a Santiago*, 1964. © ICAIC

that includes several shots of dancers and band members, the camera takes us back—playing the mirror game once again—to the woman of Santiago, who is now dancing around in circles in an evocation of the Lucumí goddess Ochún. The song ends with a final shout of "Mozambique," and the screen reads "Fin" (end).

CONCLUSION

In principle, *Iré a Santiago* moves from street scenes to the more intimate space of the black home and then continues on its playful journey, accentuating, questioning, demystifying, and correcting historic discourse—both bourgeois and triumphalist revolutionary. Likewise, in a playful way, the documentary dialogues with the discourse of the tourism industry and underscores not only the importance of the ecological-scenic heritage but also the human heritage and cultural and intellectual legacy of Santiago de Cuba. Ultimately, the film returns to the open, democratic spaces of the street and popular heritage. It is in the street space where Santiago fully expresses itself during one of the city's most important rituals—Carnival.

There is no doubt that through this simultaneously visual and musical pilgrimage Gómez is underlining the fundamental place and historic-cultural legacy of Santiago de Cuba within the Cuban nation. Santiago de Cuba, just like that other Santiago (de Compostela) in Iberian mythology, becomes a place of origin, affirmation, and pilgrimage to the roots of nationality and spirituality signified by the Cuban people in the icon of the Virgen de la Caridad del Cobre (Our Lady of Charity, or the Virgin of El Cobre) and by the Lucumí goddess Ochún. It is the same spirituality and legend to which the documentary poetically refers in the mixed intermission and, more obliquely, through the film's final shot of the woman of Santiago dancing to the beat of "Mozambique" with body language that identifies her movement with the ritual dance of Ochún. Whether these scenes make implicit reference to Cachita-Ochún, to the importance of the oral tradition, or to the hybrid religiosity of the people of Santiago and of Cuba, or whether they simply allude to the so-called predisposition of the Caribbean imagination to myth and legend, the fact is that they bring into relief the importance of spiritual discourse and position it hand in hand—and on par—with the historical one.

Last, we cannot ignore that this pilgrimage, so to speak, confronts us with contemporary images alongside a history of colonialism and oppression that necessarily includes its inverse—piracy, Maroon culture, insurgency, creolization, and transculturated myths and rituals. Ultimately, we are faced with a

Santiago de Cuba that is Antillean and Caribbean, a Santiago that is complex and, above all, a far cry from that other Santiago and that other imagined, exotic, one-dimensional Cuba—"¡Arpa de troncos vivos, caimán, flor de tabaco!" (Harp of living tree trunks, caiman, flower of tobacco)—that the (post)colonial imaginary that Lorca, the other pilgrim from overseas, brought us in a *son*.

Translated from the original Spanish by Joan Donaghey

NOTES

1. "In the most traditional sense, the term 'pilgrim' (from the Latin, *peregrīnus*) refers to a traveler who, out of devotion or because of a vow, visits a shrine or other sacred place. In its broadest interpretation, it includes all those traveling through foreign lands (foreigners). In a stricter sense, for Spanish Catholics, a pilgrim (*peregrino* in Spanish) is that person who makes his or her way to the Cathedral of Santiago de Compostela to visit the apostle's tomb" (http://es.wikipedia.org/wiki/Peregrino). Translated and adapted from the Spanish.

2. The term *son* refers to a musical genre with indigenous, African, and Spanish influences.—Trans. See West-Durán (this volume) for more on Cuban music.—Ed.

3. The year 1930 was a fruitful one for Cuban culture. Langston Hughes visited the country in February, meeting Nicolás Guillén during his stay. Coincidentally, on the same day that Langston Hughes left to return to New York, Federico García Lorca arrived in Havana after his time in New York, where, according to Romare Bearden (see Breen 1989), Hughes and Lorca had become friends. In April 1930, inspired by the US poet's friendship and guidance, Nicolás Guillén published his *Motivos de Son*. Lorca arrived in New York on June 25, 1929, and fled from the city for Havana (via Miami) on March 4, 1930. In using the verb *flee* to describe his departure from New York, I follow the terminology the author himself used in the ninth part of his *Poet in New York* collection, entitled "Huída de Nueva York" (Flight from New York) (2008). It is very likely that Lorca's fascination derived from his attraction to Gypsy culture as characteristic and yet marginalized from Andalusian culture, and Spanish culture in general, as black culture has been in the Americas.

4. It bears mentioning that the verb *perderse*, to lose oneself, refers to the poet's immersion in the world of carnal and other pleasures, sins, or vices that alter one's rational, normative/heteronormative conduct.

5. See the complete text of the poem at the end of this chapter.

6. While it is true that Lorca only wrote a single poem in Cuba, he also worked on a play titled *El público*. According to Gibson, "It is almost certain

that the bulk of the drama that he finished that summer in Granada was written in Cuba" (2009, 235). (The title of this poem has been alternately translated as "Sound of the Cuban Blacks," "Sound of the Cuban Negroes," and "Blacks Dancing to Cuban Rhythms."—Trans.) Poem translated as "Sound of the Cuban Negroes" by A. S. Kline (2007). http://www.poetryintranslation.com/PITBR/Spanish/FiveintheafternoonLorca.htm.

7. As Santiago de Compostela is to the mythology of Spain and the Iberian Peninsula.

8. The second verse makes reference to the famous Romeo y Julieta brand of cigars, the logo of which depicts act 2, scene 2 of the Shakespearean drama, in which Juliet reflects on belonging and identity assigned by a name and laments the fact that the two lovers belong to feuding families. I think Lorca's verse directly references the Cuban cigar brand, which in turn alludes to the Shakespearean drama.

9. Shakespeare, *The Tempest*, act 3, scene 1. Spoken by Caliban.

10. It is impossible to avoid associating Matamoros, who is also known as Santiago Matamoros (Saint James "Matamoros," literally, "Moor-killer") with Santiago the place. According to legend, the apostle earned his nickname when he miraculously appeared to fight alongside the Christian crusaders at the battle of Clavijo. Also, Pedro Izquierdo (Pello el Afrokán) burst onto the Cuban music scene in 1963 with his catchy "Mozambique Rhythm." The overwhelming popularity of both Pello and his newly created rhythm/dance caused quite a stir at the time—a mere four years after the Revolution—owing to what some (the Cuban bourgeoisie and middle classes in particular) considered his irreverent stage presence. It is also worth noting that it was not only the contagious Mozambique rhythm, with its evocation of that African country, that Pello el Afrokán brought to the scene; the performer was also accompanied by a troupe of dancers, some blond *mulatos* and some white with dark hair, who danced with and for Pello el Afrokán—the African? No doubt a Fanonian-style sociological phenomenon.

11. Remember that this is the Cuba of 1964 where, despite a revolutionary atmosphere and feeling of cosmopolitan revival, the country had only just begun to experiment with vanguardist cinema. The films that had been made earlier were historic reels or comedies such as Tomás Gutiérrez Alea's *Las doce sillas* (1962). In terms of camerawork and editing, the most important films produced in that period were the 1963 documentary *Salut les cubains* by French director Agnès Varda, and the 1964 film *Soy Cuba* by Soviet director Mikhail Kalatozov. Both were filmed in Cuba with primarily foreign crews and Cuban (professional and amateur) actors.

12. From the references made (tremors, juice made from fermented roots), we know that we are talking about Santiago de Cuba.

13. In regard to the displacement of the incorporeal male subject—that is, the voice-over narrator I referenced above—note that when shifting from *they*

to *we*, the commentator becomes part of the abovementioned context, no longer an observer-participant but rather a constituted, integrated subject within the context she is describing.

14. See verses 18 and 36 of Lorca's poem and note the title itself—"*Son de negros de* Cuba" (emphasis added).

15. The black family debuts in Cuban literature in Cirilo Villaverde's novel *Cecilia Valdés* (1839, 1882), but it is a family broken by the sexual violence of the colonial, slavery-based, patriarchal system.

16. This is true to such an extent that, when outside their own territory and especially in western Cuba (in the old provinces of Las Villas, Matanzas, Havana, and Pinar del Rio, but particularly in Havana), where they had been moving in alarming numbers since the 1970s, people from the eastern province were called "Palestinos." Such was the case that in the mid-1990s the musical group Van Van released a song in which they stated—and at the same time warned—"*La Habana no aguanta más*" (Havana can't take any more).

17. This woman may allude to two things: the legend of Our Lady of Charity or the Virgin of El Cobre, a statue found at sea by three fishermen, or Ochún, the Lucumí goddess worshipped in Cuba. However, taking into account the syncretic religious register of the Cuban people, it may refer to both.

18. For a brief but excellent and well-documented explanation of the origin and evolution of the Santiago Carnival, see http://en.wikipedia.org/wiki/Carnival_of_Santiago_de_Cuba.

19. *Changüí* is a style of Cuban music that originated in the early nineteenth century in the eastern region of Guantánamo Province, specifically Baracoa. It arose in the sugarcane refineries and in the rural communities populated by slaves. *Changüí* combines the structure and elements of Spain's *canción* and the Spanish guitar with African rhythms and percussive beats of Bantu origin. *Changüí* is considered a predecessor of *son montuno* (the ancestor of modern salsa), which enjoyed tremendous popularity in Cuba throughout the twentieth century. The *changüí* ensemble consists of four musical instruments—*marímbula, bongó, tres,* and *güiro* (or *guayo*)—and a singer(s). See http://en.wikipedia.org/wiki/Changü%C3%AD.

20. In fact, Act 4, "The Men and Women of Santiago," anticipates the importance of human heritage to a more comprehensive understanding of Santiago de Cuba.

BIBLIOGRAPHY

Breen, Nelson E. 1989. "To Hear Another Language." *Callaloo* 40 (Summer): 431–52.
Cabrera Infante, Guillermo. 2006. "Lorca hace llover en La Habana." In *Miradas cubanas sobre García Lorca*, edited by Manuel Iturria Savón, 89–104. Seville, Spain: Editorial Renacimiento.

Cedeño Pineda, Reinaldo, and Alexis Castañeda. 2003. "Iré a Santiago." *La Jiribilla*, no. 136. Accessed July 27, 2015. http://www.lajiribilla.co.cu/2003/n136_12/136_03.html.

Chanan, Michael. 2004. *Cuban Cinema*. Minneapolis: University of Minnesota Press.

Ebrahim, Haseenag. 2007. "Sarita and the Revolution: Race and Cuban Cinema." *European Review of Latin American and Caribbean Studies* 82: 107–18.

Fulleda León, Gerardo. 1999. "¿Quién eres tú Sara Gómez?" *La Gaceta de Cuba* (July–August): 42–46.

García Lorca, Federico. 1996. *Obras Completas*. Edited by Manuel García-Posada. 4 vols. Barcelona: Galaxia Gutengerg/Círculo de Lectores.

———. 1997. *Epistolario Completo*. Edited by Andrew A. Anderson and Christopher Maurer. Madrid: Cátedra.

———. 2008. *Poet in New York*. Translated by Pablo Medina and Mark Statman. New York: Grove Press.

Gibson, Ian. 2009. *Caballo azul de mi locura: Lorca y el mundo gay*. Barcelona: Editorial Planeta.

González Esteva, Orlando, ed. 2000. *Concierto en La Habana*. Mexico City: Artes de México.

González, Tomás. 1993. "Sara, One Way or Another." In *AfroCuba: An Anthology of Cuban Writing on Race, Politics and Culture*, edited by Pedron Peréz Sarduy and Jean Stubb, 128–36. Melbourne: Ocean Press, 1993.

Guillén, Nicolás. 1980. *Songoro Cosongo y otros poemas*. Madrid: Alianza.

Iturria Savón, Manuel. 2006. "La ruta cubana de García Lorca." In *Miradas cubanas sobre García Lorca*, edited by Manuel Iturria Savón, 17–32. Seville, Spain: Editorial Renacimiento.

Morillo Vilches, Luis. n.d. "García Lorca y Cuba: Historia de una pasión." Sociadad Filatélica y Numismática Granadina. Accessed July 27, 2015. http://www.sfng.es/Articulos/lorcaycuba/lorcaycuba.html.

Volpato, Gabriel, and Daimy Godinez. 2004. "Ethnobotany of *Pru*, a Traditional Cuban Refreshment." *Economic Botany* 58, no. 3: 381–95.

LOURDES MARTÍNEZ-ECHAZÁBAL is Emerita Professor of the Departments of Literature and Latin and Latin American Studies at the University of California Santa Cruz and Visiting Senior Professor at the Postgraduate Program in Literature at the Federal University of Santa Catarina. She is the author of *Para semiotica da mulatez* (1990), numerous articles in scientific journals, and book chapters. She is organizer and editor of the dossier "Homenaje a Manuel Granados" (2005) and coeditor of the volume *Genealogies of Displacement: Between Migration and Exile* (2005). She is currently working on a book, tentatively titled, "Building another file: race, sexuality, and affection in 20th century Cuban culture."

APPENDIX

Son en negros en Cuba	Sound of the Cuban Negroes

Cuando llegue la luna llena / When the full moon rises
iré a Santiago de Cuba, / I'm going to Santiago, Cuba,
iré a Santiago, / Going to Santiago
en un coche de agua negra. / in a coach of black water.
Iré a Santiago. / Going to Santiago.
Cantarán los techos de palmera. / The palm roofs will sing.
Iré a Santiago. / Going to Santiago.
Cuando la palma quiere ser cigüeña, / When the palm tree wishes to be a stork,
iré a Santiago. / Going to Santiago.
Y cuando quiere ser medusa el plátano, / And the plantain wishes to be a jellyfish,
iré a Santiago. / I'm going to Santiago.
Iré a Santiago / Going to Santiago
con la rubia cabeza de Fonseca. / with Fonseca's blond curls.
Iré a Santiago. / Going to Santiago.
Y con la rosa de Romeo y Julieta / With the rose of Romeo and Juliet,
iré a Santiago. / Going to Santiago.
¡O Cuba! ¡Oh ritmo de semillas secas! / Oh, Cuba! Oh, rhythm of dried seeds!
Iré a Santiago. / Going to Santiago.
¡O cintura caliente y gota de madera! / Oh, waist of fire, drop of wood!
Iré a Santiago. / Going to Santiago.
¡Arpa de troncos vivos, caimán, flor de tabaco! / Harp of living tree trunks. Caiman. Flower of tobacco.
Iré a Santiago. / Going to Santiago.
Siempre he dicho que yo iría a Santiago / I always said I'd be off, going to Santiago,
en un coche de agua negra. / in a coach of black water.
Iré a Santiago. / Going to Santiago.
Brisa y alcohol en las ruedas, / Wheels of breeze and alcohol,
iré a Santiago. / going to Santiago.
Mi coral en la tiniebla, / My coral in the twilight,
iré a Santiago. / going to Santiago.
El mar ahogado en la arena, / The ocean drowned in the sand,
iré a Santiago, / going to Santiago.
calor blanco, fruta muerta, / white heat, rotten fruit,
iré a Santiago. / going to Santiago.
¡O bovino frescor de calaveras! / Oh, fresh beef of the skulls!
¡O Cuba! ¡Oh curva de suspiro y barro! / Oh, Cuba, curve of sigh and clay!
Iré a Santiago. / I'm going to Santiago.

SIXTEEN

Her Contribution

Sandra Abd'Allah-Alvarez Ramírez

IN 1960S CUBA, WOMEN WERE decisively involved in the construction of the present and the future of the country. Most of them were young and assumed the tasks assigned to them with a sense of great responsibility. It was a time of renewal, when young people with little experience could supervise a factory or work in publishing. It was a period of transition when ingenuity, creativity, and militancy prevailed. Men, women, black, white, mestizo, poor, rich, urban, and peasant all participated in the construction of the new society. New models of men and women emerged. But this was happening in the context of tradition exemplified by this line in a children's song: *"Ella no podía jugar porque tenía que lavar"* (She couldn't play because she had to do washing that day).

Between January 1959 and August 1961, Sara Gómez participated in many tasks, but her main work was in cultural journalism for the organization Juventud Socialista (Socialist Youth). The magazine *Mella*, edited by Isidoro Malmierca, was a fortnightly publication to which Inés Martiatu contributed writings on cinema and Gómez on theater. After edition number 180, *Mella* began a cultural section called "Espectáculos, which contained sections on "Cinema Notes," "Theater Notes," "What's on TV," "Ballet Notes," and *Puntillazos* (a kind of culture brief) as well as film ratings. Gómez's journalistic collaborations were also published in *Hoy Domingo*, the cultural supplement of the newspaper *Hoy*. It was at this time that Gómez met renowned intellectuals such as Nicolás Guillén, Manuel Navarro Luna, Fayad Jamís, and Manolo Díaz Martínez.

At the same time, Gómez participated in the Seminario de Etnología y Folclore del Teatro Nacional de Cuba (Seminar on Ethnology and Folklore at the National Theater). This seminar, led by renowned musicologist Argeliers León, included a rich grouping of people: María Teresa Linares, Manuel

Moreno Fraginals, John Dumoulin, Isaac Barreal, Rogelio Martínez Furé, Miguel Barnet, Alberto Pedro Díaz, Inés María Martiatu, and others. Other relevant formative spaces included the National Library, where Gómez participated in a course on art history taught by Rosario Novoa; the Casa de las Américas, where she was a student of Eliseo Diego and Roberto Fernández Retamar; and the Museum of Fine Arts, where Professor Adelaida de Juan gave lectures on pre-Columbian art. She attended the art school of San Alejandro, which saw an increase in left-wing artists and intellectuals. There she met the artist Manuel Mendive, who would illustrate *De bateyes* (1971), the ethnographic documentary that Gómez dedicated to the sugar communities (sadly, this documentary has deteriorated and can no longer be seen). Attendance at these institutions and their training programs alternated with the tasks entrusted to Gómez and her colleagues by the newspaper *Juventud Rebelde*.

As we move to a discussion of *Mi aporte* (My contribution) and its context, it is worth pausing for a moment to consider the Cuban cultural context when *Mi aporte* and *De cierta manera* (One way or another) were filmed. Recall that the First National Congress on Education and Culture (1971) had had a narrowing effect on the concept of "revolutionary art," imposing a marked dogmatism. The events related to the UNEAC (Union of Artists and Writers of Cuba) awards, specifically the Heberto Padilla case, would leave their mark beyond the literary context. As a result, presuppositions of traditional pedagogy would flood the terrain of artistic and literary creation, turning the latter into a space of political power and marginalizing various cultural expressions. This chill was expressed in a reiteration of the historical character of national cinema and the impoverishment of intellectual debate.[1] The *parametración* (setting of parameters) in the theater and the persecution of many intellectuals for their moral behavior or opinions characterize the *quinquenio gris* (five gray years), which many say lasted ten years. Gómez herself was questioned on the issue of race. She told her friends and colleagues that she—along with Alberto Pedro Díaz, Rogelio Martínez Furé, and Tomás González—was summoned to a meeting with the then Minister of Education José Llanusa. It is precisely in these conditions, which certainly weakened the creative capacity of many artists and imposed strict formulas for "revolutionary art," that Gómez wrote and filmed *De cierta manera*. Nevertheless, she was able to construct a film showing the heterogeneity of contemporary Cuban society at a time when homogenization and uniformity were understood to be the dominant modes of socialist society. As Tomás Gutiérrez Alea (1989) said of her intentions: "Sara would have liked to do cinema without cameras, without microphones: directly."

While all of Gómez's films offer deep insight into Cuban culture and society in the first decade of the Revolution, *Mi aporte* (1972), a documentary seldom shown in Cuba, incisively addresses the contradictions that emerged from women's claims to social inclusion and the obstacles they faced to make their participation effective. As a film that folds together biography, autoethnography, and political reportage, it illuminates her contribution as a social being, as a woman, and as *una negra cubana* to the social and the aesthetic transformations of her world. More than ten years after the triumph of the Cuban Revolution, social conditions remained in place that left in doubt about whether the "New Woman" had been achieved in terms of women's participation in paid work and in the tasks required by a society under construction.[2]

Mi aporte opens with the hymn of the Federación de Mujeres Cubanas (FMC, or Federation of Cuban Women), which immediately reminds us of the ideal woman encouraged and promoted by the Revolution: "Cuban women, forward, forward, the love of work is the most important." The message of the song engages in a dialogue with the issues addressed in the documentary. The film opens in a sugar refinery, the country's economic mainstay at that time, and the voice of the film's interviewer, Consuelo Vidal (known popularly as Consuelito), describes the new role Cuban women have taken on, carrying out work traditionally assigned to men—an achievement of the revolutionary process.

The reason for the film's title soon becomes apparent. We see a series of posters calling on women to participate in the production of fruit, the sugar industry, and health care. The camera pans across all of them, stopping on the phrase *"mi aporte,"* written on a sack of sugar. The slogan foregrounds women's contributions to the *zafra*—"combatant for the 10 million"—in the 1970 sugar harvest. Gómez conceived of the film as her tribute to the harvest, which was an event of great political magnitude.[3] She decided intentionally to set this film amid the sugar industry, and specifically in the Camilo Cienfuegos sugar mill that once belonged to Hershey in the town of Santa Cruz del Norte.

To understand the contextual framework of *Mi aporte*, one must remember that the FMC was founded to achieve unity among women and guarantee their participation in building the new society. The issue of a so-called feminine revolution within another revolution was a key issue on the social agenda, and Cuban women were considered a priority sector. Fidel Castro once stated: "Women have interests that are common to all members of society; but they also have interests of their own. Above all, in working to create a different society and organizing a better world for human beings, women have very important interests in seeing this effort through, because, among other reasons, women make up a sector subjected to discrimination in the capitalist world in which we lived. In the world we are building, all vestiges of discrimination against women must disappear" (2006, 87).

To guarantee women access to paid work and public life in general, and to facilitate their incorporation into the revolutionary process, the government created social institutions and educational spaces. These spaces included daycare centers, boarding and semiboarding schools, and courses for tailoring and for driving. In practice, these changes were even broader than anticipated, and multiple contradictions soon appeared between the individual goals of women and what society expected of them—some of which are portrayed in *Mi aporte*. The Revolution opened the doors of Cuban women's homes and enabled them to step into public life, paid work, and many other forms of collaboration. Unfortunately, the reverse did not occur for men, who were not invited to participate in the domestic world—a failing Gómez makes evident in her documentary.

The only man who participates in *Mi aporte* is the women's boss at the sugar mill, and he takes a stance that is critical of women and their performance as workers. Almost without reflection, he recites a series of occurrences in the sugar mill that seem to him to demonstrate the inefficiency, ineptitude, and even opportunism of women workers.[4] The attitude of this man, who differs little from a capitalist boss, exposes the excessive demands placed on women during their incorporation into the workplace.

In the first segment of the film, each of the women interviewed presents the personal obstacles she faced when starting paid work. By the end of this segment, the accumulation of subjective and objective challenges seems to make real participation in the workplace impossible, despite the need to generate an income. The multiple, diverse, and complex obstacles include a husband who does not want his wife to work, lack of childcare, expectations of work in the home, pregnancy, and ill children. All these pretexts point toward a certain inefficiency in the measures adopted by the Revolution to resolve the problem of bringing women into the Revolution.

On the other hand, *Mi aporte* shows the intentions of women to collaborate with the Revolution beyond their own interests and profits. As Luisa Campuzano says of women's work on the Literacy Campaign, and the imprint it left on gender issues, "This [incorporation into society] was taken on by women as a concession and not as a conquest [of rights], as a contribution to the Revolution and not to their own emancipation. It did not imply in any way the development of gender consciousness" (2004, 140).[5] Far from seeing, in the first instance, the repercussions of access to paid work, women see their contribution to the process of the Revolution. Similarly, in the absence of necessary social conditions, such personalization is only expressed in terms of losses (as in the sense of it not being worth going to work if it will mean more stress and difficulty for the women).

To reinforce the reasons why women chose not to participate in paid work, Gómez deploys the children's song cited at the beginning of this chapter: "She couldn't play because she had to do washing that day." Girls and boys sing these words in a scene depicting a daycare setting. The next image shows women in the daycare center preparing and serving food. The new institution, intended to free women so they could work outside the home, in fact reproduces and legitimizes women's traditional roles. The contradiction makes evident the double discourse that exists around women's issues in Cuban society.

The topic of maternity is explored in the conversation that makes up the second segment of the documentary. Gómez presents three positions that tended to come up whenever the issue of pregnancy's influence on women's return to the home and legitimization of traditional feminine roles was addressed. Mirta Valladares, a professional, speaks about the conflict she faced between her conscious need to be in the public sphere (not only for economic reasons but also for personal ones) and her need to build a family. The problems she faced at work because she had to take care of her sick child reveal the excessive demands placed on women. Valladares has obviously experienced an extremely difficult conflict. She feels trapped and guilty, unable to be a good mother and also a good worker. She also speaks about the absence of men from the home and their lack of commitment to domestic work. The men in her life remain on the margins of home life, thus placing additional demands on her so that, even as she joins the workforce, she (like other women) continues to exercise her function as "mother-wife."

Lucía Corona, a researcher, experiences no such conflict. She says she has given up the home and the idea of motherhood to prioritize her professional aspirations. Her story demonstrates the need for rapid changes in traditional women's roles both on a social level and in individual lives. Corona recognizes that the solution cannot come only through education. Rather, deep social change is a long-term process that will demand an enormous amount of patience to obtain results for future generations. It is too much, says Corona. She wants solutions here and now—her life is being consumed every day.

Gómez, on the other hand, who appears here simply as another character in the documentary, prefers to take a more aggressive position. She does not want to make concessions and is in favor of confronting and actively demanding male cooperation. It is worth noting that during the filming of this documentary, she was pregnant with her third child, which perhaps explains the strong position she takes on the issue. She declares, "I, for one, will not give up." In an interview carried out for the documentary ¿Dónde esta Sara Gómez? (Where is Sara Gómez?) (Müller 2005), Agnès Varda, speaks about the multiple conversations she had with the Cuban filmmaker on this topic and how Gómez reiterated the fact that she would attempt to do everything at once—she would give up neither her professional life nor her aspirations as a mother.[6] In practice, Gómez took on both roles.

Particular mention should be made of the arguments of Gladys Egües, whose analysis of this issue is less personal and more sociological. She introduces the value of education and the role of the family into the discussion. She questions whether the traditional family is the one the Revolution needs and speaks of the "family in disintegration." Moreover, Egües assumes a role closer to that of an interviewer (she's a journalist, after all), and although her position is less experiential, she gives the discussion a direction that ultimately leaves the resolution of the problem in the hands of the education system.

In her assessment of maternity, however, Egües focuses on the supposed frustration of women without children who do not fulfill their social function. Here, we come to the thesis of feminine essence in cultural feminism, which emphasizes women's supreme (and supposedly enviable) role and power create human life. Egües gives voice to the fundamental components of this conflict when she says,

> Everything is a great circle, and it's a difficult and hard circle. At this moment the situation you experience is contained within all these limits: having to queue up for things, the problem of your child, the daycare, the problem of attending to your husband, having to work almost twenty hours a day, which is what happens with a woman who works. But at the same time, you have to contribute so that the material basis can exist, so that one day you will no longer have to continue with the mop, so that society advances. It's a contradiction, but I think it's a contradiction I understand, that is creating rupture but is also resolving.

Nevertheless, with an acuity that decades later still surprises, Egües argues that, in order to participate actively in society, a woman has to leave another woman in her place, whether her mother, mother-in-law, or someone else. However, even today in countries with specific legislation that guarantees women's rights, women professionals, academics, researchers, and so on might inadvertently reproduce gender inequality by leaving another woman to do the domestic work. Clearly the debate is fierce and complex. Given the rise in women's unemployment and the feminization of poverty and migration, what would happen if all women who are feminists or have gender consciousness decide not to employ other women as domestic workers—workers who generally cannot access the labor market in conditions of equality due to low or nonexistent education levels because they are immigrants or they belong to the most disfavored classes?

This discussion draws out the responsibility that Cuban women bear for the cultural reproduction of male supremacy (machismo). Corona openly declares the responsibility that women have for the reproduction of sexism: "The Cuban man," she says, is "permeated by the machismo with which he was bottle-fed by his mother.... As women, we are the great perpetuators of machismo, and women are the great creators of the myth about women's limitations, what is masculine and what is feminine, about what we do." Without completely agreeing, it is important to emphasize that these women anticipate the consequences of patriarchy and distinguish the reproductive role of women and the role of men in sustaining a myth supposedly created by women. Nowadays, we recognize the exact role that men and women have played in maintaining women's subordination over the centuries. However, the issues remain complex and difficult to analyze and address.

Corona goes even further when she emphasizes the class differences that influence women's education and jobs and how women's interests change in keeping with class conditions. Being a woman worker is not the same as being a woman intellectual. Corona highlights the need for women to question themselves—not just those women who stay at home but also those who do creative work, those who do not work in factories, and those who feel immune to machismo and the struggles other women face. This intellectual woman, supposedly disconnected from ordinary women, is not the "New Woman" needed by the Revolution. Thus, Corona makes a judgment highly valued by socialist feminism: Women workers are not the same as women intellectuals (in substituting bourgeois women). Their distinct life situations make for very different worldviews. Corona speaks about "women who belong to the masculine world" in reference to intellectual women and those involved in creative work. This is the only moment in the debate where creative work is assigned a gendered condition. At the moment a woman engages in such work she seems to pass into the "masculine world." An equivalence results between masculinity and creativity, as between femininity and reproduction. Corona alludes to a premise of feminism—that historically, the legitimized producers and products of creativity have generally been men.

The third section of the film features women tobacco workers who have been invited to watch the first two segments of the film. Their opinions about the film are often in conflict with the main ideas offered by the intellectual women. The women workers feel capable of taking on several workdays at once—at home (with the children, the husband, etc.), in volunteer work, and in paid work. Equally, they defend motherhood, and while they unanimously emphasize that suffering is linked to women's roles, they do not see it as an impediment to their happiness. Thus, the debate reinforces Corona's comments about the impact of social origins (class) on differences between women's perspectives. In the end, the professionals maintain an evidently distinct analysis from the tobacco workers.

Why was the film considered controversial enough to be banned by the FMC and shelved by the Instituto Cubano del Arte e Industria Cinematográficos (Cuban Film Institute)? Perhaps institutional motives were related to the contested or nonconformist nature of the idea that the supposed gains made by women as a result of the Revolution could potentially be experienced as disadvantages. *Mi aporte* shows how, after more than ten years, the Revolution had not been able to find effective solutions to women's marginalization. Paid work, the film suggests, becomes not an advantage but a barrier when it creates new demands on women's time and energy without the resolution of previous demands, or the reversal of men's refusal to participate in the family and the home, thus enabling women's entrance into the social or public sphere. On the other hand, the conflict about motherhood in relation to personal satisfaction and the achievement of personal projects is a critical issue that continues today.

The Revolution made a certain commitment to the fathers and husbands of Cuban women. Luisa Campuzano (2006) calls this commitment the "revolutionary pact." The denunciations of some women of the double standards of men who call themselves revolutionaries or communists but who continue to exclude women from society or complain about the forms of their participation might also partly explain why the film was not widely shown. *Mi aporte* exposes questions, contradictions, and conflicts more than it offers solutions, satisfactory results, or praise for the way things are. Gómez attempts to reveal to us precisely what she finds behind the facade, beyond the happy faces of women in the workforce—the daily reality of women's conditions, those who have children and husbands to attend to and who leave at five in the morning to go to work. We are left with the sense that there is no conclusive answer to such a complex issue that contains so many problematic aspects. There is no perfect response, as if a pat answer were ever Sara Gómez's intention. Her contribution is, after all, but one of many contributions of diverse women, both distant and close.

Translated from the original Spanish by Helen Dixon

NOTES

1. García Borrero points to the journal *Cine Cubano*, one of the most controversial magazines of the period, which from that moment on began to publish monothematic editions that limited debate and critical reflection (2002, 103).

2. According to Alexandra Kollontai (1918), the necessary condition to achieve the "New Woman" is the destruction of capitalism and the arrival of socialist society. However, it also requires women's self-awareness of their subordination and changes in women and men's social roles as well as the participation of both in childcare and family life. For a discussion on the New Man and New Woman, see Serra (this volume).—Ed.

3. See María Caridad Cumaná's interview with Sergio Giral in this volume.—Ed.

4. Both Casamayor and Benson discuss this issue in their contributions to this book.—Ed.

5. The Literacy Campaign (Campaña Nacional de Alfabetización en Cuba) is a significant legacy of the Cuban Revolution. In one year (January 1 to December 22, 1961), over 750,000 Cubans were taught to read by 250,000 volunteers, 100,000 of whom were young women. See Catherine Murphy's film *Maestra* for more information (http://www.maestrathefilm.org/).

6. Gómez said this during the filming of *Salut les cubains!* (Varda 1963), two years after the birth of her eldest daughter, Iddia Veitía Gómez.

BIBLIOGRAPHY

Campuzano, Luisa. 2004. *Las muchachas de la Habana no tienen temor de Dios: Escritoras cubanas S. XVIII-XXI*. Havana: Ediciones Unión.

Castro, Fidel. 2006. "Speech to the First National Congress of Federation of Cuban Women (I Congreso Nacional de la FMC)," Havana, October 1, 1962. *Mujer y Revolución* (Women and revolution). Havana: Editorial de la Mujer.

García Borrero, Juan Antonio. 2002. "Las aporías del gris." In *La edad de la herejía*, 95–108. Santiago de Cuba: Oriente.

Gutiérrez Alea, Tomás. 1989. In the conversation held at UNEAC to commemorate the years since the death of Sara Gómez. Section editor Frank Padrón, "Retrato multiple de Sara," *Cine Cubano*, no. 127: 37–43.

Kollontai, Alexandra. (1918) 1971. *The Autobiography of a Sexually Emancipated Communist Woman*. Translation by Salvator Attansio. New York: Herder and Herder.

Müller, Alessandra. 2004. *¿Dónde está Sara Gómez?* Savosa, Switzerland: Amka Films.

Varda, Agnès. 1963. *Salut les cubains!* Paris, France: Ciné-Tamaris.

SANDRA ABD'ALLAH-ALVAREZ RAMÍREZ is a Cuban journalist, writer, editor, and essayist. For ten years, she was editor of the website Cubaliteraria, operated by the Cuban Book Institute. She is founder and manager of the Directorio de Afrocubanas and founder of the long-established blog "Negra Cubana tenía que ser."

SEVENTEEN

Conclusion

Transculturation, Gender, and Documentary

Susan Lord

ENCOUNTERS BETWEEN TRADITION AND MODERNITY create an especially complicated yet productive space for the appearance of women as citizens and agents of social change and cultural expression. As culturally specific gender roles and temporal realities are threatened by the standard time of modernization and commodification, a view of the gains and losses brought by such encounters becomes tangible and available to critique and reflection. The appearance of the "new woman" of decolonizing and postcolonial visual culture depends on collectivities and new mobile formations of social relations. Sara Gómez is a foundational figure in this regard—she began her documentary filmmaking practice in a period when the "double vocation" of artistic and political experimentation was the norm (López 1992, 46–47), and she continued to challenge conventions through Cuba's "gray years" of intensified censorship and control until her death in 1974.

As the contributors to this volume argue, each of Gómez's documentaries represents an experiment with the conventions of the genre and with the limits of social discourse. This experimentation participated in the New Cuban Cinema's creative revolution by signifying a response to those elements of history, memory, and everyday life that were frozen out of the frame of dominant narratives of nation and subjectivity in colonial and imperialist cinemas. In the creatively robust and politically complex context of the 1960s, Gómez stood out as figure whose relationship to cinema, as she expressed in an interview in *Pensamiento Crítico* in 1970 (see chap. 1, this volume), "constitute[d] an authentic act of decolonization." Across her films, this "authentic act" challenges the whitening and masculinization of the revolutionary subject,[1] the monumental time of the Cuban Revolution, and the hypostatization of development wherein transculturation risked being mere deculturation.[2]

The purpose of this chapter is twofold: first, to offer viewing tools found in the history of documentary cinema theory and criticism, and second, to push the significance of Gómez's work forward in time. With a focus on *Mi aporte* (My contribution) (1972), but also situated more broadly in terms of her documentary practice, this essay presents a means of understanding Gómez's legacy in women's cinema and in the discourse of gendered citizenship. I sketch some lines of inquiry for analyzing documentary from a cross-cultural, feminist perspective: first, from the point of view of feminist documentary theory; second, from the typologies and history of Latin American documentary theory; third, from the contestation over "popular" culture and the meaning of transculturation; and fourth, from a decolonial reflection on ethnography.

From the beginning of my research on Gómez, I have been motivated and encouraged by friendships and collaborations with Cubans, and I have reflected on the complications of doing this work across distances of geography, economy, mobility, and identity: a white settler from the global North with tenure and research funds and (a somewhat diminishing) ignorance of the social realities of the worlds in which Gómez and her work circulate. Over the years, I have gone to Havana at least twice annually, built with colleagues a course that takes students to Havana each May, lived in Havana, and brought Cuban colleagues to Canada as visiting artists and researchers. All the projects I have done in Cuba have been realized in collaboration with Cubans, and I understand my responsibility as one of leveraging the resources of my profession to translate and translocate the incredible creativity and critical insight of Cubans about their gendered experience, thus expanding our shared social interest and expressing gratitude for all the doors and windows they have opened for me.

Afro-Cuban filmmaker Gloria Rolando was the first person I met on this journey. She has taught me a great deal about Afro-descendent culture, about gender and race and economies, and about the contemporary legacy of Sara Gómez. An ethnographic documentarist, in many ways Rolando self-consciously inherited from Gómez concerns about history and memory and about the work of documentary as an act of keeping alive the stories of those individuals and communities whose lives and cultural practices have been cast aside. This chapter ends with a sketch of the legacy Sara Gómez left to subsequent generations, with a focus on Rolando's work in an effort to offer an homage to her project and its work of keeping Gómez in the present tense.

In terms of documentary reception across time and space, I turn to Linda Williams's (1993) essay on the partial and contingent truths that form the always-receding goal of documentary. This goal is temporalized at two sites in any investigation of documentary meaning: the viewer (her subjectivity limited by forgetting and ever partial knowledge) and the film (disjunctions that form the work's present-tense viewing context as well as the ever-accruing mediations that adhere to the signifying system and the sign's receding referent). Feminist theory and epistemology have long argued the contingency of the subject, and critical ethnographic theory has brought the critique of the imperial imaginary to bear on the knowledge claims of anthropological and ethnographic records. With these conditions in mind, my positioning of Gómez's work, together with the work's positioning of me, make one of many potential lines of inquiry about the work itself and the cultural memory that it labors to produce.

Whether Gómez's subject matter concerns the local cultural and political critiques of national work programs (*Sobre horas extras y trabajo voluntario*, 1973) and election processes (*Poder local, poder popular*, 1970) or the diaspora and difference found within a family (*Crónicas de mi familia*, 1966), her films consistently bring marginal identities to the frame, respatializing and remediating citizenship. Central to both the modes of representation and the subject matter is the issue of time itself. Along with strategies that reflect on the temporality of film processes (shot duration, montage rhythm, and narrative), the cultures of time represented in the films include the subjective worlds of memory and everyday life (*Crónicas*), the uneven development of social chronotopes[3] (the Isle of Pines trilogy), and the different or contested temporalities formed by cultural memory and practices (*Y . . . tenemos sabor* and *Crónicas*) as well as by gender difference (*Mi aporte*). This temporality has a spatial extension, as noted in this book's introduction, for in all of Sara Gómez's films windows and thresholds and doorways speak volumes. They are spaces of emergence—interior frames that function to mediate or create a density of mediation by which to literally see the emergence of a new subjectivity. These spaces are arguably about deterritorializing the boundaries of domestic and public space through the dynamic transformation of identity and belonging.

Gómez's films look at marginalization as a contemporary experience, with long and deep cultural and political histories. Particularly attentive to the status of women and the weight of machismo, and to Afro-Cuban culture and enduring racism, the films address how marginalization is a cultural problem for the Revolution's political aim to unify a people, a popular culture, and a nation. Thus, rather than performing the discourse of margin versus center, the films adjust the frame to take up the radical claims of a new society based in cultural difference and expressed through popular democracy. Such a project was particularly risky in this period due to the intensifying power of the state and the concomitant disciplining of the citizenry through acts of incarceration, censorship, and banishment.

In her book about citizenship and photography, Ariella Azoulay (2008) proposes we find a mutual relationship between the various "users" of photography—and I would posit documentary as well—wherein photographed persons address the spectator, claiming their citizenship in the "citizenry of photography." Azoulay writes, "An emphasis on the dimension of being governed allows a rethinking of the political sphere as a space of relations between the governed, whose political duty is first and foremost or at least also a duty toward one another, rather than toward the ruling power" (25). For Azoulay, the history of unequal access to citizenship is linked to appearance and disappearance. With democratization of access to the image, relationships are afforded a more extensive lateral dimension and networks of appearance develop that can never be completely subsumed by the lens of the ruling power. In this space, the subjects cease to appear as "marginal" or "dissident." Rather, this activity of appearance rehabilitates or remediates their citizenship. Citizenship is not a stable status that one simply struggles to achieve, but is an arena of conflict and negotiation located in techniques and technologies of appearance.

This is precisely the legacy that Gómez leaves for the current generation of viewers and makers. Most of her documentaries present participation as something that is practiced fundamentally as critical engagement. *Mi aporte* is one of the best examples of the extent to which Gómez's filmmaking, together with the social subjects of those films, embody radical, participatory democracy (thus participating in the larger project of modernity—the democratization of culture). For that reason, there has been a particularly strong emphasis on *Mi aporte* in this volume. The next section of this chapter summarizes the argument I made in an earlier essay (Lord 2002). It is useful for its transcultural methodology. I direct the reader to the earlier version for the fuller analysis.

Collaboratively made in 1972 by six people at the Instituto Cubano del Arte e Industria Cinematográficos (ICAIC, or Cuban Film Institute) with Gómez as the premier director, *Mi aporte* begins as an ostensible report card on women in the new society. Given Casamayor's, Benson's, Serra's, and Abd'Allah-Alvarez Ramírez's contributions to this volume, my recounting of the film's content and context will be limited. The film opens with the announcement that it will show women's contributions to the Zafra de los Diez Millones—the ten-million-ton sugar harvest—and thus to the Revolution itself. An interviewer introduces women (young and old, *mulato*, black, and white) who work at the sugar plant, asking them what they do in a style typical of *cine reportaje* (reportage). Their responses about their work lead to a discussion about issues of childcare and the difficulties of working, child-rearing, and homemaking.

These testimonies are intercut—in a style that suggests an interruption of the women's stories—with a male worker's analysis of his female comrades' ineffective labor due to physical weakness, pregnancy, and the absenteeism that results from childcare exigencies. Included in this first part of the film is a short section where a paternalistic-sounding voice-over describes the progress of women's integration into the labor force while the image track shows women peering out of their windows and doors. This image track eventually syncs up with women's voices—many of them single mothers—as they explain that they are unable to go to work because there is no one to look after the children and not enough daycare in the area. One woman admits to choosing the role of wife over that of a revolutionary worker. Text appears on the screen: "The woman who lives in this house is powerless to work because her husband doesn't want her to." In "response," we see footage of a daycare setting, with children singing, eating healthy lunches, and playing. This first section ends with the didactic text: "Have we created the condition for the formation of the new woman?"

The next section of the film takes up this question and another—"Can the model traditional family subsist in the circumstances of revolutionary Cuba?"—by way of a discussion among four professional women: Gómez herself, Lucía Corona, Mirta Valladares, and Gladys Egües. This section is filmed in a cinema verité style with synced sound and little editing. The following quotation clearly summarizes the content of the discussion: "To have a job is fundamental for me . . . [it is the way to be] part of the building of society. . . . But the practical reality is very different: it is hard to have a home, a baby, and try to be active at work." Halfway through this section, the image track switches to footage from the previous section, over which the discussion continues. It ends with "*FIN*" (end).

However, a third section begins that reveals the film as a process documentary. A group of women from a tobacco factory, having watched parts one and two, are filmed as they discuss the issues raised by the film and its subjects. *Cine-debates*—controlled discussions accompanying film screenings—were common in Cuba at this time and were a practice of media education that continued until the 1990s.[4] The women's critiques echo those heard in the previous sections, and the report card Gómez submits is not so much about women's contributions as it is about the failure of the Revolution to deal with cultural issues specific to gender and machismo. The film ends with the words: "end of report [*reportaje*]."

According to Lillian Guerra's (2012) analysis of the role of most documentary and the *cine-debate*, this film, and the third section in particular, is bound to a binary between investing in the hyperreality of the grand narrative of the Revolution and producing a counternarrative. Yet, according to Casamayor (this volume), things are somewhat messier than this. Gómez articulates a "demand to transform and improve the lives of Cubans, all Cubans, but with their individual particularities sustained as men and women, black, white, and all of Cuba's diverse cultures and religions. Complicated Cubans—Cuban humans that she always sought to understand" (Casamayor, this volume). These are radical filmic acts and not just speech acts.

If we read *Mi aporte* through documentary typologies developed in the global North, such as those formulated by Bill Nichols and Julia Lesage, we gain a set of meanings and values associated with consciousness-raising, interactive and reflective structures, and feminist dialogics. This lens thus gives us a feminist documentary in the mode defined by Lesage:

> Cinéma vérité documentary filmmaking had features that made it an attractive and useful mode of artistic and political expression for women learning filmmaking in the late 1960s. It not only demanded less mastery of the medium than Hollywood or experimental film, but also the very documentary recording of women's real environments and their stories immediately established and valorized a new order of cinematic iconography, connotation, and range of subject matter in the portrayal of women's lives.... The feminist documentarist uses the film medium to convey a new and heightened sense of women's identity, expressed both through the subject's story and through the tangible details of the subject's milieu.... The realist feminist documentaries represent a use of, yet a shift in, the aesthetics of cinéma vérité, due to the feminist filmmakers' close identification with their subjects, participation in the women's movement, and sense of the film's intended effect. The structure of the consciousness-raising group becomes the deep structure repeated over and over in these films. (1984, 231, 246)

This typology yields one set of truths applicable to *Mi aporte*: Feminist collectivities develop a critical consciousness among participants; the shift in iconography based on this critical consciousness is capable of contributing to social change; direct speech and storytelling are transmissible through the film's structure, which itself reflects a decolonized reflexive structure of feminist consciousness; and, of course, the deep structure of gender roles in the determination of cultural and social value. What this perspective cannot see is the critical engagement with the deep, formal structures of Latin American documentary and tensions between gender, race, and colonialism as well as between gender and class.

In documentary literature, it is now commonplace for writers to turn to Bill Nichols's (1991) delineation of the main documentary "modes": expository, observational, interactive, and reflexive. However, this is but one version of a set of articulations he and Julianne Burton developed over the course of a decade. Burton's "Democratizing Documentary: Modes of Address in the Latin American Cinema, 1958–72" (1984) and Michael Chanan's "Rediscovering Documentary: Cultural Context and Intentionality" (1997a) present a history of the modes employed by Gómez, and I use them here to analyze for a "northern" viewer how these modes functioned within a Latin American perspective. Burton writes:

> From the inception of the social documentary movement in the mid-to-late fifties, Latin American filmmakers began experimenting with a broad range of strategies designed to eliminate, supplant, or subvert the standard documentary mode of address: the anonymous, omniscient, ahistorical "voice of God." . . . Long before the technological innovations in sound recording associated with "direct cinema" and "cinema verité" were widely available in the region, Latin American filmmakers explored indirect and observational modes in an attempt to pluralize and democratize modes of documentary address. . . . In their drive to subvert or eliminate the authoritarian narrator, some filmmakers substituted intertitles . . . [and ceded the voice of God to] on-camera and/or on-microphone presence of the filmmakers or their surrogates, and the self-presentation of social actors. (1984, 49)

The issue of voice-over and its function as a trace of the presence of the disembodied patriarchal authority has long been the subject of feminist and feminist-postcolonial critique.[5] Clearly, feminist and decolonizing cinemas overlap in their subversion of that type of authority—this is certainly true for *Mi aporte*. But Gómez goes further by offering a revolution within The Revolution—a radical redistribution of various economies, from that of labor to that of the image. The direct critique of machismo and the formal choice to have women speak directly and in voice-over—as well as the decision to have the director, her microphone, and the social actors all registered as collaborators in the construction of this representation—participate equally in feminist and decolonizing principles. However, in the case of Latin America in general and Cuba in particular, the voice of God was never only, or even initially, a patriarchal figure; it was the master, the colonizer, the imperialist. Gómez's contribution to an already highly politicized, specifically decolonizing formal strategy was to reveal machismo as another culture of authority that oppresses women by marginalizing their participation and devaluing their time (the latter point is especially clear in *Sobre horas*).

These two critiques—the decolonizing and the feminist—do not collapse into each other when viewed through the lens of Latin American documentary tradition, and gendered analysis is also not a mere supplement. By critically engaging in a decolonizing project, Gómez declares herself a full participant as critic and comrade. For example, her use of intertitles in several of her films declares her accord with the documentary project developed by her ICAIC colleague Santiago Álvarez, whose film *NOW!* (1965) is perhaps his best known. As Burton (1984) has pointed out, the genealogy of experimentalism that Álvarez embodies extends from Dziga Vertov, translated through the particular aesthetics and politics of Latin America. By understanding and taking a place in this project, Gómez underscores the experimental process of popular democracy and authorizes an Afro-Cuban woman to explicitly and critically take issue with the deeply problematic subject of women's autonomy, particularly within the increasingly complex reach of the Federation of Cuban Women,[6] which both commissioned and then censored this film.

Turning to Chanan's (1990) typology of Cuban documentary, we see how fully Gómez participated in, and experimented with, tradition. Chanan takes the ICAIC's content-driven typology of Cuban documentary and reformulates it through a lens of intentionality, thus providing a way to see the politics of form. His categories are derived from the most frequently used terms in Latin American documentary theory and criticism: *cine didáctico, cine testimonio, cine denuncia, cine encuesta, cine rescate, cine celebrativo, cine ensayo, cine reportaje,* and *cine de combate*. As Chanan explains: "The distinctive feature of all the terms listed is precisely their intentional character. They indicate a variety of purposes: to teach, to offer testimony, to denounce, to investigate, to bring history alive, to celebrate revolutionary achievement, to provide space for reflection, to report, to express solidarity, to militate for a cause. These are all needs of revolutionary struggle, both before and after the conquest of power, when they become part of the process of consolidating, deepening, and extending the revolution" (37).

Mi aporte is explicitly presented as an instance of *cine reportaje*. However, it formally provides a report card on women's progress by employing other modes. The film investigates and protests the unequal development of women and men, it rescues women's voices from silence, and, by offering women a role not only in the representation but also in the interpretation of the images produced, it extends the intention of *cine didáctico* ("to impart the means for the acquisition of more and better knowledge upon which action may be premised") into the heart of the lifeworld—home life and child-rearing. One signature of Gómez's authorship in this collaborative film is the retelling and recontextualization of images seen at an earlier instant. Clearly, this approach is not unique to her, but it does disclose her abiding commitment to provide the means of interrogating representations—even her own. Repetition recontextualizes the Vertovian "fragments of actuality," realizes a politics of time in the form, and constitutes an important part of the dialectical structure of both *Mi aporte* and her later feature film, *De cierta manera*. Given that the latter film was edited by Gómez's colleagues after her death, and that footage was lost due to damage,[7] *Mi aporte* provides an important clue to the postproduction presence of the director.

Devyn Spence Benson's chapter in this volume offers a detailed analysis of Gómez's intersection of race and racialization and provides a comprehensive history of policies and practices of the period. When we consider the nexus of race, racialization, and Afro-descendent cultural practice, performance, and position in Gómez's films, a deeper critique of the Revolution emerges—one relevant to current struggles in Cuba and to antiracist visual culture more broadly. What is "popular" and what is "folklore" in Cuba after the Revolution presents an interesting problem for Afro-descendent identity. The early work of the Revolution saw marginalized popular traditions gain centrality and authority in the project of building a new national culture. The New Theatre movement performed plays aimed at both political and aesthetic education through themes pertinent to the audience/community's concerns; see Fowler Calzada (this volume) for several examples of these types of projects. These dispersed sites of cultural practice, rooted in tradition but transformed by revolutionary purpose, did permit previously marginalized cultures to participate in the political project.

However, after Girón (Bay of Pigs) in 1961; after Padilla's incarceration; after Castro's "Words to the Intellectuals," when he infamously declared, "within the Revolution, everything; outside the Revolution, nothing"; and after the film *P.M.* (Cabrera and Leal 1960), local cultural traditions of religious connotation and ritual value were remarginalized as "folklore" and then housed in national institutions such as the Folklore Group. According to Rowe and Schelling (1996), Cuban socialism thus repeats the enlightenment-modernity trajectory of educating "the people" as a unified body away from supposed superstition and irrationalisms. In this context, we can see that the story of *P.M.* is more than a story of censorship (of a film that coincidentally has black content); it is one of struggle over how to tell the story of Afro-descendent urban culture. From Girón on, black activists, organizations, scholars, and cultural workers found their public sphere shrinking rapidly. Alejandro de la Fuente (2001) writes that 170 black organizations were closed in 1961. We do not know what Sara Gómez thought of this turn in particular. However, her film *Crónicas de mi familia* (1966) locates her family history and testimonies in relation to these spaces (see Casamayor, this volume).[8]

My reason for mapping out this trajectory is that it delineates a moment when the potential for working through the racism in Cuban identity was truncated by monocular self-understanding of "national consciousness." If the official public sphere cannot support antiracist work, then the citizenship practices of artists, cultural workers, and intellectuals become all the more vital.

Gómez's films present these shifts as a double danger in the specific films themselves and in her commitment to focus on contemporary realities across all her works. First, when placed in a museum and labeled as folklore, Afro-Cuban culture is framed as belonging to a distanced past and as a sign of underdevelopment. Thus, when wedded to Spanish colonial masculinity, problematic ritualized orders of patriarchal governance, such as those she found in Abakuá, are reproduced/repeated within social relations—which she argues in *De cierta manera*.[9] Not of the present and thus not subject to historical transformations—to coeval temporal creation and communications with other institutions, practices, identities and memories—the cultural practitioners are thus not subjects of history. Second, because these folkloric practices are primarily those of Afro-descendent peoples, this marginalization re-imposes racial difference on an already historically repressed group. Hence, Gómez's films seek to reframe these cultural practices as popular subjects of and to history. History, however, is not accorded a single formation of monumental or revolutionary time. For Gómez, the specificity of cultural memory requires that the revolutionary narrative be dispersed and popular.

The issues related to the interconnection between popular culture, race, and cultural difference are less central to *Mi aporte* than to other documentaries in Gómez's oeuvre. Nonetheless, it is the politics of documentary representation of *Mi aporte* that is important. Afro-Cuban women were the most marginalized Cubans before the Revolution, and *Mi aporte* remediates this reality by ensuring that Afro-Cuban women's voices and images contribute to the ongoing work of the popular struggle for equality. Importantly, Gómez does not collapse gender and race difference into a singular narrative of nation and revolution. This critical consciousness embodied by the films and their social subjects presents a version of Cuban culture and society as a doubled temporality of nationalism and cultural difference, first articulated as "transculturation" by Fernando Ortiz in his famous 1940 ethnographic study *Contrapunteo cubano del tabaco y el azúcar* (Cuban counterpoint: tobacco and sugar): "I am of the opinion that the word *transculturation* better expresses the different phases of the process of transition from one culture to another because this does not consist merely in acquiring another culture, which is what the English word *acculturation* really implies, but the process also necessarily involves the loss or uprooting of a previous culture, which could be defined as a deculturation" (Ortiz 1987, 102).

In section three, the *cine-debate*, the camera focuses on the women as they speak. For the first minutes, only two or three women participate. What are the others thinking? Are they experiencing the excruciating boredom discussed by Lillian Guerra (2012, 318) vis-à-vis the *cine-debate*? Are they trying to figure out how to get the beans cooked in time for dinner if the discussion continues? Midway through the section, all but two or three women are passionately discussing the issue of gendered labor—not in the factory, but in the home. "We can teach animals, surely we can educate men" is a typical statement made by one and agreed on by this group of workers. The particularity of their personhood is given the space for enunciation, for appearance, and for consensus in the film, signifying Gómez's attempt to present gender as a transcultural or transversal phenomenon.

This observation leads to the final section of analysis on the work of ethnography and the ethnographic legacy Gómez left for subsequent women filmmakers. It is a shame that we cannot include analysis of her film *De bateyes*—an ethnography about a community of sugar mill workers—due to the print's deterioration. (The film is currently being restored by us in the Vulnerable Media Lab and will be available for viewing in 2021.) Luis García Mesa, her cinematographer, tells an important story in the interview published here that goes some way to tell us why she made that film:

> I don't know what happened to it—it was a beautiful documentary. About the *bateyes*, the sugarcane workers' communities. Both here in Havana and in Camagüey, where we went. There are a lot of workers' quarters where Haitians lived, and there is tremendous prejudice against Haitians. In fact, I remember once Titón [Tomás Gutiérrez Alea] was in Santiago de Cuba with Ramiro Valdés, and he said to him, "Eh, what are you doing here, what's ICAIC doing here?" And Titón said, "We're doing a film called *Cumbite* [1964] about the Haitians." And he, Ramiro, said, … "Eh, why are

you doing a film about those people, they're just cheap labor." Titón was shocked. A commander of the Revolution talking about Haitians in that way—not even about Haitians, about anyone—it was incredible. Sara was very interested in that.

In documentary cinema, and in the history of ethnography, there are various ways to overcome the "orientalism" of the traditional anthropological gaze and to create an antiracist practice. The *cine rescate* is precisely not about entombment or preservation against the time. Rather, the intention of this mode is "to bring history alive" (Chanan 2004, 205) and to fold this history into the now-time of the nation as a revolutionary project. *Cine rescate* differs substantially from the "necrology" of salvage ethnography (and the traditional anthropologist's sense of time critiqued by Fabian [1983]) that performs rescue missions on "dying cultures." In reference to Amy Fass Emery, where she discusses the *testimonio*, we can say that Gómez, at times, produces "fables of intimacy" that authorize her to speak of and to the Other—not as a detached social scientist, but as a self intimately involved with the others she represents.[10] Yet, at other times, she is inside the process known as "native ethnography" and is informed by the feminist practice of consciousness-raising, where the social subjects and the ethnographer are the same. This mobile form of engagement—of the dynamic relation between self and other—provides Gómez with an ethical mode that is unavailable to both the "fabulists" and the anthropologists. The degree of self-reflexivity in her films is consistent with this radical autoethnography.

In these moments of interactive/reflexive subjectivity, she puts herself in the frame and, consequently, into the story of her contribution, producing a deterritorialized intimacy as a form of citizenship practice—a set of aesthetic and ethical documentary strategies that are expressive of historical and emotional geographies of belonging for the filmmaker, subject, and audience. The citizenship practices of decolonized ethnography that emerged in the 1960s is found in the work of both Gómez and Nicolás Guillén Landrián (see Cumaná, this volume) and connected to the international networks then being mobilized by decolonizing projects and new social movements: connections to Black Power, the Left Bank film projects, feminist organizing, and newsreel film—all of which combined to remap the city as a space of world citizenship and localized histories.[11]

The aesthetic and ethical documentary strategies expressive of historical and emotional geographies of belonging for the filmmaker, subject, and audience that we learn how to see and hear in Gómez are carried forward by subsequent generations. Some of the "direct descendants," such as Jorge Luis Sánchez, Magda González Grau, Enrique "Kiki" Álvarez, and Ricardo Acosta, are represented in Acosta and McIntosh's film and video program from 1992. In their program notes, which I cite at length because they are not easily accessible and they draw clear lines between *la madre y sus hijos/as*, they write:

> Throughout the decade of the 1980s, a new generation of artists began to produce work, primarily people who were born after 1959, the year of the Revolution. These new artists have enriched and complicated cultural life in Cuba.... Young artists have had to fight for creative space to express their concerns, which in some instances do not interest or are even opposed by established cultural institutions....
>
> The first program, IDENTITIES & LEGENDS, brings together works which address cultural identity—national, community and individual, a portrait of the elements which constitute Cuban society. MY NEIGHBOURHOOD—MY CONTEXT, the second program, elaborates the notions established in the first program, extending them into the realm of social relations which effect the entire community. These works attempt to examine how social power is constructed and what the responsibility of the individual is in a broader social context. We continue with LOVE AND PAIN, the longest program in the series, which presents a broad range of works which address the imaginary and the elusive.... Over all, this series has been constructed to offer insights and respond to questions which we all share as artists despite the particular nature of our practice. All of the work you will see represents the firmly held position of an individual director, but also an honest approach to understanding common realities. As we grow we learn that the "other" is not outside of "us," we are all "us." (Acosta and McIntosh 1992)

The early films by these filmmakers—such as *Querido y viejo amigo* (Dear old pal of mine) by Gloria Torres and Magda González about a ninety-one-year-old Jamaican woman living on the Isle de Juventud, or *A mis cuatro abuelos* (For my four grandparents) by Aaron Yelin Rozengway, about the contemporary Jewish community in Cuba, or *El síndrome de la soledad* (The solitude syndrome) by Ileana Aviies Pompa, about a man living with AIDS—are about identity and belonging. Other key themes in Gómez's work—such as issues that arise due to poverty and marginalization—are strongly represented in two films by Jorge Luis Sánchez: *El Fanguito* and *Un pedazo de mí* (A piece of me). The latter is about the punk scene in Havana. Sánchez humanizes the youth, takes seriously their alienation, and gives them screen time and space to express themselves in a cultural context where new and alternative forms of music are held with suspicion. *El Fanguito* is perhaps the most directly Gómez-inspired film of the program.

> After extensive research and involvement with the neighbourhood called El Fanguito (loosely translated as "muddy little place"), a very poor and mistrusted part of Havana, Jorge Luis Sánchez began this documentary profile of the neighbourhood and its very proud inhabitants. This work demonstrates the very difficult conditions the people of El Fanguito live in, the stigma that is attached to them for residing there, and the overall marginalisation, underdevelopment and "machismo" they tolerate every day, but it also examines the steps they are taking to improve their lives. These people love their neighbourhood; they have built it, it is their home and they are determined to protect it and develop it. (Acosta and McIntosh 1992)

Many of the films in the 1992 program were in fact produced in Taller de Cine Asociación Hermanos Saíz–ICAIC, and some of the filmmakers—such as Torres and González —were working in the television institute. Access to the ICAIC was complicated for filmmakers of this age who were interested in these themes. The open and experimental system of the 1960s was no longer. While the constraints of the "gray years" had loosened due to pressure from artists and intellectuals, national cultural systems of production were inadequately flexible to serve these emergent voices. This was not unique to the ICAIC in Cuba; the National Film Board in Canada in the 1970s and 1980s was a case in point. But in an environment where it was not possible to establish something like "independent" cinema organizations, organizations such as Asociación Hermanos Saíz could build a means for access to the ICAIC's production facilities. It was in this context that Ricardo Acosta, for example, was able to be tutored by Gómez's editor, Iván Arocha.

These "direct descendants" of Sara Gómez extended her interest in "quasi-alternative" environments to produce a repertoire of themes and styles that reappear in subsequent decades and in quasi-alternative spaces of production. Many of these "street filmmakers," as Anne Marie Stock (2009) has called them, took to digital formats immediately and shifted their production facilities to shared or home studios and to the art schools. One of the filmmakers who best follows the Gómez-Sánchez school of urban ethnography is Alina Rodríguez (not the beloved actor of *Conducta*), whose film *Buscándote Habana* gave space and voice to citizens living in economically and legally precarious circumstances in Havana. A student of the Facultad Arte de los Medios de Comunicación Audiovisual (FAMCA), the film school of the Instituto Superior del Arte (a postsecondary art school), Rodríguez and many of her colleagues are now working in the diaspora.

Elsewhere I have written about the *nietas,* or granddaughters, of Gómez, such as Susana Barriga and Sandra Gómez (Lord 2013; Lord and Zarza 2014). These women worked through FAMCA and/or through the Escuela Internacional de Cine y TV (or EICTV, an international film school in San Antonio de los Baños). These spaces, islands within the island, afforded opportunities for women in particular to develop a practice and build international networks. Zaira Zarza and I detail the incredible creativity of Cuban women filmmakers and cinematographers who trained in EICTV (Lord and Zarza 2014). Sandra Gómez, Susana Barriga, and Heidi Hassan are the focus of our essay. They work at the intersection of cultural citizenship, diaspora, revolutionary legacy, and globalization, and they do so through what we have described as deterritorialized intimacies. These intimacies are afforded by their documentary practices: historical and emotional geographies recorded as places of belonging and as spaces of nonbelonging. We argue that three contemporary filmmakers are having direct and indirect conversations with Sara Gómez, who was working at a time of intense internationalism for Cuba—a time not seen again until the Special Period of the 1990s, which itself was at the threshold of a wholly different meaning of internationalism involving globalized neoliberal states and subjects as well as new networks, affiliations, and world imagining. For Cuba, the Special Period was one of intense sorrow and suffering as a result of the collapse of the Soviet Union. Tens of thousands of people left the island in the 1990s, and 80 percent of the state economy disappeared. Videos of the new generation, such as *Video de familia* (2001) by Humberto Padrón and *(De)generación* (2006) and its follow-up *(Ex)generación* (2008) by Aram Vidal Alejandro directly address the emotional conflicts of the Special Period.

The remaining pages of this conclusion will focus on Gloria Rolando, an *hija* (daughter) of Gómez who works at the intersection of cultural citizenship, diaspora, and revolutionary legacy with a documentary practice of decolonized ethnography that gives a deep history of its intimacies. Rolando was born in Havana's Chinatown in 1953. Beginning at the ICAIC, her filmmaking career spans nearly thirty years. She heads an independent filmmaking group, Imágenes del Caribe, based in Havana. As of early 2020, Rolando has written, produced, and directed sixteen documentaries, and has worked on numerous others as assistant director, researcher, and writer. She has traveled extensively in the Caribbean, the United States, and recently in Canada, participating in conferences, giving workshops, and screening her films. Rolando's *Pasajes del corazón y la memoria* (2007) received the Sara Gómez Prize in 2009 at the Thirtieth International Festival of New Latin American Cinema in Havana.

Contemporary encounters with spatial and historical dislocations that form the Afro-Caribbean diaspora constitute the content of her work and form a complex and problematic imaginary for citizenship and belonging. As well, the "Africa" of Rolando's work is based on an imaginary of and for Africa. Her project also, however, records Cuba as part of the expanded Antilles—that is, a fragmented emotional geography that includes the Canary Islands, Jamaica, Haiti, Harlem, and, of course, Africa.[12] In Rolando, as in Gómez, the city also features strongly: the street where the *comparsa* (a form of Afro-Cuban dance) takes place, where the history of Afro-descendant cultural appearance was made, where the exiled Black Panther can hide, and where ancestors were brought as slaves, slave owners, Galician domestic laborers, and Chinese merchants. The emotional geopolitics of the street are, therefore, the places of reanimating historical memory in the everyday.

Rolando's film practice is best understood within the traditions of *testimonio* and *cine rescate*. Committed primarily to preserving and reanimating—remediating—the history and memory of Afro-Cuban and Afro-Caribbean communities, her films are based on interviews and archival research. Yet, more than talking heads, Rolando's films are structured through musical forms, which she understands as fundamental to Caribbean identity.

Raíces de mi corazón (2001) is a fiction/documentary hybrid about a young Afro-Cuban woman's struggle to build a memory out of fragments of the 1912 massacre of thousands of members of the Partido Independiente de Color, a national political party formed largely by Afro-Cubans after the struggle for Cuban independence. This highly charged and contested chapter in Cuban history returns to the question of belonging and to the ways in which intimacies and maternal family lines can reframe the story of a nation. In Rolando's later trilogy about the massacre, *1912: Breaking the Silence* (2010–12), the voices of the rap group Anómino Consejo join with those of sociologists and historians to perform the history of Afro-Cuban struggles for citizenship. In this way, throughout her work, the cultural traditions of Afro-descendants receive primacy not just in the film but also in the spatial politics of belonging. In the first film of the trilogy, for example, voice-over is minimized in favor of testimony and archival display, producing a powerful "field of exhibitionistic and expressionistic attractions" (Beattie 2008, 4) that highlight the main claim, according to Michael Renov, of any documentary: "Believe me, I'm of the world" (quoted in Beattie 2008, 4). In the earlier 2001 docufiction *Raíces de mi corazón*, the photographic portraits of Rolando's family that open the story—with history and the present acting as thresholds or passages between the emotional geographies and histories of Afro-Cubans—are a direct quotation of Gómez's *Crónicas de mi familia*. Through display and exhibition, Rolando's photographs testify to and perform testimony of being of the world. These archives are bridged to Rolando's living traditions, wherein the nation is dispersed and transculturated in the streets of *comparsa* and in the gardens of Jamaican descendants.

Learning to hear (as opposed to listen)—a phenomenon described beautifully in relation to Sara Gómez both in a chapter of Alexandra Vazquez's book *Listening in Detail* (2015) and in Alan West-Durán's essay in this volume—has helped me to see Rolando's films. The *1912* trilogy features a dense layering of sonorous appearance—as an intergenerational conversation through sound about the struggle for history not only about unearthing and giving space for the memories in oral and material form but also the shape of the narration, the sound of the voices, and the duration of the look. We have Cuban rap groups Anónimo Consejo and Obsesión, early twentieth-century compositions, Cantos de Santería, campesino music, and more. Through the three parts of *1912*, we experience a braided discourse about race, nation, and cultural forms. The trilogy is a history both of the formation of the Partido Independiente de Color and its massacre by the Cuban army and of how the nation-state, pre- and post-Revolution, actively *un*remembers these citizens. It is a history of silencing as a practice not only of racism but also of racialization and nationalism.

With Rolando's work, and in its relationship to Gómez's, we observe the resistance to the anthropologist's rescue of history, its entombment as though in a museum, and its distance as folkloric past. Instead, *rescate* is a process of engaging the past and making it sing. Some of Rolando's films demonstrate more of a tendency toward preservation—heritage—such as *Oggun* (1991), while others reconstitute tradition as a history of resistance, such as the *1912* films or even *The Jazz in Us* (2004), or, more recently, *Reembarque* (Reshipment) (2016), about the history of Haitian immigrants of the early twentieth century who were returned when the sugar market crashed. In *Reembarque*, the dialogue with the present is robust and sonorous.

Other of Rolando's films expand the mission of preservation by extending into neighborhoods, such as *Los Marqueses de Atarés* (2003), about the history of carnival and of street dancing/*comparsa* in Atarés in Cerro, a neighborhood of Havana. However, this film does not end with "the end." Rolando takes the film back to Atarés and projects it so that the community sees itself. This reflexive approach to autoethnography echoes Gómez's *Mi aporte* while undertaking a process of remediating and repatriating tradition. Gómez's and Rolando's films both give space to the appearance of Afro-descendent women's images of work, ritual, dance, love, and friendship. However, this place is both an acoustical and a visual space. In fact, in some ways, the auditory permits the visual.

The work of documentary in the legacy of decolonization struggles, and the place Cuba occupies in this history, forms an extended public discourse about liberation, resistance, belonging, and identity. In this public space of the image, in the context of Cuba, the appearance of women as social and political subjects has often been symbolic of certain victories within a national-revolutionary narrative. The intimacies afforded by intersecting questions of gender, race, family, private space, and so forth affords women filmmakers, their audiences, and social subjects a complex threshold of citizenship where the image forms the space for citizens to appear to one another. The works of Sara Gómez and Gloria Rolando are central to this new formation of citizenship—yesterday and today.

No es el fin.

NOTES

This essay reformulates material from three previously published essays: Lord (2002), Lord and Cumaná (2013), and Lord and Zarza (2014).

1. See Casamayor (this volume).

2. I briefly discuss Fernando Ortiz's theory of transculturation later in this chapter.

3. *Chronotope* is used in both cultural theory and film theory to refer to fundamental forms of self-understanding held by identities and cultures. The term originates with Mikhail Bakhtin when he writes, "We will name *chronotope* (literally 'time space') to the intrinsic connectedness of temporal and spatial relationships that are artistically expressed in literature.... In the literary artistic chronotope, spatial and temporal indicators are fused into one carefully thought-out, concrete whole. Time, as it were, thickens, takes on flesh, becomes artistically visible; likewise, space becomes charged and responsive to the movements of time, plot and history. This intersection of axes and fusion of indicators characterized the artistic chronotope" (2010, 84).

4. Lillian Guerra argues that the ICAIC's origins in the Partido Socialista Popular meant that "'guided viewing [*cine dirigido*]' of all films through *cine-debate*, including Cuban produced newsreels," was a form of ideological discipline. "ICAIC's founders, especially Alfredo Guevara and Julio García Espinosa, expected documentary film to represent hyper-real images of citizens consciously and visibly engaged in revolutionary struggle.... The filmic euphoria of the *hyper-real reel* thus reinforced the viability of the *real*" (2012, 318). I respond to Guerra's analysis later in this chapter.

5. The issues created by patriarchal authority are cogently analyzed in Malitsky (this volume) and Martínez-Echazábal (this volume). They also emerge in the interviews with Inés María Martiatu Terry and Luis García Mesa, also published in this book.

6. See Serra (this volume) for a discussion of the Federation of Cuban Women and the tension that *Mi aporte* brought forth.

7. In an interview with Ricardo Acosta (this volume), film editor Iván Arocha discusses the complicated environments in which damage to *De cierta manera* occurred.

8. An increasingly robust history of this period of black activism and cultural production has begun to appear during the past decade in particular. See Benson (2018) for a recent synthesis of this material.

9. Gómez's critique as shown in the film has been ambivalently received (Ebrahim 1998). Some think that the voice-over narration in the documentary section dealing with patriarchal traditions from Africa and colonial Spain, the "Secret Society," was the interfering work of Tomás Gutiérrez Alea and Julio García Espinosa. However, the script shows that she and Tomás González wrote what we hear and see on the screen. Even so, there are a couple of interesting modulations. Most of the discourse in the film is in the indicative voice (unless in the dialogue) except for this, which is in the conditional: "*puede decirse que su naturaleza de sociedad secreta tradicional y excluyente la sitúan contraria al progreso e incapaz de insertarse dentro de las necesidades de la vida moderna*" (it may be said that the traditional and exclusive nature of this secret society situates its members against progress and incapable of satisfying the requirements of modern life). Immediately after this discourse, the script has Yolanda in close-up looking at the camera, with Mario off-screen and Yolanda saying, "My life isn't as full of things as yours is. My parents working for the revolution, me in boarding school all the time."

10. Emery cited in Loss (2003). See also Emery (1996).

11. Much has been written about the Italian neorealist influence on Cuban cinema. But I wish also to draw attention to the tradition of the urban ethnographer, such as we see in Jean Rouch and Edgar Morin's important film *Chronicle of a Summer* (1961). I'd also point to Chris Marker and, of course, to Agnès Varda's films as well as Quebec filmmakers such as Michel Brault, who was instrumental in the making of *Chronicle of a Summer* (Rouch was close to and worked with Michel Leiris, who went to Cuba as the leader of the French delegation of leftist artists and intellectuals in the late 1960s). This network of urban ethnographers created an aesthetic by which to express locality and urban life inside the movement of an emergent global and decolonized consciousness.

12. For more on Gloria Rolando, see Stock (2009), Ebrahim (1998), and González Mandri (2006). For a filmography and events related to Rolando's

work, see AfroCubaWeb (http://afrocubaweb.com/gloriarolando/gloriarolando.htm).

BIBLIOGRAPHY

Acosta, Ricardo, and David McIntosh. 1992. "*Crónicas de mi familia*: New Cuban Film and Video." Film program catalog.

Arteaga, Haydee. 1989. "Recordar a Sara." Special issue on Sara Gómez, edited by Antonio Conte. *Cine Cubano* 127: 19–20.

Azoulay, Ariella. 2008. *The Civil Contract of Photography*. New York: Zone Books.

Bakhtin, Mikhail M. 2010. "Forms of Time and of the Chronotope in the Novel." In *The Dialogic Imagination: Four Essays*, 84–258. Austin: University of Texas Press.

Beattie, Keith. 2008. *Documentary Display: Re-viewing Nonfiction Film and Video*. London: Wallflower.

Benamou, Catherine. 1994. "Cuban Cinema: On the Threshold of Gender." *Frontiers: A Journal of Women's Studies* 15, no. 1: 51–75.

———. 1999. "Cuban Cinema: On the Threshold of Gender." In *Redirecting the Gaze: Gender, Theory, and Cinema in the Third World*, edited by Diana Robin and Ira Jaffe, 67–98 Albany: State University of New York Press.

Benson, Devyn Spence. 2016. *Antiracism in Cuba: The Unfinished Revolution*. Chapel Hill: University of North Carolina Press.

———. 2018. "Sara Gómez: Afrocubana (Afro-Cuban Women's) Activism after 1961." *Cuban Studies* 46: 134–58.

Burton, Julianne. 1984. "Democratizing Documentary: Modes of Address in the Latin American Cinema, 1958–1972." In *"Show Us Life": Towards a History and Aesthetics of Committed Documentary*, edited by Thomas Waugh, 49–86. Metuchen, NJ: Scarecrow.

———, ed. 1990. *The Social Documentary in Latin America*. Pittsburgh: University of Pittsburgh Press.

———. 1997. "Film and Revolution in Cuba: The First Twenty-Five Years." In *New Latin American Cinema, 2: Studies of National Cinema*, edited by Michael T. Martin, 123–42. Detroit, MI: Wayne State University Press.

Chanan, Michael. 1997a. "The Changing Geography of Third Cinema." *Screen* 38, no. 4: 371–88.

———. 1997b. "Rediscovering Documentary: Cultural Context and Intentionality." In *New Latin American Cinema, 1: Theory, Practices and Transcontinental Articulations*, edited by Michael T. Martin, 201–17. Detroit, MI: Wayne State University Press.

———. 2004. *Cuban Cinema*. Minneapolis: University of Minnesota Press.

———. 2006. "Latin American Cinema: From Underdevelopment to Postmodernism." In *Remapping World Cinema: Identity, Culture and Politics in Film*, edited by Stephanie Dennison and Song Hwee Lim, 38–52. London: Wallflower.

Conte, Antonio. ed. 1989. Special issue on Sara Gómez, *Cine Cubano* 127.

Craven, Christa, and Dána-Ain Davis. 2016. *Feminist Ethnography: Thinking Through Methodologies, Challenges and Possibilities*. Lanham, MD: Rowman and Littlefield.

Davies, Catherine. 1997. "Modernity, Masculinity and Imperfect Cinema in Cuba." *Screen* 38, no. 4: 279–93.

de la Fuente, Alejandro. 2001. *A Nation for All: Race, Inequality and Politics in Twentieth-Century Cuba*. Chapel Hill: University of North Carolina Press.

D'Lugo, Marvin. 1997. "'Transparent Women': Gender and Nation in Cuban Cinema." In *New Latin American Cinema, 2: Studies of National Cinemas*, edited by Michael T. Martin, 155–166. Detroit, MI: Wayne State University Press.

Ebrahim, Haseenah. 1998. "Afrocuban Religions in Sara Gómez's *One Way or Another* and Gloria Rolando's *Oggún*." *Western Journal of Black Studies* 22, no. 4 (Winter): 239–51.

Emery, Amy Fass. 1996. *The Anthropological Imagination in Latin American Literature*. Columbia: University of Missouri Press.

Fabian, Johannes. 1983. *Time and the Other: How Anthropology Makes Its Object*. New York: Columbia University Press.

Fulleda León, Gerardo, 1989. "Una reina desoída." Special issue on Sara Gómez, edited by Antonio Conte, *Cine Cubano* 127: 25–26.

García Borrero, Juan Antonio. 2001. *Guía crítica del cine cubano de ficción*. Havana: Arte y Literatura.

———. 2009. *Otras maneras de pensar el cine cubano*. Santiago de Cuba: Oriente.

———. 2010. *Intrusos en el paraíso: los cineastas extranjeros en el cine cubano de los sesenta / Outsiders in paradise: Foreign filmmakers in Cuban cinema of the 1960s*. Cines del Sur.

González Mandri, Flora María. 2006. *Guarding Cultural Memory: Afro-Cuban Women in Literature and the Arts*. Charlottesville: University of Virginia Press.

Guerra, Lillian. 2012. *Visions of Power in Cuba: Revolution, Redemption and Resistance, 1959–1971*. Chapel Hill: University of North Carolina Press.

Lesage, Julia. 1979. "One Way or Another: Dialectical, Revolutionary, Feminist." *Jump Cut* 20 (May): 20–23.

———. 1984. "The Feminist Documentary—Politics and Aesthetics." In *Show Us Life: Toward a History and Aesthetic of the Committed Documentary*, edited by Thomas Waugh, 223–52. Metuchen, NJ: Scarecrow.

López, Ana M. 1992. "Revolution and Dreams: The Cuban Documentary Today." *Studies in Latin American Popular Culture* 11: 45–58.

———. 2006. "The State of Things: New Directions in Latin American Film History." *The Americas: A Quarterly Review of Inter-American Cultural History* 63, no. 2: 197–203.

Lord, Susan. 2002. "Temporality and Identity: Undertaking Cross-Cultural Analysis of Sara Gómez's Documentaries." In *Women Filmmakers: Refocusing*, edited by Jacqueline Levitin, Judith Plessis, and Valerie Raoul, 249–63. Vancouver: UBC Press.

———. 2009. "Acts of Affection: Cinema and Citizenship in the Work of Sara Gómez." In *Gender and Sexuality in 1968: Transformative Politics in the Cultural Imagination*, edited by L. J. Frazier and D. Cohen, 173–93. New York: Palgrave Macmillan.

Lord, Susan, and María Caridad Cumaná. 2013. "Deterritorialised Intimacies: The Documentary Legacy of Sara Gómez in Three Contemporary Cuban Women Filmmakers." In *Hispanic and Lusophone Women Filmmakers: Critical Discourses and Cinematic Practices*, edited by Julian Daniel Gutiérrez-Albilla and Parvati Nair, 96–110. Manchester, UK: Manchester University Press.

Lord, Susan, and Zaira Zarza. 2014. "Intimate Spaces and Migrant Imaginaries: Sandra Gómez, Susana Barriga and Heidi Hassan." In *New Documentaries of Latin America*, edited by Vinicius Navaro and Juan Carlos Rodriguez, 199–217. New York: Palgrave Macmillan.

Loss, Jacqueline. 2003. "Global Arenas: Narrative and Filmic Translation of Identity." *Nepantla: Views from the South* 4, no. 2: 317–44.

Martin, Michael T., ed. 1997. *New Latin American Cinema*, 1: *Theory, Practices and Transcontinental Articulations*; 2: *Studies of National Cinemas*. Detroit: Wayne State University Press.

Montes de Oca, Dannys, and Dayamick Cisneros Rodriguez. 2004. "Labores domésticas." In *Labores domésticas: Versiones para otra historia de la visualidad en Cuba: Género, raza y grupos sociales*. Pinar del Río, Cuba: Galería UNEAC, Galería Telepinar, Centro Provincial de Artes Visuales.

Nichols, Bill. 1991. *Representing Reality: Issues and Concepts in Documentary*. Bloomington: Indiana University Press.

Ortiz, Fernando. 1987. *Contrapunteo cubano del tabaco y el azúcar*. Caracas: Fundacion Biblioteca Ayacuch.

Pick, Zuzana M. 1993. *The New Latin American Cinema: A Continental Project*. Austin: University of Texas Press.

Piedra Rodríguez, Mario, ed. 1987. *Cine cubano: Selección de lecturas*. Havana: Pueblo y Educación.

Rich, B. Ruby. 1995. "An/Other View of New Latin American Cinema." In *Feminism in the Cinema,* edited by Laura Pietropaolo and Ada Testaferri, 273–97. Bloomington: Indiana University Press.
Rowe, William, and Vivian Schelling. 1996. *Memory and Modernity: Popular Culture in Latin America.* London: Verso.
Salkey, Andrew. 1971. *Havana Journal.* London: Pelican Books.
Shaw, Deborah. 2003. *Contemporary Latin American Cinema: 10 Key Films.* New York: Continuum.
Stock, Ann Marie, ed. 1997. *Framing Latin American Cinema: Contemporary Critical Perspectives.* Minneapolis: University of Minnesota Press.
———. 2009. *On Location in Cuba: Street Filmmaking during Times of Transition.* Chapel Hill: University of North Carolina Press.
Vazquez, Alexandra. 2013. *Listening in Detail: Performances of Cuban Music.* Durham, NC: Duke University Press.
Williams, Linda. 1993. "Mirrors without Memories: Truth, History, and the New Documentary." *Film Quarterly* 46, no. 3: 9–21.

SUSAN LORD is Professor of Film and Media in the Cultural Studies Graduate Program, and Director of the Vulnerable Media Lab at Queen's University. She is co-editor of *Killing Women: The Visual Culture of Gender and Violence; New World Coming: The Sixties and the Shaping of Global Consciousness;* and *Fluid Screens, Expanded Cinema.* As a member of the editorial collective for the journal *Public: Art, Culture, Ideas,* she has co-edited the issues "Havana" and "Archive/Counter-Archives."

Epilogue

"As Time Goes By, We Are Less of a Polite, Aesthetic, Static, Sexual, and Passive Object"

Sara Gómez Yera Interviewed by Marguerite Duras

MARGUERITE DURAS: *In the capitalist countries, youth, beginning from early childhood, are subjected to a kind of duping, a kind of social climbing—being the top students in the class in order to become famous, rich, and independent. The French term for this is* percer: *to make your own through the masses and surpass them. That is the single ideal. What happened here in Cuba with respect to social climbing, with all this competitive spirit? In your present process of development, can you tell yet what will replace it?*

SARA GÓMEZ: It is necessary to consider that all the questions are based on premises that I am obliged to accept before answering, which makes me uneasy. You ask me, "What happened here with the . . . ?" Here, I would say that nothing happened in the field of the individual, but rather everything *is happening*, and it is happening through a long and painful "dissolve," to speak in cinematic terms. In regard to the changes in the economic base, I think these are produced by sector—they don't occur on the scale of individual ethical values. The "social climbing," the competitive spirit is here, present, but this doesn't worry me greatly.

What I do believe is that the basic structure tends to channel and, in fact, transform this individualistic feeling in accordance with the society. A Cuban child doesn't want to be a "vanguard," that is to say, the best in the class. And this can be achieved only by the path of serious and conscientious study, by honesty in exams, by participation in seminars and special courses, and by gaining the right to be the "monitor" (guide and helper) student of the material so that he or she can represent an interest greater than that of the Revolution.

This creates an intellectual development committed to true vocation. Do you know our actual education system?

The adolescent and the youth want to be "vanguards," "militants," for which they must be studious and work hard; actively participate in sport, cultural, and agricultural activities; and, of necessity, they must be recognized as such by the masses. Hence, the masses themselves give the student the right to "surpass" them, if I can use your term here. The masses continually test the individual's honesty. In assembly, they discuss his or her right to be a militant, to be a political, administrative, or artistic cadre. The masses will soon consist of men and women who were better children and better young people.

Personally, I'm optimistic; my experiences justify this optimism. I believe in the scholarship recipients of the schools of art, of physical education, of technology, and of languages. I believe in that generation of high school students who for forty-five days each year share a roof and food away from their homes as they perform agricultural work next to men and women whom they have never seen before and of whose existence they had no palpable awareness.

If, in any case, I did feel any worry for those men and women who were not better children, I'm confident in the reciprocal influence of their direct contact with the youth. I'm confident in the conflicts they will face logically, the triumphs of the best of each, and the impotence of those who are not capable of improving themselves. Does this mean that opportunists, mediocre people, and the wealthy do not exist? No, they are here among us—and it is possible that within me lives an opportunist, a mediocre person, and one who aspires to possess riches—but this is no cause for worry since we are willing to fight against these elements outside and within ourselves. And what I can assure you is that this is not a country of conformists. I believe more than anything in one of these young "conflictive" people who are in each classroom, on each farm, in each industry, the one who questions what no one had questioned before, demands an answer, and makes everyone think.

MARGUERITE DURAS: *Personal well-being is the only well-being in capitalist societies. Enjoying goods acquired with money and meeting family and friends in a country house—these are the only aspirations of bourgeois families. But later, despair begins to set in. Can you say what could replace this so-called well-being, considered to be the most common in European countries—a tranquil well-being that is like a nightmare?*

SARA GÓMEZ: This "tranquil well-being" that is effectively a "nightmare" has stopped being an ideal, perhaps because it has stopped being a possibility. We are too committed to be tranquil. It is evident that we are an accelerated people who are in a rush. We all have urgencies—the urgency of our collective economic problems, the urgency of our political and military problems. We have an enemy. We recognize it, we have faced it, and we have a responsibility to end it. We feel the urgency to express ourselves now, immediately, to affirm ourselves. We are desperately devoted to a true compulsion to work, to struggle, to devote ourselves. And we believe, we believe with an aggressiveness that does not allow for tranquility, but rather excites us and extends us, one and all, together.

Believe me, I have never lived one day without rejoicing, without experiencing a true and authentic state of inner celebration, and sometimes, for reasons so unfamiliar to your world, like the triumph of one of our sports teams in an international competition, or, I don't know, on a bus, for example, or during an appointment at a polyclinic, I'd meet a woman who would talk to me about her worries, her domestic problems, and I understood. I told her things about myself, too. We'd become friends. We'd affectionately engage with each other for two hours even though, and this is the wonderful part, we wouldn't see each other again (or we might, it doesn't matter). I don't know her name or her house, but I like her. I understand her, and that makes me happy.

It is possible that you think all this talk about intercommunication does not answer your question, but I believe I have given you my new concept of well-being, which is, of course, subjective, a part of my personality, which is decidedly extroverted. But there is something symptomatic here—I have never felt alone for a long time without being ashamed of it later.

MARGUERITE DURAS: *A change is underway here. What is the major difficulty in this mutation, I mean from the individual point of view, of your inner life?*

SARA GÓMEZ: I believe in the change you refer to, and I have thought about this many times. In my personal case, and in that of many others I know, the major difficulty occurs in domestic relations, in the rules of living together in a house. There are things we previously accepted intellectually or rationally that later produced a serious and terrible emotional contradiction. I know very well what I want to do with myself, what is necessary for me to do with my life, but it happens that I almost always vacillate. I vacillate to the verge of desperation, and I've even come to feel impotent in the face of my own inertia. I don't feel capable of doing anything, of breaking with those who oppose me due their old values. They are my parents, my grandmother, the people I love, and they will suffer. They might die, and I would feel responsible. I need them in some way.

We are a country that has inherited the traditional Spanish family, and we are permeated by prejudices in regard to this. It is not easy; it becomes tragic. The fact that this occurs within the frame of a revolutionary family is curious. In the case of the antirevolutionary family, it's easier. For example, I do not have problems with my father. He left for the United States as a political exile and, in fact, has disappeared. The differences, the determinants, are just too serious. Do you understand? The problem is on this side of the dividing line. In an extreme case of war, my mother will be next to me holding her gun, but in normal times, times of peace, of work, living together, it becomes distressing. There are things she doesn't understand, that she has not had to learn to understand and that I must justify. And when I talk about my mother, I talk about an entire generation of women and men forty-five years or so old, women and men who are militant and even lead large organizations, but who still believe in the myths of the previous bourgeois society. They aspire to make of us a society of virgin ladies—decent, elegant, and refined, "ladies of exceptional morals"—and serious men, gentlemen, formal and discrete men who know how to keep up appearances. They are possessive of us to the point where a rupture takes place in a violent and painful way for both sides. And the dramatic thing is that this takes place as a result of a Revolution we are all willing to defend.

MARGUERITE DURAS: *The projection of themselves in their possession of material things, this fundamental vice in humans that leads to ruin—what will replace it? Will this be the point when the major modification of the "I" will take place here? By diminishing its attributes, will it, or will it not, remain the "I" preserved from suffering? The suicides of those who "failed" in society—what does this mean here? Without such "failure," what would suicide mean? Would it be what one might call pure and metaphysical suicide?*

SARA GÓMEZ: Much of what I expressed in my answers to questions one and two is useful to respond to this question, too. We could also analyze specific facts, since I don't feel capable of speculating. Recently, my husband and I became aware that our two-year-old daughter had not developed a sense of personal property. Ever since she was forty-five days old, she has attended a daycare [*círculo infantil*[1]] where, for ten hours a day, she shares food, clothing, toys, television, and direct attention from members of the staff. This realization was a big surprise for us, but my daughter does not differentiate between *her* ball and *a* ball, *her* chair and *a* chair, *her* plate and *a* plate.

All of this made me think of working experience on the Isle of Pines, where I heard people say "my farm," "my shelter," "my dairy," and even "my island."

On the Isle of Pines, the Island of Youth, they are creating, out of the blue, a habitable place.[2] They are building, they are planting, they are the only ones responsible for the island, and, in fact, they own it. Is it that a transformation is taking place in the meaning of property without having necessarily lost it? I don't know. It's possible. I don't understand this problem very well. And I confess that I am penetrated by a feeling of possession of certain things that sometimes offers me relief and at other times . . . and other times offers me compensation. But it occurs to me that we tend to feel that we are the owners of all that in which we participate, that of which we are a part, aiding in its creation. Perhaps this new, wider sense of property would stop us from devoting ourselves to the stingy possession of a "really awesome outfit to wear to the dance tonight." Am I being clear?

Now, to suffer from the lack of a personal possession so that we feel like failures, to the point of committing suicide, isn't this rather ridiculous? I offer a tenacious resistance to accepting failure. In fact, I don't like the word. And, in regard to "pure and metaphysical" suicide, I don't understand. I don't believe it. Here we possess, and we are all possessed, even those who don't know it or have not wanted to know it. Isn't that beautiful?

MARGUERITE DURAS: *In the capitalist world, the nuclear family is something that offers relief from a universe inscribed with unhappiness. That is the only thing it offers. And here? Having children so that they are quickly freed from your tutelage—is this discouraging for some? Or the opposite?*

SARA GÓMEZ: Well, we know what has happened with the family—its values have been dwarfed by others. My family represents a small minority compared to the others, all those that are available to me. But I don't give up; I have chosen. Besides, you are mistaken. My daughter has not been freed from my tutelage. On the contrary, I am conscious that my responsibility toward her determines that I must contribute to her living in a better world. By complying with my social duty, I am complying with the biological duty.

MARGUERITE DURAS: *The idea that the child must necessarily be in conflict with his or her parents in order to take a place in this world—what do you think about this?*

SARA GÓMEZ: This time we have not entered into conflict with our parents to occupy *their* place in the world, but *another* place in the world and, what is more, another place in another world—a world precisely opposite to this one that led us to desperation and violence.

MARGUERITE DURAS: *How have the functional attributes of women in Cuba been transformed? It seems that the traditional function of woman is about to disappear. Women's behavior seems less feminine than it is in Europe. In this an illusion?*

SARA GÓMEZ: I'm not sure I completely understand your question. But if you're referring to those functional attributes that place responsibility on women through procreation, I think they have not changed; rather, they have grown. As time goes by, we are less of a polite, aesthetic, static, sexual, and passive object. Revolution has confronted us with the responsibility of our intelligence, our commitment as thinking beings. In the case of women, this change is manifested in providing us a security—a kind of self-sufficiency that we did not possess before. So when we devote ourselves, we are capable of demanding. More than ever, we are quite conscious of the precise value of how much we devote ourselves. And we reflect this in our behavior, a new sense of liberty, which, in my opinion, brings freshness, charm, and spontaneity to our relationships.

MARGUERITE DURAS: *Has the inalienable solitude of human beings changed for the better or the worse—that is, for the best, art; for the worst, suicide? Has this solitude changed its meaning?*[3]

SARA GÓMEZ: Yes, it has changed meaning. All our lives our work is in what you call "inalienable solitude for the best"; that is, our life, our behavior, our work belong to us. We are alone facing our own historical consciousness—that makes us fully responsible, and so the reason for alienation has disappeared. Our work is creative, we live to create—to create something that we will possess beyond time, beyond any possible existential anguish, like art. Is that clear?

MARGUERITE DURAS: *With work currently being in perfect correlation with the revolutionary consciousness, what will it be when the mechanization of the means of production takes place? What will people's occupations be?*

SARA GÓMEZ: Your question takes me by surprise, and I confess that I cannot answer it. I have said much, and I'm exhausted. I've tried to be honest. I couldn't do otherwise. But now, I want to add something with regard to this question. The problem you are raising here is not my problem. I'm not sure if it was [Frantz] Fanon, but someone said that each generation is obliged to resolve its own problems, and the problem of replacing people with machines is not one that will occur in my lifetime. But I will say that I wish this problem would come to me; this would imply that the problems I face now would be resolved. And yet I like these times. I feel a real generational pride. I'm confident in our historical significance. I want to clarify that I am happy, happy to live here and now. You talked earlier of the absurd, or useless, quality of life—I don't remember—I don't know exactly what I wanted to say, but I don't understand it, believe me, I don't understand it. And if you believe it, you are justifying my uncertainty of your work, your cinema. Sincerely, I hope you excuse me for this last statement. I'm full of good will for you, believe me. It's just that I cannot manage to understand it.

Translated from the Spanish by Paul Kelley and Susan Lord

NOTES

1. *Círculo infantil* is a free daycare system in Cuba for children starting when the children are forty-five days old. It has had a profound impact on families, the community, and, especially, working mothers of the Revolution. The *círculo* was created in 1961 through the leadership of Vilma Espín, president of the Federation of Cuban Women. This social advance is discussed directly in the film *Mi aporte* and by several authors in this volume. —Eds.

2. Leida Oquendo, an anthropologist and a close friend of Sara Gómez, was among the group of communist youth who went to the Isle of Pines "with the feeling that with the experiment we undertook, we carried a great burden—that of the entire future of the Revolution—on our shoulders" (Lord in conversation with Oquendo, Havana, March 2004). Sara Gómez's trilogy on the island is discussed throughout this volume. Also, while in Havana in 1967, it appears that Duras herself went to the Isle of Pines.—Eds.

3. In Spanish, the question is as follows: *¿La soledad inalienable del hombre para lo mejor y lo peor...?* Given Sara's answer—and the historical period—the meaning could well be translated as "alienation" as much as "solitude."—Trans. On the matter of the high rates of suicide in Cuba both before and after the Revolution, see Perez (2005).—Eds.

BIBLIOGRAPHY

Perez, Louis A. Jr. 2005. *To Die in Cuba: Suicide and Society*. Chapel Hill: University of North Carolina Press.

Filmography

As Assistant Director

Cumbite. Feature fiction. Directed by Tomás Gutiérrez Alea (1962, 82 min.)
Salut les Cubains. Directed by Agnès Varda (1963, 30 min.)
El robo. Feature fiction. Directed by Jorge Fraga (1965, 99 min.)
Tiempo de pioneros. Directed by Roberto Fandiño (1962)
Gonzalo Roig. Narration and text by Sara Gómez. Directed by Sergio Giral (1969)

Enciclopedia popular (Popular encyclopedia)

In 1962–1963, Sara Gómez made five short documentaries for the *Enciclopedia popular* series, a kind of training studio for new filmmakers. Except for the length, the production details for *Historia de la piratería* also apply to the other four films.

Solar habanero (Havana tenement) (*Enciclopedia popular*, Episode 31, 10 min.)
El solar (The tenement) (*Enciclopedia popular*, Special Episode, 10 min.)
Plaza Vieja (Old town square) (*Enciclopedia popular*, Episode 28, 4 min., 44 sec.)
Fábrica de tabacos (Tobacco factory) (*Enciclopedia popular*, Special Episode, 4 min., 44 sec.)
Historia de la piratería (History of piracy) (*Enciclopedia popular*, Special Episode, 10 min.)

Original Title *Historia de la piratería* (History of piracy)

Country of Production: Cuba
Year of Production: 1963
Category: Documentary
Classification: Short Film / Spanish Language
Color: White / Black
Sound: Sonora

Film Gauge: 35 mm
Footage: 274
Duration: 10 min.
Director: Gómez, Sara
Production Company: ICAIC
Head of Production: Pastor, Osvaldo
Studio: ICAIC
Designs: Morante, Rafael
Animation: Martinez
Photography: López, José
Editing: Rodríguez, Raúl
Musical Selection: Iglesias, Arturo
Script: Gómez, Sara
Narration or Dialogue: Gómez, Sara
Staff [Others]: Astorga, P. Pablo; Rodríguez, Asenneh (narrators); Iglesias, Arturo (effects); Doset (still photography)
Synopsis: Piracy in Cuba through its history. Comparison of piracy in the sixteenth, seventeenth, and eighteenth centuries with the contemporary situation.
Awards: [No Data]
Notes: Other titles: *Pirates of the Americas* and *The Defense of the Coasts of the West Indies*; music from archives; sound by the Department of Sound ICAIC; produced by the Department of Popular Encyclopedia.

Original Title: *Iré a Santiago* (I'm going to Santiago)

Country of Production: Cuba
Year of Production: 1964
Category: Documentary
Classification: Short Film / Spanish Language
Color: White / Black
Sound: Sonora
Film Gauge: 35 mm
Footage: 410
Duration: 15 min.
Director: Gómez, Sara
Production Company: ICAIC
Head of Production: Pi, Fernando
Studio: ICAIC
Photography: García Joya, Mario
Sound: García, Raúl
Editing: Bravo, Roberto
Script: Gómez, Sara

Narration or Dialogue: Gómez, Sara
Staff: Nápoles, Victoria (narrator)
Actors: [No Data]
Synopsis: Aspects and customs of the city of Santiago de Cuba
Awards: [No Data]
Notes: Music from archives; inspired by a poem by Federico García Lorca.

Original Title: *Excursión a Vuelta Abajo* (**Excursion to Vuelta Abajo**)

Country of Production: Cuba
Year of Production: 1965
Category: Documentary
Classification: Short Film / Spanish Language
Color: White / Black
Sound: Sonora
Film Gauge: 35 mm
Footage: 266
Duration: 10 min.
Director: Gómez, Sara
Production Company: ICAIC
Chief of Production: Pi, Fernando
Studio: ICAIC
Photography: Costales, Luis
Animation Camera: Palenzuela, Ramón
Editing: Vega, Justo
Script: Gómez, Sara
Narration or Dialogue: Gómez, Sara
Staff [Others]: Nápoles, Victoria (narrator)
Actors: [No Data]
Synopsis: About the world-famous tobacco production area in the province of Pinar del Río and the advances that came with the Cuban Revolution and mechanization.
Distribution: ICAIC
Awards: [No Data]
Notes: Music from archive; Sound Department ICAIC

Original Title: *Guanabacoa: Crónicas de mi familia* (**Guanabacoa: Chronicles of my family**)

Country of Production: Cuba
Year of Production: 1966
Category: Documentary

Classification: Short Film / Spanish Language
Color: White / Black
Sound: Sonora
Film Gauge: 35 mm
Footage: 363
Duration: 13 min.
Director: Gómez, Sara
Production Company: ICAIC
Head of Production: Rivero, Eduardo; Pascau, Jesús
Studio: ICAIC
Photography: Tabío, Jos; March, Luis
Editing: Vega, Justo
Music Composer: Landa, Fabio
Original Source: Gómez, Sara
Script: Gómez, Sara
Staff [Others]: [No Data]
Actors: [No Data]
Synopsis: The director, in search of her roots, presents a family picture that at the same time is a testimony to a little-known aspect of social and cultural life.
Distribution: ICAIC
Awards: [No Data]

Original Title: *Y... tenemos sabor* (And we've got flavor)

Country of Production: Cuba
Year of Production: 1967
Category: Documentary
Classification: Short Film / Spanish Language
Color: White / Black
Sound: Sonora
Film Gauge: 35 mm
Footage: 823
Duration: 30 min.
Director: Gómez, Sara
Production Company: ICAIC
Production Chief: Pascau, Jesús
Studio: ICAIC
Photography: García Joya, Mario; López, José
Lighting: Martínez, Rogelio

Sound: Hernández, Germinal; Fernández, Carlos
Editing: Vega, Justo
Musical Performers: Conjunto Changüí; Conjunto Típico Habanero; Conjunto Clave y Guaguancó; Conjunto de Santiago de Cuba; Trío Los Decanos; Trío Virgilio Almenares; Orquesta Estrellas Cubanas; Chucho Valdés, his combo and Guapachá
Script: Gómez, Sara
Narration or Dialogue: Mendoza, Isa
Staff: Zayas, Adalberto (interviews)
Actors: [No Data]
Synopsis: Cuban music and its basic instruments.
Distribution: ICAIC
Awards: [No Data]

Original Title: *En la otra isla* **(On the other island)**

Country of Production: Cuba
Year of Production: 1968
Category: Documentary
Classification: Short Film / Spanish Language
Color: White / Black
Sound: Sonora
Film Gauge: 35 mm
Footage: 1112
Duration: 41 min.
Director: Gómez, Sara
Production Company: ICAIC
Production Chief: Pascau, Jesús
Studio: ICAIC
Photography: García Mesa, Luis
Sound: Hernández, Germinal
Editing: Villalón, Caíta
Composer: González Pérez, Tomás
Musical Performers: Portuondo, Omara; Quinteto de Jazz de la Orquesta Cubana de Música Moderna
Song Titles: "On the Other Island"
Script: Gómez, Sara
Credit Design: Ávila, René
Staff [Others]: [No Data]
Actors: [No Data]

Synopsis: Documentary survey carried out on the Isla de Pinos, where a new generation of young people are living and working.
Distribution: ICAIC
Awards: [No Data]
Notes: Narration: Interviews

Original Title: *Una isla para Miguel* (An island for Miguel)

Country of Production: Cuba
Year of Production: 1968
Category: Documentary
Classification: Short Film / Spanish Language
Color: White / Black
Sound: Sonora
Film Gauge: 35 mm
Footage: 591
Duration: 22 min.
Director: Gómez, Sara
Production Company: ICAIC
Production Chief: Pascau, Jesús
Studio: ICAIC
Photography: García, Luis Mesa
Sound: Hernández, Germinal; Valdés, Arturo
Editing: Villalón, Caíta
Music Composer: Valdés, Chucho
Script: González, Tomás; Gómez, Sara
Narration or Dialogue: Gómez, Sara
Credit Design: Ávila, René
Staff [Others]: Mendoza, Isaura (narrator)
Actors: [No Data]
Synopsis: The process of reeducation of adolescents who, because of their social and economic context, were in a state of marginalization.
Distribution: ICAIC
Awards: [No Data]

Original Title: *Isla del tesoro* (Treasure island)

Country of Production: Cuba
Year of Production: 1969
Category: Documentary
Classification: Short Film / Spanish Language

Color: White / Black
Sound: Sonora
Film Gauge: 35 mm
Footage: 265
Duration: 10 min.
Director: Gómez, Sara
Production Company: ICAIC
Production Chief: Pascau, Jesús
Studio: ICAIC
Photography: García, Luis
Sound: Hernández, Germinal
Editing: Villalón, Caíta
Music Composer: Guerra, Armando
Song Titles: "The Other Island"
Script: Gómez, Sara
Narration or Dialogue: Gómez, Sara
Credit Design: Ávila, René
Staff: Mendoza, Isaura; Llauradó, Adolfo (narrators); Triana, Roberto (focus puller); Herrera, Adalberto (titles)
Actors: [No Data]
Synopsis: A vision of the Isle of Pines from its discovery until today, when it has become the Isle of Youth, where the Revolution builds a new society with the active participation of young people.
Distribution: ICAIC
Awards: [No Data]
Notes: Music: Armando Guerra and the song "The Other Island"

Original Title: *Poder local, poder popular* **(Local power, popular power)**

Country of Production: Cuba
Year of Production: 1970
Category: Documentary
Classification: Short Film / Spanish Language
Color: White / Black
Sound: Sonora
Film Gauge: 35 mm
Footage: 285
Duration: 9 min.
Director: Gómez, Sara
Production Company: ICAIC
Chief of Production: García, Guillermo

Studio: ICAIC
Photography: Riera, José M.
Sound: Sorrell, Leonardo
Editing: Arocha, Iván
Script: Gómez, Sara
Credit Design: Herrera, Alberto (Truffó)
Staff [Others]: [No Data]
Actors: [No Data]
Synopsis: Meeting of a district popular power committee and citizens
Distribution: ICAIC
Awards: [No Data]
Notes: Narration; interviews.

Original Title: *De bateyes* **(The sugar workers' quarters)**

Country of Production: Cuba
Year of Production: 1971
Category: Documentary
Classification: Short Film / Spanish Language
Color: White / Black
Sound: Sonora
Film Gauge: 35 mm
Footage: 654
Duration: 24 min.
Director: Gómez, Sara
Production Company: ICAIC
Chief of Production: Llapur, Santiago; García, Guillermo
Studio: ICAIC
Photography: García, Luis Mesa
Sound: Hernández, Germinal
Editing: Arocha, Iván
Music Composer: Salvador, Emiliano
Musical Performers: Grupo Experimentación Sonora del ICAIC
Script: Gómez, Sara
Narration or Dialogue: Gómez, Sara
Credit Design: Herrera, Alberto (Truffó)
Staff [Others]: Díaz, Alberto Pedro, Martínez Furé, Rogelio, and Molinet, María Elena (contributors); Pucheux, Jorge (special effects), Saavedra, Hilda (narrator)
Actors: [No Data]

Synopsis: Testimonies about the origins and characteristics of *bateyes*, or communities of those working the sugar mills.
Distribution: ICAIC
Awards: [No Data]

Original Title: *Un documental a propósito del tránsito* (A documentary about traffic)

Country of Production: Cuba
Year of Production: 1971
Category: Documentary
Classification: Short Film / Spanish Language
Color: White / Black
Sound: Sonora
Film Gauge: 35 mm
Footage: 455
Duration: 17 min.
Director: Gómez, Sara
Production Company: ICAIC
Production Chief: Vigil-Escalera, Orlando
Studio: ICAIC
Photography: López, Rodolfo
Sound: García, Raúl
Mix: Demósthene, Juan
Editing: Arocha, Iván
Musical Performers: Grupo Experimentación Sonora del ICAIC
Script: Gómez, Sara
Credit Design: Azcuy, René
Staff [Others]: Fernández, Omar (adviser)
Actors: [No Data]
Synopsis: Activities of the transit authority and plan for reeducation of those punished for traffic offenses.
Distribution: ICAIC
Awards: [No Data]
Notes: Narration; interviews.

Original Title: *Año uno* (The first year)

Country of Production: Cuba
Year of Production: 1972

Category: Documentary
Classification: Short Film / Spanish Language
Color: White / Black
Sound: Sonora
Film Gauge: 35 mm
Footage: 260
Duration: 10 min.
Director: Gómez, Sara
Production Company: ICAIC
Chief of Production: Gómez, Rolando
Studio: ICAIC
Photography: López, Lupercio
Lighting: González, Rafael
Sound: Hernández, Germinal
Editing: Arocha, Iván
Musical Performers: Grupo Experimentación Sonora del ICAIC
Script: Gómez, Sara
Narration or Dialogue: Gómez, Sara
Credit Design: Ávila, René; Hernández, Adalberto
Staff [Others]: Fernández, Isabel; Batet, René (narrators)
Actors: [No Data]
Synopsis: Childcare centers and their importance in child development.
Distribution: ICAIC
Awards: [No Data]

Original Title: *Atención prenatal* **(Prenatal care)**

Country of Production: Cuba
Year of Production: 1972
Category: Documentary
Classification: Short Film / Spanish Language
Color: White / Black
Sound: Sonora
Film Gauge: 35 mm
Footage: 250
Duration: 10 min.
Director: Gómez, Sara
Production Company: ICAIC
Chief of Production: Rouco, Jorge
Studio: ICAIC
Photography: García, Luis

Sound: Hernández, Germinal
Editing: Villalón, Caíta
Musical Performers: Grupo Experimentación Sonora del ICAIC
Script: Gómez, Sara
Narration or Dialogue: Gómez, Sara
Credit Design: Ávila, René
Staff [Others]: López, Lilia Rosa; Navarro, Miguel (narrators)
Actors: [No Data]
Synopsis: Prenatal care and the advice for pregnant woman to enable a safe and healthy birth.
Distribution: ICAIC
Awards: [No Data]

Original Title: *Mi aporte* **(My contribution)**

Country of Production: Cuba
Year of Production: 1972
Category: Documentary
Classification: Short film / Spanish Language
Color: White / Black
Sound: Sonora
Film Gauge: 35 mm
Footage: 905
Duration: 33 min.
Director: Gómez, Sara
Production Company: ICAIC
Production Chief: Llapur, Santiago
Studio: ICAIC
Photography: García Mesa
Sound: Hernández, Germinal
Editing: Arocha, Iván
Script: Gómez, Sara
Credit Design: Ávila, René
Staff [Others]: Pucheux, Jorge (Special Effects); Vidal, Consuelo (narrator)
Actors: [No Data]
Synopsis: Through interviews and debates, the difficulties that women still find being accepted in the workplace while balancing their ongoing domestic responsibilities are presented and discussed.
Distribution: ICAIC
Awards: [No Data]
Notes: Narration; interviews and debates; music from archive.

Original Title: *Sobre horas extras y trabajo voluntario* (**Extra hours and voluntary work**)

Country of Production: Cuba
Year of Production: 1973
Category: Documentary
Classification: Short Film / Spanish Language
Color: White / Black
Sound: Sonora
Film Gauge: 35 mm
Footage: 239
Duration: 9 min.
Director: Gómez, Sara
Production Company: ICAIC
Chief of Production: García, Guillermo
Studio: ICAIC
Photography: Riera, José M.
Sound: Borrés, José
Mix: Hernández, Germinal
Editing: Arocha, Iván
Script: Gómez, Sara
Narration or Dialogue: Gómez, Sara
Credit Design: Rodríguez, Adalberto; Hernández, Adalberto
Staff [Others]: Hernández, Bárbara; González, Tony (narrators)
Actors: [No Data]
Synopsis: A group of workers in the textile industry offer their opinions on different aspects of the Thirteenth Workers' Congress of the Cuban Workers' Confederation pronouncements related to the two topics of the title.
Distribution: ICAIC
Prizes: Mention in the group of documentaries made on the occasion of the Thirteenth Congress of the Cuban Workers' Confederation. Annual Selection of the Review, Havana, 1973.
Notes: Music from archive.

Original Title: *De cierta manera* (**One way or another**)

Country of Production: Cuba
Year of Production: 1974. Postproduction completed and film released in 1977.
Category: Fiction
Classification: Feature Film / Spanish Language
Color: White / Black
Sound: Sonora

Film Gauge: 35 mm
Footage: 2,147
Duration: 79 min.
Director: Gómez, Sara
Assistant Director: López, Rigoberto
Production Company: ICAIC
Director of Production: Vives, Camilo
Studio: ICAIC
Photography: García Mesa
Camera Operator: Valdés, Julio
Animation Camera: Hernández, Adalberto
Lighting: Ruiz, Carmelo
Sound: Hernández, Germinal
Editing: Arocha, Iván
Music Composer: Vitier, Sergio
Musical Performers: González, Sara
Song Titles: "La nueva escuela" (The new school); "Cantos rituales abakua" (Abakuá ritual songs)
Composition of Songs: Rodríguez, Silvio
Script: Gómez, Sara; González, Tomás
Narration or Dialogue: Gómez, Sara
Scenography: Larrabure, Roberto
Props: Moreno, Joaquín
Credit Design: López, Ricardo
Staff [Others]: Valdés Dones, Alberto (assistant animator); Pucheux, Jorge (special effects); Ramírez, María (Continuity); Rouco, Jorge (production assistant); Cedeño, Rafaela (costume designer)
Actors: Balmaseda, Mario; Cuéllar, Yolanda; Limonta, Mario; Mendoza, Isaura; Carcassés, S. Bobby; Reyes, Sarita
Synopsis: The neighborhood of Miraflores, built in 1962 by the very people who would inhabit it, is a result of the first efforts of the Cuban Revolution to eradicate marginal neighborhoods. The film tells the story of this neighborhood through a relationship between a Black worker and a White teacher. The film combines documentary and fiction to reveal the complexities of marginalization, revolutionary modernization, race and gender.
Premier: October 6, 1977, at the following cinemas in Cuba: Acapulco, Yara, Metropolitán, Monaco, City Hall, Florida
Distribution: ICAIC. Tricontinental Films in the United States. IDERA in Canada.
Prizes: Selected by the Critics of Cuban Cinema as among the ten most significant films of the year. Havana, 1977

Index

26th of July Movement, 230, 332

Abakuá, 217, 258n1
Abd'Allah-Alvarez Ramírez, Sandra, 10, 21, 299, 362, 371, 375
Acosta, Ricardo, 4, 7, 8, 24, 188, 201, 306, 316, 384, 385, 390n7
Afro-Cuban religions, religiosity, 37, 64, 105, 253, 332; Abakuá society and practices, 52, 53, 70, 76, 83, 135, 139, 207–208, 211–213, 216–218, 265, 268, 269, 335, 337, 351, 381; Arará ceremonies, 339; ñañiguismo, 76, 135–137, 139; Santería, 72, 76, 104, 110, 115, 119n13, 153–154, 212, 230, 242, 332, 335; Yoruba religions, 115
Afro-Cuban/Afro-descendent history and culture, 7, 41–42, 223–231, 374, 381, 387, 388; Afro-Cuban societies (Sociedades de color), 71, 228–230, 278, 381; pre-revolutionary history, 37, 41, 251
AfroCubana (Afro-Cuban Women's) Activism, 21, 223; Afro-Cubana project, 26n15, 242, 246n21
Afrocubanas: Historia, pensamiento y prácticas culturales (Afro-Cuban women: History, thought, and cultural practices), 27

Agrarian and Urban Reform Laws, 224
Al duro y sin careta (No holds barred), 48, 104, 118
Álvarez Román, Santiago, 5, 51, 59, 197, 252, 265, 267, 275, 276, 280, 283, 328, 329, 379
Amparo: Millo y azucenas (Amparo: Millet and Lily), 103, 108
anthems: "Las mujeres cubanas, adelante, adelante," 299; "Ser comunista para triunfar" (To be a communist is to win victory), 301
Anthology of Black and Madagascan Poetry, 42
Antiracism in Cuba: The Unfinished Revolution, 21, 26n15, 244n2
Año uno (The first year), 45, 46, 411
Arduengo, Amalia, 38, 50
Arocha Montes de Oca, Iván, 4, 7, 11, 24, 26n9, 54, 56n7, 118n10, 186, 215, 246n12, 268, 269n1, 306, 316, 339n5, 385, 390n7, 410–415
Asamblea del Poder Popular (Popular Power Assembly), 290. *See also* Órganos del Poder Popular
Astorga, P. Pablo, 404
Atención prenatal (Prenatal care), 45, 201, 412

Ávila, René, 407–409, 412, 413
Azcanio, Manuela "La Mexicana," 106, 108
Azcuy, René, 411

Balmaseda, Mario, 12, 48, 101, 104, 118n11, 177, 178, 210, 266, 268, 336, 415
Barceló, Amadito "Guapachá," 44
Barnet, Miguel, 293, 363
Barreal, Isaac, 363
Barriga, Susana, 386
Batet, René, 412
Batista, Fulgencio, 4, 92, 106, 107, 110, 224, 235
Bay of Pigs attack (Girón), 62, 109, 227, 380, 381
Beatles, The, 196, 197, 231
Beauvoir, Simone de, 42
Benson, Devyn Spence, 11, 20, 21, 25n5, 26nn8,15, 223, 250, 302n2, 375, 380
Betancourt, Juan R., 225
black consciousnesss: Black Panthers, 18; Black Power, 51, 55, 230, 231, 383
black identities, culture, and history, 64–65, 68, 70–73, 81, 82, 252, 349, 350, 356
Black Women as Custodians of History, 225
Borrés, José, 414
Bravo, Roberto, 84, 404
Brecht, Bertolt, 102; Brechtian effect, 328
Brene, José R., 103, 104, 113
Burton, Julianne, 25n4, 378
Bustamante, José Oriol, 131
Butterworth, Douglas, 88, 89, 93, 102

Cabrera Infante (Guillermo), 343, 344
Cabrera, Lydia, 42, 208
Cabrera, Sabá, 67, 227, 380
Calderón González, Jorge, 103, 108

Calixta Comité, 107, 113
Campaign against racial discrimination (1959), 224
Campaña Nacional de Alfabetización en Cuba, 26n11, 370n5. See also literacy campaign
Carbonell, Walterio, 55, 73, 74, 225, 230, 231, 245n10
Carcassés, Bobby, 268
Carmichael, Stokely, 19, 56n4, 240, 265
Carpentier, Alejo, 42, 195, 221n3
Casa de las Américas, 363
Casamayor-Cisneros, Odette, 12, 16, 20, 21, 58, 79
Castro, Fidel, 11, 18, 61, 62, 82, 84, 93, 106, 107, 109, 116, 119, 224, 226, 227, 231, 235, 243, 282, 284n16, 288, 289, 292, 295, 298, 303n10, 332, 345, 346, 351, 352, 364, 380
Castro, Raúl, 241, 332
Cayo Hueso, 35, 36, 38, 40, 44, 53, 95, 111, 112, 116, 120, 124, 163, 260, 313
Cedeño, Rafaela, 415
Centennial Youth Column, 333
Césaire, Aimé, 18, 19, 262
Chanan, Michael, 102, 256, 344, 378, 379
Chaplin, Charlie, 5, 272
Chávez, Rebeca, 7
Christensen, Theodore, 252, 265
Chronicles of my family (Guanabacoa: *Chronicles of my family*), 43, 70, 218, 228, 405. See also *Crónicas de mi familia* (Guanabacoa: Crónicas de mi familia)
Cine Cubano (Cuban Cinema magazine), 8, 26, 47, 315, 370n1
cine imperfecto (imperfect cinema), 10, 13, 26n9, 54, 118n10, 244, 315
cine-debate(s), 5, 299, 301–302, 376, 377, 382, 389n4

cinema fields and styles: didactic and educational cinema, 32, 52, 53, 69, 99, 153–156, 235, 271–275, 329, 379, 380; experimental cinema, 6, 12; political cinema, 45, 56n1, 226, 364; postcolonial cinema, 6; sociological practices, 44, 80, 206; Third cinema, 12, 21; women's cinema, 5, 6, 373; world cinema, 6;

citizenship, 13, 14, 23, 89, 110, 374, 375, 381, 383, 387, 389; blacks' citizenship, 223; cultural citizenship, 20, 21, 89, 386; gendered citizenship, 373; political and social activism, 114, 231, 245n10; women's citizenship, 372

Coffea Arábiga, 95, 96, 185, 196, 197, 205, 311, 316

Cofiño, Manuel, 84, 109, 110

Coloquio "Sara Gómez: Imagen múltiple. El audiovisual cubano desde una perspectiva de género," 10

Comité de Defensa de la Revolución (CDR), 107, 108, 119n14, 126, 167, 168. See also Committee for the Defense of the Revolution (Revolutionary Defense Committee)

Committee for the Defense of the Revolution (Revolutionary Defense Committee), 107, 126, 167, 263. See also Comité de Defensa de la Revolución (CDR)

Communist Party (Partido Comunista de Cuba), 58, 84, 271, 295; Central Committee, 92

Conjunto Changüí, 407

Conjunto Clave y Guaguancó, 407

Conjunto de Santiago de Cuba, 407

Conjunto Folklórico Nacional (National Folklore Company), 204

Conjunto Típico Habanero, 407

Consejo Nacional de Cultura, CNC (National Culture Council), 227

Contrapunteo cubano del tabaco y el azúcar (Cuban counterpoint: tobacco and sugar), 382

Conversaciones con un cineasta incómodo, 98

Corona, Lucía, 75, 240, 301, 366, 368, 369, 376

Cortázar, Octavio, 44, 272

Costales, Luis, 405

Crítica: Cómo surgió la cultura nacional (Critique: How national culture emerged), 73, 231

Crónicas de mi familia (Guanabacoa: Crónicas de mi familia), 13, 17, 20, 25n5, 70–73, 218, 229, 243, 245n12, 273, 275, 276, 278, 279, 283, 292, 349, 374, 381, 388, 405. See also Chronicles of my family (Guanabacoa: Chronicles of my family)

Cruz, Celia, 330

Cuando la sangre se parece al fuego (When blood seems like fire), 109, 113

Cuban Missile Crisis, 50, 62

Cuban Revolution: cosmology and ideology, 58–63, 73, 102, 103, 111, 256, 287–288, 374, 377. See also women's rights; marginalization and marginality; race, racism, and racial consciousness

Cuéllar, Yolanda, 336, 415

Cumaná, María Caridad, 6, 10, 20, 24, 80, 86, 181, 222, 251, 259

Cumbite, 43, 52, 56n6, 99, 192, 193, 261, 403

Danza Nacional (National Dance Company), 50

Davis, Angela, 51, 203

De bateyes (The sugar workers' quarters), 192, 193, 195, 198, 221n2, 363, 382, 410

De cierta manera, 3, 7, 10, 12, 13, 17, 22–25, 26n9, 45, 48, 51, 52, 54, 56n7, 75–77, 87, 88, 91, 92, 94–98, 102, 104, 107–110, 116, 117n1, 118nn10–11, 123, 124, 181, 206, 209, 212, 218, 257, 258n4, 263, 264, 266–268, 298, 309–311, 314–315, 328, 332, 335, 336, 339n5, 351, 363, 380, 381, 390n7, 414. See also One way or another

Delgado, Livio, 311

Demósthene, Juan, 411

Depestre, René, 262, 265, 284n9, 293

Díaz Martínez, Manuel (Manolo), 50, 362

Díaz, Guillermo, 268, 335, 337, 338

Díaz, Rolando, 298

Díaz, Telmary, 6

documentary modes: cinema vérité, 216, 252, 376, 377, 378; cine reportaje, 46, 364, 375, 379; cine rescate, 379, 383, 387, 388; cine testimonio, 383, 387; direct cinema, 16, 378; ethnographic and autoethnographic practices, 4, 5, 7, 12, 14, 16, 20, 21, 52, 59, 205, 228, 232, 235, 239–240, 252, 300, 363, 364, 373, 382, 383

¿Dónde está Sara Gómez?, 26n8, 245n9, 302n5, 328, 367

Doset (still photography), 404

Duchesne, Marina, 50

Dumoulin, John, 363

Duras, Marguerite, 18, 19, 24, 302, 395–400, 401n2

Ebony, 42

Education and Culture Congress, 55. See also First National Congress on Education and Culture

Egües, Gladys, 75, 187, 240, 292, 300, 301, 367, 376

Egües, Rembert, 44

el Ambia, Eloy, 264, 268

El Fanguito, 384, 385

El negro (The black man), 258n1

El negro en Cuba, 1902–1958 (Black people in Cuba), 251

El otro Francisco, 264

El premio flaco (The skinny price), 103

El Puente, 245n10

El robo, 403

"El socialismo y el hombre en Cuba," 60. See also "Socialism and Man in Cuba"

El solar (The tenement), 403

Emilio, Frank, 346

Enciclopedia Popular (Popular encyclopedia), 5, 7, 13, 22, 45, 59, 69, 184, 272–276, 403

En la otra isla (On the other island), 1, 13, 14, 16, 17, 20, 46, 59, 68, 75, 183, 187, 189, 190, 232, 233, 243, 256, 280, 281, 292, 294, 407

En un barrio viejo (In an old neighborhood), 252, 253

Episodes of the Cuban Revolutionary War, 289

Espín, Vilma, 11, 82, 298, 301

Estenoz, Evaristo, 251

Estudios afrocubanos (Afro-Cuban studies), 251

Excursión a Vuelta Abajo (Excursion to Vuelta Abajo, Trip to Vuelta Abajo), 43, 338, 405

Exhibition: "Crónicas de mi familia: New Cuban Film and Video," 8, 56n2

Fábrica de tabacos (Tobacco factory), 273–275, 277, 403

Fandiño, Roberto, 42, 403

INDEX

Fanon, Frantz, 19, 55, 202, 203, 234, 262, 334, 400
Federación de Mujeres Cubanas, FMC (Federation of Cuban Women, also Cuban Federation of Women), 11, 12, 74, 82, 126, 149, 225, 235, 236, 238, 239, 241, 243, 298–302, 364, 369
feminist aesthetic and consciousness-raising, 12, 20, 45, 242, 243, 347, 377–378, 383, 398, 400
Fernández, Omar, 411
Fernández, Raúl, 329
Fernández Retamar, Roberto, 363
Fernández Robaina, Tomás, 251
Fernández, Isabel, 412
First National Congress on Education and Culture, 69, 73, 363. *See also* Education and Culture Congress
"For an Imperfect Cinema," 5. *See also* "Por un cine imperfecto"
Formell, Juan, 331
Fornet, Ambrosio, 17, 84
Fowler Calzada, Víctor, 12, 13, 22–24, 87, 122, 260, 269, 299, 380
Fraga, Jorge, 84, 85, 403
Fulleda León, Gerardo, 13, 58, 72, 344

García Alonso, Aida, 106
García Borrero, Juan Antonio, 77, 293, 370n1
García Espinosa, Julio, 5, 10, 14, 77, 84, 98, 102, 215, 267, 315, 335, 389n4, 390n9
García Joya, Mario "Mayito," 184, 214, 263, 313, 354, 355, 404, 406
García Lorca, Federico, 22, 228, 276, 341–49, 357n3, 358n8, 405
García Márquez, Gabriel, 18
García Mesa, Luis, 11, 24, 26n9, 181–221, 246n21, 280–308, 311, 316, 382, 412, 413, 415
García Yero, Olga, 10

García, Raúl, 404, 411
genre and song: "Mozambique," 331, 346, 354, 356, 358
Giral, Sergio, 6, 24, 53, 80–86, 103, 231, 246n21, 247n28, 252, 258n1, 264, 403
Gómez, Carlos, 2
Gómez, Manuel Octavio, 14, 252, 267
Gómez, Sandra, 386
Gómez, Sara: authorship, 204–205, 280, 380; biography and personality, 2–4, 37–40, 58–59, 81, 181–182, 186, 200, 218, 226, 245n9, 261–263, 307–309, 312–313; documentary practice, 373, 383; journalism, 49; legacy, 373, 375, 382, 384–388; parodic discourse, 345; and the Revolution, 23, 32, 302, 380, 395, 399–400; style, 190–192, 210–211, 218–219, 281–283, 294, 296, 297, 347, 349, 351, 376. *See also* feminist aesthetic and consciousness; marginalization and marginality; race, racism, and racial consciousness
González Grau, Magda, 8, 384
González Pérez, Tomás, 22, 23, 42, 44, 48, 49, 55, 59, 87, 124, 231, 243, 262, 308, 309, 335, 363, 390
González, Rafael, 412
González, Sara, 337
González, Tony, 414
Gonzalo Roig, 403
Granados, Manuel (Manolo), 242, 245n10
Grenet, Ernesto, 346, 348
Grupo de Experimentación Sonora del ICAIC, 5, 335
Guerra, Armando, 409
Guerra, Lillian, 11, 12, 377, 382, 389n4
Guevara, Alfredo, 5, 47, 48, 80, 84, 199, 267, 292

Guevara, Ernesto "Che," 11, 14, 60–64, 69, 256, 287–298, 301, 302, 329, 334
Guillard Limonta, Norma Rita, 10
Guillén Landrián, Nicolás (Nicolasito), 5, 6, 10, 20, 44, 55, 56, 82, 95, 96, 185, 186, 196, 231, 245nn10–11, 251–258, 264, 272, 294, 311, 383
Guillén, Nicolás, 35, 42, 63, 231, 357n3, 362
Güines, Tata, 346
Gutiérrez Alea, Tomás "Titón," 5, 23, 42, 43, 52, 59, 77, 83, 87, 98, 99, 101, 116, 118n8, 124, 192, 215, 252, 261, 272, 293, 298, 310, 313, 315, 335, 338, 358, 363, 382, 390n9, 403

Hassan, Heidi, 386
Hasta cierto punto, 52
Havana Cultural Congress, 17, 19, 230, 231
Hernández, Adalberto, 412, 414, 415
Hernández, Bárbara, 414
Hernández, Germinal, 3, 53, 83, 182, 183, 207, 208, 209, 292, 302n5, 309, 311, 407, 408, 409, 410, 412, 413, 414, 415
Hernández Espinosa, Eugenio, 103, 107, 108, 113, 118
Hernández Gómez, Alfredo, 3
Hernández Gómez, Ibis, 3
Herrera, Alberto "Truffó," 409, 410
Herrera, Georgina, 225, 242, 245
Historia de la piratería (History of piracy), 14, 15, 42, 43, 59, 273, 276, 403

ICAIC Newsreel, 5, 45, 265, 296. *See also* Latin American News of the ICAIC; *Noticiero ICAIC Latinoamericano*
Iglesias, Arturo, 404
illustrated essay: "Rumba" (by Sara Gómez), 317–328
INDER (National Sports and Recreation Institute), 146, 160, 162

Instituto Cubano del Arte e Industria Cinematográficos, ICAIC (Cuban Film Institute), 2, 4–8, 12, 14, 19, 20, 24, 42–45, 47, 48, 53, 55, 80, 83–85, 87, 98, 99, 181, 183, 185, 186, 188, 189, 192, 197–199, 203, 204, 205, 207, 210, 223, 227, 231, 240, 243, 245n12, 246n21, 251, 252, 261, 264, 266, 267, 272, 275, 292, 294, 306, 307, 310, 313, 316, 328, 346, 375, 379, 382, 385, 386, 389n4, 404–415: archives, 22, 221n2; Cinemateca de Cuba, 272; Documentation Center, 23, 87; documentary production (division), 22; Ediciones ICAIC, 10. *See also* Grupo de Experimentación Sonora del ICAIC; ICAIC Newsreel; *Noticiero ICAIC Latinoamericano*
Instituto de Etnología y Folclore (Institute of Ethnology and Folklore), 42, 49, 58
International Women's Congress, 315
Iré a Santiago (I'm going to Santiago), 10, 12, 13, 22, 25, 59, 65–67, 184, 223, 228, 229, 243, 265, 273, 275–277, 283, 284n8, 339n2, 344–348, 350, 351, 353, 355, 356, 404
Isla del Tesoro (Treasure island), 14, 46, 59, 183, 187, 331, 332, 408
Isle of Pines trilogy, 20, 59, 187, 230, 279, 280, 283, 374
Ivens, Joris, 206, 252

James, C. L. R., 18
Jamís, Fayad, 50, 362
Jiménez Leal, Orlando, 67, 227
Juan, Adelaida de, 363
Junco, Tito, 118
Juventud Socialista (Socialist Youth), 49, 362

INDEX 423

Kurosawa, Akira, 5, 217

La Lupe, 330
La Rose, John, 19
Landa, Fabio, 406
Larrabure, Roberto, 415
Las Yaguas, 103, 105, 113
Latin American News of the ICAIC (ICAIC Newsreel), 5, 42. See also *Noticiero ICAIC Latinoamericano*
Law against Idleness (Law 1231/1971), 92, 172
Leiris, Michel, 18, 390
León, Argeliers, 293, 362
Lesage, Julia, 25n4, 377
Lewis, Oscar, 18, 93, 103, 117n4, 205, 246n22
Lewis, Ruth, 93
Ley de Familia (Family Code), 299
Ley de la Infancia (Law of Childhood), 299
Ley de Maternidad (Maternity Law), 299
Limonta, Mario, 177, 178, 336, 415
Linares, María Teresa, 362
literacy campaign, 14, 18, 26n11, 270, 272, 284n16, 365, 370n5. See also Campaña Nacional de Alfabetización en Cuba
Llanusa Gobel, José, 55, 363
Llapur, Santiago, 410, 413
Llauradó, Adolfo, 409
López, Israel "Cachao," 331
López, José, 404, 406
López, Lilia Rosa, 413
López, Lupercio, 185, 412
López, Ricardo, 415
López, Rigoberto, 5, 24, 25n5, 77, 215, 245, 260–269, 315, 415
López, Rodolfo, 411

Lord, Susan, 1, 31, 56n2, 221n2, 225, 227, 244n3, 279, 372, 394
Lores, Edelmira "Mirita," 38, 40
Los del baile (Those of the dance), 185, 245n11, 254
Loy Hierro, Amparo, 108

Maceo y Grajales, José Antonio de la Caridad (José Maceo), 40, 221n7
Maceo, Antonio, 202, 213, 223, 267
Machado, (Gerardo), 332
Machado, Julio, 302n5
Malcolm X, 19, 155, 224
Malitsky, Joshua, 22, 270, 286, 390n5
Manuela, la mexicana (Manuela, the Mexican), 103, 106, 108
Mañach, Jorge, 251
March, Luis, 406
marginalization and marginality, 14, 16, 17, 20, 21, 23, 51, 52, 58, 59, 62, 63, 73, 76, 77, 85, 90, 93, 95, 100–109, 111–116, 117n4, 124, 137, 153–155, 160, 163, 186, 209, 210, 217, 226, 235, 241, 257, 335–338, 369, 374, 379, 380, 381, 384
María Antonia, 103, 118, 258n1
Marker, Chris, 200, 206, 252, 390
Martí, José, 63, 262, 332
Martiatu Terry, Inés María "Lalita," 4, 11, 24, 25n5, 26n15, 35–56, 58, 118n11, 119n13, 225, 226, 230, 232, 234, 241, 242, 243, 245n12, 246n21, 362, 363
Martínez (animation), 404
Martínez Furé, Rogelio, 55, 203, 245n10, 292, 293, 363, 410
Martínez Pedro, Alberto, 203
Martínez-Echazábal, Lourdes, 12, 22, 24, 35, 57, 181, 221, 341, 360
Massip, José, 252, 258n1
Matamoros, Santiago, 358n10
McIntosh, David, 4, 8, 56n2, 316, 384

Medea en el espejo (Medea in the mirror), 103
Memoria sobre la vagancia en la Isla de Cuba (Memoir about idleness on the island of Cuba), 89
Memorias del subdesarrollo (Memorias), 100, 101, 116, 118n8, 265, 298. See also *Memories of the Underdevelopment*
Memories of Underdevelopment, 99, 154, 298. See also *Memorias del subdesarrollo*
Mendive, Manuel, 363
Mendoza, Isa, 407, 408, 409, 415
Mi aporte (My contribution), 2, 12, 13, 17, 21, 47, 48, 74, 75, 78, 82, 187, 190, 198, 201, 235–239, 241, 243, 246n12, 247n25, 294, 297, 299, 301, 363–366, 369, 373–375, 377–381, 388, 390n6, 401n1, 413
microbrigades, 111, 116, 119n16, 168
Military Units to Aid Production, 18
Molinet, María Elena, 410
Moore, Carlos, 225
Morante, Rafael, 404
Moré, Benny, 330
Morejón, Nancy, 38, 225, 242, 245
Moreno Fraginals, Manuel, 293, 362
Moreno, Joaquín, 415
Müller, Alessandra, 26n8, 245n9, 302n5, 328
music and cinema, 12, 20, 22, 24, 51, 67, 70, 197, 228, 278, 328–335, 337, 338, 345–348, 352–354
Mutual Aid and Self-Help Plan (Plan de Ayuda Mutua y Esfuerzo Propio), 87, 111, 116, 119n16, 128

Nápoles, Victoria, 405
narration: voice-over narrator, 13, 14, 52–54, 59, 65, 76, 87, 88, 111, 116, 207, 208, 213, 216, 273–280, 297, 328, 346–348, 350, 376, 378, 390n9
National Library (Cuba), 99, 154, 245n10, 265, 363
National Penitentiary for Crimes against the Safety of the State, 334
Navarro Luna, Manuel, 362
Navarro, Miguel, 413
New Man, 11, 14, 18, 20, 21, 59–64, 68, 70, 256, 268, 287–291, 293–296, 298, 302, 334
New Woman, 11, 75, 240, 288, 300, 301, 364, 368, 370n2, 372, 376
Noticiero ICAIC Latinoamericano, 5, 42, 267. See also Latin American News of the ICAIC (ICAIC Newsreel)
Novoa, Rosario, 363
NOW!, 51, 275, 283n2, 379

Ociel del Toa, 254
One way or another, 7, 45, 75, 82, 91, 124, 181, 257, 298, 328, 363, 414. See also *De cierta manera*
Operación Pedro Pan (Operation Peter Pan), 18
Oquendo, Leida, 26n12, 401n2
Órganos del Poder Popular, 295. See also Asamblea del Poder Popular (Popular Power Assembly)
Orquesta Estrellas Cubanas, 407
Ortiz, Fernando, 251, 330, 382; Ortizian ethnography, 13
Otero, Lisandro, 103

P.M., 67, 227, 228, 245n11, 380
Padilla, Heberto, 363, 380
Palenzuela, Ramón, 405
parametración, 293, 363
París, Rogelio, 331
Parqueando el carro (Parking the car), 310

Partido Independiente de Color (Independent Party of Color), 251, 387, 388
Partido Socialista Popular (Popular Socialist Party), 50, 389n4
Pascau, Jesús, 280, 406, 407, 408, 409
Pastor, Osvaldo, 404
Pedro Díaz, Alberto (Alberto Pedro), 23, 55, 87, 124, 231, 262, 308, 309, 363, 410
Pedro Mendive, Alberto, 55
Pello el Afrokán (Pedro Izquierdo), 254, 346, 354, 358
Pensamiento Crítico, 24, 32, 235, 372
People's Task Force (organizaciones de masa), 114, 148, 160
Pérez Prado, (Dámaso), 328, 330
Pérez Sarduy, Pedro, 225, 242, 245n10
Pi, Fernando, 404, 405
Pick, Zuzana, 25n4
Piñeiro, Ignacio, 331
Plaza Vieja (Old town square), 59, 273, 274, 276, 277, 403
Poder local, poder popular (Local power, popular power), 21, 294–297, 300, 374, 409
poems: "Son de negros en Cuba," 228, 342, 343, 344, 349, 361; "Sound of the Cuban Negroes," 358n6, 361
Poet in New York, 344, 357n3
Portuondo, Omara, 44, 49, 407
"Por un cine imperfecto," 102. See also "For an Imperfect Cinema"
Prado, Rosa, 18
Presidio Modelo, 334
Prieto, Abel, 270, 284n16
Pucheux, Jorge, 410, 413, 415

quinquenio gris (Five gray year period, or "gray period"), 14, 17, 48, 230, 291, 302n2, 363, 372, 385

Quintela, Carlos, 49, 50, 51
Quinteto de Jazz de la Orquesta Cubana de Música Moderna, 407
Quinteto Instrumental de Música Moderna, 346

race, racism, and racial consciousness, 17, 20, 23, 40, 41, 54, 55, 62, 68, 69, 76, 220, 223–227, 228, 232–235, 238–240, 243–244, 251–252, 257, 265, 270, 275, 276, 374, 381
Ramírez, María, 415
Ramos, José Antonio, 251
Randall, Margaret, 18
Reglamento de Círculos (Rules of Daycare Centers), 299
Reportaje, 294
Residencial Miraflores, 23, 87, 99, 101, 104, 112, 113, 117n1. See also Residential Miraflores
Residential Miraflores, 124–179
Retornar a Baracoa (Returning to Baracoa), 255
Retrato de Teresa (Portrait of Teresa), 299
revista *Mella* (Mella magazine), 2, 5, 49, 50, 51, 58, 261, 307, 362
Revolutionary Offensive, 94, 95, 117n5, 163
Reyes, Sarita, 268, 415
Rhythm and Blues, 42
Rich, B. Ruby, 25n4
Riera, José M., 410, 414
Risquet, Jorge, 299
Rivero, Eduardo, 406
Rivero Caro, Adolfo, 51
Rocha, Glauber, 265, 266
Rodríguez, Abraham, 118n11
Rodríguez, Adalberto, 414
Rodríguez, Alina, 385, 386
Rodríguez, Anita, 183
Rodríguez, Asenneh, 404

Rodríguez, Nelson, 5, 311
Rodríguez, Raúl, 404
Rodríguez, Silvio, 415
Rolando, Gloria, 26, 85n1, 373, 386–389
Romeu, Antonio María, 346
Rouco, Jorge, 412, 415
Rubiera Castillo, Daisy, 26n15, 242
Ruiz, Carmelo, 415

Saavedra, Hilda, 410
Saco, José Antonio, 73, 89, 90, 91, 262
Saladrigas, René, 116
Salkey, Andrew, 18, 19
Salut les Cubains, 5, 56n5, 263, 328, 358n11, 370n6, 403
Salvador, Emiliano, 410
Sánchez, Roberto, 44
Sánchez González, Jorge Luis, 8, 48, 186, 384, 385
Santa Camila de la Habana Vieja (Saint Camila from Old Havana), 103, 104, 113, 119
Sara Gómez: Un cine diferente, 10
Seminario de Etnología y Folclore del Teatro Nacional de Cuba (Seminar of Etnology and Folklore), 2, 19, 362
Septeto Habanero, 329
Serra, Ana, 11, 21, 74, 284n9, 287, 305, 375
sexism, machismo, and masculinity, 20, 23, 52, 54, 74, 76, 77, 98, 104, 118n9, 136, 137, 187, 201, 218, 239, 241, 244, 268, 270, 336, 338, 368, 374, 376, 378, 379
Si me comprendieras, 298
Sobre horas extras y trabajo voluntario (Extra hours and voluntary work), 21, 294, 297, 374, 414
"Socialism and Man in Cuba," 11, 60, 69, 287, 288, 290, 291, 293. See also "El socialismo y el hombre en Cuba"

Solar habanero (Havana tenement), 59, 284n6, 403
Solás, Humberto, 118n9, 252, 272
songs: "Drume negrita," 346, 348; "La nueva escuela" (The new school), 415; "Son de la loma," 346, 348; "Take five," 334; "Tres lindas cubanas," 346, 353
Sóngoro Cosongo, 78n2
Sorrell, Leonardo, 410
soundtrack: "Cantos rituales abakuá" (Abakuá ritual songs), 415
Special period, 292, 386
Stock, Anne Marie, 25, 385

Tabío, Jos, 406
Taller de Línea y 18 (Línea and 18th Street Workshop), 95, 96, 197, 206, 294
Tiempo de pioneros, 403
Torres, Gloria, 384, 385
Triana, José, 103
Triana, Roberto, 409
Tricontinental Films, 25, 415
Trío Los Decanos, 407
Trío Matamoros, 346
Trío Virgilio Almenares, 407

Un día en el solar (One day in the tenement), 103, 104
Una isla para Miguel (An Island for Miguel), 12–14, 19, 20, 25n7, 44, 46, 59, 60, 183, 187, 191, 206, 234, 256, 257, 280, 282, 294, 334, 408
Union of Communist Youth, 334
Union of Rebel Youth, 307
University of Havana, 2, 99, 154
Up to a certain point, 52, 338. See also *Hasta cierto punto*

Valdés Dones, Alberto, 415
Valdés, Arturo, 408
Valdés, Chucho, 44, 329, 330, 334, 407, 408
Valdés, Julio "El Pavo," 183, 415
Valdés, Oscar, 258n1, 272
Valdés, Ramiro, 192, 382
Valladares, Mirta, 75, 240, 301, 366, 376
Valle Casals, Sandra del, 10
Varda, Agnès, 5, 6, 19, 52, 56n5, 59, 186, 200, 263, 328, 358n11, 367, 370n6, 390n11, 403
Vega, Justo, 405, 406, 407
Vega, Pastor, 84, 268, 299, 338
Veitía Gómez, Iddia, 2, 3, 8, 370n6
Veitía, Héctor, 3, 220, 292
Vera, Maité, 103, 105, 113
Vertov, Dziga, 379; Vertovian (aesthetic), 380
Vidal, Consuelo (Consuelito), 74, 236, 364, 413
Viewers' Dialectic, The, 5
Vigil-Escalera, Orlando, 411
Villalón Mesa, Dulce María (Caíta), 44, 308, 407, 408, 409, 413
Vitier, José María, 335
Vitier, Sergio, 268, 335, 415

Vives, Camilo, 415
voluntary work (voluntary labour program), 21, 46, 51, 297
Vulnerable Media Lab, 7, 26n7, 221n2, 382

West-Durán, Alan, 22, 328, 340, 388
women's rights, 10, 21, 47, 62, 74–77, 82, 223, 235–239, 240–241, 243, 268, 298–300, 301, 364–369, 372, 374, 375, 376
Words to the Intellectuals, 226, 380

Y... tenemos sabor (And we've got flavor), 13, 22, 44, 102, 328–331, 374, 406, 44, 102, 328, 406
Yelín, (Saúl), 186
Yera, Juana, 2, 38
Young Rebel, The, 14
Youth reform camps (Isla de Pinos project), 14, 231

Zafra de los Diez Millones (Ten-million-ton harvest), 14, 21, 82, 92, 198, 235, 291, 295, 299, 364, 375
Zarza, Zaira, 6, 386
Zayas, Alberto, 329, 330–331, 407

www.ingramcontent.com/pod-product-compliance
Lightning Source LLC
Chambersburg PA
CBHW051241300426
44114CB00011B/841